P9-EMP-147

DISCARD

LINCOLN AVE 60625

SEP − 2006

The

UNITED STATES

of

ARUGULA

The
UNITED STATES
of
ARUGULA

HOW WE BECAME A GOURMET NATION

David Kamp

BROADWAY BOOKS
NEW YORK

PUBLISHED BY BROADWAY BOOKS

Copyright © 2006 by David Kamp

All Rights Reserved

Published in the United States by Broadway Books,
an imprint of The Doubleday Broadway Publishing Group,
a division of Random House, Inc., New York.
www.broadwaybooks.com

BROADWAY BOOKS and its logo, a letter B bisected on the diagonal,
are trademarks of Random House, Inc.

Book design by Jan Derevjanik

Library of Congress Cataloging-in-Publication Data
Kamp, David.
The United States of Arugula : how we became
a gourmet nation / David Kamp.— 1st ed.
p. cm.
1. Gastronomy. 2. Cookery, American. I. Title.

TX633.K36   2006
641'.0130973—dc22
2006042599

ISBN-13: 978-0-7679-1579-3
ISBN-10: 0-7679-1579-8

PRINTED IN THE UNITED STATES OF AMERICA

1 3 5 7 9 10 8 6 4 2

First Edition

R0400058394

TO AIMÉE

CHICAGO PUBLIC LIBRARY
SULZER REGIONAL
4455 N. LINCOLN AVE.   60625
DISCARD

CONTENTS

CHICAGO PUBLIC LIBRARY
XX TX REGIONAL
XSS N. LINCOLN AVE. 60625

PREFACE

MOST OF US HAVE AT LEAST ONE RAPTUROUS FOOD MEMORY FROM CHILDHOOD—OF fresh-baked Saturday-morning popovers, of sweet little strawberries picked in the wild, of a Cantonese lobster dish unveiled from beneath a dome at some dimly lit place with a name like Jade Pagoda. But I must confess, in defiance of societal pressure to view one's bygone youth as a magical idyll of unsurpassable delights, that these memories pale completely in comparison to those I have of, oh, last week. Virtually every day of my adult life, I've been fortunate to eat something I simply never tasted as a young child. I'm talking not only about fancy foods, like white truffles and aged balsamic vinegar, but about commonplace, nonevent stuff: a tortilla chip dipped in salsa, a handful of picholine olives, a pat of goat cheese on a cracker, a crumble of aged pecorino, a fresh croissant.

Amazingly, these things were either unavailable in my youth or sufficiently scarce that my family didn't know about them. I remember attending a wedding in 1984, when I was in my teens, at which a cousin from San Diego, where they were more food-forward than us East Coasters, grimly surveyed the restaurants and markets of the dire Pennsylvania town where we'd gathered, and said, "Dude, you people need to learn about salsa." My response: "What's salsa?" I remember my mother, in 1978, returning from a business trip to Palo Alto, California, and telling us that her associates had taken her to a Japanese restaurant where they served something called sushi, and that when some of this sushi was placed before her, the restaurant's watchful Japanese proprietor, somehow sensing that my mother was a sushi novitiate, sped across the room, and, like a Secret Service agent taking a bullet for the president, inserted himself bodily between my mother and the table, crying *"Raw fish! Raw fish!"*

Suffice it to say, salsa, if I may toss out an oft-cited food factoid, has sur-passed ketchup as America's most popular condiment, and sushi has become so unthreatening that Schnucks, the St. Louis–based supermarket chain whose eminently Midwestern, howdy-do slogan is "The Friendliest Stores in Town," now features a sushi bar in many of its locations. In other words, I'm not the only one who has come a long way culinarily. Judy Rodgers, whose San Francisco restaurant, Zuni Café, was named the Outstanding Restaurant in America at the 2003 James Beard Foundation Awards, and who herself won the foundation's Outstanding Chef Award the following year—the food-world equivalent of winning Best Picture and Best Director at the Oscars—was originally a St. Louis girl, and she recalls that in her youth in the 1960s, *white corn* was considered outré. ("I didn't like it," she says. "I liked yellow corn.") Today, as you might expect of a chef whose restaurant is named for a Southwestern Indian tribe but whose primary influences are country French and rustic Italian, Rodgers has gotten a lot more adventur-ous. Her menus feature items as varied as house-cured anchovies, homemade spaetzle, short ribs braised in ale, pasta alla carbonara, grilled meats marinated in the Argentinian chili-vinegar mixture known as *chimichurri*, roast chicken with bread salad (her signature dish), and *esqueixada*, a pungent Catalan salt-cod concoction.

The very fact of such cornucopian variety buoys me. I love the speed with which the food world moves, ushering forth new taste sensations and better ideas with the let's-top-ourselves alacrity of Apple Computer and the anything's-possible ambition of 1960s NASA. I love the way each new month brings with it some strange, unexpected, or simply delicious new ed-ible to try, whether an artisanal Kentucky bacon whose down-home produc-ers have just figured out e-commerce, an unfamiliar peach variety that some small-time farmer has grown from heirloom seeds, or the utterly bizarre "bubble tea" drinks that leapt from Taiwanese street stalls to American cities a few years ago, replete with giant tapioca balls that are slurped through an extra-wide straw.

I love the way that even the seemingly mundane staples of our daily life are being tapped for all the depth and complexity they can offer—to the point of ridiculousness, but benign ridiculousness. Butter is now something you can get in a variety of regional pedigrees and butterfat contents: 86 percent for the artisanal "cultured" version made by the Vermont Butter and Cheese Company, 85 percent for the butter from California's Straus Family Creamery, 82 percent for the commercially manufactured but high-end Plugrá, and 80 percent for your basic supermarket Land O'Lakes. Sugar, too, is making a play for our attention, its enthusiasts arguing that there's a whole world out there beyond the yellow Domino box, a world populated by varieties with such Dr. Seussian names as jaggery, piloncillo, muscovado, and demerara. What about salt, then? Well, at the restaurant widely regarded as the best in the United States, Thomas Keller's French Laundry, in Yountville, California, I was soberly presented with a salt tasting—*a salt tasting!*—as an accompaniment to my foie gras course. The waiter, like some particularly elegant cocaine dealer, gently spooned nine mini-mounds onto a little board, each salt a different hue and consistency from the next—one as fine and white as baking powder, another as dark and chunkily crystalline as the inside of a geode.

It is, in short, a great time to be an eater. And how often do we get to say something as unreservedly upbeat as that? Nowadays, it's all too common—and, alas, valid—to complain that things just aren't as good as they used to be: movies, music, baseball, political discourse, ladies' millinery, what have you. But food is one area of American life where things just continue to improve. If we're cooking at home, we have a greater breadth and higher quality of ingredients available to us. If we're dining out, we have more options open to us, and a greater likelihood than ever that we'll get a good meal, no matter what the price point. Our culinary elites—the chefs, cookbook authors, cooking-school instructors, purveyors, and food writers who lead the way—are suffused with feelings of boundless possibility, having liberated themselves from the old strictures and prejudices that hemmed in their predecessors. It's okay for the traditions of peasant cookery to inform those of haute cuisine, and for haute flourishes to inform regular-guy food.

I daresay we're in the throes of an American food revolution! Well, I *would* daresay, were it not for the fact that the national media have been declaring the advent of the American food revolution for decades, since way back in those primordial dark ages before people knew what salsa and sushi were. In November of 1966, *Time* put Julia Child on its cover, an acknowledgment of the huge following she'd acquired via her program on public television, *The French Chef*, and the best-selling cookbook she'd co-written in 1961, *Mastering the Art of French Cooking*. The story inside declared, "If 1966 is the year that everyone seems to be cooking in the kitchen with Julia, this is partially because Julia is just right for the times . . . Supermarkets have found that their gourmet counters are their handsomest profit earners, and are rapidly expanding them . . . [The] Bon Vivant supermarket in San Diego stocks more than 3,000 kinds of fancy foods, from kippered sturgeon and kangaroo tails to pickled rooster combs and 4-lb. tins of Caspian Sea caviar."

Almost a decade later, in the summer of 1975, *Newsweek* featured the French chef Paul Bocuse on its cover, using his prominence as the Sinatra of the nouvelle cuisine Rat Pack as a pretext for examining the new culinary savvy afoot in America: "From Seattle to Savannah, sales are up on gourmet kitchenware. New York's The Bridge Kitchenwares Co. has a six-month waiting list for the $20 porcelain mortars and pestles necessary for grinding fresh herbs. Chicago's Crate and Barrel chain, whose revenues have tripled since 1970, can't keep up with demand for woks, crepe pans or the $190 Cuisinart food processor that does everything to food but cook it." And in 1976, James Villas wrote a landmark essay in *Town & Country* entitled "From the Abundant Land: At Last, A Table of Our Own," in which he noted "our country's present obsession with fine food and drink" and felt it was only a matter of time before "we could boast a cookery with all the subtlety and refinement of *la cuisine française*," complete with a "formal codification of dishes and cooking techniques, so that people everywhere can truly understand this nation's complex culinary heritage."

In truth, the American food revolution has really been more of a food *evolution*, a series of overlapping movements and subtle shifts, punctuated by the occasional seismic jolt. If there's a major difference between now and the sixties and seventies, it's that the scale is so much larger; culinary sophistication is no longer the province of a tiny gourmet elite. The historically unrivaled run of prosperity in the United States in the eighties and nineties, compounded by the culinary advances that had so excited *Time* and *Newsweek* in the previous decades, has led to the creation of an expanded leisure class that treats food as a cultural pastime, something you can follow the way you follow sports or the movies.

The food world has its own ESPN (the Food Network, founded in 1993), its own constellation of marketable stars (Emeril Lagasse, Rachael Ray, Bobby Flay, etc.), its own power elite (Alice Waters, Wolfgang Puck, Charlie Trotter, Daniel Boulud, Jean-Georges Vongerichten, etc.), its own literary lights (Ruth Reichl, Calvin Trillin, Anthony Bourdain), and its own high-end glossies (*Saveur* and *Food & Wine*, as well as the old dowager *Gourmet*, revivified under Reichl). You can be a non-cook and still be a food obsessive, attending new restaurant openings like a theatergoer, religiously consulting the Zagat guides (launched in 1979), and ordering the finest prepared foods from Whole Foods, Dean & DeLuca, or Williams-Sonoma. Or you can be a serious cook and fill your kitchen with professional-grade equipment—the six-burner Viking Range, the Sub-Zero refrigerator, the supersharp Global knives from Japan—and buy your produce and artisanal edibles from the local farmers' market that didn't exist ten years ago, and exhibit your disdain for mere "feeders" by subscribing to and following the recipes of *Cook's Illustrated*, the meticulousy researched, trend-averse antiglossy that has thrived since its founding in 1980 without the benefit of any advertising revenue. While I don't think we have realized Villas's vision of a unified, codified national cuisine like France's, nor do I think we ever will—America is just too big, unwieldy, multiregional, and multicultural for that—we have come that much closer to being a nation where, as in France (and Italy and Japan), food is a fundamental facet of our cultural life, a part of the conversation, something contemplated as well as eaten.

This is a big deal, for America has long struggled with the very idea of culinary sophistication, viewing it warily as a sign of elitism (an unforgivable sin in a populist land), weirdness, or worse. Booth Tarkington captured this attitude in an amusing passage in his 1918 novel, *The Magnificent Ambersons*, in which an Indianapolis commoner reacts skeptically to the latest highfalutin delicacy to hit the city, olives: "Green things they are, something like a hard plum, but a friend of mine told me they tasted a good deal like a bad hickory-nut. My wife says she's going to buy some; you got to eat nine and then you get to like 'em, she says. Well, I wouldn't eat nine bad hickory-nuts to get to like *them*."

Much more recently, in 1989, in the black comedy *Heathers*, the movie's teen protagonists were able to pass off their murder of two mean jocks as a gay suicide pact by leaving *bottled mineral water* at the scene. ("This is Ohio . . . If you don't have a brewski in your hand, you might as well be wearing a dress.") To this day, there are those who make alarmist hay of suspect food preferences. In her best seller *Treason*, the conservative commentator Ann Coulter derides liberals who opposed the invasion of Iraq as having "sulked with their cheese-tasting friends," the French, as if being buddies with someone who appreciates a good Morbier is an act of sedition (and notwithstanding the fact that America's foremost cheese expert, Steven Jenkins, of New York City's Fairway Market, is a political conservative). And during the 2004 presidential election, an Iowa conservative group paid $100,000 to air a television commercial that excoriated supporters of the former Vermont governor Howard Dean as "tax-hiking, government-expanding, latte-drinking, sushi-eating, Volvo-driving" freaks.

But these food phobics are the laggards, the ones who haven't gotten the message that Americans are increasingly sophisticated about what they eat and expansive in their tastes. Indeed, it's getting harder, in a good way, to define what constitutes a "gourmet" product nowadays. Is brie really gourmet anymore, or extra-virgin olive oil, or prosciutto, or fresh pasta? Is it gourmet to use fresh herbs instead of dried ones from a McCormick tin? Technically, the millions of people who get their coffee from Starbucks every morning are purchasing, to use the trade term, "specialty" coffee, but at this point, with 5,000-plus U.S. locations and 10,000-plus worldwide, is drinking Starbucks coffee really that much of a specialty-food experience, or simply a better one than gulping down the watery deli swill we all used to put up with?

THIS IS A BOOK about how we got to this point—how food in America got better, and how it hopped the fence from the ghettos of home economics and snobby gourmandism to the expansive realm of popular culture. The paterfamilias of this saga is James Beard, who announced his corporeal presence on this earth in 1903 as an enormous, thirteen-pounds-plus newborn, and remained, until his death in 1985, a literally and figuratively outsize character in the food world, the undisputed dean of American gastronomy. There were plenty of other cookbook writers and cooking teachers before Beard, but none who had his knack for engaging so large and varied an audience, and for legitimizing American cookery as both a heritage to be drawn upon and a cause to be advanced. That's why the action of this book begins, give or take a few digressions, in 1939, the year a despairing Beard, who had moved to New York from his native Oregon to pursue a life in the theater, recognized that he was no Lionel Barrymore and decided to supplement his meager income by co-founding a catering company—the first step in his massively influential food career, taken at a time when the words "food" and "career" did not sit comfortably together.

And onward the story continues to Julia Child, the beloved, warbling giantess from Pasadena who demystified sophisticated French cookery for average Americans; Craig Claiborne of *The New York Times*, who turned food writing into a bona fide arm of journalism and invented the make-or-break, starred restaurant review; Alice Waters, the untrained Berkeley counterculturist whose co-creation of the iconoclastic restaurant Chez Panisse was as much a political mission to enlighten the masses as it was a culinary pursuit; Wolfgang Puck, the Austrian-born, Los Angeles–based chef who unabashedly embraced American capitalism, expanding a business that started with one restaurant, Spago, into a multifarious empire that encompasses upscale dining establishments, inexpensive cafés, and supermarket products; and dozens of other influential figures, some of whose names are recognizable as national brands (Chuck Williams of Williams-Sonoma; Joel Dean and Giorgio DeLuca), and some of whom have been forgotten or are unsung heroes whose names were never well-known in the first place.

It's a rich cast of characters, because the American food world, though often perceived as a precious refuge for aesthetes, adorable eccentrics, and saintly earth-mother figures devoted to sustainable agriculture and arranging baby lettuces just so, is, in reality, like any other creative milieu—full of passionate, driven, talented, egocentric, sharp-elbowed people, some congenial, some difficult, most of whom know one another and regard one another with varying degrees of fraternity, rivalry, warmth, and malice. (One reason Bourdain's scabrous memoir, *Kitchen Confidential*, resonated with so many food professionals is that it gave lie to the old PBS image of the kitchen as a becalmed place where Concerto No. 1 from Vivaldi's *The Four Seasons* is always playing.)

The raggedy tale of Chez Panisse alone is rife with moments of idealist struggle, druggy abandon, screwball comedy, workplace romance, seat-of-the-pants innovation, and serious dissension—some of its participants extolling Waters as a magnetic, kindhearted soul of extraordinary vision and ingenuity, and others deriding her as an imperious, disengaged credit hog who can't even cook that well. There have been personal friendships in the food world that, more by accident than design, have had nationwide repercussions—like the one Claiborne struck up in the fifties with the chef of Le Pavillon, Pierre Franey, which resulted in nearly three decades of collaboration at *The New York Times*, and the one Boulud struck up with Vongerichten in the mid-eighties, when both were young chefs on the rise in New York, egging each other on with fantasies of what it would be like to be not only chefs but chef-owners. And there are tiffs: the two chef-authors who have done more than anyone to educate Americans about authentic Mexican food, Rick Bayless and Diana Kennedy, don't care for each other.

The two most brilliant marketers of specialty foods in New York City, Eli Zabar and Giorgio DeLuca, nearly had a smackdown in Zabar's shop in the late seventies when the former suspected the latter of stealing ideas. (Fortunately, tempers cooled before any vials of aged balsamic vinegar were toppled and shattered.) There is still simmering controversy, more than three decades after the fact, over who invented pasta primavera, and precisely what ingredients should be in it.

There are so many plots and subplots to the American-food saga, such a wealth of characters, that this book could potentially be several books, a multivolume epic of Proustian length. But in the interests of serving forth a digestible narrative—if you'll indulge the gastronomical metaphors; then I'll stop, I promise—I've sacrificed certain plotlines. Not every region gets its due (sorry, Lydia Shire, Jasper White, and all you great Boston-area chefs; sorry, Norman Van Aken and company down in Florida), nor do the whizzes and wunderkinds of the dessert and chocolate worlds (sorry Jacques Torres, Sherry Yard, John Scharffenberger, etc.). And I've given admittedly short shrift to the extraordinary American wine boom that's accompanied the food revolution—a subject that really deserves a book all to itself.

I'm compelled to acknowledge, however, that every so often I encountered an interviewee who cocked an eyebrow and questioned this book's very premise, arguing that food in America has, in fact, been going down the tubes for years. "Oh, it's definitely gotten much worse, with all the processed foods and meals eaten outside the home—hardly anyone cooks at home anymore," Marion Cunningham told me as we sat at her dining-room table in Walnut Creek, California, adjacent to the very kitchen where she tested the recipes for her landmark 1979 revision and modernization of *The Fannie Farmer Cookbook*. Cunningham, a Beard protégé for whom fame and success in the food world did not come until she was well into middle age, has been around long enough—since 1921, to be precise—to remember when mothers did most of their own baking, put up their own preserves, routinely used ingredients from their own gardens, and yoo-hooed their husbands and children to the table for a shared meal and a lively discussion of the day's events.

I don't mean to turn a blind eye to the issues Cunningham raises, or even to those she hasn't—such as the epidemic that has seen the number of Americans classified as "overweight" or "obese" rise to 64 percent, and the threat that rapacious agribusiness poses to small farmers, and the health dangers posed by farmed salmon and hormone- and antibiotic-treated beef, and the commercial food industry's infliction upon us of ever-more-shuddersome products like green Heinz ketchup and stuffed-crust pizza. There are food- and nutrition-related problems out there that warrant serious consideration and action, and while these issues are acknowledged in this book, they are not its main subject. (I would suggest two excellent books by Marion Nestle, *Food Politics: How the Food Industry Influences Nutrition and Health* and *Safe Food: Bacteria, Biotechnology, and Bioterrorism*, for further reading on these topics.)

But I must respectfully disagree with Cunningham's conclusion that we as a nation have slid backward culinarily. We enjoy a vastly greater choice of goods and eating options than our forebears did, and, if we choose well, we can eat better, and more healthfully, and with a greater knowledge of culinary cultures outside our own, than our grandparents ever could have imagined. Furthermore, the very fact that the aforementioned issues have come to the fore, and are now the subject of symposia and debate, is yet another indication of how far food has come in the American consciousness. You wouldn't have McDonald's scrambling to shore up its death-burger image by offering salads with Newman's Own dressing, abolishing its Super Size portions, and switching to vegetable oil for its french fries, or Burger King angling for health and foodie cred by hiring Bayless to promote its Santa Fe Fire-Grilled Chicken Baguette Sandwich, or Alice Waters taking on the sorry state of school lunches as a pet cause, if the food world hadn't acquired some muscle and cachet that it lacked even a decade ago.

I feel I should also address those dissenters who, rather less graciously than Cunningham, have condemned as their idea of hell the very climate of ferment and ambition that so excites me. The same James Villas who abounded with optimism in *Town & Country* in the seventies is now an unfettered (albeit whip-smart and entertaining) crank who proudly trumpets his abhorrence of sushi and salsa, refers to these times as the "era of gastro-pornography," and believes that the heyday of American food came and went in the sixties, when fine-dining traditions were still prevalent and chefs kept to one kind of cuisine, in just one kitchen. "Contrary to all the ecstatic proclamations by the ever-gullible food press, the proliferation of trendy cookbooks, and the wildly buoyant Zagat restaurant surveys," he wrote in his 2002 memoir, *Between Bites*, "gastronomy in America [has] evolved into nothing more than a sick joke" that would mortify the likes of Beard and Claiborne if they were alive today.

Likewise, Robert Clark, at the end of his otherwise impressive and co-gent 1993 biography of Beard, *The Solace of Food*, throws a hissy fit about what the food world has become in the wake of its patriarch's death, blast-ing it as shallow, trend obsessed, and in suicidal thrall to celebrity chefs and myopic Manhattan tastemakers who delude themselves into believing that "the whole country [is] greedily feeding on chanterelles and mâche." Like Villas, he imagines that Beard would be horrified by it all, surveying the scene like the weeping Indian in the old Keep America Beautiful ad: "We seem as a people less inclined to gather at our stoves and our tables and take succor in the good things that happen around them . . . and James Beard would have thought that a tragedy."

These laments bring to mind the wounded, I-was-there-first bitterness of the early R.E.M. or Nirvana fan who has never gotten over the fact that his favorite indie band got big, and who therefore sees a positive develop-ment—the mass acceptance of what was once a small movement—as some kind of unforgivable sellout. There's no doubt that chefs and food editors do indeed get caught up in risible trends (for example, blackened fish in the eighties, lemongrass abuse in the nineties, foams in the early twenty-first cen-tury), and that the celebrity-chef machinery coughs up the occasional vain-glorious twit, but these are mere glitches in what has been a remarkable culinary evolution. While the whole country most certainly is not "greedily feeding" on mâche, things are moving fast enough that, in the decade-plus

since Clark launched his gratuitous, unprovoked attack on the perfectly innocent salad green, a Chez Panisse alumnus named Todd Koons has started
up a company called Epic Roots that distributes bagged, fresh mâche to supermarkets in thirty states. In the same period, an alumnus of Wolfgang
Puck's kitchen, Nancy Silverton, has rapidly expanded her La Brea Bakery,
whose artisanal baguettes and sourdough loaves are par-baked in Southern
California, shipped frozen to supermarkets across the country, and baked to
completion on the premises the day they're sold, allowing people all over the
United States to enjoy fresh-baked bread of a sort that was once available
only in expensive West Coast specialty shops.

So maybe it's not the worst thing in the world that the bustling, ever-
busy, aromatic home kitchen of yore has been replaced by an ad hoc arrangement of dining out, ordering in, toting home prepared foods, and *occasionally*
whipping up something from scratch. And maybe it wouldn't be so horrible
if those who flat-out don't want to cook never had to, provided they had options and inclinations beyond processed fast food. Indeed, to some culinary
thinkers, like the brilliant Chicago chef Charlie Trotter, this represents an
exciting new frontier. "From an opportunity standpoint, it's gonna be an
amazing time to be a cook or a chef twenty, twenty-five years from now,"
he says. "It's a weird time at the moment, because you have a massive part
of the population that doesn't cook, maybe doesn't even know how to cook,
and yet is conversant in several food languages, knows its way around a sushi

Besides, I'm not entirely sold on the guilt trip that some in the food
elite like to lay on non-cooks and infrequent cooks. Though I'm an enthusiastic home cook myself, I recognize that this is America, and part of what
has made America America is its drive, its impatience, its demand of long
hours in the workplace, its two-career couples, its lack of Mediterranean lan-
guor. It's all well and good to pine for the vanished America in which moms
stayed home and issued forth three hot meals a day, or to gaze across the Atlantic with envy at Europeans who still take three hours off for a midday
meal with wine—and it sure is nice to appropriate the rhythms of these
places over the weekend or while we're on vacation—but that ain't us.

menu. And then there's this whole 'nother segment of non-cooks that eats nothing but fast food and processed food, which is part of the reason we have the obesity problem. Either way, you have people who, whether for personal reasons, time-commitment reasons, or financial reasons, aren't cooking. I think there's extraordinary potential behind that, to feed people who aren't feeding themselves, and to do it right. We can't be afraid of progress in the food world."

But this is getting ahead of the story. There are beans to be shelled, roasts to be trimmed, oysters to be shucked, big fish to be gutted . . .

The

UNITED STATES

of

ARUGULA

INTRODUCTION

A WORLD WITHOUT
CELEBRITY CHEFS

"IF SOMEONE SUGGESTS A 'PIZZA PIE' AFTER THE THEATER, DON'T THINK IT IS GOING to be a wedge of apple. It is going to be the surprise of your life." So began the April 21, 1939, column of the *New York Herald Tribune* food editor, Clementine Paddleford, the doyenne of America's then tiny contingent of food journalists. Her column went on to promote pizza as a "nice stunt to surprise the visiting relatives, who will be heading East soon for the World's Fair. They come to be surprised, and pizza, pronounced 'peet-za,' will do the job up brown."

That Paddleford, in 1939, had to explain how to pronounce "pizza" (in an article sub-headlined ITALIAN PASTRY APPROPRIATE WITH BEER AND WINE) speaks volumes about the gastronomic world Americans inhabited at the time. Dining out was for special occasions, ordering in was nearly unheard of, and most Americans adhered to a diet of what was familiar to them locally and culturally. Italian foods such as "peet-za" were alien to all but Italian Americans and a small minority of urban culinary adventurers. To America's wealthy elite, eating Italian food was beneath contempt, irredeemably déclassé and stinky—a sentiment that Frank Capra, himself a Sicilian immigrant, exploited marvelously in a scene from his most famous film, *It's a Wonderful Life* (1946), in which the movie's moneybags villain, Mr. Potter,

chides George Bailey, the big-hearted, immigrant-assisting director of the local building and loan, for "frittering his life away playing nursemaid to a lot of
garlic-eaters."

Paddleford, to her credit, harbored no such prejudices. A first-rate
journalist with an endearingly loopy sensibility, she plunged uninhibitedly
into New York's ethnic markets, where, she wrote, "all the queer fish of the
sea are congregated to sell wholesale or retail to Italians, Spaniards, Portuguese, Chinese, any one who knows the goodness of queer fish." Paddleford was also shrewd and adventurous enough to recognize that within the
3,000-mile span of the continental United States lay a wondrous variety of
homey regional foods, there for the discovering. In her single-engine Piper
Cub airplane, she flew low over the land, using the one- and two-lane roads
of the countryside as her guide, following their twists and curves to wher-
ever a promising farmhouse or local café appeared.

But Paddleford didn't have an audience of well-heeled food sophisticates to applaud her, no pulpit on National Public Radio or the Food Network from which to delight her followers with tales of eating wine-jelly pie
in the South or Maine lobster stew in New England. Her work—her life—
was relegated to what was then called the women's page of the newspaper, a
home-economics ghetto of recipes, advice columns, and helpful household
hints. What's more, her culinary fearlessness was undercut by her fealty to her
role as the *Herald Tribune*'s resident wifey (though Paddleford was actually a
divorcée) and the presumed conservativeness of her lady readership. Try as
she might to zest up her readers' lives with exotica once in a while, Paddleford knew that she couldn't go too far—a frustration that revealed itself in
her "queer fish" column, in which she suddenly implored her audience to
"Be a kitchen rebel and glory in rebellion. Raise the eyebrows of your
friends. Serve sea urchins after an evening at bridge." She probably knew as
she was typing those words that the urchins-after-bridge thing would never
catch on.

James Beard was in a similarly awkward spot in '39, having taken a
role as a junior partner in a new Manhattan catering company called Hors

d'Oeuvre, Inc. This was something of a comedown for the thirty-six-year-old Beard, "Jim" to all his friends, who'd moved to New York City a year and a half earlier (having already lived briefly in the city in 1924–25) with dreams of making it in the theater, either as an actor, set designer, or costumer. Talk about a queer fish: the hulking, gay, six-foot-four Oregonian had a head the shape of an upended potato and huge ears that jutted out like pull tabs. He'd grown up as the spoiled, overfed only child of a sexually ambiguous Englishwoman named Mary Jones, who, prior to her marriage of convenience to a man named John Beard, had run a boardinghouse in Portland. Devoted to this mother—a stout, forceful hospitality-aholic who laid out stunning buffets of home-prepared breads, salads, cold dishes, roasts, soups, cakes, and sweets for her friends and neighbors—Beard had become a dab hand in the kitchen at a young age; by the time he was eight, he was baking his own bread. This kitchen precocity kept Beard afloat in New York when that big theater break proved not to be forthcoming. A born charmer with an affinity for bohemian types—two more traits inherited from his mother—Jim Beard made friends easily, and when money was tight, he could always cook for these friends in exchange for a seat at the table with someone else footing the grocery bill.

The prime mover at Hors d'Oeuvre, Inc. was the well-connected man-about-town William Rhode. Beard had met Rhode at a party, and the two men developed an instant rapport over their mutual love of food. The catering company they dreamed up together, with assistance from Rhode's sister, Irma, and Beard's friend Mack Shinn, was a success from the outset. Rhode was well acquainted with the sorts of Upper East Side ladies who needed canapés for their cocktail parties, and he was a gifted self-promoter, adept at planting items about himself in the papers; among the first to tout Hors d'Oeuvre, Inc. publicly was Rhode's friend Lucius Beebe, the *Herald Tribune* society writer, who, in his "This New York" column, described the company as "a brand new sort of gastronomic agency [that] already shows signs of being a minor Klondike." While Rhode's tastes in edibles skewed fancier, more in the caviar-and-foie-gras direction, Beard's kitchen creations drew upon his mother's straightforward American repertoire. Hors d'Oeuvre, Inc.'s most popular item was a miniature sandwich of sliced Bermuda onion served between little rounds of fresh brioche that were spread with home-made mayonnaise and then rolled along the edges in minced parsley—essentially, a gussied-up version of a Mary Beard snack.

Beard didn't know in 1939 that he'd found his calling, nor was he yet aware that he was in possession of a preternatural gift, a highly cultivated palate that was every bit as special, in its way, as the extraordinary eyesight of Ted Williams, the rookie Red Sox left fielder who claimed he was able to see the stitches of a speeding baseball as it spun toward home plate. On the precipice of middle age and bereft of any theater prospects, Beard was just happy to have a steady job. No one thought of a food career as prestigious, and few even entertained the concept.

Julia McWilliams certainly didn't; by 1939, her experiment in New York City life was already well behind her, and food hadn't even factored into it, apart from the occasional trip to the lunch counter at Schrafft's. After graduating from Smith College in 1934, she found a job as an advertising copywriter for a Manhattan furniture company, W. & J. Sloane. Though she flourished as a career gal, by 1937 she had quit Sloane's and returned to her hometown of Pasadena, California, because she was approaching age twenty-five, and, unlike most of her Smith friends, had failed to hook a man. And so, while Beard was rolling his onion sandwiches in parsley, the well-born McWilliams was living with her recently widowed father, attending Junior League functions, golfing, dating, halfheartedly pursuing new jobs, and not knowing what the future held for her. It wouldn't be until the late forties, after she'd married a sophisticate named Paul Child and moved to France, that she even began to cook seriously.

The third future member of the food elite's original Big Three, Craig Claiborne, spent the late thirties flailing miserably through college in his home state of Mississippi, unable to abide the premed program at Mississippi State University or the paddlings of his putative fraternity "brothers." Claiborne wound up transferring to the University of Missouri with vague thoughts of becoming a journalist, and would endure an inept tour of duty in the navy, a stint at a Swiss hotel-management school, and a few years scrapping around New York as a freelancer before he would emerge, in the late fifties, as *The New York Times'*, and therefore America's, foremost food journalist.

As ragged and itinerant as the Big Three's pre-food careers were, it wasn't as if there was a coherent food world that was excluding them, keeping them from their destinies. While the women's pages plied their readers with recipes for butterscotch squares and "Lacy Valentine Salad," a terrifying concoction of marshmallows, apricots, maraschino cherries, dates, celery, and canned grapefruit suspended in gelatin and garnished with curly endive and mayonnaise piping,* the "gourmets" of the time occupied their own, equally perverse little universe. Mostly male, they dined at fine old hotels like the Biltmore and the Astor in New York, and made a habit of lamenting the fast-vanishing ways of the previous century's Gilded Age, when mustachioed men of means gorged themselves gouty on endless feasts of oysters, crabs, canvasback duck, prime rib, and terrapin.†

The ringleader of this gang was Crosby Gaige, a theater producer who fancied himself New York's greatest epicure, oenophile, and bon vivant. His offices housed the New York chapter of the London-based International Wine and Food Society, and, when he wasn't producing plays, Gaige was putting his name to such books as *The Cocktail Guide and Ladies' Companion* and *The New York World's Fair Cookbook*. But the foremost public gourmet was Lucius Beebe, the *Herald Tribune*'s top-hatted, extravagantly turned-out

---

*This recipe appeared in the *Chicago Tribune* in 1937 under the byline of Mary Meade, the pseudonym of the paper's longtime food editor, Ruth Ellen Church.

†The terrapin, an aquatic sea turtle, used to flourish off the shore of Maryland and in the brackish waters around Brooklyn and Queens, and was a staple of nineteenth-century menus in polite New York society. Overharvesting led to their disappearance from the rich man's diet in the early twentieth century. Edith Wharton's work abounds with references to terrapin, for example, this passage from her short story "The Blond Beast": "Draper, having subsisted since infancy on a diet of truffles and terrapin, consumed such delicacies with the insensibility of a traveller swallowing a railway sandwich."

exemplar of the high life, whose columns often detailed his gustatory intake at such hoity-toity spots as "the Stork" and "the Colony." Beebe found a new outlet for his florid prose in 1941, when Earle MacAusland, a former advertising manager for *Parents* magazine, founded *Gourmet*, a monthly that, at its inception, was more of a primer on fine living and worldly elegance than a place to look for recipes. In a characteristically showoffy-nostalgic piece about a visit to Locke-Ober, the venerable Boston restaurant, Beebe wrote, "Locke's came into being in a grand era of ornate electroliers, floriated mahogany, and barroom nudes, when Tom and Jerry* was a standard commodity at all bars during the cold months and when two Southdown mutton chops complete with kidney, bacon, and appropriate quantities of potatoes, coffee, and hot cakes were considered the absolute minimum on which people might safely breakfast."

Somewhere between the women's-page ladies and the gourmets fell Sheila Hibben, the food editor of *The New Yorker*, Harold Ross's literature-and-culture cavalcade for the smart set. As bracingly prophetic and contemporary as her "Markets and Menus" columns read today—visiting a small grocery on the Upper East Side in 1941, she found "a substantial reserve of that good Droste cocoa from Holland" and "a farm cheese from Wisconsin" that was "one of those honest products that prove ours is going to be a great cheese country once the flood of processed stuff subsides"—Hibben had little reach into the mainstream. Cecily Brownstone, who was the food editor of the Associated Press and was one of the few members of the old food brigade to survive into the twenty-first century, living until 2005, recalled Hibben in an unpublished interview with Laura Shapiro as "a very good writer, but not read by the masses. That's the difference between now and then. You wouldn't be looked at askance now if you mentioned the food books you like to your friends, but you would have then."

In a rarefied food-lit category all her own was California's M.F.K.

---

*A hot alcoholic beverage made with eggs, rum, and brandy, falling somewhere between a toddy and a nog.

Fisher (Mary Frances or M.F. to her intimates), who, in the thirties and early forties, published a series of piquant essay collections with pertinent recipes, starting in 1937 with *Serve It Forth*. Tougher, earthier, and altogether less twee than the waistcoated fops back East—ruminating on her title subject in 1941 *Consider the Oyster*, she wrote, "Life is hard, we say. An oyster's life is worse. She lives motionless, soundless, her own cold ugly shape her only dissipation"—she carved out her own niche and was adored by the media intelligentsia: *Look* magazine profiled her, film stars sought her out for meals, and Paramount Pictures gave her a screenwriting contract.* But Fisher's was a boutique audience. The general public had no idea who she was, Jim Beard included; he later admitted that he'd not heard of her until a friend presented him with Fisher's third book, *How to Cook a Wolf*. Fisher wouldn't have much company in the food-lit stakes until after World War II, when *The New Yorker* journalists A. J. Liebling and Joseph Wechsberg, both of whom had spent substantial amounts of time eating their way through France, started writing delightfully evocative culinary memoirs.

As for chefs, they seldom encountered the phenomenon known as celebrity. Though the Lucius Beebes of the world knew who Charles Ranhofer and Louis Diat were—the former had presided over Manhattan's greatest restaurant of the nineteenth century, Delmonico's, and the latter had, since 1910, run the kitchens of the Ritz hotel on Forty-sixth and Madison, where he famously invented vichyssoise—chefs generally toiled in anonymity. Ranhofer and Diat also happened to be Frenchmen, conveniently foreign and "other"—as the whole concept of fancy eating was to most Americans. It simply wasn't socially acceptable for an American-born man to aspire to a career in the kitchen.

"I would say that any child who told his family that he wanted to be a cook in a restaurant would be sent to his room and told to stay there until he came to his senses," says Chuck Williams, the founder of the kitchenwares

---

*One Paramount executive, besotted with Fisher's author photo, wanted to sign her as an actress.

retailer Williams-Sonoma, who was born in 1915. "The parents weren't about to have a son who was a fry cook in some beanery."

It would be decades, in fact, before chefs were even recognized by the U.S. government as professionals. Only in 1977, after years of ardent lobbying by Louis Szathmáry, a colorful, rotund Chicago chef straight out of central casting—with his tall toque and walrus mustache, he looked like he should have been feverishly pursuing a runaway chicken with a cleaver in a Warner Brothers cartoon—did the U.S. Department of Labor elevate the occupation of chef from its "Services" category (lumped in with domestics and dogcatchers) to its category of "Professional, Technical and Management Occupations."

In today's context of Wolfgang Puck and Emeril Lagasse, this seems shocking, as belated a delivery of justice as the American Psychiatric Association's 1973 removal of homosexuality from its list of mental disorders. But the very unprestigiousness of America's food culture was what left the door open for people like Beard, Child, and Claiborne to come in and make it their own. The Big Three didn't fit into conventional mid-century society: Beard and Claiborne were gay men who had endured the pain of feeling "other" their entire lives, and Child was six foot two and unpretty, on a perilous path to becoming, in her own future husband's words, "an old maid." In their stumbling, halting efforts to figure themselves out, Beard, Child, and Claiborne found their salvation in cooking and eating. Their sheer joy in this discovery set them apart from the existing food establishment. Bound by neither the conventions of the Jell-O-abusing women's-page ladies nor the froufrou affectations of the terrapin-eating boulevardiers, the future Big Three simply appreciated food as a source of pleasure. Funnily enough, this was a novel concept in America at the time.

CHAPTER ONE

AMERICA'S DYSFUNCTIONAL RELATIONSHIP WITH GOOD FOOD

Hogs are in the highest perfection, from two and a half to four years old, and make the best bacon, when they do not weigh more than one hundred and fifty or sixty at farthest: They should be fed with corn, six weeks, at least, before they are killed . . .

—prepping instructions for curing bacon,
The Virginia House-wife, Mary Randolph, 1824

SPAM, SPAM, SPAM, SPAM / Hormel's new miracle meat in a can / Tastes fine, saves time / If you want something grand / Ask for SPAM!

—radio jingle for Spam, sung to the tune of
"My Bonnie," 1937

"IN THE BEGINNING, THERE WAS BEARD," JULIA CHILD FAMOUSLY SAID, IN A CHARACteristic display of generosity. But precisely *what* Beard began bears some explaining. Though she's among the foremost of Beard's protégés, the cookbook author Barbara Kafka can't contain her exasperation at the received wisdom that there were no good meals to be had in America until her mentor reared his enormous head. "It's like there was no food in this fucking city, or this country, until this miraculous apparition came along!" she says. "Or there was no cooking at home until Julia. Don't tell me this kind of nonsense! I think that Le Chambord,* which I went to as a child, was

---

*The Café Chambord, as it was properly known, was on Third Avenue near Fiftieth Street in Manhattan, and was a popular celebrity haunt in the 1940s and 1950s. Jackie Gleason and his *Honeymooners* cast dined there regularly after their live Saturday-night telecasts.

PAGE 11: *John Harvey Kellogg, cereal pioneer and renowned quack, presides over his health sanitarium in Battle Creek, Michigan, 1937.*

probably the best French restaurant that New York has ever seen and will ever see. And in the West Forties, way over, there were bistros lined up and down. Guys got off the ships right opposite the biggest harbor, practically, in the world—off the *Normandie* and the *Ile de France*. And they were French guys."

So, yes, it is wrongheaded to presume that Americans did not eat well until the Big Three became big. The very first American cookbook, *American Cookery*, written by a Connecticut woman named Amelia Simmons and published in 1796,* demonstrates that there were both cooks and eaters in those days who appreciated fine ingredients and flavorful food. *American Cookery* is considered the "first" American cookbook because, though several cookbooks had been published before it in the colonies and the young republic, they were adaptations or reprints of European cookbooks, mostly British. Simmons's book, on the other hand, was expressly aimed at born-and-bred Americans who used ingredients not available in Europe, such as the "pompkins" she used in a "pudding" recipe that differed very little from our current ones for Thanksgiving pumpkin pie. Her "Indian Slapjack," a cornmeal pancake of the sort now found on the menus of upscale Santa Fe bruncheries, would have gone very nicely with her "Beft bacon" (printers had not yet sorted out their use of *f*s and ornamental *s*'s), which, in a manner that would excite today's aficionados of artisanal foodstuffs, was cured in molasses, sea salt, and saltpeter for six to eight weeks and then smoked over corncobs.

Further evidence of a culinarily attuned America comes in the most celebrated cookbook of the nineteenth century, *The Virginia House-wife*, by Mary Randolph, a pillar of late-eighteenth-century Richmond society (her brother was married to Thomas Jefferson's daughter), who, after her husband experienced some reversals of fortune, ran a boardinghouse and collected her

---

*The book's full title was *American Cookery, or the Art of Dressing Viands, Fish, Poultry, and Vegetables, and the Best Modes of Making Pastes, Puffs, Pies, Tarts, Puddings, Custards and Preserves, and All Kinds of Cakes, from the Imperial Plumb to Plain Cake. Adapted to This Country, and All Grades of Life. By Amelia Simmons, An American Orphan.*

recipes into a book, published in 1824. Not only was *The Virginia House-wife* a work of astonishing breadth and worldliness—Mrs. Randolph knew how to cook everything from the expected Ye Olde dishes like roast goose and Indian-meal pudding to seemingly very contemporary offerings like polenta and ropa vieja (Cuban- or Spanish-style shredded beef)—but her respectful use of vegetables was downright Alice Waters–ish. Randolph cautioned against overcooking asparagus, and advised that a perfect salad should have "lettuce, pepper grass, chervil, cress &c.," which "should be gathered early in the morning, nicely picked," and served with a lovely tarragon vinaigrette.

President Jefferson was himself quite the epicure and procurer of exotic foodstuffs, importing seeds from Europe to plant in his garden and cultivating Mediterranean fig, olive, and almond trees at Monticello. In his personal "Garden Book," he kept records of what produce was available at Washington's vegetable market during the years of his presidency, 1801 to 1809, and the sheer variety sounds much like what a latter-day foodie might gush over at San Francisco's Ferry Plaza Farmers Market on a bountiful summer day: sorrel, broccoli, strawberries, peas, salsify, raspberries, Windsor beans, currants, endive, parsnips, tomatoes, melons, cresses.

All this said, not for nothing is the United States known as a meat-and-potatoes kind of place. In the early years of the republic, it wasn't uncommon for Americans to have beefsteak not only for dinner, which was consumed at midday, but for *breakfast*—a habit only exacerbated as the country expanded westward, opening more land for ranching. Foreign visitors to the United States in the nineteenth century routinely expressed their shock at the huge, meaty smorgasbords set out on groaning boards in the public rooms of hotels at all hours of the day, not to mention the joyless, gluttonous dispatch with which the natives went about the business of eating. Charles Dickens declared that Americans ate "piles of indigestible matter." Thomas Hamilton, another Englishman, wrote an account of his journey to the United States in 1833 called *Men and Manners in America*, in which he observed, "In my neighborhood there was no conversation. Each individual seemed to *pitchfork* his food down his gullet, without the smallest attention to the wants of his neighbor." The food in these places wasn't of high quality, either, with vegetables boiled to a fare-thee-well and starchy potatoes and puddings served in great quantities. The Canadian historian Harvey Levenstein, in a droll study of early-American dietary habits called *Revolution at the Table*, notes that "the enormous amounts of meat and starch and the short shrift given to fresh fruits and vegetables made constipation the national curse of the first four or five decades of the nineteenth century in America."

It's hard to square this bleak picture with the Edenic one painted by Mary Randolph and Thomas Jefferson, and, indeed, the feisty old culinary historian Karen Hess, who edited and wrote the introduction to the facsimile of the first edition of *The Virginia House-wife*, dismisses the work of Levenstein, her rival, as that of a "stupid idiot." (As she points out, the Randolph cookbook alone presents clear evidence to refute Levenstein's assertion that in the nineteenth century "herbs were used mainly for medicinal rather than culinary purposes" in America.) Still, it's possible for an unbiased observer to use Hess's and Levenstein's works complementarily and draw the conclusion that while the United States had some terrific cooks, cornucopian markets, and an abundance of wonderful homespun culinary traditions, it also had some serious food issues. The novelist James Fenimore Cooper, author of *The Last of the Mohicans*, spent several years in France as a U.S. consul, living in Lyons, the nation's gastronomic capital. Upon his return home in 1833, he recorded his horror at the state of American food, calling his fellow Americans "the grossest feeders of any civilized nation ever known," a culinarily clueless people who subsisted on a diet of "heavy, coarse, and indigestible" fare. The chasm between French and American food was all the more appalling to Cooper because he grew up wealthy in the woodsy hinterlands of upstate New York, where all manner of wild game roamed and edible plants grew, and knew that his country could do better.

But the United States, a country wary of elitism and susceptible to populist, xenophobic demagogues, would always have mixed feelings about taking culinary cues from the French. Long before the age of "freedom fries" and the efforts by an adviser to George W. Bush to damage John Kerry's 2004 presidential campaign by saying the Massachusetts senator "looks French," the advisers to the Whig presidential candidate of 1840, William Henry Harrison, tried to smear the Democratic incumbent, Martin Van Buren, as a fey monarchist aristocrat—on the evidence that he drank champagne and had hired a Frenchman to be White House chef. The scrappy old soldier Harrison, on the other hand, subsisted on "hard cider" and "raw beef and salt," and won the election.*

Whether it was a matter of this country's Puritan origins, its early inheritance of British culinary stodginess, or just a general don't-tread-on-me stubbornness, America would always have a dysfunctional relationship with the idea of culinary sophistication. A strain of the Harrison campaign's plainspoken beefy populism persists to this day: in 2004, the CEO of the fast-food chain Hardee's, Andrew Puzder, touted the company's Monster Thickburger—a 1,420-calorie sandwich composed of two one-third-pound beef patties, three slices of cheese, and four strips of bacon on a buttered, mayonnaise-spread bun—as "not a burger for tree-huggers." (Many of whom, presumably, look French.) Similarly, the thickset founder of the Wendy's chain, Dave Thomas, did a commercial in the nineties in which he addressed a grateful roomful of 300-pounders who called themselves the "Big Eaters Club." In another spot, Thomas portrayed himself as being trapped at a pretentious cocktail party where a mincing waiter offered him a dainty, absurd-looking hors d'oeuvre and said, "Crab puff, sir?" Cut to a shot of a relieved Dave back at Wendy's, sinking his teeth into an enormo-burger.[†]

On the other end of the spectrum were those who shied away from fancy feeding for ascetic or religious reasons. Many preachers, such as the Presbyterian minister Sylvester Graham (1795–1851), inventor of the graham cracker, inveighed against spicy and heavily seasoned foods because of their

---

*And promptly died of pneumonia, having served just thirty-two days in office.

†Thomas had quadruple-bypass surgery in 1996 and died of liver cancer in 2002.

supposed aphrodisiacal qualities. (Despite this, Graham was later embraced as a hero by sex-mad 1960s hippies for his advocacy of vegetarianism and early opposition to refined white flour, which, he sensibly argued, had less flavor and nutritional value than whole wheat flour.) Even when the robber barons of the Gilded Age *did* embrace the sophistication of French cuisine in all its glory, hiring French chefs for their New York mansions and Newport cottages, they were countered in the late nineteenth and early twentieth centuries by quack food faddists who were suspicious of pleasurable eating. Among the most famous was Horace Fletcher (1849–1919), a retired businessman with no scientific background who developed a huge following by advocating that all food be "thoroughly masticated"—chewed and chewed and chewed until it became flavorless and involuntarily shushed its way down the esophagus, thereby aiding the digestive system. (In fact, the probable health benefit from Fletcherizing, as this chewing process came to be known, was that it took so long that it made overeaters eat less than they would have otherwise.)

Marginally more credible was Dr. John Harvey Kellogg (1852–1943), who, in addition to developing a breakfast-cereal empire with his brother, Will, ran a "health resort" in Battle Creek, Michigan. Though he later rescinded his 1902 endorsement of Fletcherizing, Kellogg had his own peculiar thoughts on food, arguing that eating meat encouraged masturbation (a bad thing) and urging his guests to take yogurt enemas, the concept being that the active cultures in the yogurt would provide healing benefits to bowel walls aggravated by a lifetime's worth of steak-eating and boozing.*

In a sense, the home economists and food-company executives who held sway over the women's pages at the time of Beard's move to New York were quacks in their own right. As the nineteenth century turned into the twentieth, and as the United States grew more industrialized and urbanized, the sensualism and agrarian seasonality of home cooking gave way to the rise of processed foods and rigorous, supposedly scientific methodologies in the

---

*Kellogg's quackery was later the subject of a novel by T. Coraghessan Boyle, *The Road to Wellville*.

kitchen.* Even Fannie Merritt Farmer, whose 1896 *Boston Cooking-School Cook Book* is still considered a lodestar of honest American home cookery (and was renamed for her in subsequent editions), was a humorless home-ec lady, inordinately obsessed with couching her instructions in laboratory-speak. The first edition of *The 1896 Boston Cooking-School Cook Book* kicked off with, "Food is anything that nourishes the body. Thirteen elements enter into the composition of the body: oxygen, 62½%; carbon, 21½%; hydrogen, 10%; nitrogen, 3%; calcium, phosphorus, potassium, sulphur, chlorine, sodium, magnesium, iron, and fluorine the remaining 3%"—not exactly a mouthwatering lead-in. Farmer also expressed her hope that the day would come when "mankind will eat to live," the implication clear that doing the opposite—living to eat—was reprehensible. On and on she went in this dour, lab-coated way, defining ingredients in terms of chemical compounds—for example, sugar as "$C_{12}H_{22}O_{11}$"—and describing buttermilk, rather disquietingly, as "liquid remaining after butter 'has come.' "

While Farmer, at least, was well-intentioned in her commitment to nutritionally correct (if not particularly palatable) food, the new wave of big food companies cynically used pseudoscientific claims of healthfulness to appeal to customers. General Mills, the food conglomerate responsible for the creation of the fictional homemaker-sage Betty Crocker, launched an offensive to proclaim the "wholesomeness" of white flour and white bread, even though the very advances in industrialized milling that made white flour possible were the ones that removed the germ and the bran from a wheat kernel—and therefore, most of the nutrition. C. W. Post, the main competitor of the bowel-obsessed Kellogg brothers, plugged his first ready-to-eat breakfast cereal, which he called Grape-Nuts, as "brain food"; taking his chutzpah a step further, he intimated that Grape-Nuts were also effective in fighting malaria and consumption. After chemists in the 1910s and 1920s dis-

---

*The founder of the home economics discipline, also known as "domestic science," was a chemist named Ellen Richards, who in 1873 was the first woman ever to graduate from the Massachusetts Institute of Technology.

covered vitamins—naturally occurring nutrients in foods that aid in meta-bolic processes—Post's company seized upon the opportunity to play up the cereal's calcium and phosphorous content in magazine ads that portentously asked readers, "Are you bringing up your children properly?" Even the Schlitz brewing company got in on the "health" act, boasting, oddly, that its beer was so pure that "when your physician prescribes beer, it is always Schlitz beer."

James Beard had no time for factory foods, health fads, or pseudo-science. Well before he became a professional food person, he was reveling in the pure, the regional, and the homemade, even as his country's cuisine, if it could even be called that, became ever-more processed and standardized. His unbridled enthusiasm, his pure love of *taste*, was so infectious that he could excite people even when he was describing eating experiences that, frankly, sound repellent. In his 1964 memoir, *Delights and Prejudices*, he doc-uments his earliest "taste memory"—a phrase he is credited with coining—as he recalls being bedridden with malaria at age three. His family's male Chinese cook, Jue-Let, who worked in tandem with his mother, Mary, in the kitchen, spoon-fed him a cure of chicken jelly: chicken broth with the white of an egg and its shell mixed in, then strained, then chilled into quiv-ering blobs. To Beard, this icky stuff was "superb . . . magically good," and "the true essence of chicken . . . [with] a texture that was incredibly delight-ful." Likewise, the slightly older Beard reveled in shopping with Mother in a fine-poultry shop where "I would come away with two pounds of gizzards and hearts for myself." Few people today would ever want to eat chicken jelly or chicken hearts—or, for that matter, the raw onions that Beard so adored—but fewer still could remain impervious to the sensual joy he took in eating these things, or to his conclusion that "the flavor of perfectly pre-pared chicken [has] remained a stimulant to my palate ever since."

The dinners he prepared for his bohemian friends in New York in the 1930s were every bit as sensual and always made from scratch, with none of the canned foods or "ready mixes" such as Bisquick (which General Foods had introduced in 1931) that were proliferating on grocery shelves. Even if Beard was just making a poor man's repast of mushrooms on toast—a favorite snack of his—he bought his mushrooms fresh from an Italian corner grocer and used good bakery bread. Earlier still, while knocking around the Portland, Oregon, theater community in his twenties, he cooked unpretentious backstage meals for appreciative casts and crews with ingredients he'd procured from the city's open-air farmers' market on Yamhill Street, where he and his mother shopped when he was a boy. The Yamhill Market was crucial in shaping his culinary sensibility, as were the meals he and his family ate outdoors in Gearhart, the coastal Oregon resort town where the Beards kept a modest summer cottage. Right on the beach, Mary Beard boiled crabs and grilled razor clams that she and Jim had caught and dug themselves; Beard also picked the strawberries and the huckleberries that appeared in the pies and tarts the family and their guests ate for dessert.

So by the time Beard finally recognized that cookery was his vocation as much as it was his avocation—the success of Hors d'Oeuvre, Inc. led to a contract for his first book, *Hors d'Oeuvre and Canapés*, in 1940—he realized that part of his mission was to defend the pleasures of real cooking and fresh ingredients against the assault of the Jell-O-mold people and the domestic scientists. His second cookbook, published in 1941, was called *Cook It Outdoors*, and while it didn't have an exhortatory exclamation point at the end of its title like the one at the end of *Awake and Sing!*, the social-realist play written by the leftist playwright Clifford Odets six years earlier,* it might as well have. By the time of his fourth cookbook, and his first attempt at a comprehensive masterwork, the 1,217-recipe *The Fireside Cook Book: A Complete Guide to Fine Cooking for Beginner and Expert* (1949), Beard was pointedly telling *The New York Times* that what he'd written was no "laboratory manual."

The opportunity to write *Hors d'Oeuvre and Canapés* arose through the good graces of a social butterfly named Jeanne Owen, the secretary and day-to-day manager of the International Wine and Food Society chapter that

---

*Odets's producer, Cheryl Crawford, was among the wealthier members of Beard's bohemian circle, and frequently had the cash-poor Beard out to her estate in Connecticut. She also used her connections to get him his first paid catering job in New York City, before Hors d'Oeuvre, Inc.

operated out of Crosby Gaige's office. The American-born but Paris-raised Owen saw promise in Beard and took him under her wing, educating him about French cookery and securing him the book contract. The book, however, was the undoing of Beard's partnership with Bill Rhode, who resented Beard's solo effort to profit off the business and his references in the text to "my shop"; upon joining the staff of *Gourmet* as an editor in 1943, Rhode saw to it that Beard didn't write for the magazine, and this blacklisting lasted until Rhode's death in 1946.

While *Hors d'Oeuvre and Canapés* was a minor work, it sold well enough to prompt its publisher, M. Barrows & Company, to commission *Cook It Outdoors*, Beard's paean to grilling. The book had sixteen different recipes for barbecue sauce and twelve for hamburgers, but it was no Dave Thomas–style sop to dumb, torpid lugs; it included, audaciously for the time, a recipe for a "Pascal Burger" of ground lamb and lamb kidneys and a "Bagdad [*sic*] Burger" served between two slices of grilled eggplant. There were also elaborate instructions on how to build one's own backyard barbecue pit, and a recipe entitled "If You Should Run Over an Old Hen" that began, "Such things happen, this running over a farmer's hen . . ." Clearly, Beard was eager to get the fellas involved in the dying art of home cookery, too, by appealing to their machismo. The jacket copy, if anything, protested too much: "It is a man's book written by a man who understands not only the healthy outdoor eating and cooking habits, but who is an expert at the subtle nuances of tricky flavoring as well . . . A good workable book that will take a heck of a lot of wear and be a darned good companion to the outdoor cook."

"It's very important that Jim was a man," says Barbara Kafka. "That's how he made a difference. Historically, you had cookbooks and cookery writing by two groups of people, women and chefs. And, as in so many things, Jim was a crossover person. Also, because he wasn't afraid to be enthusiastic, he went right to the heart of people. His real talent was for the American voice." Beard's considerable girth, far from turning people off, abetted his crossover appeal, because he wasn't some fussy schoolmarm or a flaming gadabout like the tails-wearing, Rolls-Royce-driving Lucius Beebe.

"He was not seen as gay by the public," Kafka says. "If they'd met Jim in person, they might not have been so sure, but he was just seen as a big man, and big is good, in terms of cooking."

What Beard began, in essence, was a new perception of American food and cookery. If there was no going back to the halcyon days of Mary Randolph's sumptuous feasts of pure goodness—which were laborious to prepare, and, to face facts, made possible by slaves in the South and servants in the North—there was at least a way to reclaim the pleasures of real cooking and unrushed food, even if only as a leisure activity, as outdoor grilling increasingly became in the 1940s. Whereas Irma Rombauer, the author of *The Joy of Cooking*, represented a sane middle ground for housewives of the thirties and forties, urging them to make their own stocks in the early editions of her book* but advising that "a can of bouillon should be kept for quick aspics and for use in the place of stock"—and explaining that *The Joy of Cooking* had been compiled "with one eye on the family purse and the other on the bathroom scale," with "occasional lapses into indulgence"—Beard transcended the very notion of cooking as part of homemaking. To him, cooking and eating comprised a fulfilling cultural pastime, to be pursued as ardently as golf, opera, painting watercolors, or any other activity that aroused one's passions. In the bargain, with his charisma and approachability, he also made a better case for the preservation of regional foods than the zany Clementine Paddleford† or the highbrow Sheila Hibben.

But even as Beard was coming to prominence as a cookbook author,

---

*Rombauer, a bourgeois St. Louis housewife of German descent, compiled the first edition of *The Joy of Cooking* in 1931, when she was fifty-four, as an exercise in getting over the 1930 suicide of her husband. The first edition was just a private printing of 3,000 copies, but the subsequent edition, published by Bobbs-Merrill in 1936, became a national best seller. At the time of Rombauer's death in 1962, more than 26 million copies of the book, in its various editions, had been sold. Though Rombauer kept her distance from the "gourmet" ranks, she forged close friendships with both Beard and Cecily Brownstone.

†Beard admired Paddleford, though, remarking that she is "surely the getting-aroundest person I have ever known, except for Eleanor Roosevelt," and he socialized with her frequently.

he saw that the state of American gastronomy would get worse before it got better. Throughout and immediately after the war years of the forties, the big food conglomerates were putting ever-more grotesque packaged products on the market, many of which were by-products of their efforts to produce tinned or freeze-dried field rations for the troops. (However, Spam, George A. Hormel & Co.'s "miracle meat" in a can, predated America's involvement in the war, appearing on grocery shelves in 1937.) In time, the packaged-food companies would abandon any pretense of claiming their processed and frozen products were superior in taste, instead stressing their convenience. Cannily (and often with canned foods), these companies' advertising campaigns actually stigmatized the experience of spending hours in the kitchen. As Laura Shapiro puts it in *Something from the Oven*, her history of 1950s American cookery, "During the postwar era, time became an obsession of the food industry and eventually of American homemakers as a manufactured sense of panic pervaded even day-to-day cooking." Shapiro cites an ad for Minute Rice that sounds like it was written by someone hopped up on Dexedrine: "Baby fussing? Dinner to get? When baby wants attention and Daddy wants dinner, your best friend is *quick-quick* Minute Rice!"

Beard despaired of such developments, and of the nonsensical recipes that were urged upon readers by the women's pages, such as a popular one for "Flapper Salad," an atrocity that called for a canned pear or peach to be decorated with carrot slivers and/or pimientos to simulate the face of a 1920s flapper, with the fruit then covered in aspic, surrounded by lettuce, and covered in a sweet dressing. "I showed [the recipe] to someone who took it seriously," Beard wrote to his friend Helen Evans Brown, a Californian and cookbook author and kindred-spirit food purist. "God, where can their sense of humor be?"

Fortunately, Beard and Brown didn't have to fight their battle alone. One of the salutary effects of the war was that it caused an influx of talented kitchen workers whose cooking abilities and regard for real food complemented Beard's nicely. Though William Henry Harrison's cronies might not have approved, these influential newcomers were French.

CHAPTER TWO

LIBERTÉ, EGALITÉ, SOULÉ

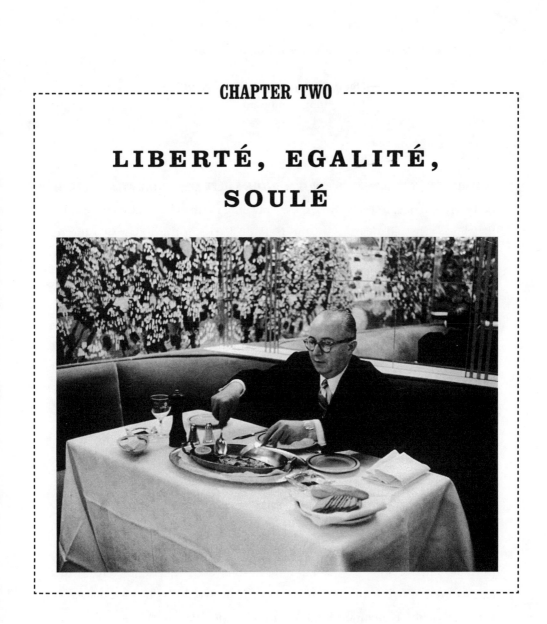

Henri Soulé is not a *marchande de soupe*!

—Henri Soulé, proprietor of New York's
Le Pavillon restaurant

IN APRIL 1939, THE OCEAN LINER *NORMANDIE* SAILED ACROSS THE ATLANTIC FROM Le Havre, France, to New York City. Traveling in first class was Henri Soulé, the thirty-year-old manager of the Café de Paris; in third class was Pierre Franey, the eighteen-year-old second assistant to the *saucier* at the Restaurant Drouant. Both restaurants were owned by the Drouant family, which ran several high-end dining establishments in and around Paris. The family's de facto CEO, Jean Drouant, had petitioned his government to let him operate a sophisticated, 400-seat restaurant at the French Pavilion at the 1939–40 World's Fair in Flushing Meadows, Queens. Once his request was granted, Drouant dipped into his own pool of employees, rounding up the best of them to represent his country. Though Soulé (pronounced, explained *The New Yorker's* Joseph Wechsberg, "like 'soufflé' without the f's") was not yet forty years old, he had already made a name for himself as Paris's most formidable front-of-the-house figure. Short, balding, and stout—a Gallic Alfred Hitchcock—he transcended his physical shortcomings with elegantly tailored suits, a graceful gait, and a general air of owlish imperiousness. He also spoke fluent English and had the grandiloquent habit of referring to himself in the third person, as "Soulé"—making him, in sum, the perfect choice to be the face of French haute cuisine in America, as he would be in his capacity as maître d' of the Restaurant Français at the French Pavilion.

Franey, in time, would be every bit as important a figure in American gastronomy as Soulé, if not more so. But on the *Normandie* voyage, his first trip to America, he still looked like the provincial Burgundian peasant he was,

PAGE 25: *The great restaurateur Henri Soulé, in his element at New York's Le Pavillon, 1962.*

a stocky little fellow with a moon face and raccoon eyes set deep beneath a thick, charcoal-dark monobrow. Just four years earlier, he'd arrived in Paris from his village of St. Vinnemer in short pants (much to the mortification of the cosmopolitan older cousins who received him) to begin his apprenticeship at a restaurant several notches in stature below the Restaurant Drouant. Starting at the bottom of the ladder, with the female vegetable-peelers and the rheumy-eyed dishwasher drunks with no aspirations to chefdom, Franey plugged away at a series of ever-more reputable joints until he landed at the Drouant, where he worked his way up to the rank of first *commis*, or assistant, to the fish cook—no small feat in a restaurant especially renowned for its seafood. Shortly before the World's Fair, having mastered the fish station, Franey was rotated to the more prestigious *saucier* station, where he began as second *commis* with the expectation of again working his way up.*

But in Queens, his reputation as an excellent fish cook preceded him: he was tapped to reprise his old role as the *poissonier*'s lieutenant, in which he would put to good use his skill at preparing such challenging Drouant dishes as the turbot soufflé, which called for the fish to be carefully deboned and butterflied; filled with a mousse of ground fish, egg yolks, and beaten whites; folded back together; and baked in white wine until the stuffing inside rose soufflé-style, theatrically inflating the turbot back to its live-fish dimensions.

As elaborate as preparations like this were, the chefs and *commis* who prepared them were anything but *haute* characters themselves. Many came

---

*The French kitchen hierarchy in fine-dining restaurants went as follows: At the top was the exalted *chef de cuisine*, who was in charge of planning the menu, deciding the day's purchases, and overseeing the kitchen. Next was the *sous chef*, the man operationally in charge of running the kitchen and the de facto hatchet man for his boss. Reporting to the *sous chef* were eight *chefs de partie*, department heads: the *saucier*, who handled sauces, stocks, and the task of sautéing meats; the *entremetier*, or vegetable cook, who also handled soups and omelets; the *poissonier*, or fish cook; the *rôtissier*, or roast cook, who broiled and roasted meats and also made *pommes frites* and other fried foods; the *garde-manger*, who handled cold dishes like pâtés; the *pâtissier*, or pastry chef; the *boucher*, or butcher, who carved the meat and poultry; and the *chef tournant*, the all-rounder who could fill in at any one of these stations in a pinch. The *chefs de partie* typically had three or four *commis* working for them, themselves ranked by ability and experience. In some especially elaborate and expensive French restaurants, there were as many as six *commis* in a department.

from dirt-poor families and grew up in conditions that bordered on the feudal—indeed, it seemed that every French chef who came to define luxe New York dining in the fifties and sixties had some sort of heartbreaking story to tell of childhood privation and hard knocks. Jean Vergnes, later to become the chef at the Colony and Le Cirque in New York, was just thirteen when he left his little village in the southeast of France to apprentice at a restaurant in the nearest city, Grenoble. So ruthlessly demanding were his kitchen superiors that even on the rare occasions when Vergnes got to see his mother—when she appeared at the screen door at the back of the restaurant, having taken the train to Grenoble to drop off some clothing and a few francs for her son—young Jean was allotted only a few seconds to touch her fingers longingly through the wire screen before returning to his potato peeler.

Jacques Pépin, who emerged on the American scene a bit later, arriving in 1959 to work for Franey, began his apprenticeship at thirteen. And when he was only six, he had been literally farmed out by his parents for the summer, sent from the comfort of his family's apartment in the town of Bourg-en-Bresse to a farm in the countryside. There, he lived with an unfamiliar family and worked as a junior cowherd in exchange for room and board, since his parents couldn't afford to keep him fed and occupied during the summer-vacation months. When he *was* at home, young Jacques and his brother, Roland, were saddled with the unenviable task of chasing after the horse that pulled a delivery cart through their town's streets, shoveling up the horse's droppings so that the Pépin family would have fertilizer for their modest plot in the community garden.

If there was any advantage to growing up in such penury and rusticity, it was that the French cooks were rooted in the earth. As America was marching inexorably toward processed, manufactured, packaged food, the French still felt the pull of the seasons and lived off food they grew and raised themselves. From a young age, Franey knew how to trap and dress rabbits, catch and clean pike, kill and bleed chickens, and forage for dandelion greens for salad, choosing the leaves that sprouted from molehills rather than the ones that grew out in the open because the stalks of the sunlight-deprived, molehill-cosseted dandelions tasted sweeter. Like the Virginian Mary Randolph more than a hundred years before them, the Franeys lived without refrigeration, waiting until fall to slaughter their pigs so that their spare ribs and hams would cure in the cool months without fear of spoilage, and letting no part of the animal—not the blood, the lungs, the caul fat, nor the intestines— go to waste.

In this regard, the French chefs who established themselves in America in the forties and fifties would prove surprisingly simpatico with the California foodie counterculturists who embraced French cookery in the sixties and seventies: both camps were underwhelmed by the quality of the ingredients offered by the big suppliers in America, and the Frenchmen appreciated the hippies' efforts to make America hospitable to artisanal cheese makers, boutique farmers, paid foragers, and organic ranchers. But the French would never warm to the very American concept of the self-taught chef. Franey and his contemporaries were rigorously put through their paces by martinet bosses, repeating the same techniques thousands of times, earning only grudging respect from their be-toqued superiors, and rotating from one kitchen station to the next in order to learn the repertoire of classic French cuisine in all its nuance and variety. Nothing would ever convince the Frenchmen of Soulé's brigade that there was a better way than their way to learn how to be a professional cook. "Young cooks today with culinary-school diplomas may view it as somewhat anachronistic," Franey wrote in the 1980s, "but classic French cuisine is without question the mortar upon which all of today's cooking is based."

The notion of "classic French cuisine" bears some explaining. Since the age of Taillevent,* who was the cook to the first Valois kings in the fourteenth century and compiled his recipes into a book entitled *Le Viandier*, French cookery has been governed by two principles: that it is superior to all other

---

*Taillevent was the *nom de chef* of Guillaume Tirel (1310–1395), still a revered figure among the French. In Paris, there is a Michelin-rated three-star restaurant named for him, where America's current preeminent genius chef, Thomas Keller of the French Laundry and Per Se, trained in the 1980s.

nations' cookery, and that the current generation's chefs are mavericks who are simplifying their forebears' fussy, anachronistic methodologies and developing a new way forward, a "nouvelle cuisine." (The mediagenic French chefs of the 1970s who moved away from butter- and flour-rich sauces—among them Paul Bocuse, Michel Guérard, Jean and Pierre Troisgros, Alain Chapel, and Roger Vergé—are but the most famous in a long line of Frenchmen to unite under the banner of nouvelle-ness.) In the seventeenth century, the prevailing expert on French cuisine was François Pierre de la Varenne, a court chef during King Louis XIV's reign, whose 1651 cookbook, *Le cuisinier françois*, presented an organized if not comprehensive set of recipes of what the French nobility ate; it was La Varenne who invented duxelles, the paste of chopped mushrooms, shallots, and melted butter that's still omnipresent in French cookery, and is so named because the chef was working for the Marquis d'Uxelles when he created it.* La Varenne was followed in the eighteenth century by Vincent La Chapelle, who pointedly called his 1735 cookbook *La cuisinier moderne* to set himself apart from his predecessors, and another chef, known simply as Menon, who is thought to have actually coined the phrase "nouvelle cuisine" when he used it as the title of the third volume of his epic 1739 treatise *Nouveau traité de cuisine* (New Culinary Processes).

But classic French cuisine as Franey and his ilk understood it was created by Antonin Carême (1784–1833) and Auguste Escoffier (1846–1935). Carême was a fervent nationalist who had no doubt, as he declaimed in his multivolume 1833 masterwork, *L'art de la cuisine française au dix-neuvième siècle* (The Art of Nineteenth-Century French Cuisine), that "nineteenth-century French cuisine will remain the model of the beautiful in the culinary

---

*La Varenne's preparations, so recognizably "French" in hindsight, give lie to the notion, often posited by Italian chefs exasperated by the Francocentrism of culinary history, that classical French cuisine derives wholly from the Florentine cooks who accompanied Catherine de Medici from Italy to France in 1533—when, at age fourteen, she married the Duke of Orléans, later to become King Henry II. While the Florentines were indeed a huge modernizing influence on France, popularizing green vegetables and the separation of sweet courses from savory, La Varenne's *Le cuisinier françois* reveals a chef working in his own distinct idiom, a creative force in his own right.

art." He may have been a ringleted, vain pretty boy wholly immodest about his own culinary talents, but Carême proved to be a prophet.

Born a few years before the French Revolution of 1789, Carême came of age in a time when the aristocratic culinary traditions of the prerevolutionary ancien régime were still very much in evidence, yet the bourgeoisie, too, were taking an increased interest in eating well. Carême straddled these two worlds. He always worked for a wealthy patron—most notably for the French diplomat Charles Maurice de Talleyrand—but he also recognized that the future of cuisine depended on a wide audience, not just a bunch of wealthy, titled banqueters. (Carême was himself a self-made man who, he claimed, was born to a poor family of twenty-five children and abandoned in the streets of Paris at the age of eleven. He stumbled into a job as an apprentice in a pastry shop, thereby kicking off his illustrious career.) "My book is not written for great houses alone," he wrote in the introduction of *L'art de la cuisine française*. "On the contrary, I want it to have a general utility . . . I would like every citizen in our beautiful France to eat delicious food." Ambitious and prescient, Carême realized that publishing was his way to posterity, and, between the many books he wrote and his high-profile commissions for European nobility (in addition to Talleyrand, he also worked for Czar Alexander I of Russia, the Prince Regent of England, and Baron James de Rothschild), he became famous throughout Europe—truly, the first celebrity chef.

Carême's books were the first to collect his nation's traditions, methodologies, and usages of kitchen equipment into "French cuisine" as we think of it today, with exhaustively thorough chapters devoted to the preparation of various kinds of bouillons, soups, sauces, quenelles, breads, fish dishes, and meat dishes—some of the very same processes that Julia Child and her collaborators would painstakingly deconstruct and reconstruct for an American audience in the early 1960s. It was also Carême who popularized such terms as béchamel, velouté, and soufflé, ensuring that, as one of his biographers put it, "like ballet (another art formed in seventeenth-century France), cuisine would continue to speak in French."

All that said, Carême's most avid readers were not ordinary French citizens but the burgeoning ranks of restaurant chefs, the foremost of whom, Escoffier, streamlined Carême's grand, fanciful visions into recipes and techniques that could be pragmatically applied in a professional kitchen. (Whereas Carême never worked in a restaurant—hardly any good ones existed in his heyday*—Escoffier never worked for a private patron.) The Provence-born Escoffier was something of a boy wonder, establishing himself in the 1860s at Le Petit Moulin Rouge, Paris's most popular restaurant of the time. By the 1880s, he was working at the Grand Hotel in Monte Carlo, where he befriended César Ritz, a Swiss up-and-comer on the management side of the hotel. In 1890, Escoffier and Ritz were hired in tandem by the theater impresario Richard D'Oyly Carte[†] to run the restaurant and hotel operations, respectively, of his new luxury hotel in London, the Savoy. The Savoy gave Escoffier a platform from which to put his Carême-lite theories into practice: the repertoire would still be based on Carême's principles as set forth in *L'art de la cuisine française*, but without the rococo presentations and cumbersome *service à la française* of Carême's day, in which a profusion of dishes was laid out on the table all at once. Escoffier helped popularize *service à la russe* (Russian-style), in which courses were brought out in succession by waiters (with diners no longer obligated to pass their plates around to get a taste of this and

---

*Though Europe has several restaurants that claim to date as far back as the Middle Ages, the restaurant in the modern sense—an establishment that offers waiter service and a varied bill of fare to paying customers—dates back only to the late eighteenth century. The word "restaurant" is attributed to a Paris soup merchant named Boulanger who believed his soups had curative, or restorative, properties. Boulanger's establishment, which opened in 1765, was said to have been adorned with a sign that read *Boulanger débite des restaurants divins*, which translates, more or less, as "Boulanger provides divine sustenance." The first fine-dining restaurant of consequence, complete with a good wine cellar, is generally thought to be La Grande Taverne de Londres, which opened in Paris in 1782 under the auspices of Antoine Beauvilliers, who challenged Carême in the cookbook-publishing stakes with his own *L'art du cuisinier* (1814).

†D'Oyly Carte made his fortune as the producer of Gilbert and Sullivan's operettas. He built the Savoy Theatre first, in 1881, and conceived of the hotel as a posh après-show spot for well-to-do theatergoers. The hotel ended up being a bigger earner than his theatrical endeavors.

that), and he pioneered the practice of à la carte dining, wherein one guest could order a completely different set of courses from another.

Escoffier also devised the *chefs de partie* system of function-specific kitchen stations, eliminating the old jumble of redundant, overlapping departments, and furnished his kitchens with state-of-the-art iron ranges, making his operations more efficient than the hearth-based kitchens of Carême's day. (Hearth cooking would remain a backward abomination in restaurants with serious intentions until Americans such as Alice Waters and Peter Hoffman invented urban-farmhouse chic in the 1980s.) Such was the success of the Ritz-Escoffier team that they soon went into business for themselves, with Ritz managing the eponymous Hotel Ritz in Paris and the Carlton in London, and Escoffier serving as these hotels' head of restaurant services and acting in a similar capacity for the luxury cruise lines that sought his imprimatur.* Escoffier's 1903 book, *Le guide culinaire*, became the primer for all cooks seeking to understand the complete repertoire of proper French haute cuisine, its 5,012 recipes effectively standardizing the fancy French menu and giving us the hit parade of rich dishes that, until the final decades of the twentieth century, defined four-star dining: velouté of chicken soup, lobster *à l'américaine*, poached Dover sole in champagne sauce, filet mignon with bordelaise and béarnaise sauces, veal kidneys in mustard-cream sauce, crêpes suzette, etc.

HENRI SOULÉ AND his charges were hardly the first people to offer fancy French food in the United States. Lorenzo Delmonico cemented his reputation as New York City's greatest restaurateur of the nineteenth century by hiring the Frenchman Charles Ranhofer to run his kitchens in 1861, and, among

---

*In 1910, the New York Ritz, to which César Ritz had licensed his name, opened on Madison Avenue, with Louis Diat as the executive chef. In 1950, as this hotel was about to close, Diat told *The New Yorker*, "I am not of the school of Escoffier, but of the schools of M. Jules Tissier, of the Bristol, in Paris; of M. Georges Gimon, of the Paris Ritz; and of M. Emile Malley, of the London Ritz"—a curious remark, given that Messieurs Gimon and Malley were presumably following the directives of Escoffier.

the wealthy families of the nineteenth century's second half, it was a status symbol to employ a French chef at one's Fifth Avenue mansion or Newport "cottage."

But Soulé made his mark as haute cuisine's great disseminator in America. Delmonico's represented an old way, with menu items numbering in the hundreds and multicourse banquets that stretched on for hours—a Ranhofer meal typically progressed from oysters to soups (one clear, one stewlike) to hors d'oeuvres to fish to game to viands to terrines to salads to a variety of desserts, among them Baked Alaska, invented by the chef to honor Secretary of State William Seward's 1867 purchase of Alaska from Russia. It was Gilded Age gorge-athon eating for wealthy robber barons, probably fantastic to have experienced, but not as *raffiné* as the Escoffier-derived cookery and modern service that the French Pavilion offered fairgoers in 1939. (Soulé had actually waited on Escoffier several times in the 1920s, when the great chef was retired and lunched twice weekly at Soulé's place of work, the Hôtel Mirabeau in Paris.)

Soulé's timing was good, too. As the fair began in May, the U.S. restaurant industry was recovering not only from the Depression but from the effects of Prohibition. Though the Volstead Act of 1919 had been repealed in 1933, making booze and undiluted wine legal again, the alcohol ban had already exacted a devastating toll on the hospitality industry, wiping out the luxury pleasure palaces of the previous century, Delmonico's included.* For the Manhattan swells old enough to remember the good old days before Prohibition, the Restaurant Français at the French Pavilion was a gustatory reawakening. Crosby Gaige, Lucius Beebe, and their epicurean comrades from the International Wine and Food Society made a pilgrimage to Queens and were duly impressed, as was the still-unknown Jim Beard, who went as

---

*Delmonico's had begun in 1827 as a café operated by Lorenzo's uncles, John and Peter—born in Switzerland as Giovanni and Pietro Del-Monico—and by 1831 had upgraded itself to a self-described "Restaurant Français." The entrepreneurial Lorenzo, the Jean-Georges Vongerichten of his time, extended the brand aggressively, opening a new Delmonico's location every time New York's social center of gravity crept northward.

a guest of the Society's Jeanne Owen. For those traveling to the World's Fair from other parts of the United States, the restaurant was an outright revelation, its capons in tarragon aspic and noisettes of lamb with stuffed artichokes unlike anything the folks were eatin' back home in Wichita. Even with prices that were high for 1939—$1.60 for *Coq au Vin de Bordeaux*, $5.50 for a bottle of 1929 Cheval-Blanc—Soulé was doing overflow business, making room for customers on benches meant for his exhausted staff when all the regular tables were full.

The success of the Restaurant Français, which served upward of a hundred thousand meals over the two-summer run of the World's Fair, stoked Soulé's ambition. New York, he recognized, was essentially an untapped market, with only a handful of restaurants serving haute cuisine, such as the Colony and the Café Chambord, and even there not with his flair. Few in his homeland believed that a decent French restaurant could even exist in New York. The *New Yorker* writer and self-styled epicure Joseph Wechsberg, one of Soulé's earliest boosters in America, recounted in print a conversation he'd had with the chef Fernand Point, whose restaurant just south of Lyons, La Pyramide, was widely thought to be France's greatest in the first half of the twentieth century. "After all," said Point, an intimidating man who stood six foot three and weighed upward of 300 pounds, "how French can *any* French restaurant be in America?" Though Soulé revered Point, he took umbrage at these words and set out to prove the big man wrong.

The ominous news reports issuing forth from the other side of the Atlantic made the idea of a permanent American venture even more appealing. As the first summer of the World's Fair drew to a close, France had already entered into war with Germany. By the fair's second summer, in 1940, Soulé was working with a drastically reduced staff, since most of his men had been conscripted into the army, and the crowds were noticeably thinner and less lively than the previous year. In mid-June, Paris fell to the Nazis, and the French signed a surrender agreement with Germany, leaving the country in the hands of the puppet Vichy government, and leaving the French Pavilion employees wondering what kind of life awaited them back home.

For Soulé, the die was cast when, shortly after the World's Fair came to an end, the U.S. government decreed that French refugees could obtain permanent work visas provided that they had jobs lined up and that they ritually reentered the country. In 1941, after a few months of uncertainty, a contingent of the Restaurant Français staff that included Soulé, Franey, and even Jean Drouant himself traveled to the Canadian side of the Niagara River for the purpose of ceremonially crossing the Peace Bridge that connects Fort Erie, Ontario, to Buffalo, New York. In a remarkable stumble out of character, Soulé was the sole member of the group not to have his immigration papers in order; to his embarrassment, he had to stay in Canada for three weeks. Nevertheless, he made it back to New York, and when he did, he found himself completely in charge of the new restaurant he'd planned on opening with Drouant—though Drouant had arranged the financing for the new enterprise (reputedly by hitting up Joseph Kennedy, who in turn reeled in other investors), he decided at the eleventh hour that he missed France too much and returned home. With Drouant out of the picture, it was Soulé's show.

The restaurant that he finally opened in October 1941 at 5 East Fifty-fifth Street, strategically situated opposite the plush St. Regis Hotel, was called Le Pavillon, in honor of its Flushing roots. On opening night, Soulé staged a bacchanal for an invitation-only guest list of Kennedys, Rockefellers, Vanderbilts, and the like, none of whom were charged. The menu included copious amounts of beluga caviar, a mousse of sole with lobster and champagne sauces, a roasted fillet of beef in truffle sauce, and magnums of Chateau Pétrus, the great Bordeaux, which had theretofore never been sipped by Americans on their own soil. "There were no concessions to 'American taste,' " recalled Franey, who, clearly a favorite of the demanding Soulé, was brought aboard as the *chef poissonier*, a *commis* no longer. "The menu was in French, of course, and most of our educated and wealthy customers could work their way through it with at least some comprehension, but if they did not understand a particular term, I am certain they would hide the fact for fear of seeming gauche."

Le Pavillon was a big step forward in American fine dining, the template for the fine French restaurant with Escoffier-derived cuisine and exqui-site, tiered service administered by a battalion of captains, headwaiters, and waiters. In the 1940s, much more was expected of the waitstaff than the mere delivery of plated appetizers, entrées, and desserts—the waiters did a great deal of tableside preparation themselves, carving roasts and birds, and portioning out servings of poached salmon and crabmeat omelet from the *buffet froid*, the prominently displayed cold buffet table that was another req-uisite flourish of the time. (Franey was granted plenty of latitude in prepar-ing dishes for the *buffet froid*, and his prowess there is probably what convinced Soulé that he would one day be worthy of being Le Pavillon's head chef.)

Le Pavillon was important in and of itself, but it became even more so as the decades advanced and its employees opened their own places. Directly or indirectly, Soulé's palace begat the "Le" and "La" restaurants that reestab-lished New York as a major gastronomic city in the mid-twentieth century: La Caravelle, Le Périgord, La Côte Basque, La Grenouille, Le Cygne, and Le Mistral, to name but a few. (Charles Masson, who opened La Grenouille, the only direct descendant of Le Pavillon still in operation at the time of this book's publication, was part of the original '39 World's Fair crew.) As New York's contingent of sophisticated diners grew, the phrase "He worked un-der Soulé" became a tipster's catchphrase, the mark of a place worth check-ing out.

For a quarter of a century, until his death in 1966, Soulé was the undis-puted godhead of American fine dining, and even Fernand Point conceded that Soulé had gotten it right—in a gesture of acknowledgment, Point, in 1949, let Soulé in on a share of his supply of a rare first-growth Burgundy. Though New York never lacked for flamboyant restaurateurs, Soulé was a new breed of food figure, an object of obsession, curiosity, and sycophancy among his wealthy clients and the press. The *New York* magazine restaurant critic Gael Greene, who endeared herself to Soulé late in his life, described the proprietor as "a flirtatious five-foot-five cube of amiability" (to *her*, any-way) who was also a "showman, snob, perfectionist, martinet, con man, wooer, and wooed master of haute cuisine." Le Pavillon itself, she wrote, smelled "buttery, with hints of rum from the sauce anglaise and vague whiffs of almond."*

The New York rich had never encountered a character quite like Soulé, a man of peculiar prejudices and ceremonies—Franey remembered him always beginning the dinner service by "raising both of his arms above his head and vibrating them the way a minstrel singer might," evidently so that the sleeves of his shirt would jut out of his tuxedo just so, revealing the gold cuff links given to him by the Duke and Duchess of Windsor. Despite being comically *pingouin*-like in appearance, Soulé glided rather than waddled, and showered favored guests with his peculiar brand of obsequiousness, which, utterly devoid of warmth, put *them* on point, obligating them to try the special *plat du jour* whose last portions he had reserved, he insisted, just for them. The VIPs, like the Windsors and the Kennedys, were seated by Soulé in the front of the restaurant, in the section that came to be known as the *royale,* while lessers were seated farther back, and nobodies were seated in an alcove off to the side, out of view of the *royale.* Here, the very American notion of a "power table" was born.†

His clientele reveled in exchanging tales about Soulé. There was the time that a customer, dispassionately informed by the proprietor that no table would be available for at least an hour, flew into a rage and slapped Soulé smack on his bald pate. With one right uppercut, Soulé knocked the man unconscious and had his busboys collect the interloper and carry him out to

---

*Wechsberg, too, attempted to capture Le Pavillon's aroma in words, as "a delicate blend of *beurre noisette* [brown butter] and *sauce homard* [lobster sauce], Périgueux truffles and broiled Chateaubriand, Fine Champagne 1843 and a fine Havana—and the lovely scents of lovely women."

†Doing his bit for the war effort, that irrepressible boulevardier Lucius Beebe devoted several column inches to the quandary of how men in uniform should be seated at fancy restaurants: Do nobodies of high military rank deserve better seating than somebodies of low rank? Evidently not, thought Beebe: "When Alfred Gwynne Vanderbilt, long an ornament of the plushier puddles, turned up in a boatswain's mate's uniform, he wasn't to be discarded, even momentarily, in favor of some provincial colonel who, until the week before, had never encountered a French menu."

the curb. In another instance, some Pavillon regulars, vacationing one summer in Soulé's native Basque country, made a rare spotting of the chubby restaurateur out of context, strolling his old stomping grounds in Saubrigues, near Bayonne in southwest France, dressed in baggy shorts and a white cap. Asked by the tourists if he was indeed who they thought he was, Soulé brusquely said, "You must be mistaken," and moved on.

Willfully remote, Soulé resisted even his most famous customers' incursions into his personal life and was repulsed by any physical displays of familiarity, including attempts by his female guests to kiss him. Nevertheless, everyone in New York society knew of his peculiar arrangement: that there was a mysterious, never-seen Mrs. Soulé who lived back in France, and that Le Pavillon's coatroom lady, Henriette Spalter, known to all as Madame Henriette, was his mistress.

THAT A RESTAURANT such as Le Pavillon could storm out of the gates during wartime, with a full reservation book and adoring press write-ups, while rationing was in effect and the Depression still cast a pall over the economy, speaks volumes about the esteem in which educated Americans held French culture and French cuisine. Among the upper classes, Francophilia had held sway for some time, and it was de rigueur for society mothers to hire French governesses for their children. ("I spoke French before I spoke English!" boasts Dinah Lord, the smart-alecky kid sister of Tracy Lord, Katharine Hepburn's heiress character, in the 1940 film *The Philadelphia Story*.) *Gourmet*, in its early incarnation as an unabashedly clubby, elitist publication, leaned heavily on the talents of charter contributor Samuel Chamberlain, a wellborn Boston artist even better versed in *la vie française* than the magazine's founder, Earle MacAusland. Chamberlain and his wife, Narcissa, had lived in Burgundy for a dozen years before World War II. Under the pseudonym Phineas Beck, Samuel wrote a serialized narrative for the magazine called "Clémentine in the Kitchen," a somewhat fictionalized, rather precious account of his family's bumpy readaptation to life in Yankee Massachusetts, to which it fled as the war geared up. The rosy-cheeked Clémentine of the title, putatively the "Beck" family's imported country-girl cook, forever befuddled by the plastic-wrap ways of *les américains*, was not a real person but a composite of the French cooks the Chamberlains had employed. Not that this bit of artifice mattered to the readers—"Clémentine in the Kitchen" was *Gourmet*'s most popular feature in its first year of publication.*

But the war unleashed a tide of pro-French sentiment well beyond the provinces of the wealthy and well-traveled. Though it was this very war, and the collaborationist Vichy regime specifically, that later engendered the "cheese-eating surrender monkeys" epithet popular among twenty-first-century American Francophobes,† the truth is that World War II and the decade that followed it represented a high-water mark in Franco-American goodwill. The GIs who fought in France became besotted with the country they were liberating; the French reciprocated, expressing their love of America. "I'd always wanted to go to America, since I don't know how long," says the chef Roger Fessaguet, who remembers being smitten with Sonja Henie, the va-va-voomish Norwegian-born figure skater who'd turned pro in the United States in the 1930s. (Fessaguet, later the founding chef of La Caravelle, got to realize his dream in 1948, when he was seventeen, crossing the Atlantic to join the staff of Le Pavillon.)

Pierre Franey, returning to his homeland as a U.S. infantryman, discovered firsthand the high regard in which the French held the United States. The kid of Le Pavillon's staff, he'd been conscripted into the U.S. Army and uprooted from the kitchen for three years, participating in the Allies' taking of Normandy. In 1945, in the war's closing months, while his unit was

---

*Chamberlain collected his Clémentine pieces into a book in 1943. Fifty-eight years later, *Clémentine in the Kitchen* was reissued as the first title in Random House's Modern Library food series, with a new introduction by *Gourmet*'s Ruth Reichl.

†This epithet was first used to satirical effect in a 1995 episode of *The Simpsons* in which the character Groundskeeper Willie, an ever-irate Scotsman, utters the phrase to express his disdain for the French. It was repurposed by conservative commentators as an angry taunt during the run-up to the 2003 U.S. invasion of Iraq, which the French government opposed.

bivouacking near his hometown of St. Vinnemer, Franey sought and received his commander's permission to ride with another GI into the village so that he could see his family for the first time in five years. As his Jeep rumbled through the countryside, word spread among the excited French locals that the liberators, the Americans, were coming. By the time the Jeep rolled into St. Vinnemer, Franey, still unrecognized beneath his U.S.-issue helmet, saw a throng of cheering villagers gathered in the town center, one of whom, waving a homemade American flag, was his mother.

As more and more Americans voyaged to France in the postwar era, abetted by the dollar's strength against the weak franc and the advent of jet travel, they came to understand France as the home not only of swank Parisians eating Escoffier food but of bistros and auberges that served *la cuisine de bonne femme*, the cookery of women, of comfort, of the home: potato-leek soup, pot-au-feu, omelets. "The magic that France had at the time was felt by so many of us," says Chuck Williams, a Florida native, who, after completing his wartime duty in the air force, built himself a house in the undiscovered hinterlands of Sonoma County, California. "It was roaming on the side streets of Paris and eating in the small mom-and-pop restaurants where you might be sitting next to a charming dog or cat," he says. "It was the haunting music and songs sung by Edith Piaf that I heard everywhere. It was the wonderful pastry and chocolate shops in every block, the butcher shops, the crepe and waffle stands, the standup bars where you stopped for an espresso, a café au lait, or a cognac."

So taken was Williams with Parisian culture that he eventually put aside his career as a building contractor and, in 1956, opened a kitchenwares store that he called Williams-Sonoma. "I wanted to capture the magic of Paris in my shop, and I think I achieved it by making it completely French," he says. "Imagine a wall of every mold and baking tin in every size, a display of all the French tools, wooden spoons, knives, and spatulas. Another wall of heavy copper and aluminum pots and pans. A display of fish poachers and couscous cookers in every size. Even the roll-down awning for the front of the shop was the French flag."

Judith Jones, later Julia Child's editor at Knopf, was another young

American who chose to live the Parisian expat life after the war. "It was all so heady," she says. "Cooking at home had all been sort of boring and traditional and English. You weren't supposed to say, 'Mmm, wasn't that yummy?' It was like sex—you just didn't talk about such a thing. We had a maid who cooked, and my mother was always closing the kitchen door, 'cause she didn't want the smells to come out. We weren't allowed to have onions in the house. And garlic! That was really beyond the pale. So you can imagine how excited I was by France. I loved the way people shopped, the care they took. It was right after the war, and people would stand in line at the charcuterie, with their toes sticking out of worn-out carpet slippers, and spend four times what I spent. They'd spend their last penny for something good."

THOUGH JIM BEARD had been steadily making a name for himself as cookery's Mr. U.S. of A. when the war broke out, and though 1944 saw the publication of his latest volume of culinary Americana, *Fowl and Game Cookery*, he, too, was caught up in the era's Francophilia. Beard had been to France in the 1920s, when, having been sent by his mother to London to study with a renowned voice coach, he was unable to resist an extended side trip to the spiritual home of gastronomy. Even on his student budget, Beard ate well at the sorts of homey Paris bistros that A. J. Liebling would later romanticize in his backward-looking *New Yorker* pieces of the fifties: places where "the food was good bourgeois fare and exceedingly cheap," Beard remembered. "We ate good *pot-au-feu*, calf's feet *poulette*, *blanquettes* and *boeuf à la bourguignonne*, with an occasional roast chicken or bit of game." An intrepid market-goer, Beard became a regular at Paris's enormous central market, Les Halles, which made his beloved Yamhill Market in Portland look like a roadside farm stand. To cap off these wonderments, Beard found himself, for once, able to enjoy sexual freedom, and had a brief fling with a young man named Hans.

In 1942, despite being thirty-nine and in no shape to fight, Beard tried to enlist in the armed forces, partly out of a genuine sense of national duty, and partly out of a desire to once again travel to France. Beard's weight didn't make him an attractive prospect to the United States Army, but by 1943, he found a place where he was welcome: the United Seamans Service (USS), which was responsible for providing food, shelter, and recreation to sailors in the merchant marine. It was a cushy post—he essentially managed the officers' clubs and devised comfort-food menus for the wounded and homesick sailors—but Beard applied himself well. It took him a couple of years and three stints in the Western Hemisphere—in Puerto Rico, Brazil, and Panama—before he got to France, but finally, in 1945, the USS sent him to the bustling Provençal port city of Marseilles, where he explored southern France for the first time and soaked in its garlic- and olive-oil-suffused cookery. When his USS duty was up, Beard spent a few days in liberated Paris, where he took advantage of the city's depressed economy to load up on steeply marked-down copper pots and pans to take back to New York.

AS UNLIKELY A MAN in uniform as Beard was, he had some competition in the navy's Craig Claiborne, yeoman, third class. Claiborne was a troubled soul, a queer, squinty-eyed kid from Indianola, Mississippi, with a set of psychosexual complexes worthy of a Tennessee Williams character. Born to a proper Southern family just as it was experiencing a reversal in fortune—his father, Luke, had some investments go sour and abruptly lost his considerable landholdings—Claiborne, as a small boy, saw his home transformed into a boardinghouse. Young Craig was forced to share a bed with his father, a melancholy, devout soul who was given to uttering the gloomy, baffling phrase: "This world and one more and then the fireworks." One night, as he later revealed in his squeamishly received confessional memoir, *A Feast Made for Laughter*, Claiborne ran his arm along his sleeping father's, down to the hand, to discover his father's fingers "enfolded around the throttle of his lust." It was a transformative moment for the pubescent boy, who, for the rest of his life, would prefer the company of older men, and who proceeded to "begin an exploration of his [father's] body" every night once Dad had (apparently) drifted off to sleep. Neither father nor son ever acknowledged these "explorations" in conversation.

Slight, unathletic, and hopeless at fitting in with the other Mississippi boys, most of whom played football and baseball, Claiborne found solace in the kitchen, where his mother, Miss Kathleen, and her retinue of black servants whipped up an amazing assortment of dishes for the boarders in a variety of idioms: Creole, soul food, down-home, Fannie Farmer. Like Beard, Claiborne had an adventurous palate at a young age and reveled in everything from chitterlings (pig's small intestines) to oyster gumbo to barbecue to homemade coconut cake. Unlike Beard, Claiborne was more aggravated by than devoted to his mother, whose grandeur in the face of the family's debts he found mortifying, and whose efforts to lend direction to his directionless life he found smothering.* As unsuited to the military as he seemed, the unhappy Claiborne, who had bounced from Mississippi State University to the University of Missouri, decided that the navy was his ticket out of Miss Kathleen's stifling embrace. A month after graduating from Missouri with a bachelor's degree in journalism in 1942, he was doing clerical work for the navy's intelligence division in Chicago. By autumn, Claiborne was aboard the naval cruiser the USS *Augusta*, charging across the Atlantic to participate in Operation Torch, the Allied invasion of North Africa, overseen by Rear Admiral H. K. Hewitt of the navy and General George S. Patton of the army.

Operation Torch was a success, opening up a second front for the Allies against the Nazis, who were pushing westward from Egypt. That November, off the coast of Morocco, the *Augusta* officers and crew celebrated with a shipboard Thanksgiving meal whose courses were jokingly gussied up

---

*Claiborne also never forgave his mother for withholding from him for six months the information that his boyhood friend and biggest crush, Gordon Lyon Jr., an air force pilot, had been shot down over the Solomon Islands in 1943. Like Gore Vidal's great teen love, the baseball prodigy Jimmy Trimble, who was also killed in combat in the Pacific theater, Lyon was a handsome, sensitive jock with a unique tolerance for "dear boys," though he didn't have an affair with Claiborne, as Trimble did with Vidal.

with French words and allusions to commanding officers and North African locales: Cream of Tomato Soup à la Casablanca, Baked Spiced Spam à la Capitaine de Vaisseau, Chantilly Potatoes à la Patton. But Claiborne, who was scheduled to return to America on the *Augusta*, itched to go ashore and explore Casablanca, whose parapets and domes he could see through binoculars from the deck. In an uncharacteristically brazen move, he asked the vessel's admiral, John Leslie Hall, if he could join the command group that was staying behind in North Africa, perhaps as a secretary to the admiral himself. Hall agreed, and the elated Claiborne proceeded to undertake his own little gustatory tour of Casablanca, eating Moroccan couscous for the first time— "with sweet dried fruits and that best of all hot sauces, harissa, a fiery blend of chilies and coriander," as he later recalled—and also enjoying his first real French cooking, at a bistro called La Comédie whose mom-and-pop proprietors invited him to their home for roast chicken and omelets.

The motives behind Claiborne's long, multi-stint naval career were not wholly cynical—"To die in [World War II] for the cause of humanity and justice was to elevate your soul to God, and I would have willingly given my life," he said—but he certainly knew how to manipulate the navy bureaucracy's apparently boundless need for warm bodies to his advantage. His Operation Torch experience and college degree somehow made him a plausible candidate for officer training—even though, as a communications specialist, he never did any shooting—and so, after being accepted into a training program in 1943, he enrolled at Notre Dame University, from which he emerged the following year as Ensign Claiborne. "In all of Navy history there has probably never been a more incompetent navigator or communications expert than I," Claiborne later admitted. But being Ensign Claiborne allowed him to fulfill his boundless curiosity about other cultures—which would later serve him in good stead as a journalist—and afforded him the opportunity to keep his distance from Miss Kathleen, who nevertheless tormented him with bagfuls of letters that he characterized as "a giant-sized umbilical cord wrapped unceremoniously and noose-like around my neck." (In one characteristic missive, she wrote, "I harbor but one single wish in this life, that you may know that there is no perfect love except that of a mother.") The veteran naval officers, for their part, seemed not to mind the eccentric, ingratiating kid with the mush-mouth Mississippi accent and courtly "If ah do say so" locutions. Claiborne simply loved navy life—he exulted in the cushy officers' barracks, worshipped his superiors, and harbored secret crushes on a number of them, including the *Augusta*'s Admiral Hall, whom he admired as "one of the most . . . handsome men I have ever encountered."

Shrewd enough, barely, to bluff his way through naval maneuvers— when given the command of a submarine chaser at war's end in Okinawa, he relied on his underlings' navigational expertise and God's graces to get the boat safely back home to Hawaii—Claiborne turned again and again to the navy for salvation when civilian life grew drab. Marooned in the late forties in an unfulfilling job in the advertising department of the *Chicago Daily News*, Claiborne cashed in on the GI Bill in early 1950 to enroll at the Alliance Française in Paris, purportedly to learn French, but more realistically to goof around France as so many other Americans were doing. "If I could have named my one major dream in life since I learned to reason, it was to visit and live in France," he later said. "It is not to exaggerate to say that all my life I had felt an alien in America . . . It is a bit mawkish, I know, but the moment the taxi turned the corner on the Champs Élysées, driving toward l'Étoile, I was possessed with the most extraordinary feeling of coming home after years and perhaps centuries of absence, and I started to cry."

In Paris, Claiborne ordered a simple meal of scrambled eggs with fresh tarragon, then an unknown quantity in the United States, and reveled in its "heavenly" qualities. He went to an upscale suburban restaurant called Le Pavillon Henry IV (no relation to Henri Soulé's Le Pavillon) and rapturously received his baptism in béarnaise, enjoying the tarragon-infused sauce atop tournedos of beef. He splurged daily on fruit tarts and pastries from Paris's numerous patisseries. His transformative moment, though, came on the ship back to New York, when he was flat broke, and, with some money borrowed from a friend, managed one last great meal: *turbotin à l'infante*, slow-cooked young turbot in a white-wine and fish-stock reduction, garnished with a puff-pastry crescent. "Somewhere out there, and I don't know where," he thought to himself, "there are secrets to be learned." He asked for, and got, the recipe from the chef.

Compelled by a lack of funds to return to Chicago, where he grudgingly worked as a copywriter for a public relations firm, the thirty-year-old Claiborne was one of the few Americans who registered delight at the news of the Korean conflict, as the nascent "proxy war" to the Cold War was called in the summer of 1950. He again volunteered for overseas duty with the navy, again somehow avoided anything resembling the dirty business of warfare (and exasperated the commander of a British battleship, who shouted "Render honors!" as his vessel sailed past Claiborne's, to which the perplexed Claiborne responded, "Do *whut?*"), and again hoarded his pay and counted on a GI Bill scholarship to get him back to Europe. Indeed, it was while ostensibly doing his duties as the "operations officer" on a destroyer escort during the Korean War that Claiborne, his mind wandering, put two and two together: he liked writing; he liked food—perhaps he could make a living writing about food.

But how to receive the proper credentials for such a career? After admitting to his increasingly loathed mother that he was contemplating enrolling at Paris's famed Le Cordon Bleu cooking school, Claiborne was surprised when Miss Kathleen countered with a genuinely constructive suggestion: that he apply to a Swiss hotel school she had heard good things about, L'École Hôtelière, L'École Professionnelle de la Société Suisse des Hôteliers, the Professional School of the Swiss Hotel Keepers Association. The school, in Lausanne, was a training ground for people who hoped to become managers of luxury hotels—not exactly what Claiborne had in mind for himself, but he was happy to be accepted, and he matriculated there in 1953. One of the few other Americans in his class was James Nassikas, a New Hampshire kid who later became well-known in food circles as the owner of the Stanford Court hotel in San Francisco, Jim Beard's de facto West Coast home and the site of many of his cooking classes in the seventies. "I said to

Craig, 'Gee, what kind of hotel do you want?' and he said, 'I don't want to be in the hotel business,' " Nassikas says. "I remember that he proudly showed me a letter he'd written to the editor of the *Chicago Tribune* where he was commenting on a recipe for filet of sole marguery, a real classic French preparation. He was so proud they printed it. I was just puzzled—I didn't understand."

While the navy had been an effective means to an end, L'École Hôtelière was the first place Claiborne felt he belonged. In his eighteen-month program, he learned the ins and outs of proper table service, using the summertime break to *stage* (pronounced "stahj"), or get on-the-job training, as a waiter at a Swiss mountain resort. Even more exhilarating was the cooking curriculum, which called for Claiborne to learn the fundamental methodologies of an Escoffier-style kitchen. A world away from Miss Kathleen's country cookin', Claiborne, under the tutelage of tubby elders in toques, made puff pastry, quiches ("wholly unknown to Americans at the time"), hollandaise sauce, consommé, pâtés, quenelles, roasts, and soufflés. In 1954, Claiborne graduated eighth in his class, with the conviction that if he was going to make it as a food writer, he would have to move to New York. His native Mississippi had no place for a food-loving sissy boy, but in Manhattan, he would find a way to fit in.

JULIA McWILLIAMS WAS as eager as Claiborne and Beard to do her part for the war effort in the early 1940s, but, ironically, in light of her future fame, she was the least hell-bent on getting to France. In Pasadena, she'd divided her time between volunteer work for the Red Cross and socializing within her family's wealthy circle, even rejecting a 1941 marriage proposal from Harrison Chandler, of the prominent family that owned the *Los Angeles Times*. For a six-foot-two woman pushing thirty, in a social milieu in which there was intense pressure to "marry well," this was a risky move, but McWilliams knew she wasn't in love with the amiable but stiff Chandler, and, like Claiborne, she desperately craved a life change. In 1942, she left Pasadena for

Washington, where she first worked in the typing pool at the State Department, and then, not long thereafter, at the Office of Strategic Services (OSS), the precursor to the Central Intelligence Agency.

McWilliams fit the profile of the plumy, blue-blood OSS: from a good family, educated at a fine East Coast school, and wealthy enough not to care about a salary. She worked in the office of the OSS director, FDR crony William "Wild Bill" Donovan, who cherished employees of her pedigree on the grounds that they were free thinkers, unburdened by lockstep military thinking, and unbribable to boot. Not that McWilliams was spying on anyone—in D.C., she was an administrative assistant. Eager for adventure, she leaped at the OSS's solicitation of volunteers to go to India in 1944, and wound up working on a tea plantation in Kandy, a resort city in Ceylon that the OSS had commandeered as its base of operations from which to plot attacks on the Japanese.

Even late in her life, Julia Child remained circumspect about the specifics of her OSS duties, but it's known that, as Julia McWilliams, she had a high security clearance and was, at the very least, responsible for processing classified papers about the OSS's various espionage and sabotage schemes in the war's Southeast Asia theater. Off duty, McWilliams found that Ceylon, with its lush flora and encampments of ginned-up British and American officers, provided a seductive backdrop for the sort of drunken frolics with sophisticates that she had enjoyed as a party girl in Pasadena. The men she met in Kandy, though, were of an altogether more worldly breed, especially Paul Child, ten years her senior, a Bostonian by birth, an artist by training, and a cartographer for the OSS.

Prematurely bald and a good six inches shorter than McWilliams, Child nevertheless exuded a bohemian charisma—he'd lived in Paris in the twenties, loved to cook and dine out, and was a black belt in jujitsu. McWilliams fell hard for Child, but the feeling was not mutual at first—he adored the gangly, bawdy Julia as a drinking buddy and fellow adventurer, but as an older man with lots of affairs in his past, he thought her too sexually naïve and, initially, not especially attractive. As time went on, though, and both

McWilliams and Child were relocated by the OSS to Kunming, in southern China, Child realized that he, too, was falling in love. His long letters to his twin brother, Charlie, provide a chronicle of his softening stance toward "Julie," as he called her. By the end of the war, as he headed home from China, Paul was eager for Charlie to meet this girl, even with the caveat that—as every PBS viewer would know in twenty years—she talked kind of funny. "You will appreciate her warmth," Paul wrote to Charlie late in 1945, "and you can quickly learn, as I have, to discount the slightly hysterical overtones of her manner of talking."

It was in Kunming, in the last stages of the war, that Paul Child effectively "switched on" his future wife's palate, taking her to Chinese restaurants where, for the first time, she became alive to flavor—the hams and slurpy noodles of the Yunnan Province (of which Kunming is the capital), the chilies of Szechuan, the sweet-and-sour soups and sauces of Peking-style cooking. "That is when I became interested in food," Julia later said. And as Paul baptized Julia in the ways of various Chinese cuisines, he regaled her with tales of the great French meals he'd eaten in Paris two decades earlier, when he'd moved in the same circles as Ernest Hemingway, Gertrude Stein, and Alice B. Toklas.

McWilliams came to the realization that if she wanted this man, it was in her best interests to learn how to cook. During a short reacclimation period after the war, when she and Child were living on opposite coasts—she staying with her father in Pasadena temporarily, he working for the State Department in Washington—Julia, not yet sure that marrying Paul was a foregone conclusion, took a cooking class in Beverly Hills. She recounted her halting progress to her beau in letters—and it *was* halting, with runny omelets and a duck that exploded in the oven—but Paul was pleased and, from the sound of it, aroused by her efforts. "Why don't you come to Washington and be my cook?" he wrote. "We can eat each other."

Julia McWilliams married Paul Child on September 1, 1946, in a civil ceremony at a family friend's home in New Jersey, with a reception across the Delaware River in Bucks County, Pennsylvania. They went ahead with the wedding even though they'd been in a serious car accident the day before, while driving from Charlie Child's home in Pennsylvania to New York City, where the McWilliams family was to host a wedding-eve cocktail party. The wedding photos show Julia beaming with a huge wad of gauze held fast above her left eye with white adhesive tape, and Paul leaning on a cane—a suitable beginning, somehow, to their eccentric but abiding, rollicking union.

In October of 1948, the Childs boarded the SS *America* en route to Paul's new State Department appointment as an exhibits officer for the United States Information Service (USIS) in Paris—essentially, he was to serve as a benign propagandist for the Marshall Plan to rebuild Europe. Paul's USIS duties would keep them abroad for eleven of the next thirteen years, with stints in Marseilles, the German town of Bad Godesberg, and the Norwegian capital, Oslo. But it was the Paris stint, the Childs' first and longest, stretching into early 1953, that catalyzed Julia's transformation from mere wife-hostess and good-time gal to TV's future *French Chef*.

Like Claiborne, Julia found in France, and in French food, the focus that her life to that point had lacked. Her very first meal off the boat, at a restaurant called La Couronne, in Rouen, Normandy, blew her away: sole in a basic meunière sauce, made with lemon and plenty of local butter, book-ended by oysters to start and salad and brie to finish. "I couldn't get over it," Julia recalled years later, still aghast that she'd spent the first thirty-odd years of her life eating "Middle-western, ladies'-magazine type of food." A late-comer to Francophilia, she plunged into Paris like a woman with some catching up to do. She and Paul took an apartment on the rue de l'Université (to which she referred, with characteristic Julia-ness, as the "Roo de Loo"), in the city's seventh arrondissement, and she set about learning French, walking the streets for hours, familiarizing herself with the stalls of Les Halles, having her coffee at Les Deux Magots (as opposed to at the Café de Flore—you fell into one or the other), and, above all, reveling in restaurant meals, in "the gentle garlic belches after eating escargots," as her biographer, Noël Riley Fitch, put it.

A year into her Paris life, Julia decided she wanted to learn how to cook in French—not only the *cuisine bourgeoise* of sophisticated French housewives but the haute cuisine of professional chefs, who were, by tradition, men. The logical next step was to enroll at the Cordon Bleu. As strongwilled as she was towering, Julia agitated to get out of the program for amateurs, to which she was initially assigned, and into the professional course for American war veterans, GI Bill guys learning to become chefs. She was the only woman in a class of twelve. Her teacher was Max Bugnard, a bespectacled, droopily mustached old fellow straight out of Audrey Hepburn's Cordon Bleu scenes in *Sabrina*, who'd apprenticed under Escoffier himself.

Though he joked to friends that he had become a "Cordon Bleu widower," Paul was thrilled by this development, especially since Julia, in her dogged determination to master the art of French cooking, often attempted to re-create her lessons with Bugnard the very evening after she'd learned them. In a letter to Charlie in December 1949, Paul described, for the first time, the sight of his wife, in their home kitchen, cooking French food— most likely a cassoulet, given the details: "The oven door opens and shuts so fast you hardly notice the deft thrust of a spoon as she dips into a casserole and up to her mouth for a taste-check . . . Now & again a flash of the non-cooking Julie lights up the scene briefly, as it did the day before yesterday when with her bare fingers, she snatched a set of cannellini [beans] out of the pot of boiling water with the cry, 'Wow! These damn things are as hot as a stiff cock.' "

CHAPTER THREE

THE FOOD
ESTABLISHMENT, PART I

It began with curry. Curry with fifteen little condiments and Major Grey's mango chutney. The year of the curry is hard to pinpoint, but this much is clear: it was before the year of quiche Lorraine, the year of paella, the year of vitello tonnato, the year of boeuf Bourguignon, the year of blanquette de veau, and the year of beef Wellington . . . It was the beginning, and in the beginning there was James Beard and there was curry and that was about all.

—Nora Ephron, *New York* magazine, 1968

JIM BEARD RETURNED FROM FRANCE AFTER THE WAR FEELING "ROOTLESS AND WITH-out purpose." He'd written three cookbooks, catered his share of parties, and dished out Provençal stuffed eggplant to the boys in Marseilles, but in mid-1940s America, there was simply no lucrative niche for a jolly male culinary authority to fall into. Fortunately, the National Broadcasting Company, which had started out in the twenties as a radio network, was in desperate need of ideas and programming for its upstart television operation, and it contacted Beard in 1946 to see if he was interested in doing cooking demon-strations on a new TV show.

Elsie Presents, as the show was called at first, was a hodgepodge of household hints and stilted interviews with radio and theater celebrities, with segments introduced by a puppet version of Elsie the Cow, the spokes-mascot of the Borden dairy company, the program's sponsor.* (Elsie was

---

*Like Henri Soulé, Elsie the Cow was a prominent figure at the 1939 World's Fair. Having existed to that point only as a daisy-wreathed cartoon cow in print ads, Elsie was made flesh when, at the fair's

PAGE 53: *James Beard (left) converses merrily with the ladies of the old-line food world at a Greenwich Village garden party, 1950s.*

operated by Bil Baird, the great puppeteer who later did the "Lonely Goatherd" sequence in *The Sound of Music*.) Beard was given a fifteen-minute segment at the end of the show called "I Love to Eat!"—in its modest way, the first cooking program ever on TV. The face Beard presented to the public was that of the manly man who'd written *Cook It Outdoors*, the big fella who built barbecue pits and roasted enormous birds. *Elsie Presents* ran on Fridays, fight night at Madison Square Garden, and, in its short run, immediately followed NBC's boxing telecasts. In that era, TV sets were less likely to be found in private homes than in public gathering places, and the throngs that convened in taverns and hotel lobbies to watch the fights stuck around to watch Beard, too. Charlie Berns of the 21 Club, the exclusive restaurant on Fifty-second Street in New York that began its life as a speakeasy (known colloquially as Jack and Charlie's), called Beard to tell him that one night his diners had refused to leave the bar to go to their tables until they'd finished watching Beard make spare ribs.

Though *Elsie Presents* helped Beard achieve greater name and face recognition, the show lasted only through 1947, by which time Borden had pulled out and Birds Eye Frozen Foods had assumed sponsorship—incidentally beginning Beard's long, uneasy relationship with corporate sponsors whose products and methods ran counter to his culinary values. And, for all his ability to charm a live audience at an in-store cooking demonstration, Beard was curiously stiff on TV, not his ebullient self. "Jim wasn't much good on television for some reason," says Judith Jones of Knopf. "He started out to be an actor, and I think that was probably his downfall, because the minute he got in front of a mike, he'd suddenly be acting. He couldn't be himself."

After Beard, the reigning TV cook was Dione Lucas, an Englishwoman who had graduated from the Cordon Bleu and founded her own cooking

---

Borden exhibit (which featured an automatic milking machine called a Rotolactor), the public kept demanding to know which of the 150 Jersey cows present was *the* Elsie. The Borden people selected the most attractive cow to play the role, and in 1940, this cow returned to the fair with her own special exhibit, a hay-strewn boudoir done up in what the company called "Barn Colonial" decor.

school, L'École du Petit Cordon Bleu, in London in the thirties. Lucas moved to New York after the war and started up the Dione Lucas Gourmet Cooking School (so named because the Cordon Bleu in Paris wouldn't license the name to her), landing her own one-hour program on CBS for the 1948–49 season, *To the Queen's Taste* (later retitled *Dione Lucas's Cooking Show*). Lucas was no more charismatic on TV than Beard—she was small, stocky, and dour, with her hair pulled back tightly like a suffragette's—but she was undeniably a good teacher, and her specialty was French cookery, the field of cuisine that aspirational housewives most wished to learn.

The CBS show lasted only one season, but Lucas resurfaced again in the fifties with a syndicated program and a popular restaurant next door to Bloomingdale's called the Egg Basket, where she popularized two then exotic egg preparations, the omelet and the quiche. Among Lucas's students in the fifties was Paula Wolfert, a Barnard student and young bride-to-be from a "boiled-and-broiled" background who later achieved renown, in the seventies, for her Moroccan and Mediterranean cookbooks. "For fifty dollars I took six lessons in her huge kitchen, on the second floor of the Dakota," says Wolfert. "I flipped. I loved it. I had never eaten food like that—all that cream and butter. I had to go off and have my gallbladder removed after it was over, and I wasn't even twenty yet." Nan Robertson of *The New York Times* happened to be writing up Lucas's cooking school at the time of Wolfert's attendance; the resulting article captured Lucas complimenting the youngster on her first lobster bisque ("Jolly good, Mrs. Wolfert!") while also noting, "Mrs. Wolfert then cut her finger and was rushed to the bathroom for first aid."

"Dione was a bitter woman, not warm or cuddly, like a mentor should be," says Wolfert, who stayed on for a time as Lucas's unpaid assistant in the cooking school, helping her teach rich housewives how to make *filets de sole à la meunière* and *soufflé Plaza Athenée* (with lobster and vegetables). Perhaps this bitterness was attributable to the uncertain, catch-as-catch-can life of a cooking guru in 1950s America, even one with a TV show. "She was tremendously talented and worked like a dog," Julia Child later recalled of Lucas, "but money just slipped through her fingers." Nevertheless, says

Wolfert, "Dione was important in the fifties because at least *something* was happening."

Indeed, the rising public profiles of Lucas and Beard marked the emergence of a true food establishment in America, a small group of New York–based sophisticates who, via newspaper columns, magazine work, and cookbooks, had national and even international reach. (In 1961, when asked by Judith Jones whom she wanted to meet while visiting New York to promote *Mastering the Art of French Cooking*, Child named Beard, while her collaborator, Simone Beck, requested an audience with Lucas.) In addition to Lucas and Beard, this group included Helen McCully, the food editor at *McCall's*; Jane Nickerson, her counterpart at *The New York Times*; Cecily Brownstone of the Associated Press; good ol' Clem Paddleford of the *Herald Tribune*; and the voluptuous Ann Seranne, who had started out as Crosby Gaige's mistress and ghostwriter in the forties before moving on to *Gourmet* to be Earle MacAusland's deputy, eventually assuming the full editorial duties of the magazine while "Mr. Mac" attended to the publishing side. The members of this group kept one another's counsel, exchanged gossip, and stood united in opposition to the quick-bake, canned-soup mores of the domestic scientists.

McCully, an elegant, gray-haired, tartly opinionated Nova Scotia native, presided over a culinary salon in her penthouse apartment on the Upper East Side, while Brownstone and Beard hosted more casual get-togethers at their West Village homes. Brownstone and Seranne, like McCully, were Canadian-born, further testament to the outsider makeup of the American food world; and Paddleford, though born and raised in Kansas, lived on a planet all her own, where her kitty cat Pussy Willow slept curled in a ball in her In basket, and spring was celebrated in print as that time of year when "Mr. Merolla at 963 Third Avenue has fresh catnip for puss."*

A 1956 photograph captures members of this group gathered at a sum-

---

*Beard, ever amused by Paddleford, reported to his friend Helen Evans Brown in 1959 that "Clementine . . . is hoping now to go out for a cruise on an atomic submarine to see how they all eat."

mertime reception in Brownstone's garden on Jane Street: a motley collection of ladies in mumsy frocks and snoods, teeming around a giant, balding
man in shirtsleeves and a bow tie who is eyeing a platter of chicken skewers.
Beard thrived as the only man in this group, the affable Buddha who remained on good terms with all the ladies even as they feuded with one another (Brownstone had little tolerance for Paddleford, who "didn't know
much about food" and "always wanted to find a man and get him into bed"),
and despite his own behind-the-back criticisms (Lucas, Beard confided to his
friend Helen Evans Brown, was "a great, great technician who doesn't know
food," and he resisted her overtures to run a cooking school together). It was
in this decade that Beard made his name as "James Beard," the brand name,
the face and belly of American gastronomy. He published eight books in the
fifties, including the remarkable *James Beard's Fish Cookery* (1954), which included recipes for just about every variety of fish that could be taken from
American waters (and contained the wonderfully barmy Beardism "Here are
grunions at their best"); *The Complete Book of Barbecue & Rotisserie Cooking*
(1954) and *The Complete Book of Outdoor Cookery* (1955), both of which capitalized on an American craze for backyard barbecues that had grown exponentially in the years since *Cook It Outdoors**; and *The James Beard Cookbook*
(1959), a comprehensive, generalist trade paperback for beginners that remains Beard's best-selling work.

But it was on the strength of his fourth book, *The Fireside Cook Book*
(1949), that he rose to the top of the heap. The title referred not to hearth
cooking but to the name of the Simon and Schuster imprint that published
it. Fireside Books specialized in oversize, riotously colorful edutainment
tomes on subjects from chess to folk music. For Beard, working with Fireside was his chance to do a big, all-purpose cookbook in the vein of *Fannie
Farmer* and *The Joy of Cooking*. His approach was to present a basic recipe—
for a "Plain Chicken Sauté," say—and then offer an array of variations, such

---

*It was in a favorable *New York Times* review of *The Complete Book of Barbecue & Rotisserie Cooking*
that Beard was first called the "Dean of American Cookery," an epithet that, with minor variations
(such as ". . . of American Gastronomy") stuck for the rest of his life.

as a Sauté with Mushrooms, a Sauté Provençale, a Sauté Amandine, and so on. Like *The Joy of Cooking*'s Irma Rombauer, who couldn't help but interject choice Rombauerisms into her recipes ("Why not give the cucumber the benefit of the doubt—at least once—to see whether it has really been maligned?"), Beard infused *The Fireside Cook Book* with his own distinctive voice; in his recipe for Baked Boned Shad, he declared, "A good shad boner is born, or, at the very least, highly trained; not developed at home. If you have no one to bone your shad, have it dressed whole, but be prepared for countless fine bones in the delicious meat."

The Fireside Cook Book was not exempt from the culinary unpleasantries of the period—Beard advocated beginning his "American Dinner" menu with fruit cup, and devoted an entire chapter to the joy of frozen foods—but it was fun and user-friendly, its recipes airily laid out for easy reading and decorated with cheery rural-kitsch illustrations (anthropomorphic vegetables, mice in chef's toques) by the husband-and-wife team of Martin and Alice Provensen, who that same year provided the artwork for the Golden Books perennial *The Fuzzy Duckling*.

The Fireside Cook Book sold well and got good notices, and its publication also marked the moment when Beard first explicitly made his case for an American cuisine, arguing in the introduction that "America has the opportunity, as well as the resources, to create for herself a truly national cuisine that will incorporate all that is best in the traditions of the many people who have crossed the seas to form our new, still young nation." Riding high, Beard also landed the job as *Gourmet*'s restaurant critic in 1949. But critical writing was not really his métier, and Beard, acting on the wrongheaded assumption that every *Gourmet* reviewer needed to channel the voice of Lucius Beebe, sounded little like his exuberant cookbook-author self in these pieces. He preciously used the royal "we" and larded his columns with overwrought Beebe-isms, as when he indulged in a reverie about restaurants "where one may be wafted to Olympian heights on magic gastronomical carpets."

In any event, Beard's time at *Gourmet* was short-lived. MacAusland gave him the heave-ho in 1950 for reprinting one of his *Gourmet* columns almost verbatim in the catalog of the Sherry Wine and Spirits Company, the upscale vintner on Madison Avenue. Sherry's owners, brothers Sam and Jack Aaron, adored Beard and functioned as his angels, always providing work and income for him, whether it was writing for their catalog, assisting customers on their sales floor, or—after the *Gourmet* fiasco—embarking on fact-finding tours of Europe as their consultant.* On a trip to Paris, Beard got to meet another West Coast misfit who had found her métier as a cook and sparkling *saloniste*, the San Francisco–born Alice B. Toklas, who had been Gertrude Stein's companion and had late in life made her food-publishing debut with *The Alice B. Toklas Cookbook* (1954)—a work whose unself-conscious charm as an evocation of Stein-Toklas nuttiness ("The carp was dead, killed, assassinated, murdered in the first, second, and third degree. Limp, I fell into a chair with my hands still unwashed, reached for a cigarette, lighted it and waited for the police to come . . .") was overshadowed by its inadvertent inclusion of a recipe for hashish fudge.†

Beard won further exposure in the fifties as a food columnist for *Argosy*, America's oldest pulp-fiction magazine, which had repurposed itself at the dawn of the fifties as a proto-*GQ* men's lifestyle magazine. Liberated from writing about the Olympian heights of gastronomy, "Jim" Beard, as he was bylined for the occasion, was free to dispense folksy advice on grilling steaks and mixing cocktails. *Argosy*'s editor, Jerry Mason, also underwrote the

---

*That Beard was more of a Scotch man than a wine man—his tipple of choice was a tall glass of Glenlivet on the rocks—seemed not to matter.

†Toklas, though a gifted home cook who had absorbed well the lessons of French bourgeois cookery, felt a need to flesh out her book with recipes submitted by friends. One, from the young Surrealist painter, writer, and Beat generation adjunct Brion Gysin, was for a delicious sweet that "might provide an entertaining refreshment for a Ladies' Bridge Club or a chapter meeting of the DAR," as well as "euphoria and brilliant storms of laughter; ecstatic reveries and extensions of one's personality on several simultaneous planes." The recipe called for butter, sugar, pepper, nutmeg, cinnamon, coriander, dates, figs, almonds, peanuts, and "canibus [*sic*] sativa." For all her bohemianism, the seventy-seven-year-old Toklas had no idea what the last ingredient was, and let the recipe run as submitted in the book's British edition. She was mortified when the press alerted her to her oversight, and saw to it that the American edition ran sans the marijuana-munchie recipe.

publication of *Barbecue & Rotisserie* and two other paperback quickies, *Complete Cookbook for Entertaining* (1954) and *Casserole Cookbook* (1955). And by 1956, Beard had also set up his first cooking school with André Surmain, a flashy, vainglorious entrepreneur who, five years later, would open the restaurant Lutèce with André Soltner, a young recruit from Alsace-Lorraine. The partnership with Surmain lasted only a year, but the James Beard Cooking School persevered in the test kitchens of Restaurant Associates, the hospitality group whose hard-charging visionary, Joseph Baum, had sought out Beard as a consultant for his expanding portfolio of restaurants, which by 1959 would include the Four Seasons.

Though Beard still didn't reach as many readers as newspaper columnists like Brownstone, Paddleford, and Nickerson, he eclipsed them in fame through force of personality. "Jim was an enthusiast," says Barbara Kafka, who insinuated herself into the food world in 1957 as a young writer for *Vogue.* "One of the things I learned from him was not to be afraid of all the words we're taught to eschew as writers: 'wonderful,' 'fabulous,' 'divine,' 'sublime,' 'great,' 'extraordinary'—the hyperbole words. People wanted them about food, and they still do."

There was also something to be said for Beard's sheer oddball magnetism: people were drawn in by the very sight of him, the Bosc pear body draped in a striped apron, the glint in the eyes set deep in the unusually contoured head, the suave theatricality with which he plunged into his cooking demonstrations. John Ferrone, who edited *The James Beard Cookbook* and remained close to Beard until Beard's death, recalls that his then employer, Dell, had reservations about the cover of the book's first edition, a photograph of the bow-tied Beard grinning almost dementedly as he proffered to the reader a serving platter heaped high with pork chops, cold cuts, and sausages—sausages that, in their shiny, bulging casings, somehow seemed to be miniature representations of the shiny, bulging Beard. "A lot of people thought the cover was gross—too much meat, too much fat, *yecch!*" says Ferrone. "But I think people loved that about Jim. He looked like a poster boy for good eating. I felt that he wouldn't have had the same impact if he'd been short and skinny."* The book, which had an initial print run of around 150,000, sold out almost immediately.

Learning to love the hustle, Beard took his act on the road, signing on as a consultant for Edward Gottlieb Associates, a public relations firm that had the account of the French cognac industry. Simultaneously pleasing his benefactor and his audiences, he finished off his demonstrations of lobster *à l'américaine*—a French dish, despite the name—with a showy dousing of the crustacean with cognac and a flaming finale. (He succinctly concluded this recipe in *The James Beard Cookbook* with the direction "Ignite and blaze.") Beard also entered into an endorsement deal in the late 1950s with Green Giant, the canned-vegetable company, agreeing to tout its Corn Niblets and wax beans in his recipes.† In his heart, Beard knew that lending his name to processed foods was a betrayal of his core beliefs in seasonality and regionality—on more than one occasion, to more than one acquaintance, he flagellated himself for being a "gastronomic whore"—but his cooking school required a lot of money to operate, and his ever-increasing number of writing commitments required a full-time retinue of testers and ghostwriters. By the sixties, he would also be lending his name to French's mustard and Cross & Blackwell Seafood Cocktail Sauce (the latter owned by Nestlé). Never adept at managing his finances in the first place, Beard swallowed his principles and learned to love Niblets.

Beard could more comfortably reconcile his culinary principles with his work for Joe Baum and Restaurant Associates (RA), which paid him a handsome retainer to be its "hired palate." RA was a company way ahead of its time, with a varied portfolio of restaurants of different themes and menus.

---

*Ferrone frequently had Beard to dinner at his West Thirteenth Street town-house apartment, whose tiny galley kitchen could barely accommodate Beard's girth. "If Jim turned around too quickly," says Ferrone, pointing to the belly-level knobs on his stove, "he'd turn the gas on."

†Green Giant was founded in 1903 as the Minnesota Valley Canning Company, based in the town of Le Sueur. Initially known for its "cream-style corn" and tiny, early-harvest green peas, the company introduced a larger, sweeter pea in 1925 called the Green Giant, which sold so well that the company renamed itself in the pea's honor.

Significantly, it broke away from the French template for fine dining and was willing to try, well, *anything*. The Newarker, which opened in 1953, was a bravely crazy attempt to lure non-travelers to Newark Airport with white-linen service, exquisite continental cuisine, and a variation of the word "Newark" for a name. Beard first worked with RA on the Hawaiian Room, a splashy place in the Hotel Lexington that capitalized on the Trader Vic's–style Polynesian craze with skewered meats and rum drinks.

Baum, a sharp, hard-charging graduate of Cornell University's hotel management school, was a born showman and a font of ideas, lots of them ridiculous, like adorning desserts with sparklers and serving "three-clawed lobsters" at the Newarker. By no means immune to bad taste, he often undermined his good ideas with gaudy excess—another of his RA creations, the Forum of the Twelve Caesars, which opened in 1960, was the restaurant equivalent of a Cinerama swords-and-sandals epic: a huge restaurant in Rockefeller Center meant to evoke the Roman Empire, with Cecil B. DeMille decor, cutesy menu descriptions (a salad was called "The Noblest Caesar of Them All"), and silver gladiator helmets for ice buckets. Even though it actually served good food—Mimi Sheraton, at that time an ex–*Village Voice* restaurant critic who was doing menu research for RA, remembers an "herb-scented chicken baked in clay that was cracked open most fragrantly at the table"—the Forum wasn't taken seriously as a fine-dining destination. Like a lot of Baum brainstorms, it hemorrhaged money and didn't last long.

Yet Baum, unlike many later theme-joint impresarios, actually cared about food; in fact, many in the food world credit him with coining the term "foodie" to describe a person inordinately obsessed with restaurant-going and cooking fashions. And when he and RA's president, Jerry Brody, were opening a restaurant in the Seagram Building that was to change its decor and its menus with the seasons, he turned to Beard for his intimate knowledge of traditional, seasonal American cooking. The Four Seasons, which opened in July of 1959, was and is best known for its stunning Philip Johnson design, its giant Picasso tapestry, its needly Richard Lippold sculpture that hangs above the bar, its Mies van der Rohe chairs, its undulating beaded drapes, its Zen-graceful Pool Room, and its muscular, masculine Grill Room. But its eclectic menu had Beard's fingerprints all over it, those of "a citizen of Oregon with the wish list of an always-hungry American," to quote the restaurateur George Lang, who was in charge of new projects for RA.

There were dishes that Henri Soulé would never go near, like an Amish ham steak with rhubarb, a minted lobster parfait, springtime shad roe from the Hudson, and Miami stone crabs. The menu was so eclectic, in fact, that it skewed more internationalist than American-panoramic, but it introduced a lot of ideas that, twenty years down the line, would shape the so-called New American cuisine. The restaurant grew its own fresh herbs, had a network of small purveyors who provided ingredients when they were just *à point* (including the famous avant-garde composer John Cage, who brought in the mushrooms he foraged on his upstate property in Rockland County), and featured a large number of American wines on its list.

The Four Seasons was prescient and justly celebrated upon its opening, but curiously uninfluential in terms of spearheading a movement toward a less Frenchified, more Americanized cuisine; it was its own phenomenon, and the French paradigm continued to hold sway. Nevertheless, Beard, now well into his fifties, was growing ever-more influential in other realms of the culinary whirl. In particular, he reveled in being a mentor and talent scout, using his connections to secure work for up-and-comers he felt were worthy, among them the seafood specialist John Clancy, who was installed as chef at Chillingsworth, a Cape Cod restaurant for which Beard was doing consulting,* and Paula Wolfert, who needed a new opportunity in the food world when she discovered, upon recovering from her gallbladder attack, that an unsympathetic Dione Lucas wouldn't take her back. Through a family friend, Wolfert won an audience with Beard at his town-house apartment at 86 West Twelfth Street.

---

*Among the most successful of Beard's protégés, Clancy went on to become chef at the Coach House, the venerable Southern-style restaurant in Greenwich Village, and later had his own seafood restaurant in New York.

"I go to his house, he's wearing this puffy shirt like the *Seinfeld* puffy shirt and gold chains and gold bracelets,* and he gives me a pack of recipes to make then and there," she says. The baking expert Paula Peck was coming over for dinner that evening, so Beard put Wolfert to the test immediately. Pleased with her efforts—a very late-fifties, very caloric extravaganza of lobster bisque, chicken Rafael Weill (a San Francisco dish of braised chicken in a cream-sherry sauce, named for a founder of California's Bohemian Grove camp for wealthy businessmen), and some kind of strawberry-pastry cream dessert—Beard shortly thereafter dispatched Wolfert to the Connecticut home of Mrs. Joshua Logan, wife of the Broadway director, who was throwing a dinner for 150 guests. "He gives me the recipes, she pays me, and he doesn't take any money for it," Wolfert says. "I mean, it was insane, I didn't know how to cook for 150 people, but he told me everything to do."

BY 1957, THERE WAS another man besides Beard in the ranks of the food establishment: Craig Claiborne. Claiborne's ascent, while hardly of supernova proportions, was evidence of how wide-open the food world was to anyone with sufficient industriousness and intelligence.

Armed with his degree from the Swiss hotel school, Claiborne moved, penniless, to New York in 1954. Having worked for a public relations firm in Chicago, Claiborne had an appreciation of how desperate the service sections of newspapers were for story ideas, so, summoning all the moxie he had in him, he placed a call to *New York Times* food editor Jane Nickerson to suggest that she write a story on . . . him, Craig Claiborne, recent Swiss-hotel-school graduate. Nickerson took the bait, and on May 10, under the headline GRADUATE OF SWISS HOTEL SCHOOL TELLS OF STUDY OF FRENCH COOKING, ran Nick-

---

*Beard's "private" wardrobe was far more flamboyant than the avuncular tweeds and bow ties he favored for public appearances. His theatricality and heft dictated a love for caftans, kimonos, brocade pajamas, and just about any kind of loose-fitting articles of chinoiserie. "He was almost a cross-dresser, except that he was too big," says Barbara Kafka.

erson's write-up of the "fresh-faced young man"—the food-world equivalent of a gossip-column puff piece on a promising stage ingenue:

> He was eating a lunch that included, among other things, a Martini and a shrimp cocktail. One put down Mr. Claiborne's choice of such Americanisms to his gladness about being back in the United States, where he plans to write about food professionally.

The sense of novelty with which Nickerson described the techniques Claiborne had learned overseas—such as clarifying butter, preparing pasta (a word Nickerson was compelled to define as "macaroni products"), and cooking with white wine (which, *Times* readers learned, imparts a "savory flavor" to meat and fish)—demonstrated how much work Claiborne would have cut out for him when, in a turn of events that no one foresaw, he would succeed Nickerson in 1957.

But that coup was still three years away. The *Times* article, alas, did precisely nothing for Claiborne's job prospects. So, one Friday that summer, he once again summoned all the moxie he had in him, and strode into *Gourmet's* offices (which the grand Earle MacAusland had situated in the penthouse of the Plaza Hotel) to request a meeting with Ann Seranne, the editor. Seranne, for some reason, indulged the stranger with a few minutes of her time, listening to his monologue about his hotel-school and journalism degrees. Rather skeptically, she assigned him, on spec, a 3,000-word article on tea.

Early the following Monday, Claiborne, having spent the weekend at the New York Public Library main branch in midtown, reading every old book and article on tea he could find, positioned himself just outside *Gourmet's* offices. As Seranne strode in, he presented her with his finished story, entitled "Steeped in History." She admitted to Claiborne that she'd just been trying to get rid of him on Friday, but she took the time to read the article, liked it, bought it, and, in due time, became Claiborne's sponsor. "Steeped in History," with Claiborne's title intact, ran in the January 1955 issue of *Gourmet*.

Seranne gave Claiborne more assignments and, after a few months, landed him a low-paying but steady job as a receptionist, researcher, and all-around gofer at the magazine. As his talent became evident, Claiborne was soon given editing responsibilities, such as handling the column published under the name of the esteemed, elderly ex-Ritz-Carlton chef Louis Diat (but actually written by Diat's assistant, Helen Ridley). But just as Claiborne was beginning to feel that his place at *Gourmet* was secure, Seranne had a falling out with MacAusland and quit the magazine. She persuaded Claiborne to join her at the food-industry public relations firm she was starting, Seranne and Gaden. Around this same time, Seranne introduced Claiborne to Beard. Though too Francophilic and independent-minded to become a full-fledged Beard acolyte à la John Clancy, Claiborne endeared himself to the elder man with his enthusiasm and grace, and, before long, Claiborne was a semi-regular guest and kitchen helper at Beard's West Twelfth Street dinner parties.

Claiborne soon realized that working for a public relations company proved no more satisfying in New York than it had in Chicago. By 1957, he was restless. Too old to turn once more to the navy for relief, he was saved from vocational limbo by what appeared to be an act of divine providence: one spring day, Seranne's partner at the firm, Eileen Gaden, announced to the office that Jane Nickerson was moving with her husband and children to Florida and had submitted her resignation to the *Times*. Seranne and Gaden decided then and there to take Nickerson to the 21 Club for a good-bye lunch, and invited Claiborne along. As the ladies gossiped and talked shop, he listened with frustrated longing as Nickerson explained that the *Times* editors had interviewed every lady "who can type with one finger who has ever scrambled an egg," yet had still not found a successor they deemed worthy. It had not occurred to the management that a man might want the job.

Immediately after the lunch, Claiborne, aflush with white wine and cognac, typed a letter to Nickerson in which he apologized for even bringing up the subject, but, "Do you think that the *Times* might even remotely consider an application from me?" He sent the letter off, but weeks went by without a response. Finally, while on vacation in Fire Island, unable to relax, Claiborne called Nickerson, who hesitantly acknowledged she'd received the letter and said she'd passed it on to the powers that be. "Don't get your hopes up," she advised him. "A man as a food editor . . ."

But two days later, Claiborne was on a Long Island Rail Road train racing back to the city, having received a call from Nickerson, who'd announced that Betty Howkins, the women's-page editor, wanted to meet with him. Among the last of the women's-page dowagers, whose era would soon seem as distant as the Civil War, Howkins greeted Claiborne wearing white gloves and a designer hat, the requisite look of working ladies of her generation. She proved surprisingly receptive to the idea of a male food editor, though she said that only the higher-ups could approve such a hiring.

In this matter, Claiborne's Southern background turned out to be a boon. The paper's new assistant managing editor, Clifton Daniel, was a North Carolina–born fop with long, swept-back white hair, a Savile Row wardrobe, and an interest in expanding the paper's cultural coverage, including the women's page. (He also happened to be married to Margaret Truman, the daughter of former president Harry Truman.) With Daniel warmly disposed toward the idea of hiring Claiborne, the decision went up to the *Times* managing editor, the man in charge of the whole paper, Turner Catledge. Catledge was one of New York's professional Southerners, a man who, rather than assimilate, as Claiborne had been trying his level best to do, flaunted his Southern-ness, exaggerating his honeyed vowels and cultivating an image as a manly exotic in a sea of bland, gray-flannel poindexters. Claiborne was aware that Catledge had attended Mississippi State College, as he had, albeit briefly. So when Catledge asked Claiborne where he'd gone to school, the writer responded "Missippi State"—*Missippi*, as opposed to *Mississippi*. Catledge smiled. Three days later, Claiborne was informed he'd gotten the job.

IN 1979, LOOKING BACK on more than twenty years of affiliation with the *Times* and the "gastronomic revolution" to which he'd borne witness, Claiborne wrote, "Before the seeds of the food revolution, there was one dish of foreign inspiration that reigned supreme: curry. It was the one great dish for special occasions." On that subject, Claiborne was in agreement with Nora Ephron. Ephron made her name in the 1960s as the New Journalism movement's designated foodie, filing stories for *Esquire* and *New York* magazine that mischievously examined the burgeoning "gourmet" world and its increasing equity as a pop-cultural phenomenon. In a 1968 essay for *New York*, she coined the phrase "The Food Establishment" (it was the essay's title), and cast a backward glance at this establishment's origins in the 1950s, when she was in her teens:

> Historical explanations of the rise of the Food Establishment do not usually begin with curry. They begin with the standard background on the gourmet explosion—background that includes the traveling fighting men of World War Two, the postwar travel boom, and the shortage of domestic help, all of which are said to have combined to drive the housewives of America into the kitchen.
>
> This background is well and good, but it leaves out the curry development. In the 1950s, suddenly, no one knew quite why or how, everyone began to serve curry. Dinner parties in fashionable homes featured curried lobster. Dinner parties in middle-income homes featured curried chicken. Dinner parties in frozen-food compartments featured curried rice. And with the arrival of curry, the first fashionable international food, food acquired a chic, a gloss of snobbery it had hitherto possessed only in certain upper-income groups. Hostesses were expected to know that iceberg lettuce was *déclassé* and tuna-fish casseroles *de trop*. Lancers sparkling rose and Manischewitz were replaced on the table by Bordeaux.*

---

*The curry craze may well have been instigated, or at least stoked, by the Associated Press's widely read Cecily Brownstone, who started at AP in 1947 and was most famous for her recipe for Country Captain, a chicken dish served in a curry sauce studded with almonds and currants. The recipe is alleged to have originated in Savannah, Georgia, its source a nineteenth-century sea captain who had been to India.

Glib as this summation sounds, "I was totally serious," says Ephron, who moved on from print journalism to become a novelist, screenwriter, and director whose oeuvre has a conspicuous foodie undercurrent to it (most acutely in *Heartburn*, her roman à clef about the unraveling of her marriage to the reporter Carl Bernstein—which comes with recipes). "Curry opened the door for this gourmet transformation," she says. "In the late fifties and early sixties, sophisticated cooking became *the* thing to do: you were an adult, and therefore you cooked. And bought Le Creuset pots and good knives. It was just *what you did*—sort of like smoking dope became a few years later."

As such, Claiborne came along at a propitious time, when Americans were ready to up their game in the kitchen, to go beyond the mere "maintenance cooking" of harried housewives. His hiring by the *Times*, Ephron says, "was an amazing moment, a symbolic moment—the whole way the old food section was reinvented for the upper-middle-class reader. If you think about it, all newspaper food sections are unjustifiable journalistically. A lot of what they do is just recipes. The *Times* found a way to stay in food journalism without sullying themselves. Craig did all this stuff on the French chefs, and he also threw all his muscle behind the idea that food could be inexpensive and ethnic."

Claiborne wasted little time in setting himself apart from the pack. While journalists like Joseph Wechsberg and A. J. Liebling had written about food in a memoirist vein, recounting this transcendent meal and that eccentric *tavernier* for *The New Yorker*, Claiborne treated food as a journalistic beat, a daily responsibility to sniff out what was going on in America's more creative kitchens. "Craig Claiborne spent as much time writing about home cooks as he did professionals," says Ed Giobbi, an Italian American artist based in Katonah, New York, whose prowess at Italian cooking was captured in several *Times* articles in the early 1960s, leading to a close friendship and, for Giobbi, a side career as a cookbook author.

Claiborne also introduced the idea of the *Times* restaurant review, an authoritative evaluation that could make or break a place. His November

1960 review of La Caravelle, among the first of the big breakaway republics from Le Pavillon (its chef, Roger Fessaguet, had worked in Le Pavillon's kitchen, and its owners, Robert Meyzen and Fred Decré, had been Soulé's maître d's), proclaimed, "In one recently opened restaurant, New York has inherited an embarrassment of riches. It is an establishment of such caliber, there is an inclination to use such expressions as 'first rank' and 'ne plus ul-tra.' The name is La Caravelle. It is situated at 33 West Fifty-fifth Street, and it is conservative to say that there are no more than four restaurants in the city that can equal its cuisine." Just like that, La Caravelle was on the dining map—though Claiborne, marking his turf as an expert, still expressed some reservations, namely that "the placement of the silver borders on the care-less" (that hotel-school training!) and that "a restaurant of La Caravelle's genre and deserved prestige should not admit corned beef and cabbage to the menu even on a trial basis."

By positioning himself way above the heads of the ladies in snoods who had until recently dominated what passed for mainstream food journalism—he later proclaimed, rather unfairly, that "Clementine Paddleford would not have been able to distinguish skillfully scrambled eggs from a third-rate omelet"—Claiborne might have seemed to be setting himself up for a fall. But generally, the food-world reaction was one of cowed awe. Here was a man writing about food and cooking with the same intellect and rigor with which the *Times* theater critic Brooks Atkinson wrote about Eugene O'Neill and Samuel Beckett. Beard, who had hoped that his Californian friend Helen Evans Brown would get the *Times* job, wrote to her with palpable re-lief to report that Claiborne was treating him as an ally rather than a rival, and that "he is a sweetheart, really." Brown herself applauded Claiborne's journalistic approach, writing to Beard, "This country needs more writers who will tell the truth about food."

The *Times* itself was slow to pick up on the magnitude of what Clai-borne was doing and of the public's interest in sophisticated cooking, eating, and dining. In 1959, having fielded several inquiries from publishers inter-ested in doing a cookbook with the paper's imprimatur, Claiborne sent a memo to the publisher, Arthur Hays Sulzberger, to alert him to the situation. To his surprise, Claiborne received a response from Sulzberger's deputy informing him that he, Claiborne, was welcome to the rights to the title *The New York Times Cook Book*; the paper simply didn't view the project as a hot property. That would change within a few years, however, as Claiborne's 1961 book bearing that title—an encyclopedic kitchen bible of *Joy of Cooking* dimensions but with clearer instructions and more upscale recipes—became a best seller, one that, in its various editions, has sold more than three million copies.

By 1963, Claiborne's restaurant reviews, which to that point had appeared erratically, became a regular feature of the Friday paper. That same year, Claiborne introduced a star system to his reviews in which "one star denotes restaurants of more than routine interest, two stars denote those of superior quality, and three stars pertain to restaurants regarded as among the finest in the city." A wallflower no longer, Claiborne had reinvented himself as an arbiter—the culmination of a long struggle, as he put it, "to stop writhing and to emerge from the straitjacket of my childhood."

This process had begun shortly after his move to New York, when he started seeing a psychotherapist. Ironically enough, these sessions were initially bankrolled by Claiborne's mother, the oppressive Miss Kathleen, after mother and son had had one last, epic dustup—effecting what Claiborne described as "my *final* and *total* estrangement from my mother" (italics his). Paying her then struggling son a visit in the city, Miss Kathleen took Claiborne to the theater, and, as usual, irritated him to the point of exasperation—nagging him and sitting, he later recalled, "too close to me for filial comfort." As he dropped her off at her hotel, Claiborne could take his mother's calculated inducements of guilt no longer ("I'm your mother and that's all I've ever wanted to be!"), and blurted out with unfiltered venom, "Mother, listen to me . . . Why must you be so eternally, so God-horribly, a *mother?*"

Claiborne and Miss Kathleen never spoke to or saw each other again. But a few days after their conflagration, he received a check from her, accompanied by a letter that said: "My darling son, I think you are ill. I want you to take this money and go to a psychiatrist." Heeding her advice even as he cut her out of his life, Claiborne worked through his bizarre childhood, the boardinghouse, the strange Daddy frottage, the psychic vise grip of Miss Kathleen, the navy years, his dangerous, hormone-fueled meanderings through the streets of nighttime Manhattan, ogling uniformed cops. He emerged from this process a more confident man, albeit one whose resultant candor threw his *Times* friends for a loop. Whereas Jim Beard was never fully comfortable with his sexuality, not speaking of it in public and lurching from one furtive assignation to the next, Claiborne talked about sex compulsively, especially when he had a few drinks in him.

"With Craig, the pleasure of food and the pleasure of sex were all mixed up—a tremendous dinner with wonderful sauces was on the edge of sexual experience for him," says Arthur Gelb, who was the *Times* chief cultural correspondent when Claiborne came on board and later became Claiborne's most important ally as the paper's "culture czar," and, later still, its managing editor. "You can't talk about Craig without talking about sex," says Gelb. "He was over the top. He told me once, when we were drinking, that he and this little black kid, when they were small boys, would fool around with the farm animals. They would have sex with chickens."

As freewheeling as he was around his intimates, Claiborne, in his capacity as a Francophile, Southern gentleman, and food editor of the *Times*, was the picture of reverence around Henri Soulé—all the more so when, a couple of years into his tenure at the paper, he decided that Le Pavillon was one of the few restaurants in New York, nay, in America, that upheld the standards of fine dining. In a calculated move to stir up some controversy, Claiborne wrote a sweeping critique of the industry that was headlined ELEGANCE OF CUISINE IS ON WANE IN U.S., and, remarkably, published on the front page of the *Times* on April 13, 1959. The lead paragraph read, "Two time-honored symbols of the good life—great cuisine in the French tradition and elegant table service—are passing from the American scene."

It was actually a pretty shoddy piece of journalism, not up to Claiborne's usual standards. The argument was muddled: in the very next paragraph, Beard was quoted as saying, "This nation is more interested in preserving the whooping crane and the buffalo than in perpetuating classic cookery . . . We live in an age that may someday—with all justification—be referred to as the time of the decline and fall of the American palate." So was the article also lamenting the decline of American foodways? No, the subject of cooking in specific American idioms was never broached. Was it an attack on the popularity of such dubious convenience-food advocates as Poppy Cannon, author of *The Can-Opener Cookbook* (1952), and Peg Bracken, author of the soon-to-be-published *The I Hate to Cook Book*? No, this phenomenon was never mentioned. Was it about the heartland's ignorance of the riches French cuisine had to offer? No, in fact, Claiborne remarked that "oddly, while most restaurant cooking is deteriorating, the American housewife, in this time of tourist air travel, has become familiar with classic, continental cuisine. Sales of so-called gourmet foods have increased greatly."

The piece's main point, inasmuch as there was one, was that the age of lavish hotel dining in places like the Plaza and the Waldorf was on the wane because their chefs and waitstaff were aging and dying without adequately trained replacements waiting in the wings, and because corporate efficiency experts were cutting costs and insisting on substandard steam-tray food. Claiborne made a couple of valid points that still hold true today: that hotel food, even in luxury hotels, is unaccountably bad, and that America is severely lacking in trained, multiskilled waiters who are happy to be career waiters. He also noted the lack of educational options for aspiring chefs apart from the twelve-year-old Culinary Institute of America, then located in New Haven, Connecticut. But he was way off the mark in asserting that "French cuisine, the foundation of the world's great dining rooms . . . is rapidly becoming extinct in the United States"—as he would happily discover in the next three years, when La Caravelle, Lutèce, and La Grenouille opened in rapid succession. And even as he wrote, the food at the Colony—an ex-speakeasy long known more for its café-society fizz than the quality of its fare—had already risen to near-Pavillon levels under the stewardship of

Pierre Franey's chef friend Jean Vergnes, who'd come to New York from France in 1950.

Claiborne's "Elegance of Cuisine" article succeeded in further setting him apart from the nicey-nice lady food journalists, though its ultimate significance was not reportorial but historical: it's what caused Claiborne to meet Pierre Franey. By the mid-fifties, Franey had succeeded Le Pavillon's head chef, Cyrille Christophe, an old-timer who had fallen victim to the occupational hazards of burnout and drunken misanthropy. Claiborne, needing some kind of illustration for his piece in the *Times*, telephoned Soulé, explained the article's premise, and asked if he might bring a photographer over to capture Le Pavillon's chef in action. Soulé agreed, and a sequence of photos captured the thirty-eight-year-old Franey, identified in the caption as "one of the few young European chefs left in the U.S.," as he stuffed a striped bass with sole mousse, baked it, and finished it with champagne sauce.

Claiborne attended the photo shoot, shook hands with Franey, and the two men—the same age, both small-town boys, both propelled to success in New York by their love of French cookery—quickly hit it off. Before long, Franey was accompanying Claiborne on his restaurant rounds, offering an insider's critique of what emerged from the city's kitchens; and allowing Claiborne to hang around in Le Pavillon's kitchen for hours at a time.

Meeting a reporter was a new experience for Franey—he had never ventured into the dining room or sought press attention. But if 1959 had countenanced the notion of celebrity chefs, he would have been the biggest, with a regular slot on the *Today* show and a book deal. He oversaw not only Le Pavillon's kitchen, but also that of a second restaurant Soulé had opened the previous year, La Côte Basque. The newer restaurant, named in sentimental tribute to Soulé's home turf, with custom-painted wall murals to match, was actually located in the East Fifty-fifth Street location where Le Pavillon had been until 1957; Le Pavillon itself had moved to 111 East Fifty-seventh Street in 1957 after a protracted battle of wills between Soulé and Harry Cohn, the head of Columbia Pictures, which had acquired the Fifty-fifth Street building in 1955. It was a true clash of the titans: the snobbish, anti-Semitic Soulé didn't want his café-society customers to have to look at Cohn, whom he considered an uncouth Jewish vulgarian, so he gave Cohn bad tables at Le Pavillon even though he knew full well that Cohn was his landlord. The notoriously foul-tempered Cohn, who reveled in his reputation as the most hated man in Hollywood, effectively gave Soulé the boot by nearly tripling his rent. Unbowed, the defiant Soulé marched Le Pavillon up to its new home on Fifty-seventh and Park, and then, after Cohn died the following year, seized upon the opportunity to open La Côte Basque in the old space (albeit at a significantly higher rent than he'd paid before). Soulé posited La Côte Basque as a lower-priced, slightly less formal restaurant than his flagship, "my Pavillon for the poor." But, just as Daniel Boulud would discover forty years later when he opened Café Boulud as a homespun alternative to the elaborate Daniel, the "cheaper" place still attracted the same old crowd.*

Running the kitchens of both Le Pavillon and La Côte Basque was taking its toll on Franey, and, to top it off, he also had to work summers at the Hedges, Soulé's seasonal restaurant in eastern Long Island. Recognizing that "his people" retreated in the summertime to their stately homes in the quiet fishing villages known as the Hamptons, Soulé had in 1954 purchased an old inn in East Hampton that had been built in the 1700s by William Hedges.† (Soulé also purchased a home for himself in Montauk.) Every summer since, between July 4th and Labor Day, Franey, Roger Fessaguet, and a sizable contingent of Le Pavillon's staff toiled at the Hedges, attending to the summer appetites of their city clientele.

For Franey, married with two children, the salutary effect of working at the Hedges was that it exposed him to East Hampton and prompted him to buy a small home for his family in the northern hamlet of Springs, over-

---

*Soulé's comment on the difference between his two restaurants was "The Pavillon is elegant and the Côte Basque is amusing." He advised his gentlemen customers to "take their wife to the Côte Basque and the other lady to the Pavillon."

†This old English name would prove a challenge for Soulé and his French staff to pronounce—his uninitiated customers were often baffled by his allusions to "The Ai-chess."

looking Gardiners Bay. It's fair to say that he and Soulé played some role in making the Hamptons the glutted weekenders' playground it later became. "The Hedges became a very special place for people who never even lived in the Hamptons at that point," says Arthur Gelb. "The Hamptons were so sleepy back then. You never saw anyone, and the whole area was WASP." But at the end of the fifties, Soulé was encountering hostility from locals who thought that his restaurant, by virtue of his and his clients' celebrity, was attracting what Gelb characterizes as a "bohemian, homosexual, and Jewish influx from Manhattan." The locals might have been reprehensible in their bigotry, but their demographic profiling was dead on—though Soulé himself had no great love for anyone in these categories, he was a media and society darling, and where he went, the Manhattan circus followed. Claiborne tipped off Gelb to the Soulé–East Hampton battle and to the fact that the locals were also agitating for the closing of an upstart summer stock theater on similar grounds. Early in 1960, Gelb wrote up the imbroglio for the *Times*.

"The story ran on page one," says Gelb. "The townspeople were furious that Soulé was bringing in show people and gays. In the middle of the night, they were overturning his trash cans and dumping his garbage all over the lawn. He was a proud Frenchman and he went crazy. He wept while I interviewed him. The story got a tremendous reaction, and it resulted in an apology from the town fathers."

A few months later, it was Claiborne who had a scoop on the latest Soulé ruction—this time, between the restaurateur and Franey. Soulé, an obstinate man, had frequently done battle with his staff over wages and hours, and had endured his share of short-term walkouts. "He treated us like garbage. He was not sentimental," says Robert Tréboux, who was a waiter at Le Pavillon in the fifties and later purchased Le Veau d'Or, a venerable French bistro on East Sixtieth Street.* In the spring of 1960, Soulé an-

---

*Still open at the time of this book's publication, with Tréboux acting as proprietor, maître d', headwaiter, bartender, and salty after-hours raconteur, Le Veau d'Or is an extraordinary time warp of a restaurant, the last place in New York where you can still get uncompromised Escoffier cuisine and have your roast carved tableside by a man who worked directly under Soulé.

nounced that he was eliminating the kitchen staff's overtime pay. Franey protested angrily, but Soulé refused to hear him out. "It was very difficult, because the French chef has to protect his workers, like the captain going down with his ship," says Tréboux. "So Pierre left. That was it."

Franey had been encouraged to take this action by his diminutive but tough new deputy, Jacques Pépin, a hotshot twenty-four-year-old who'd arrived in New York less than a year earlier, having worked as the personal chef to France's president, General Charles de Gaulle. In France, Pépin explains, kitchen walkouts were so common that there was a special French phrase for the event: *la brigade saute*, "the brigade jumps." But in New York, Pépin soon found himself cornered by a couple of oversize goons from Local 89 of the restaurant employees union, who pinned him to a wall and said, "You better watch your step, understand? Think you're a big shot, just off the fuckin' boat?"

Neither Franey nor Pépin ever set foot in Le Pavillon again.

Claiborne announced the Soulé-Franey split to the world with an article headlined RESTAURANT MEN SIMMER AND MENU GOES TO POT; LE PAVILLON SHUT IN A GALLIC DISPUTE. Reading this report, Howard Johnson, a Pavillon regular and the founder of the orange-roofed ice-cream-and-clam-roll chain bearing his name, stepped in to try to mediate between the men, but to no avail. So, instead, Johnson hired Franey as a "vice president in charge of quality control" at his corporation, with a mandate to improve the HoJo chain's food. Soon enough, Pépin, too, was on board, again as Franey's deputy.

For a brief period in the early 1960s, after the Pavillon exodus, mass-market American food companies subjected themselves to the intriguing experiment of letting trained French chefs tell them what to do. Franey and Pépin standardized a system wherein the filling of HoJo's chicken potpies was thickened with a real butter-and-flour roux, and the beef bourguignonne was flavored with real (if inexpensive) Burgundy. The Campbell Soup company hired Marcel Theuil, a former Pavillon *saucier*, as a consultant and research chef. And the Stop & Shop grocery chain hired the Colony's Jean Vergnes to devise a series of high-end heat-and-serve prepared meals for people to purchase on their way home from work. "I used to make everything," Vergnes says, "Coq au vin, *escalopes de veau* . . . They would have a life existence of one week in the Frigidaire."

But the concept of prepared gourmet foods for the home, in that pre–Whole Foods, pre–Wolfgang Puck era, was before its time—from a corporate standpoint, anyway. While consumer reaction was positive, all of these experiments ultimately foundered on the premise that the Frenchmen's methodologies and ingredients cost too much. Franey and Pépin lasted the longest at their jobs, for the whole of the sixties, quitting only when they felt that the younger Howard Johnson, Howard B., was failing to uphold the standards set by the elder Johnson, their benefactor, Howard D.*

For Franey, anyway, the best part of the HoJo's job was that he got to work normal hours, nine to five, Monday to Friday. His friendship with Claiborne, originally more of a professional acquaintanceship, intensified into a close personal bond in the early sixties. In 1962, Claiborne used the unexpected windfall from his *New York Times Cook Book* royalties to buy land and build his own house on Gardiners Bay, right near that of Franey and his wife, Betty—a house that, as the sixties advanced, became, along with the West Tenth Street town house that Beard purchased at the dawn of that decade, the major gathering place of the American food intelligentsia. Though Franey didn't get his own byline in the *Times* until 1976, he functioned blissfully for fifteen years as "Craig's hands," preparing recipes that Claiborne was testing while Claiborne observed, half-glasses perched on his nose, stationed at an IBM Selectric typewriter on the kitchen counter, calling out in his Mississippi lilt, "Now, how many cups of flour was that, Pierre?"

---

*Less enchanted with Howard Johnson was Roger Fessaguet, who followed Franey and Pépin out the door of Le Pavillon. Before securing his job as the founding chef of La Caravelle, Fessaguet spent three unhappy months working for the roadside restaurant chain. His assigned task was to pay surprise visits to the HoJos along the New Jersey Turnpike and the New York Thruway, to see what the concessionaires were doing right and wrong—an assignment that did not endear him to those being inspected. "Exit number four, about six, seven miles after the Tappan Zee Bridge," Fessaguet recalls. "When I came out of the restaurant, the doors of my car were smashed on both sides."

As for Soulé, he carried on, more than creditably, with a new chef at Le Pavillon, Clement Grangier. But his final years were full of ill will and recrimination. When his maître d's from La Côte Basque and Le Pavillon, Robert Meyzen and Fred Decré, respectively, joined forces with Franey's loyal sous-chef, Roger Fessaguet, to start La Caravelle—which, in French, translates, more or less, as "schooner"—Soulé told the press that "The Caravelle will sink." "We were on West Fifty-fifth Street, not east, and our customers told us he was calling us 'the busboys of the West Side,' " says Fessaguet.

Franey saw Soulé one last time, shortly before the latter's death. The younger man was strolling along Fifth Avenue and noticed Soulé walking in his direction. Figuring that bygones were bygones, Franey pleasantly called out, "Mr. Soulé!"

Soulé cast his eyes downward, pretending he hadn't heard Franey. Franey kept at it, shouting, "Mr. Soulé!"—again, to no avail. By now, Franey was furious, and stalked Soulé for a city block, walking alongside him, shouting, "Mr. Soulé, look at me! Look at me! It's Pierre!" But Soulé, stubborn and unsentimental as ever, stared ahead and walked on.

Soulé died of a heart attack on January 27, 1966. Le Pavillon straggled along for another five years under new ownership, but it was never the same. La Côte Basque, however, soldiered on under the iron hand of Soulé's most loyal servant—his mistress, Madame Henriette—and then under the aegis of the chef Jean-Jacques Rachou, who acquired the restaurant in 1979.*

Just eight days after Soulé passed away, Lucius Beebe, that great bon vivant, boulevardier, and *Herald Tribune* columnist, who revered Soulé as one of the last avatars of the high life he held so dear, took his ritual morning Turkish bath, toweled off, and promptly dropped dead—of a broken heart, his friends said.

---

*When his rent was raised, Rachou was forced to move La Côte Basque to a new location on East Fifty-fifth Street, and in 2004, waving the white flag, he morphed the restaurant into a more casual place called LCB Brasserie. The original site of La Côte Basque, which was the original site of Le Pavillon, is now a Disney store.

CHAPTER FOUR

THE FOOD ESTABLISHMENT, PART II

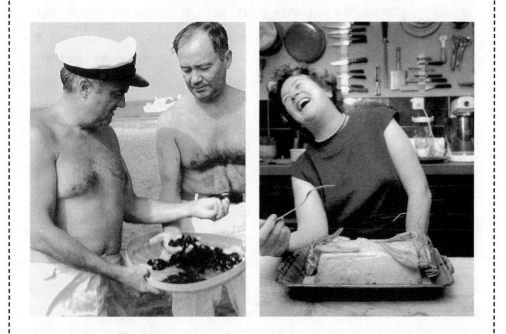

I don't expect we will ever appear on television, but possibly we will give demonstrations if we are successful.

—Julia Child, in a 1954 letter to Simone Beck,
one of her collaborators on *Mastering
the Art of French Cooking*

BEHIND THE KOOKY, HAPPY-GO-LUCKY PERSONA THAT JULIA CHILD PRESENTED TO THE
world was a determined, competitive woman. In the first three decades of
her life, she had few outlets for this drive, save the theater stages and tennis
courts of the schools she attended and the country clubs she belonged to. In
her early thirties, she found some semblance of mission in her fervent pursuit of Paul Child. But it wasn't until she was thirty-eight years old—when,
in the spring of 1951, she at last received her Cordon Bleu diploma—that
she started to channel her formidable energy into her belatedly discovered
main purpose: to educate Americans about French cookery.

A novice just three years earlier, literally fresh off the boat, Child
opened a cooking school, L'Ecole des Trois Gourmandes, in January 1952.
Her students were mostly rich American wives, brought abroad by their husbands' jobs in business or government. The other two "Gourmandes" were
a pair of Frenchwomen seven years Child's senior, Simone Beck, who preferred to be called Simca, and Louisette Bertholle. Child and Beck, a fellow
tall, spirited food obsessive, had become close friends through their membership in a Parisian women's gastronomical club called Cercle des Gourmettes.
Beck introduced Child to Bertholle, with whom she had written and self-
published *What's Cuisine in France*, a modest booklet of French recipes that

PAGE 81: *Pierre Franey (in captain's hat) and Craig Claiborne organize a clambake in
East Hampton, while Julia Child cracks up on the set of* The French Chef.

they'd had translated into English for American women living in France. Working on this project had given Beck and Bertholle the idea of writing a larger book for American wives in America; Bertholle had visited the United States with her husband and witnessed the groundswell of Francophilia there, and correctly deduced that there was an audience for such a book—if only there was some way to adapt French measurements, methods, and ingredients to the American kitchen.

By the time Beck and Bertholle had attracted interest in this new book from a small American publisher, they had already opened L'Ecole des Trois Gourmandes with Child. So when their publisher suggested that the book would work only if the Frenchwomen took on an American collaborator, there was no question about who this might be. Child proved to be their greatest asset, a ferocious researcher, typist, recipe tester, and networker. One of her first orders of business was dumping the small-time publisher and securing a contract with a major American house, Houghton Mifflin. Adept at working her connections, Child had struck up a friendly correspondence with the Boston-based Avis DeVoto, a fellow culinarian and the wife of the historian Bernard DeVoto, a Houghton Mifflin author. Mrs. DeVoto gladly obliged Child's request to forward some of the ladies' recipes and manuscript samples to her husband's publisher. By early 1953, Child had a $200 advance for *French Home Cooking*, as the book was called at that point.

As time went on, Child emerged as the project's de facto leader, with Beck a strong second-in-command and Bertholle, the only woman of the three who had children to raise, functioning as more of an adjunct. (Child and Beck eventually worked out an agreement whereby they both received 41 percent of the royalties for the finished book while Bertholle received 18 percent; all three women were credited as co-authors on the book's cover.) The Houghton Mifflin deal coincided with the end of Paul Child's USIS stint in Paris, which meant that much of the Julia-Simca collaboration took place via correspondence over the next six years, as the Childs bopped from one posting to the next—from Marseilles to Germany to Washington, D.C., to Norway, with visits to Paul's native New England interspersed throughout, including one, in 1959, to purchase a house on Irving Street in Cambridge, Massachusetts, where Paul and Julia planned on settling down when he retired.

Tireless in her enterprise, Child consulted all manner of French texts, from Escoffier's *Le guide culinaire* and the culinary encyclopedia *Larousse gastronomique* to local, regional cookbooks, the French equivalents of spiral-bound Junior League recipe booklets (though Frenchwomen never offered recipes that called for mini marshmallows and carrot-flecked Jell-O). She canvassed grocers, butchers, and fishmongers for their takes on the best way to prepare whatever dish she was researching, whether a *navarin printanier* (lamb stew with spring vegetables) or a bouillabaisse. She took a private course with Claude Thillmont, the pastry chef of the Café de Paris (where Henri Soulé had worked); cultivated her old Cordon Bleu teacher, Max Bugnard, as a sounding board; and befriended Paris's most famous writer-gastronome, the aged but still influential Curnonsky (né Maurice Edmond Sailland),* a sort of proto–James Beard figure of massive girth and unimpeachable taste who was so revered by the city's best restaurateurs that they all kept a table open for him every night, just in case he happened to toddle in. Child also assiduously vetted the competition, worrying that her book's impact might be blunted by Louis Diat's mid-fifties cooking columns for *Gourmet*, and such hot sellers *The Dione Lucas Meat and Poultry Cook Book* (1955) and the popular 1958 gastro-tourist primer *The Food of France*, written by an American named Waverly Root. "With our snail's pace," she wrote to Beck, "we have a chance to study our competitors."

Taking their time, testing, tweaking, and teaching their recipes to the point of exhaustion, Child and her collaborators effectively road-showed their book for the better part of a decade; there was no sense of quick-buck expediency to the project, no desire to hustle the thing out into the marketplace. Indeed, Child, at one point in 1957, agitated for a long-term multi-

---

*Given, like many a food writer, to whimsy, Sailland (1872–1956) fashioned his pen name from the Latin words *cur non*, meaning "why not," and added the "-sky" because of the vogue for all things Russian in the late nineteenth century.

volume approach, arguing that Houghton Mifflin publish a "Volume I" devoted just to sauces and poultry in 1958, and then allow her and Beck
another few years to do the meat and fish chapters. But Houghton Mifflin insisted on a single, well-rounded volume, which took Les Trois Gourmandes
until 1959 to complete.

The triumph of *Mastering the Art of French Cooking* lies as much in its
long gestation as it does in Child's charismatic publicizing of it. Like a band
that had played live for years before entering a studio, Child and Beck (and,
to a lesser extent, Bertholle) had developed into a tight little unit by the time
they committed their recipes to print. There's probably no other cookbook
in American history that better combines breadth, thoroughness of explanation, culinary authenticity, distinctive authorial voice ("There is something
un-French and monotonous about the way the blender reduces soup to
universal baby pap"), and reliability. Whereas Escoffier's *Le guide culinaire* was
effectively written in shorthand, presupposing that its reader was already
schooled in "mother sauces" and other fundaments of French cookery,
Mastering did the amateur cook the best favor possible—it assumed that she
knew nothing. The recipe for a basic omelet ran to seven pages and six illustrations, and advised what kind of pan should be used and where such a
pan could be procured ("from one of the shops importing French kitchenware").

While Beck's contribution is not to be underestimated—much of the
book's content originated in her collection of recipes—it was Child who
went the extra mile to make *Mastering* America-friendly. So that Americans
could experience the flavor of crème fraîche, then unavailable commercially
in the United States, Child figured out a way to thicken American whipping
cream by adding buttermilk to it at low heat and letting the mixture sit
for a day, resulting in something very much like the real thing. When she
devised her recipe for bouillabaisse, she researched which American fish
would work as substitutes for such Mediterranean fish as the red rascasse—
rockfish and cod seemed to do the trick—and didn't guilt-trip her readers if
all they had at their disposal were "frozen fish and canned clam juice," because "the other essential flavorings of tomatoes, onions or leeks, garlic,

herbs, and olive oil are always available." Similarly, when she explained how to cook with frozen peas, she did so not, as Beard had, as a sop to her corporate benefactors—she had none—but in fairness to American housewives who didn't have enchanting spring gardens of *petit pois* from which to harvest.

The finished manuscript of *French Recipes for American Cooks*, to use the book's circa-1959 working title, was a marvel of pan-social recipe compiling. It covered aspects of French cookery from the *grande cuisine* of upscale restaurants (the very involved *suprêmes et mousse de volaille en chaud-froid*, breasts of chicken coated in an aspic of cream, stock, and vermouth, chilled until set, decorated with tarragon leaves, and arranged on a platter around a little mountain of chicken mousse) to the *cuisine bourgeoise* of bistros and servant-equipped homes (the dinner-party standby *boeuf bourguignon*) to the simpler *cuisine de bonne femme* of rustic households (*potage parmentier*, a humble potato-leek soup, deliberately chosen by Child to be the book's very first recipe so that her audience would not be intimidated). All things considered, the book was even a triumph of brevity, whittled down as it was from the thousands of recipes tested by Les Trois Gourmandes over the years.

Too bad, then, that Houghton Mifflin rejected it. In November 1959, Child received word that the publisher simply found the 800-page-plus manuscript too big, and therefore too expensive, to publish; the projected sales didn't justify the projected costs. It was a huge blow, one that prompted bitter flailings from Paul Child, who railed against a stupid, bovine, home-ec'd, blinded-by-science America that wanted cheap, quick dinners made of chemicals. "It has GLYCODIN-32 in it! Only 89 cents!" he said mockingly. (In the same era, Beard privately despaired of "hearing a lot of people talk about saturated fats, atomic cookery, nuclear feeding, and all the rest of the shit.") But Julia's Boston friend Avis DeVoto took the initiative once again, sending the manuscript off to the publishing house Alfred A. Knopf, where she had once worked. The boxful of pages landed with a thud on the desk of the young editor Judith Jones, who had distinguished herself a decade earlier, when, working in the Paris office of Doubleday, she urged her bosses to print an English-language version of *The Diary of a Young Girl*, by Anne Frank. "When I came back from living in France, I realized there wasn't really a book that taught you how to cook French food at home," says Jones, "so I got this in 1960 and thought, 'This is it!' "

In this same period, the manuscript floated around the New York publishing world. Among those who got their hands on it was the great food-establishment dowager Helen McCully, who'd moved from *McCall's* to *House Beautiful*. Bowled over and shocked that Houghton Mifflin had opted out— she deemed the book "an amazing piece of work"—she passed on the manuscript to one of her favorite members of her salon, the dashing young Jacques Pépin, to see what he thought. "I read it like you read a novel, turning the pages fast, late into the night," he says. "I couldn't believe that someone had broken it all down like that. I was jealous."

Jones was convinced that she had an important book on her hands, but she was insufficiently senior at Knopf to green-light the manuscript's publication. The decision to publish, she says, came straight from Alfred Knopf himself, over the fervent objections of his wife and business partner, Blanche. "Alfred Knopf was interested in food, if more from a connoisseur point of view—I mean, he never chopped an onion," Jones says. "Blanche wasn't interested in cooking. She was too concerned about her figure. She drank martinis."

With the Knopf deal in place, Child refined the manuscript still further, beefing it up, literally, with more red-meat recipes to suit American tastes, and obliging specific requests of Jones's, such as a recipe for cassoulet, the winter-night feast traditionally composed of sausage, beans, and confit of duck or goose. (Child, perhaps sensing that preserved duck and goose were not going to be easy sells to the American public, recommended using pork loin and mutton instead, with goose confit mentioned only as a possible variation if you could find it in "one of the food-importing stores.") This still left Child and Beck with reams of unprinted recipes, but much of their fifties work would later get a proper airing in *Mastering the Art of French Cooking, Volume Two* (published in 1970 and credited just to Child and Beck, with

Bertholle out of the picture) and, for that matter, in the books that Child and Beck wrote later in their lives.*

The autumn of 1961 was a triumphal time for Julia and Paul Child. He had served out his final USIS posting, in Oslo, Norway, enabling the Childs to settle at last into their Cambridge house. In September, they received their first hardbound copy of the big book. The graphic designer Warren Chappell had devised the austere, soothing, soon-to-be-iconic fleur-de-lis pattern for the cover, the Knopf staff had come up with the title *Mastering the Art of French Cooking*, and Paul had written the book's dedication, as eloquent and characteristic a summation of the era's gastronomic Francophilia as any:

> To *La Belle France*. Whose peasants, fishermen, housewives, and princes—not to mention her chefs—through generations of inventive and loving concentration have created one of the world's great arts.

ON OCTOBER 18, Craig Claiborne gave *Mastering the Art of French Cooking* a rave in *The New York Times*, calling it "probably the most comprehensive, laudable and monumental work on this subject" and correctly predicting that it would endure as "the definitive work for nonprofessionals." Jones recalls having to do a little arm-twisting to get Claiborne to review the book. "The trade-off was, my husband and I had a little penthouse apartment, and we got an outdoor grill, and we used to cook quite a lot on the outdoor grill," she says. "People would look down from other buildings at this crazy couple, cooking.

---

*Beck, who died in 1991, never achieved the level of fame and adulation that Child enjoyed, though her first solo outing, *Simca's Cuisine* (1972), was well-received. "I think she was envious and could never quite understand why she couldn't acquire the same reputation," says John Ferrone, who worked on Beck's cookbooks as well as James Beard's. "She didn't understand that television was the magic ingredient." Child, for her part, grew agitated at what she perceived as Beck's Gallic intractability and refusal to deviate from culturally prescribed cooking formulas, and was relieved to be free of their collaboration after *Volume Two* was published. Nevertheless, the two women remained friends for the rest of Beck's life and continued to cook together at their neighboring homes in the Provençal village of Plascassier.

Well, Craig loved that story. He was very good at getting stories about home cooks." So, two months before *Mastering's* publication, the *Times* ran an article headlined THE JONESES DELIGHT IN KEEPING UP WITH CUISINE, featuring a large photograph of Jones and her husband, the author Evan Jones, grilling a spitted leg of lamb. Judith was never described by her first name, being merely "Mrs. Jones" or half of "the Evan Joneses," and the focus was much more on the manly, outdoorsy cooking of the bearded Evan, who, Claiborne wrote admiringly, "has the burly build of a Northwoodsman."

Even without Judith Jones's cajoling, though, Claiborne would have fallen for *Mastering*. One after another, the members of the food establishment lined up to sing its praises. Beard gave the book his blessing and had the Childs and Beck to the town house on West Tenth Street, where he now conducted his cooking classes. Though he didn't yet fully grasp the book's significance—he confided to Helen Evans Brown that the "Knopf French book" was "wonderful until they get into the chicken and meat department," which he criticized for overlong cooking times—he adored Julia and Simca personally, and, a few weeks later, took them to dinner at the Four Seasons, where they were introduced to the restaurant's mad-scientist visionary, Joe Baum, and its ornery Swiss chef, Albert Stockli. Beard and Dione Lucas, the incumbent French-cookery expert in the United States, also threw a party for Child and Beck at Lucas's restaurant, the Egg Basket, with Clementine Paddleford in attendance. Child and Claiborne never became close—"really just acquaintances," she later said—but she and Beard, similarly exuberant, generous of spirit, and endowed with enormous hands that made even their ordinary gestures seem theatrical, became quite *ahn-teem*, as Julia was wont to say. In the years to come, Child was a frequent guest instructor at Beard's cooking school. And as the sales of *Mastering* allowed the Childs to build a getaway home in Provence near Beck's that they named La Pitchoune (the Little One), Beard became a frequent houseguest, spending entire days in the kitchen with Julia, conjuring what Paul called *la cuisine de l'enfant barbu*, "of the bearded child."

While the food establishment's embrace no doubt helped along its sales, *Mastering* took off of its own volition, going through five printings and selling more than 100,000 copies within a year of its publication. Fortuitously, given its long gestation and delayed publication, the book captured an aspirational spirit newly afoot in America's middle-class homes and in the White House, where the young Francophile First Lady (née Jacqueline Bouvier) had hired a French chef, René Verdon.* The *Times*, in its evolving role as not only the paper of record but the lifestyle manual of culturally correct postwar upper middlebrows, played Verdon's hiring on page one, with an article by Claiborne that described Verdon's first official assignment, a luncheon for the British prime minister, Harold Macmillan, that included trout cooked in Chablis, fillet of roast beef au jus, and "artichoke bottoms Beaucaire—filled with a fondue of tomatoes simmered in butter."

Even Verdon himself seemed surprised by how fashionable French food was becoming. "When I came to America in 1958, people were talking more about gravy than sauces, but that changed fast," he says. "Mrs. Kennedy, she was like a lot of wives, very interested in understanding French food. She really wanted to talk about it and learn about it. Like, she would ask for a soufflé with asparagus. She would also want noodles. I would have to tell her, 'You cannot have two starches, soufflé and noodles, in the same meal,' but she understood."

Twenty years after the opening of Le Pavillon, the notion of an aspara-

---

*Then as now, the White House struggled to find a chef who was willing to sacrifice the bustle and lucre of a commercial kitchen for the "prestige" of preparing state dinners for visiting dignitaries and Sunday-football munchies for the First Family. The Kennedys, loyal Pavillon customers from day one, had a falling out with Henri Soulé in 1960 and switched their allegiance to La Caravelle when it opened that year. When John F. Kennedy was elected, his father, Joseph, asked one of La Caravelle's owners, Robert Meyzen, to recommend a French chef. Meyzen put the question to his chef, Roger Fessaguet, who recommended Jacques Pépin. But Pépin, having already served as Charles de Gaulle's cook, was eager to stick with his mentor-protector Pierre Franey and followed him to Howard Johnson (Pépin recalls the choice as "Camelot versus HoJo's"). Instead, the job went to Verdon, who had previously worked at the Carlyle and Essex House hotels in New York. In preparation for his new job, Verdon spent a few weeks in La Caravelle's kitchen with Fessaguet, getting a crash course in Kennedy food preferences.

gus soufflé wasn't as intimidating as it used to be. "In food terms, we middle Americans were all nouveaux riches, giddy with a cornucopia of goods and techniques that poured in from Europe, along with its refugees, after the Second World War. To put it another way, we didn't know how poor we'd been until we hit it rich," writes Betty Fussell in her 1999 memoir, *My Kitchen Wars*. Fussell was, in the sixties, one half of a New Jersey couple that went out of its way to showcase its erudition, worldliness, and exquisite taste; her then husband, the historian Paul Fussell, was a professor at Rutgers University, and the Fussells lived an *Ice Storm*–like life of suburban status consciousness and adulterous intrigue in tony, verdant Princeton, where they and their professorial-class ilk competed to see who could put on the best, most menu-accomplished dinner party, with the finest selection of French wines to match. *Mastering the Art of French Cooking* functioned as a sort of domestic equivalent of Sun Tzu's *The Art of War*, and the French term for kitchen equipment, *batterie de cuisine*, never sounded more appropriately martial.

Child's recipes, as plainspokenly and patiently as they were explained and laid out, were still elaborate and time-consuming, and the Betty Fussells of the world deliberately chose the most difficult of them to execute when company was coming. "*Veau Prince Orloff* was [a] display piece consumptive of enough money and time to garner status," Fussell writes. "This one, Julia assured us, could be made in the morning and reheated the same evening— provided, you did nothing else all day. It required you to bone and tie a five-pound roast of veal, prepare a *soubise* of rice and onions, a *duxelles* of mushrooms, and a *velouté* from a *roux* enriched with heavy cream and a pinch of nutmeg. You puréed the *soubise* and the *duxelles* together to spread on each slice of the roasted meat, then covered the entire roast with thick sauce and grated Swiss cheese so that it would brown when you reheated it. The dish was so rich that after the first two mouthfuls you were ready to gag or go home, but these were headier times, less obsessed with cardiovascular health and liposuctioned bodies than with strutting your stuff with the best ingredients money could buy."

"It wasn't about entertaining, it was about showing off culinary skills," says Fussell now, somewhat chastened in old age but still in proud possession of her sixties-vintage KitchenAid mixer and the copper pots she picked up at E. Dehillerin, the upscale kitchenwares shop in Paris, near the old Les Halles, that became a pilgrimage destination for hardcore American gastro-tourists and Juliaphiles. "And *absolutely* competitive," she says, "because Julia was supplying us the tools for astonishing our friends."

Kitchenwares suddenly attained the status of fetish objects in certain American circles, where you just *had* to have a Le Creuset casserole dish and a crepe pan the size of a manhole cover. Chuck Williams saw this phenom-enon unfold in his store, Williams-Sonoma, which had migrated from bu-colic Sonoma to the heart of San Francisco, on Sutter Street near the expensive shops of Union Square. "We were on the same block as Elizabeth Arden, which in those days was where all the ladies got their hair done," he says. "Across the street from the best women's club, the Francesca Club. On the next block was the Metropolitan Club, another women's club. I became part of their beat."

Fussell points out that men, too, were caught up in the *Mastering* craze, graduating from being mere grazers and grill meisters to being wine collec-tors and foie gras aficionados. "That lent the Julia book even more prestige," she says. "For the first time, the men really had to know what was being served them, even if they weren't cooking it. It had to be part of the con-versation, so you better not be stupid, because it also had to do with the pres-tige of travel. And people were also saying, 'Oh, have you read Craig today?'—calling him 'Craig,' this person who none of us had met. Because everybody read *The New York Times*. We would have long, professorial dis-cussions about that day's restaurant review."

Fussell isn't overstating how seriously she and her husband took their Julia and their Craig—their Princeton kitchen and Paul's French wine col-lection became so fabulous, and their culinary skills so brilliant, that the great Claiborne himself, with his nose for news, found out about them and wrote them up in the *Times* in 1969 as part of his home-cooks series. As was the case in Claiborne's write-up of the Evan Joneses, Betty was never identified by her first name, only as "Mrs. Paul Fussell," and her beauty was ignored while Claiborne admired the "pipe-smoking, tousle-haired, tweedy" Paul—though it was Betty's recipes for charcoal-grilled lamb *Provençale* and *soupe au pistou* (the latter a *Mastering* standout) that the *Times* printed.

"YOU KNOW, THE OTHER day, when I was *mmmuck*ing about in the supermarket, looking for something to eat—I was sort of in a *bad mood* and nothing I looked at appealed to me a'*tall*. I looked at all the chickens and the ducks and the fish and the steaks and the lamb, and I just didn't want to cook any *bit* of it! I found myself staring at a fresh *beef tongue*, and I said to it, 'You *ugly* old thing, I'd like to *fix you up*!' And I thought to myself, 'Why not? It will be a change, anyway!' So I *trotted* home with my tongue under my arm—and I *braised* it!"

How could TV viewers not be mesmerized? There stood a towering, skinny, middle-aged woman in pearls and an unreconstructed Smith '34 hairdo, hovering behind a kitchen counter that rose only as high as her thighs, unspooling this bizarre monologue in a fluted voice and uncertain cadence, gasping for breath in the wrong spots.

The French Chef, produced by Boston's public television station, WGBH, in two spurts, from 1963 to 1966 (in black and white) and from 1970 to 1972 (in color), expanded Child's already considerable following exponentially. The show's genesis lay in Child's 1962 appearance on WGBH's book-chat program, *I've Been Reading*, hosted by Albert Duhamel, a professor of English at Boston College. Correctly deducing that programs of this sort tended to be dull, static affairs, Child, with Paul in tow, arrived at the studio with a copper bowl, a whisk, and a dozen eggs, so she could merry up the proceedings by preparing an omelet as she and Duhamel chatted. The episode was broadcast live and not committed to tape, meaning its proto–*French Chef* charms are lost to the ages, but it's well documented that WGBH was surprised by the passion of its audience's response; unused to feedback from its viewers, the station received twenty-seven letters demanding more cooking lessons from the loony tall woman. By 1963, *The French Chef* was on the air in Boston, its first half-hour episode (of more than 200 that were eventually made) devoted to *boeuf bourguignon*. Though Child never claimed that she herself was a chef, she agreed to the title because it was catchy and concise enough to appear in full in the *Boston Globe* TV listings.

Like all public television stations, WGBH operated on a shoestring, with corporate benefactors kicking in some dollars here and there. Julia did her shows on a rinky-dink budget, in a demonstration kitchen borrowed from the Cambridge Electric Company, with groceries that she and Paul bought themselves. He carted in the food and did the dishes. The low-budget, low-tech aspect of *The French Chef* actually worked in the program's favor, necessitating that the focus remain squarely on the cooking and on Child herself, with no travelogue filler or postproduction jiggery-pokery. Child was all the show needed; unlike Beard, who froze up on TV, she was a natural. She called tomatoes "to-MAH-toes" and shallots "shuh-HAL-ots." She never met an oversize kitchen implement she didn't like, whether it was a mallet, a potato ricer, a cleaver, a rolling pin, a bow saw (to cut an enormous tuna into steaks), or a blowtorch (for caramelizing the top of a crème brûlée). She held up a roasting chicken and promised to help it realize "the full glory of its chickendom." She unapologetically patched back together a potato fritter that had fallen apart as she tried to flip it, saying "You can always pick it up. If you are alone in the kitchen, who is going to see?" She editorialized that "I think a lot of us get into a terrible *meat rut*! It's always steaks, chops, saddle of lamb, beef Wellington, or hamburgers. Well, here's a little [*breathless gasp*] change of pace. With *sweetbreads* and *brains*!"

Like Howard Cosell, an unhandsome, querulous Brooklyn lawyer who, in the same era, somehow circumvented TV's vetting process and became the biggest star in sports television, Child was theoretically ill-suited to the medium, which is precisely why viewers were drawn to her. (Indeed, no broadcast personalities would prove more imitable to comedians than Cosell and Child.) Having lived abroad for half of her adult life and only just returned to America in 1961, and having long moved in intellectual circles that paid little heed to glitz and popular culture, she was oblivious to the lacquered, c'mon-a-my-house ethos of contemporary showbiz, and stomped about her stage with the goofy, anachronistic enthusiasm of a Roaring Twenties girl in a summer-camp revue.

Child's antics and locutions were so alien that many viewers presumed she was drunk,* respiratorily unwell, or actually French. Still, *The French Chef* was anything but slapdash: according to her biographer, Noël Riley Fitch, Child put nineteen hours of preparation into each half-hour episode. She was both a bracing entertainer and an excellent cooking instructor, and quickly became the most popular attraction on WGBH.† What's more, Child's half-hour shows proved so durable and repeat-watchable that *The French Chef* would enjoy a long afterlife in reruns, to the point that even in December 1978, when Dan Aykroyd did his famous gross-out Julia parody on *Saturday Night Live* ("Now I've done it! I've cut the *dickens* out of my finger!"), the premise seemed fresh rather than shopworn.

Within a year of its 1963 premiere, *The French Chef* had become a word-of-mouth sensation, picked up by public television stations throughout the country. If Chuck Williams thought that the publication of *Mastering* had caused his sales to spike, now he was really in for something. "The program was aired on KQED in San Francisco once a week, but we never knew what was gonna be on," he says. "But by the next morning, we'd know, because our customers were watching it. They'd come into the store demand-

*In fact, Child was anything but sauced on the show. Due to budget constraints, she and the program's producers couldn't afford drinking wine for her closing toast of "*Bon appétit!*" She saluted her audience not with a real glass of wine but with a glass of water darkened with GravyMaster, a coloring agent.

†Child could also be counted on to enliven that most dreaded of public-television events, the pledge drive. "Hello, I'm Julia Child. If this goose could lay golden eggs, then we'd all be sitting pretty," she said in one WGBH fund-raising appearance in the mid-sixties, propping up a plucked, headless bird. "But it c-*hhan't*! And that's why we need your help . . ."

ing a charlotte mold or whatever pan Julia had used, and it had to be the exact size. Because they had to make what she'd made *that night*." Likewise, grocers found themselves facing demand for shallots, then not a common item, because Julia had used them on TV.

"Let Julia Child so much as mention vanilla wafers, and the shelves are empty overnight," said *Time* magazine in the cover story of its November 25, 1966 issue. The cover painting looked almost like devotional art, with Child's head ringed by a nimbus of copper pots with steam rising out of them. "Amid an avalanche of new cookbooks—206 last year alone—Julia Child's five-year-old *Mastering the Art of French Cooking* has grown to be the new bestseller in the field, with close to 300,000 copies sold at $10 apiece," the story declared. "But what really makes her just about everybody's chef of the year—and the most influential cooking teacher in the U.S.—is that her specialty, French cuisine, is the central grand tradition for the growing multitude of home gourmet cooks."

The *Time* story, which also tipped its hat to Beard ("today's king of gourmets") and Claiborne ("a discriminating one-man *Guide Michelin* to restaurants not just in Manhattan but throughout the nation"), was a watershed for the food establishment. It affirmed that Child, Beard, and Claiborne, food sensualists rather than food scientists, were now at the top of the heap, and that a genuine culinary culture had taken hold in America—even if it still had a long way to go toward matching France's.

"WE FRENCH CHEFS have to thank Julia a lot," says André Soltner. "I don't say she was the best chef—she didn't have to be. It was not her role. I mean, I was surprised a few times, because she could do things on television which we could not do, ever. She dropped something on the floor, she picked it up. If we did that, they would take us to court. But even that was good, because it showed home cooks that French cooking is not always sophisticated."

As Jacques Pépin had foreseen, *Mastering the Art of French Cooking* became an object of fascination among the Frenchmen whose cooking defined sophisticated New York dining in the sixties. Yet these chefs were by and large appreciative rather than affronted or dismissive. "I'm sure when the book came out, there were some older chefs who thought 'This is a joke,' even more so because she was a woman, but come on! Look at what she did for us," says La Caravelle's Roger Fessaguet.

Already flattered that Claiborne cared enough to identify them by name in his articles, the French chefs were still more flattered that their nation's cuisine was now being appreciated in American homes. The *French Chef* phenomenon and the profusion of new "Le" and "La" restaurants fed off each other, and a lot of the surviving old-timers look back upon this era as a halcyon period, their favorite time. The Big Three, Beard, Claiborne, and Child, were at their peak of influence, yet the scene still had some intimacy to it. Many of the French chefs spent winter weekends together skiing on Hunter Mountain in the Catskills—"Saturday evening, close the restaurant at 1 a.m., arrive in Hunter at 4 a.m., on the slopes at 8 a.m., leave Monday morning at 6:30, back at Lutèce by 9:30," says Soltner. They also hunted deer in season, caught frogs for their own consumption, and foraged for mushrooms, momentarily re-creating the bucolic rhythms of their childhoods.

In the summers, many of these same chefs, most regularly Fessaguet, Pépin, Verdon, and Jean Vergnes, joined Franey and Claiborne at their homes on Gardiners Bay, swimming, boating, playing *pétanque* (the French lawn-bowling game), and assembling feasts in Claiborne's enormous, glass-walled kitchen with floor-to-ceiling views of the bay. Most of these multicourse meals found their way into Claiborne's recipe columns for the Sunday *New York Times Magazine*. "We were natural partners," Franey later wrote of Claiborne in his memoir. "Our tastes in cooking merged . . . If I liked the shad I saw, I might pick it up and then decide how to prepare it. Perhaps there would be some good cherry tomatoes in my garden. Maybe I would think of making shad and roe garnished with those tomatoes—the tomatoes briefly sautéed with garlic—and I would call it Provençale . . . I would line up my ingredients in Craig's kitchen: the shad, its roe, salt and pepper, milk and flour for dredging, oil and butter for cooking, those tomatoes, some garlic, and of course, the parsley that I can't resist . . . I would start to cook things in the logical way, heating the skillet, cooking the fish, setting it aside while preparing the tomatoes and so on. As I would proceed, Craig would sit at a typewriter set up in the kitchen. I would call out weights and measurements: 'It's a quarter cup of milk. . . . Eight tomatoes, no, better make it ten.' "

"They had something great together, which was funny, because they were so different," says Franey's widow, Betty, of her husband and Claiborne. "Pierre was a real down-to-earth person. He liked hunting, he liked fishing, he liked cooking, and he was very basic. Whereas Craig, he liked the arts, classical music, the theater. I took my husband to the opera once or twice and he fell asleep. And Craig couldn't get up on a ski. I think he tried once and ended up with a bloody nose. Pierre took him hunting once, to Gardiners Island, and it was a joke. He didn't like holding a gun or shooting an animal."

Still, Claiborne was never happier than when he was in the kitchen with Franey in the sixties and early seventies, recalling this period as "a golden age of gastronomy in my home." Around five o'clock each Saturday, the two men would start with Scotch and sodas and the prep work. They'd begin the meal with hors d'oeuvres and a soup, then move on to a fish course accompanied by a white Burgundy; a meat or game course accompanied by a Bordeaux; a cheese course accompanied by a red Burgundy; a dessert accompanied by champagne; and, finally, coffees and stinger cocktails. In the regular rotation of guests (not counting the other French chefs and their wives) were the elder Howard Johnsons, the Joseph Hellers, the Arthur Gelbs, and other *Times* people who had homes in the Hamptons or were visiting. There was even a celebrity groupie, the entertainer Danny Kaye, who prided himself on his adeptness at Chinese cookery and wangled invitations to Claiborne's house so he could plunge into the kitchen scrum.

Also present for most of these dinners was Henry Lewis Creel, a retired Shell Oil executive and "confirmed bachelor" who was Claiborne's on-again, off-again companion.* While they never lived together, and, according to Claiborne's friends, were not necessarily monogamous, Creel brought a measure of stability and comfort to Claiborne, staving off his loneliness and tempering his depressive tendencies. "Craig told us, when we first met him, that he had—at that time he called it a 'problem,' " says Betty Franey. "But he had Henry, who was just a lovely man who lived by himself in an apartment on Sutton Place, very elegantly." While the French chefs, all natural men suffused with hairy-chested hetero machismo, were aware of Claiborne's sexual orientation, they never heard the bizarre sex talk that Claiborne foisted upon more worldly friends such as Gelb and Heller, and more or less operated in a "don't ask, don't tell" mode around the writer. "Me, I never mind," says Vergnes. "The question of gay, I don't have any problem, because Craig respect me. The rest, I don't want to know."

The sixties also found Claiborne at his most intrepid, his influence as a tastemaker never greater. In addition to reviewing restaurants, hobnobbing with the Franeys, and providing his readers with recipes for such quintessentially sixties dishes as Spanish paella, that de rigueur centerpiece of Burt Bacharach–soundtracked dinner parties ("One or another version of paella has been among the most requested recipes for several years," he wrote in 1966), Claiborne was turning on his readers to other cuisines, introducing them to home cooks and cooking-school teachers who, through his exposure, won book contracts and became the authorities in their field. It was he who first wrote about the authentic Mexican cookery of Diana Kennedy, an Englishwoman who was married to the *Times* Central American correspondent, Paul Kennedy. When Paul died suddenly in 1967, Claiborne encouraged Diana to pick up the pieces of her life by opening a cooking school in New York where she could teach the dishes and techniques she'd learned during the Kennedys' residency in Mexico. "Probably about eight months after my husband's death, Craig invited me to dinner with Pierre Franey and

---

*Creel was himself a gifted home cook, and, with Claiborne's help, got two cookbooks of his own published, the poignantly titled *Cooking for One Is Fun* (1976) and *Cooking on Your Own* (1980).

told me I should do this," says Kennedy. "It was a very important moment. And when I did set up the cooking school, he did an article on it for *The New York Times.*" (Wrote Claiborne, "Don't go to [Kennedy's cooking school] expecting chili con carne and hot tamales.") In 1972, again with a push from Claiborne, Kennedy came through with the authoritative cookbook that made her name, *The Cuisines of Mexico.*

Claiborne introduced *Times* readers to the Chinese cooks Grace Zia Chu and Virginia Lee, collaborating with the latter on *The Chinese Cookbook*, which came out in 1962. He also convinced Marcella Hazan, a reluctant Italian housewife who could barely speak English to let him profile her after he'd heard she was giving cooking lessons in her New York apartment. "The experience of telephone in another language is a monster, no?" says Hazan, recalling her first contact with Claiborne. "I understood only this: it was from *The New York Times*. Was coming—wanted to come to speak about the lesson. They wanted to come at 12:30. I said that I was sorry, but at 12:30 we had lunch. I said, 'Look, if you really want to come at 12:30'—because I was getting mad and could not understand the rest of the thing—'come for lunch.' When Victor, my husband, came home, I said, 'Someone from *The New York Times* called and he's coming for lunch Thursday.' He said, 'Who is it?' 'I don't know, something like "Crack-Crack"—I don't know what.' He said, 'Craig Claiborne?' 'I think so.' So Craig came, he wrote an article, and the rest is history." By the mid-seventies, Hazan had published two books with Judith Jones at Knopf, *The Classic Italian Cook Book* and *More Classic Italian Cooking*, and had become known, flatteringly if a bit reductively, as "the Julia Child of Italian cooking."

PAUL AND JULIA CHILD, meanwhile, were enjoying a new chapter of their life that they never could have imagined in their itinerant USIS days, with the fiftysomething Julia experiencing rock-star-like celebrity as she crisscrossed the country for book signings and cooking demonstrations, and the sixtysomething Paul happily serving as her pot-scrubber, factotum, bodyguard, and de facto manager, schlepping her all-important "sacred bag," a black satchel that held Julia's favorite knives, scoops, and other indispensable equipment. At La Pitchoune and in Cambridge, she worked with Beck on volume two of *Mastering*, which was published in 1970 and included Child's legendary nineteen-page, two-years-in-the-testing recipe for *pain Français*, or what Child called "plain French bread, the long crackly kind a Frenchman tucks under his arm as he hurries home to his family lunch." (Paul tested his own versions and was instrumental in developing the alternative "Simulated Baker's Oven" method offered in *Mastering II*, which involved using a flat piece of asbestos cement as a baking surface and dropping a stove-heated brick into a pan of water in the oven to steam the baking dough.)

Beard's sixties were more complicated. His entourage of helpers and staff at West Tenth Street grew ever-more burdensome, particularly because he had taken on the dead weight of Gino Cofacci, a ne'er-do-well architect with whom he'd been briefly involved in the fifties and somehow ended up supporting in perpetuity, with Cofacci living in Beard's house as a nonpaying boarder, "like an orphan child," says John Ferrone, who found the architect unbearable.* Beard's health also began to suffer, all those years of gorging catching up with him. His legs were ravaged by the circulatory ailment phlebitis, and, on doctor's orders, he was regularly hospitalized for spells of restricted diets and "reducing," which were, at least, marginally successful. "The fat Jim we know today, that you see pictures of, is after he'd slimmed down," says Barbara Kafka. "Jim *really* looked like a stuffed pig when he was younger."

All that said, Beard was pleased with his elder-statesman status, as "kind of a Buddha that you went to to get a blessing," as Nora Ephron puts it. By the decade's end he'd been welcomed back into the fold at *Gourmet*, for which he wrote a column called "Cooking with James Beard," and he'd also secured a lucrative deal to do a syndicated column that appeared in more than a hundred newspapers, dictated to and polished by José Wilson, a

---

*Before Cofacci, Beard had a boyfriend about whom little is known, except that he was a Dutchman and his name was Ate de Boer. Evidently, de Boer broke up with Beard, leaving him brokenhearted and reluctant to ever again enter into a serious relationship.

former food editor of *House & Garden*, who, despite the spelling of her first name, was not a Latino man but an Englishwoman who called herself "Josie." Beard's 1960s cookbooks were not particularly noteworthy, but the decade did bring his one true attempt at memoir in 1964, *Delights and Prejudices*, which, while slender and afflicted with a slight touch of the twees, was a charming evocation of his culinary coming-of-age in Oregon. Ferrone, who edited the book, recalls Beard spiriting himself away to a rented farmhouse in Saint-Rémy-de-Provence in the spring of 1963 to complete the manuscript. He blissfully made the most of the setting, Ferrone says, "cooking a rump steak over a fire of vine cuttings, fig-tree twigs, a branch of dried bay, the root of a rosemary plant, and two thyme bushes, which gave off a heady perfume and delicately flavored the meat but left no char." It's no wonder that, in the next decade, he would get on like a house afire with the young Americans Alice Waters and Jeremiah Tower, who couldn't fathom why Americans thought such lovely culinary experiences had to be restricted to France.

AS COZY AND INTIMATE as the food world was in the late sixties compared to what it would become by the turn of the twenty-first century, it nevertheless began to suffer some of the consequences of success: competitiveness, power struggles, bitchery. No member of the food establishment stirred up more trouble than Michael Field, alluded to in *Time* magazine's Julia Child cover story as "a relative newcomer who gave up a successful career as a concert pianist to conduct socialite cooking classes in his Manhattan apartment," and as "the consulting editor for *Life*'s forthcoming 16-volume series, *Foods of the World*."

All but forgotten today, Field was, for a brief period, as big as the Big Three. Indeed, Ephron's infamous "Food Establishment" essay alludes not to the Big Three but to the Big Four, with Field ranked alongside Beard, Child, and Claiborne. A Juilliard-educated concert pianist, Field prospered through the forties and fifties as one half of the classical-piano duo Appleton and

Field, all the while nursing an antique-cookbook-collecting habit and an indefatigable urge to prepare elaborate meals.

In 1958, when he was forty-three, Field decided to run a cooking school out of the home he shared with his wife and young son in Scarsdale, New York. Blending French classicism and American eclecticism with a then radical interest in northern Italian food—he was one of the first to teach students how to make pesto, the puree of basil, garlic, olive oil, pine nuts, and Parmesan cheese—Field attracted a large following and, inevitably, the attention of Claiborne. At the time of Claiborne's 1962 reportorial visit to Scarsdale ("Michael Field can execute a cadenza or cassoulet, grace note or galantine with approximately the same flourish," the article in the *Times* began), Field was still performing piano duets with his partner, Vera Appleton. But soon thereafter, he took an apartment in Manhattan and devoted himself to cooking, writing, and teaching full-time. By the mid-sixties, he had a regular column in *McCall's* called "The World of Fine Cooking" that combined prodigious research with kitchen know-how and an authentic literary voice (very much foreshadowing Jeffrey Steingarten's later columns for *Vogue*), and was spending his summers running the kitchen of the Maidstone Arms, an upscale inn in East Hampton, New York. He also wrote two very good cookbooks, *Michael Field's Cooking School* in 1965 and *Michael Field's Culinary Classics and Improvisations* in 1967, the latter an inventive pairing of traditionalist recipes with day-after leftover strategies—the excess meat from his "classic" recipe for braised lamb shoulder with white beans, for example, could be applied to his "improvisation" for moussaka.

Wiry, smirky, twitchy, and nerdy-looking, with thick-framed Jerry Lewis glasses and a cap of close-cropped black hair, Field was invariably described by his contemporaries as "tense" or "intense," a neurotic, tightly wound oddball in the generally loose, cheery, jowly, inebriate food world. "He was a prickly guy, very amused and turned on by his own prickliness," says Ephron, who interviewed Field for the *New York Post*. He was also a brilliant critic, turning out incisive, cutting essays on the cookbooks that flooded the market in the 1960s for *The New York Review of Books*. Claiborne could be exacting and snobby in his restaurant reviews and occasional book write-ups, but Field was a different animal altogether, a pit bull who operated more in the mode of Pauline Kael reviewing films for *The New Yorker* or Kenneth Tynan in his heyday as the theater critic of the London *Observer*. "Disastrous examples [of quasi-French recipes] could be cited endlessly" in the latest edition of the *Fannie Farmer Boston Cooking-School Cook Book*, revised by Farmer's niece, Wilma Lord Perkins, Field wrote in 1965. "Almost without exception they are technically inaccurate and historically incorrect." Even Perkins's straightforward recipe for roasted chicken had been "turned into a fiasco," Field added. "A 2½ pound chicken roasted as Mrs. Perkins suggests—that is, for two hours at 350 degrees F., including 15 minutes at 450 degrees F.—would literally fall apart before it could be carved."

In a roundup of French cookbooks the same year, Field had high praise for *Mastering* and for Child, Beck, and Bertholle ("Every recipe, simple or complex, clearly shows that these are authors who cook") but totally dismantled an English-language translation of a book called *La Cuisine de France*, written by the food editor of French *Elle*, who went by the curious name of Mapie, the Countess de Toulouse-Lautrec: "Her suggestion that the cook baste roast beef every five or ten minutes with hot water is absurd, and her advice to the cook making mayonnaise to beat into one yolk 'as much oil as you like' is even worse. Mapie has evidently never made mayonnaise by hand or she would know that the maximum amount of oil a large egg yolk will absorb is three-quarters of a cup."

Field was even less forgiving in 1967 of the 926-page *Thousand Recipe Chinese Cookbook*, an audacious attempt by its author, Gloria Bley Miller, to do for Chinese cooking what Child, Beck, and Bertholle had done for French. Claiborne had hailed the book, but Field suspected that Miller, in over her head, had neither tested nor fully comprehended many of the recipes she'd found in her research. "It would be interesting to know why, for example, Mrs. Miller's recipe for hot mustard requires the cook to bring one cup of water to a boil and then allow it to cool before adding one half cup of dry mustard?" Field wrote. "Surely, Mrs. Miller must be aware that drinking and cooking water in China was boiled because it was often con-taminated. To suggest this procedure to a contemporary American cook without a word of explanation makes us suspect that Mrs. Miller is either putting us on or that she really believes in the culinary properties of boiled water."

When "Mrs. Miller" countered in a letter to the *Review* that her book had received "fifty or so reviews since publication, all but [Field's] have been unqualified cheers," Field had at her again: "As for the 'fifty or so' critical 'cheers,' Mrs. Miller refers to with pride, I have read them and they are in-deed 'unqualified' in more ways than one. Generally, they consist of enthu-siastic comments about the size of her book (one newspaper even mentions its weight—'exactly 4½ pounds')."

Field's writing appealed to a crossover audience of smart, curious read-ers who didn't necessarily cook—the *Times* daily book reviewer, Christo-pher Lehmann-Haupt, approvingly mentioned his "intriguing culinary criticism in *The New York Review of Books*" and praised his books on their literary merits rather than their culinary ones—but the food community was wary. "He was a very good teacher, but he was sort of a hysteric," says Ju-dith Jones, who edited two of Field's books for Knopf. And yet, for a time, he was tolerated and even embraced because he knew his stuff, his recipes worked, and he was the New Big Thing, there to be investigated, gossiped about, and feared. As Child put it in a letter to M.F.K. Fisher, with whom she became friends in the mid-sixties, "Michael is the glamour boy around New York at the moment, a dabbler, a charmer, a word-monger, a butter-fly, and ambitious." Beard, a music buff impressed with Field's concert-pianist credentials, was the newcomer's biggest benefactor. When Time-Life de-cided to capitalize on the "trend toward better eating," as the *Time* story on Child had put it, by issuing a multivolume series called *Foods of the World*, Beard lobbied for Field to be the series' consulting editor. The books, over-size and full-color, part *National Geographic* photo-travelogue and part recipe compendiums, were to be sold by subscription to Time-Life's built-in read-ership of magazine subscribers—a surefire moneymaker.

In a professional milieu that didn't pay well unless you were Julia Child, where even Jim Beard sweated out the wait every month for that check from Green Giant, *Foods of the World* was a godsend, "nothing less than a potlatch at which Time-Life freely distributed its considerable bounty to New York's food writers, editors, cooking teachers, and recipe testers," as Beard's biographer, Robert Clark, put it. The first book in the series was *The Cooking of Provincial France*, and it had a formidable lineup: M.F.K. Fisher was selected to write the text, Beard's protégé John Clancy was testing the recipes, and Child was retained as a "consultant"—a job that she didn't particularly need but accepted, she later admitted, because she wanted to be "in the swim" of things and felt she owed *Time* for the cover story.

Field rented La Pitchoune, the Childs' French country house, in order to do research for the book. It wasn't long before Fisher and Child started to have their misgivings about him. "M.F.K. Fisher stayed at Julia's house right after Michael had stayed there," says Jones, "and she said she opened the refrigerator door and there wasn't anything in it. She said, 'How could a person who loves food be in the south of France and not at least have a piece of cheese in the refrigerator?' With Julia and Jim, it was in their bones. They loved cooking. You'd swing open their refrigerator door and it would be bursting, and they'd say, 'What would you like for dinner?' Whereas everything about Michael was nonspontaneous."

The Cooking of Provincial France was attractive in a coffee-table kind of way, but many of its recipes were more restaurant-haute than rustic and provincial (for example, a very fancy *coquilles Saint-Jacques à la Parisienne*, scallops with mushrooms in white-wine sauce), and the region-by-region approach of Fisher's introduction wasn't repeated in the text, which never explained any dish's geographical origin. Overwhelmed by the scope of the *Foods of the World* project, Field appears to have panicked and just thrown together a bunch of French and quasi-French recipes, including some lifted more or less straight from *Mastering*, without attribution. Child, embarrassed by her association with the book, privately conceded that many of the recipes were "AWFUL," while Fisher grumbled that the Time–Life people had neutered her spiky prose.*

Though he had been the first to give Field wide exposure, Claiborne had grown to resent what he perceived as Field's uppitiness and panzer-division treatment of cookbooks that he himself had liked, such as *The Thousand Recipe Chinese Cookbook*. So when *The Cooking of Provincial France* came out early in 1968, Claiborne teed off with the most bilious Michael Field imitation he could muster. "It is said that the popularity of Americans in France is at its lowest ebb in history," he began. "After the Gauls read *The Cooking of Provincial France* by Time–Life Books, things are very likely to get worse. They might even start a small war in Normandy, Alsace, or Provence, and I might very well join them." Claiborne argued Fieldishly that the dessert recipes had nothing to do with provincial France and probably came from "somebody's files," while the sauce for a sole recipe called for so little liquid that it would end up "something like mucilage." Of Field himself, Claiborne icily commented that he was "a former concert pianist who might be excused on the grounds that he never played in the provinces."

The review came out the very day of the book's publication party at the Four Seasons, driving up Field's already-high blood pressure. To cub reporter Ephron, he spluttered, "Essentially, the whole food establishment is a mindless one, inarticulate and not very cultivated. These idiots who attack me are furious because they think I just fell into it. Well, let me tell you, I used to make forty soufflés in one day and throw them out, just to find the right recipe." The situation also caused a frost in the relationship between Claiborne and Beard, who thought the *Times* review unreasonably harsh and was busy consulting for Field on other books in the series.

None of this skirmishing prevented *The Cooking of Provincial France* from earning the money it was expected to earn, nor did it prevent Time-

---

*A few stray Fisherisms did manage to make it through untouched, though, such as her dark, out-of-place anecdote about the only French village she had ever known to lack its own local bread, the reason being that its baker had committed suicide. He "was felt to have betrayed his trade and his village by leaving so unexpectedly, with nothing edible in his ovens," she wrote.

Life from hiring Claiborne and Franey to oversee the *Classic French Cooking* volume, a book for which Beard and Pépin were also retained as consultants. (It was the first time Franey was acknowledged in print as Claiborne's collaborator.) Field, fortunately, did not have to deal too much with Claiborne directly—Claiborne was charged with writing the narrative text with Franey, while Field handled recipe instructions—but the experience took its toll on a man who was a bundle of nerves on his best day. Field managed one more solo-effort cookbook for Jones and Knopf, the appealing *All Manner of Food*, before dying of a massive heart attack in 1971, when he was just fifty-six. "In a way, he became his own worst enemy," says Jones. "He overexplained, overwrote, over-everythinged. He just was compulsive, and he didn't know how to let go."

CHILD SQUEAKED OUT of the *Foods of the World* situation untarnished, as she generally would in these internecine food-establishment skirmishes, a credit to her integrity both as a cook and as a human being, as well as her geographical remove from New York. Her occasional indiscreet, eye-rolling references to the "fairies" of the food world, meaning Claiborne, Beard, and such gay Beard lieutenants as John Clancy, weren't appreciated, but no one mistook Child, a political ultraliberal who socialized in Harvard circles and had seen her own husband smeared as a suspected Communist during the McCarthy era, for a bigot.

Yet even Child acquired her own tormentor, in the form of Madeleine Kamman, a Parisian who had studied at the Cordon Bleu and, briefly, under Simone Beck at L'Ecole des Trois Gourmandes before moving to the United States in 1960. Though she initially taught French cooking classes in Philadelphia, Kamman had by the late sixties settled with her American husband in the Boston area, Child's turf. Child was initially welcoming to the newcomer. Kamman was a brilliant teacher with an uncanny knack for adapting French techniques to whatever fresh ingredients were available in the American marketplace, and her 1971 book, *The Making of a Cook*, became, and remains, a lodestar for preprofessional cooks who want to understand the scientific underpinnings of French cookery rather than just follow step-by-step instructions. But before long, word got back to Child that Kamman was bad-mouthing *Mastering the Art of French Cooking* to her students and deriding Child as a charlatan who was "neither French nor a chef"—this, even though Child took pains to note that she did not consider herself an actual chef and resisted all attempts by magazine photographers to make her pose in a toque.

Over the years, even as she built a name for herself as the head of the Modern Gourmet cooking school and Chez la Mère Madeleine restaurant in Newton, Massachusetts (and, later, as the director of the School for American Chefs at Beringer Vineyards in Napa Valley, California), Kamman continued to sling arrows Child's way, deriding her TV shows and knocking Child for not advancing the cause of women in professional kitchens. Child chose not to engage Kamman in a pissing match, keeping a dignified silence. But at a couple of public symposia late in her life, when audience members raised the subject of criticism, Child alluded to a "certain woman" who had antagonized her, "and people who know me know who I'm talking about." At one of these symposia, Child remarked with a smile on her face that if this woman ever approaches her, "I will grind her alive, piece by piece, in my food processor."

Kamman, for her part, remains unrepentant about critiquing the beloved Julia, but insists that the matter has been overblown. "As a person, she was a sweet, dear lady," she says. "As a cook, I had seen better. America has a tendency toward stardom. I never wanted to be a star, and I resisted it very strongly by saying what I thought all the time. I'm not a very popular person. But you know what? So what!"

AS DIVISIVE AS FIGURES like Kamman and Field could be, there was one figure in the late 1960s about whom everyone in the food world (save the ever-magnanimous Child) could agree they hated: Graham Kerr. Whereas the entertainment quotient of *The French Chef* was a by-product of Child's goosey charm, Kerr's TV show, *The Galloping Gourmet*, which premiered late in 1968, committed the cardinal sin of *wanting* to entertain its viewers. Six foot four, handsome, English, prodigiously sideburned, and unable to resist an innuendo-laden wisecrack about a cake pan's dimpled bottom, the thirty-four-year-old Kerr was part Hugh Grant and part Austin Powers, with a soupçon of Julia thrown in.* He opened each half-hour episode of his syndicated daytime cooking program by bounding onto his kitchen stage and hurdling over a chair, often with a full glass of wine in hand. A prefilmed travel clip would then be shown, revealing whichever exciting locale Kerr had visited of late. He'd proceed to prepare some sort of outrageously rich dish—a Brisbane prawn soufflé, for example—and banter with his studio audience of bedazzled housewives, the bouffanted aunties of the girls who'd swooned over the Beatles. Kerr added an extra frisson of naughtiness by periodically raising a crystal goblet to his lips and saying, "I think I'll have a short slurp!"

"In actual fact, I probably drank less than a half a glass of wine in the entire night of making three shows, back to back," Kerr says. "That mechanism came about because we had to find a way of being able to call for a commercial break. So when I would say, 'I think it's time for a short slurp,' that would be the cue to the director that I was going to commercial. I would grab ahold of the glass, raise it to my lips, and 'CUT!'—they would then go through the two minutes of black for the commercial, I would chat with the audience, then they would go '5-4-3-2-1,' I'd lift the glass to my lips again, and I would put it down. But the perception came about that I couldn't be like I was, having the fun that I was having, unless I was three sheets to the wind. People felt that by the end of the program, I had to be ready to fall into the soufflé."

An instant hit, Kerr proved that Child's success on television was not an anomaly, and that America was a ripe market for TV cooking shows,

---

*One ungentlemanly reviewer of *The French Chef* described Child as "two parts Broderick Crawford to one part Elizabeth II."

notwithstanding the fact that *The Galloping Gourmet* was produced by the Canadian Broadcasting Company in a studio in Ottawa. But the food establishment regarded Kerr as a vile interloper. When *Life* magazine did a four-page pictorial story on Kerr in 1969, it patched on an extra page in which, under the headline A BRISK SAUTÉING BY THE FOOD ESTABLISHMENT, it recorded the opinions of several authorities on the new star. Field, characteristically, was severe: "I think he's awful—the Liberace of the food world, except that Liberace plays the piano a lot better than the Galloping Gourmet cooks. I don't think he has any sensibility. I don't think he's funny." Beard chastised Kerr as someone "who has very little respect for food" and "hasn't done much to increase the cause of good food." Claiborne professed never to have even seen the program. René Verdon, the former White House chef, said, "From the point of view of culinary arts, I don't think an American woman can learn from watching him. From my own point of view, he's sloppy." Only Child was kind, saying, "I think anyone who is going to interest people in cooking is fine."

"Well, I got the fifth page in *Life*, anyway," says Kerr. But the condemnations wounded him. "It was something that I found extremely difficult," he says. "You see, all of the food intelligentsia would write their one book a year or do twenty-six episodes for PBS. And here was I, doing 195 shows a year, absolutely exhausted. The moment we finished a series of sixty-five, which we did in six weeks, we would jump on a plane and fly around the world, visiting places that we had set up through the National Tourist Bureau to be the authentic locations where we could see the real thing. And we would visit up to eight restaurants a day to film those. We would be given those recipes. And then I'd come back and test every single recipe myself, and rewrite them to the degree that I felt they needed to be rewritten, for the U.S. market in particular. That is a tremendous amount to do. And, therefore, to go to that trouble, and to be accused of being a playboy showman—I mean, I hated that side of it."

In fact, Kerr had more in common with the food establishment's members than they supposed. He'd spent his childhood hanging around in the kitchen of his parents' small hotel in England, soaking up technique from the kindly Provençal chef who worked there. Like Claiborne, he'd attended hotel school on his government's dime, so impressing his superiors while serving in the British Army Catering Corps that they sent him off to Brighton Tech—"arguably the best hotel school in England," he says—to learn classic, Escoffier-style cuisine. Upon graduation, he was made a "corporal chef instructor," a ranking officer whose specialty was fancy French cooking, usually for the top brass at military events. His television career even predated Child's: having accepted a catering post with the Royal New Zealand Air Force in 1958, he was discovered two years later by a producer who worked for the country's fledgling national TV network. His cheeky cooking demonstrations (initially performed in his officer's uniform, much to the consternation of the military) propelled him to mid-sixties television stardom in the bigger market of Australia, where, way ahead of the curve, he hosted a program that devoted specific episodes to local foods—"drawing a circle of about fifty kilometers around a certain city or town," he says, "and only using the produce which came out of the ground, in season, to be able to construct dishes which I would call the 'new regional cuisine of Australia.'"

For *The Galloping Gourmet*, though, Kerr's wife and producer, Treena, encouraged him to place an emphasis on comedy—it was she who conceived of the leaping-over-a-chair entrance and cultivated the program's anarchic, Peter Sellers–movie feel. By the later standards of the Food Network's *Emeril Live* and *Iron Chef*, *The Galloping Gourmet* was not particularly assaultive, and, viewed today, it's harmless fun—certainly Kerr's enthusiasm for cooking was infectious, even if the instructional value of the individual episodes was dubious. The food establishment's revulsion at Kerr's success was a kind of separation anxiety, a realization that the culinary awareness they'd helped raise had taken on a life of its own, beyond the control of a few New York tastemakers. For plenty of future chefs who were children when Kerr's program first aired from 1968 to 1971, among them his big fans Emeril Lagasse and Charlie Trotter, the establishment's fuddy-duddy distinction between the acceptable Child and the distasteful Kerr was lost; they simply saw two tall people who had strange accents, stood behind stoves, and were awesome on TV.

KERR'S ASCENDANCY COINCIDED with that of *New York* magazine, another manifestation of foodmania's new reach in the swinging late sixties. Originating as a Sunday supplement in the *New York Herald Tribune*, the foundering paper where Lucius Beebe and Clementine Paddleford had long labored over their rococo sentences, *New York* established itself as a font of New Journalism, the hipster's clubhouse where Tom Wolfe, Gay Talese, and Jimmy Breslin tried on groovy new writing voices and widgety flights of onomatopoeia. *New York* was also a food-obsessed publication from the get-go, if more in the cause of dining out than cooking in. From the beginning, in its Sunday-supplement days, the magazine featured a column called "The Underground Gourmet" in which two accomplished graphic designers and zealous food hobbyists, Milton Glaser and Jerome Snyder, alerted New Yorkers to the possibilities of inexpensive gastro-tourism in their own town. Glaser and Snyder were frustrated by Claiborne's focus on fine dining (in his restaurant reviews, if not his food journalism), and set about canvassing the city's ethnic eating places on behalf of the "greater-numbered followers of good food" who, they thought, would be better off "getting their money's worth and perhaps adding a certain measure of adventure to their gastronomic pursuit." Thus did readers in the greater New York area learn for the first time what intrepid food insiders like Beard and Claiborne already knew: where to find good Syrian pita bread, Southern sweet potato pie, Argentine empanadas, Indian Samosas, Lebanese tabbouleh, and Japanese tempura and negimaki (though even Glaser and Snyder were squeamish about sushi back then).

But it was in 1968, after the *Herald Tribune* had folded and *New York* had been reconstituted as a stand-alone weekly by Glaser and the editor Clay Felker, that Gael Greene was unleashed upon the food world. Having gotten her start writing sex-and-the-single-gal pieces for *Cosmopolitan* and *Ladies' Home Journal*, Greene—a Detroit native from "Plastic White Bread Country . . . [with]

a cruel addiction to peanut butter," as she described herself in a dust-jacket bio—was bitten by the gourmet bug in the early 1960s. She soon found herself taking classes with Dione Lucas and joining the ranks of the foodie cult, "attending to the catechism of Craig Claiborne in the forming of our floating islands, warming our bowls and yolks and whisks after the teaching of Julia Child, macerating the livers of our chickens in the style of James Beard." Felker, having read one of her early forays into food journalism, thought it worth the gamble to try out Greene as *New York*'s restaurant critic.

Inspired by the conversational style of Tom Wolfe, Greene invented her own choppy, unhinged, status-obsessed style: "Dinner at La Grenouille. How gauche. *Nobody* has dinner at La Grenouille. The lunch bunch dines after dark at La Seine or Elaine's or at their own fiendishly chic little supper parties. The 'frogpond' at twilight is mostly a beaded, sequined, no-name crowd." And: "New York is a tall box. In the summer They put the top on. It is stifling. Here is how we restoreth our cool. Icy white wines. Muscadet. Sancerre. Sauvignon blanc."

While Claiborne had been the first to apply journalistic rigor to the restaurant beat, coaxing formerly anonymous chefs out of their kitchens to talk about their craft, Greene held up the entire dining-out experience to scrutiny, albeit in a gossipy, most un-*Time*sian way. She carefully evaluated the food, but she also felt her readers needed to know how to impress snobby maître d's, which society figures ate where, and what kind of cuisine was chic this month. Flaunting a saucy "food = sex" ethos much like the one that Claiborne revealed to intimates but suppressed in print, Greene ladled on the suggestiveness, christening herself "The Insatiable Gourmet" and turning even a trip to the lavish but unglamorous Jewish grocery Zabar's into an orgiastic reverie: "Imagine that all your modest secret sexual fantasies have suddenly materialized in the living room. Scary? That's exactly the delicious panic that overcomes a modestly disciplined gourmand upon first inhaling the fantasy of Zabar's. It's too much. Disciplined Gourmand has only one mouth, one liver, one life, one slightly used digestive system . . ."

With her first-person dispatches, obsessive referencing of her male companion (aka the Kultur Maven or Grape Nut), and nutty, elaborate disguises of wigs, hats, and makeup—ostensibly worn to preserve her anonymity so she wouldn't receive favorable treatment—Greene established a new, pop branch of food lit that existed in noisy Day-Glo opposition to the fireside contemplativeness of M.F.K. Fisher, A. J. Liebling, and Joseph Wechsberg. Whereas Claiborne gave Lutèce demerits for the loud apparel of its original proprietor, André Surmain, priggishly stating, "One could wish that the owner, Monsieur Surmain, would dress in a more reserved and elegant style to better match his surroundings," Greene pointedly *dug* Surmain's threads, writing. "He is not a super butler. He is your host, a zany country squire with his fat lapels, the bluff blend of pinstripe, tattersall, stripe, and Art Deco abstract. It is a highly aristocratic vulgarity, especially those crepe-soled rust suede Hush Puppies."*

Greene was equally turned on by chef André Soltner ("a master in the kitchen . . . driven by good demons"), and grew progressively more aroused over the master's "mousseline de brochet nantua ($4.75), a mini-mousse of pike in a heady lobster-scented cream sauce," "the pâté of pike ($4.75) in a pastry crust," the "mignon de boeuf en croûte Lutèce ($9.50), tender rare slices of beef Wellington," and the "carré de Pauillac, rack of lamb ($18 for two) . . . served pink as a howling infant."

YET EVEN IN THESE heady times for the food world, shot through with arrogance and possibility, there remained a major shortcoming: the quality of American ingredients was pretty lousy. Soltner, for all his great reviews, was flabbergasted that he still couldn't get ingredients of the quality he'd enjoyed during his trainee years in war-scarred 1950s France. "We couldn't work with fresh herbs, because we had only parsley—not even fresh chives," he says. Soltner

---

*Claiborne and Surmain clashed personally, says André Soltner, who notes that Lutèce, for all its reputation as the best and most expensive French restaurant of the post–Le Pavillon era, didn't receive its fourth star from the *Times* until 1972, the year Soltner bought out Surmain's share and took sole ownership of the restaurant.

was able to convince one of his milk suppliers, Sol Zausner, who happened to be a gastronome, to take a shot at making crème fraîche—America's first—but he found it maddening that he couldn't serve the classic French dish *médaillons de veau aux girolles*, veal medallions with chanterelle mushrooms (girolles).

"When I ask for girolles, they send me a can," Soltner says. "I still remember the can, a half-liter can, yellow and green, from Germany. But we wanted to cook only with fresh, so we didn't do nothing with girolles. Then, maybe about 1980, some people from Oregon came and offered me fresh girolles. I said to one of these guys, 'I don't understand—I'm here fifteen years, and there were no girolles. You're going to tell me now girolles just started to grow?' He said, 'No, André. We always had tons and tons of girolles in Oregon. But we had no market. So we had a contract with Germany for tons of girolles. We packed them up and sent them over.' The Germans, they were putting them in cans and sending them back to us!"

Though the success of the Big Three had encouraged grocers to stock imported provisions like brie, smoked salmon, niçoise olives, and canned foie gras, the American mid-century was also the techno-futurist period when large corporations successfully posited supermarkets, processed foods, and out-of-season produce as great advances in domestic life. Sales of fresh fruit per person per year dropped from 140 pounds in the 1940s to 90 pounds in the 1960s, and the difference was made up by the purchase of canned fruits, often packed in syrupy liquid. Even when consumers sought out fresh produce, "fresh" was a relative term. New refrigeration technologies made it possible for strawberries and tomatoes to travel long distances from the warm climes of Florida and Southern California to the chilly Northeast and Midwest, theoretically rendering seasonality and regionality moot.* But while

---

*While the advent of the refrigerated rail car in the nineteenth century had gone a long way toward eradicating regional limitations on produce sales, the invention in the 1930s of an automatic refrigeration system for long-haul trucks made America's food supply more mobile than ever—now meats and produce could be delivered directly to the markets where they were to be sold. A self-taught black inventor named Frederick McKinley Jones developed the first reliable refrigeration unit for trucks in 1935. He used the same technology to create a portable refrigeration unit that was used during World War II to transport blood serum and medicines on the battlefields.

these berries and tomatoes looked beautiful for perishables that had journeyed hundreds or thousands of miles from farm to market, it was because they were hybrids developed to stand up to shipping and long display (if not to gastronomic scrutiny). On top of that, these flavorless frankenfruits were often picked underripe (for the purpose of longevity) and gassed with ethylene so they'd turn a lovely, deceptive shade of farm-fresh red, ideal for display on supermarket shelves.

The supermarket itself was a descendant of such chains as the New York–based Great Atlantic & Pacific Tea Company (A&P) and the Memphis-based Piggly Wiggly, each of which contributed a crucial innovation to the industry in the early twentieth century—the former buying its wares directly from wholesalers, enabling the chain to undercut the prices of smaller, independent groceries, and the latter pioneering the self-service store where the customer selected goods straight from the shelf, without ever presenting an order to a counterman.

In the years after World War II, the same housing boom that saw farmlands razed and turned into tract-house developments encouraged urban grocery chains like A&P and Piggly Wiggly to build wide-aisled, boxy supermarkets on the new highways that serviced the new suburbs. Factor in the introduction of the shopping cart in 1937, the new affordability of automobiles, and the acceptance of the home refrigerator as a standard piece of kitchen equipment—like the home computer in the eighties, the fridge, over the course of the thirties, went from expensive status symbol to unremarkable necessity—and the result was that large quantities of food could be purchased in one fell swoop, hauled back to one's split-level ranch, and placed in cool storage, thus eliminating the need for the daily a-marketing-we-go ritual that Beard held so dear. By 1956, according to food historian Harvey Levenstein, 62 percent of America's groceries were purchased from supermarkets, and a further 28 percent from smaller self-serve "superettes," leaving only 10 percent of the nation's spending dollars to the old butcher-baker-greengrocer agglomeration of yore.

As an immigrant from Italy in the fifties, living in Forest Hills, Queens, Marcella Hazan found her local Grand Union supermarket to be at once disturbingly alien and marvelously convenient. The prebutchered chicken parts in cellophane-sheathed white Styrofoam containers, arrayed in a refrigerator case and illuminated by fluorescent lights, were like something out of an Arthur C. Clarke sci-fi tableau, "everything strange to me, everything wrapped, the chicken pieces dead in their little coffins," she says. On the other hand, Hazan, though she was an educated woman with a Ph.D. in biology, was terribly intimidated by the English language and appreciated the fact that she could pick and choose her groceries, however strange and antiseptic, without speaking to a soul. Likewise, Julia Child, during the 1956 to 1958 period of Paul's USIS career that saw the couple living in Washington, D.C., rather than abroad, was shocked and disturbed upon her return to America to see acquaintances eating Swanson's frozen TV dinners (introduced in 1954), but she welcomed the new fangled supermarket as a pleasant innovation, informing Simone Beck in a letter that "one thing I do adore is to be shopping in these great serve-yourself markets" where "you pick up a wire push cart" and "just trundle about looking and fingering everything there is."

The Big Three and their allies had woken up America to the possibilities of good cooking and good eating, but they were not by nature oppositional, agitational folk. Thus, while they had no use for Tang instant orange drink (trademarked in 1957 and popularized in 1965, when the Gemini astronauts took it into space) or Cool Whip nondairy whipped topping (introduced in 1966), they offered little in the way of advocacy against such products. In private notes scribbled in 1969, Beard mocked the convenience-food apologists Poppy Cannon and Peg Bracken as, respectively, "the commercialist (Poppy's putting everything in a can!!)" and "the enemy camp," but publicly he held his tongue.

In part, this was a matter of pragmatism—Beard was on the payroll of Green Giant, which, while hardly the most culinarily egregious of the big food processors, was by the early sixties pushing not only canned goods but frozen vegetables in "flavor-tight" plastic pouches that also contained butter sauce. Claiborne had no trouble being snippy about bad service and the dress sense of André Surmain, but he still touted the virtues of Procter & Gamble's Fluffo shortening (a public relations account of his old friend Ann Seranne), and, eager not to alienate *Times* readers and advertisers, allowed that "chipped beef properly spiced is easily turned into festive fare" and "canned minced clams can be put to dozens of palatable uses." Even Child, though she stubbornly resisted Madison Avenue's overtures and sicced her lawyers on anyone who tried to profit off her name,* opted to work within the limitations of the American marketplace rather than push its boundaries. She shopped at her local A&P and informed Beck that U.S. supermarkets contained "everything . . . that is necessary to allow a good French cook to operate." To the end of her life, Child was reluctant to plunge into any expressly political foodie fracas, gingerly sidestepping the late-eighties debate over the use of the allegedly carcinogenic pesticide Alar on apples, and privately dismissing concerns about the potential dangers of irradiated foods, which she in fact "deeply believed in," according to her last TV producer, Geof Drummond, "because she didn't want to see food spoil or get infected with E. coli or whatever."

There were a few individuals in the food world, such as Beard's dear friend Helen Evans Brown, who dared to raise their voices publicly against the big food companies, despairing over toast "made from bread that looks and tastes like facial tissue" in her book *Breakfasts & Brunches for Every Occasion* (1961) and cheekily averring in her best-known work, *West Coast Cook Book* (1952), that "if . . . a dish composed of tuna fish, canned mushroom soup, and corn flakes is in any danger of becoming a dish of the region, I prefer to ignore it." Even earlier, in 1946, *The New Yorker*'s Sheila Hibben sounded an alarm in her volume *American Regional Cookery*, whose introduction included this surprising blurt of embittered candor:

---

*In 1974, *The New Yorker* reported that the Childs' lawyer had put a halt to a TV commercial that featured "Julia Chicken, a fowl who spoke in the French Chef's unmistakably rich and breathy accents."

I say to people that I am writing a cook book and they ask if it will tell how to make a cake with the new better-than-butter shortening and how to use all the latest dehydrated wonders and if there will be a set of rules for balanced meals and charts showing the vitamin superiority of parsnips over nectarines. And when I say, "No, I shall write of none of these things," they are a little shocked and wonder whether the book will sell. To this, too, the answer may well be no.

Hibben's prediction proved all too correct: her book didn't sell well, and for the next twenty years or so, the food establishment uneasily coexisted with "Plastic White Bread Country." But by the early seventies, out on the West Coast, a group of culinarily minded young radicals had gotten mad as hell about the supermarket state, and they decided that they were not going to take it anymore.

CHAPTER FIVE

RADICAL NOTIONS

Just because you're a revolutionary doesn't mean your idea of a good meal should be Chef Boyardee ravioli reheated in a dog dish.

—Alice Waters, circa late 1960s,
per her friend Tom Luddy

I'm the headwaiter. This is a vegetarian restaurant only, we serve no animal flesh of any kind. We're not only proud of that—we're smug about it.

—Michael Palin, *Monty Python's Flying Circus*,
"Restaurant Sketch"

"THE MIXED-GREEN SALADS—FOR SURE, YOU CAN BLAME ME FOR THEM," SAYS ALICE Waters. "We were doing those very early on. I think lettuce was my first passion. I was bringing seeds over in the early seventies from France and planting 'em in my backyard, wanting a French kind of salad, with frisée and mâche. I'm sure I have contributed to the awful demise of the concept of mesclun, just by promoting it in many, many, many ways. And now, of course, one of those big companies has grabbed on to the idea, and they cut up big lettuces and put 'em in a bag, mix 'em up, and call 'em mesclun. Who is it—Dole pineapple or somebody?"

Well, Dole actually uses the term "Salad Blends," but the point is, Waters, beneath the veil of self-effacement, is taking credit, rather than blame, for transforming the American concept of salad from shredded iceberg and tomato wedges to a jungly mixture of whole, just-picked tiny leaves of various textures, shapes, hues, and flavors.

PAGE 121: *Future restaurateur and food evangelist Alice Waters (center) lets her hair down with friend Judi Johnson and boyfriend Tom Luddy, 1968.*

Waters's restaurant, Chez Panisse, which opened in 1971, has some legitimate claim to being the most influential dining establishment in America since Le Pavillon, and there are many more things for which she and/or it can take credit: the mantra of "fresh, local, seasonal ingredients" now chanted by any chef or home cook of integrity; the high profile the organic movement currently enjoys, particularly where professional cooks are concerned; the popularization of such gourmet name brands as Laura Chenel's Chèvre and Niman Ranch meats; the formalization of the position of "forager," the person at a restaurant whose job it is to seek out the best local ingredients and establish working relationships with farmers and suppliers; and the early careers of, to name but a few chefs of national reputation, Jeremiah Tower, Judy Rodgers, Deborah Madison, Mark Miller, Paul Bertolli, Jonathan Waxman, Mark Peel, and Joyce Goldstein.

Chez Panisse is a pretty but unassuming place that sits on an okay but not particularly attractive stretch of Shattuck Avenue in the northern part of Berkeley, California. It doesn't feel like "an important restaurant"—there's a downstairs dining room done up in woody Mission style where a single bill of fare is served at a set price every night, and an upstairs café with an à la carte menu and an open kitchen where you can watch the cooks work the grill and bake pizzas in the wood-burning oven. The waiters are friendly without being affrontingly informal, and the prices are eminently fair—the most a meal can cost (as of this book's publication) is $85 a head for a weekend-night prix fixe, or about a third of what you'll end up paying at the French Laundry or Alain Ducasse. The food is unfussy and ingredient-driven, usually constructed around a main course that's essentially an idealized version of your standard "meat and two veg" combo—one night it might be an aged Niman Ranch shell steak with spring peas and truffled mashed potatoes; another night it might be a Hoffman Farm chicken stuffed with wild mushrooms and greens, served with Chino Ranch carrots, turnips, leeks, and a horseradish sauce; and still another night it might be Laughing Stock Farm pork cooked in the fireplace with cardoon gratin, served with black kale and rosemary roasted potatoes. You might smirk at the menu's relentless use of proper-noun pedigrees, but the overall Chez Panisse experience is, in a word, unpretentious.

Yet, paradoxically, no restaurant in America has inspired, yea, *invited*, more cultish worship and precious food-crit overdrive. Chez Panisse is the ultimate manifestation of the baby boomers' contribution to the American food revolution, tracing its bloodlines directly to the Free Speech Movement that rocked the University of California's Berkeley campus in late 1964. As with all things great and boomerish—the rock music of the sixties, the civil rights movement, *Rolling Stone* magazine in its heyday—the magnitude of Chez Panisse's achievements is tempered by a certain cloying self-aggrandizement. This is a restaurant that never lacked a sense of its own importance, and was celebrating its birthday with commemorative limited-edition posters as early as 1973. Not for the Panissers the just-a-cook humility of a Pierre Franey or the shruggy nonchalance of a Marcella Hazan—these are folk who revel in the fact that they changed the landscape, man.

"We've always had this joke, those of us who have been exposed to Chez Panisse or worked there, that Alice thinks she invented food," says Bill Staggs, who joined the restaurant's staff as a cook in 1972 and wound up its maître d', working there on and off until 1993. Not that Waters is the only culprit; in February 1973, when the restaurant was desperately in need of a new chef, she met her match in Jeremiah Tower, a strikingly handsome libertine full of vim, vigor, vintage Krug, ambitious menu ideas, royalist pretensions, and himself. Tower would soon emerge as the Lennon to Waters's McCartney, the combustible half of a wondrously complementary partnership that would produce magical results but engender perpetual arguments (even among those who had never met either person) over who deserved credit for what.

It's a backhanded compliment to Chez Panisse, a measure of its significance, that credit is such a bugaboo. Some of the restaurant's early principals feel they've been expunged from its history and haven't been sufficiently acknowledged for their contributions in making the restaurant what it is. Some of Waters's forebears in the Bay Area feel that they don't get enough credit for having done what Chez Panisse did before Chez Panisse even existed. In the sixties, for example, a Berkeley restaurant called the Potluck took a very similar approach, serving a fixed-price, French-influenced menu, and its industrious manager, Narsai David, was foraging for fresh, seasonal ingredients before the practice had a name, "going out to the ocean to harvest mussels when no one dreamed of putting mussels on the menu," he says, "and going up to Napa Valley in April and harvesting bushels of wild mustard blossoms and using them to marinate a lamb loin for our spring festival." Some old-timers on the East Coast are irked that Chez Panisse is credited for innovating practices that have long been commonplace in Europe; even the ever-gracious Jacques Pépin, remembering the humble garden plot outside of Lyons that his family tended during the worst days of wartime privation, can't help but note with a twinge of annoyance, "My parents were organic gardeners before the word 'organic.' They grew our vegetables with horse manure we gathered from the streets and never used chemicals. But they didn't make this big deal of it!"

Factor in Chez Panisse's status as the springboard for the whole California cuisine movement, and the self-regard becomes even more acute. When *Saveur* published its special California road-trip issue in May 2001, the centerpiece of which was a reunion of Chez Panisse alumni for a potluck dinner on the Bolinas estate of Esprit founder Susie Tompkins Buell, it was arguably the smuggest issue of a food magazine ever put together. "This is one of those 'If they dropped a bomb . . .' events," wrote the road trip's organizers, native Californians and *Saveur* editors Colman Andrews and Christopher Hersheimer, as they chronicled the progression of their gang of California food royalty from cocktail hour—"little groups of us walk back inland, glasses in hand, like characters in some romantic French movie, through dense, low, golden sunlight"—to the "old Portuguese dairy barn" where the meal was eaten.*

Yet Chez Panisse must be given its due, for it expanded the possibili-

---

Saveur's then editor in chief, the East Coast–bred Dorothy Kalins, smiled through gritted teeth as she wrote of her friends Andrews and Hersheimer in the issue's introductory letter, "I cannot tell you how many times I have had to sit still for an enumeration of the joys of that Pacific-only fish the sand dab, or smile stiffly when every seafood salad failed the test against the Crab Louie at Swan Oyster Depot, or endure yet another reminiscence of Trader Vic's or Chasen's in the old days, or watch almost any East Coast produce suffer in comparison with the perfect rapture of Santa Monica Farmers' Market fare."

ties of what food could be in America, and of who could be a chef. Whereas Le Pavillon's Franey and Pépin went about their training very much the old-fashioned way in their native France, literally going from short pants to apprenticeships in professional kitchens, Waters and Tower, in their hubris and naïveté, simply threw out the rule book; neither had ever worked in a professional kitchen until Chez Panisse. That they pulled it off, using their self-taught lessons in French cuisine as a launchpad for their own intuitive take on Franco-Californian cookery, is remarkable. Like the original Haight-Ashbury flower children who attracted legions of young seekers to the Bay Area in 1967, Waters and her cohorts have exerted a magnetic pull on smart young men and women with big culinary dreams in their heads. Charlie Trotter, now one of America's most esteemed chefs, remembers being so "caught up in the whole West Coast, Bay Area, Napa Valley, Chez Panisse, Jeremiah Tower mystique" as a young Illinois nobody in the early eighties that, on a whim, he upped and moved west one day with nothing but his bicycle and a backpack, knocking on Chez Panisse's door like a just-off-the-bus Duluth homecoming queen banging on the gates of Paramount Pictures—"and they promptly shooed me off the property," he says.

"ALICE AND I GAVE frequent dinner parties," says David Goines, who was Waters's live-in boyfriend in the mid to late 1960s. "It became more and more obvious that what was needed were ingredients that we couldn't get, or ways of cooking that weren't common. The whole trend of American family cooking, since the 1940s, had been toward faster and easier, and things that were already prepared. It was gradually whittling away the very essence of what it meant to cook dinner for your family. It's like the story of the farmer who decided that his mule was eating too much, and he gradually fed the mule less and less. And just when he'd trained the mule to live on nothing, the damn mule died on him. That's kind of what'd happened to American family cooking."

In 1966, the year he and Waters became a couple, Goines was an intense, bespectacled kid with a stentorian speaking voice and deeply held convictions—not just on food but on civil rights and free speech. He had been, in fact, one of the prime movers in the Free Speech Movement (FSM), which erupted on the Berkeley campus of the University of California in the autumn of 1964, his sophomore year at the school. Between the civil rights movement, the antinuclear movement, and rising discontent with America's military presence in Vietnam, student activism was snowballing, and the Berkeley administration had moved on September 21 to ban all political organizations from soliciting on campus. Goines was suspended from school on September 30 for violating this ban, though the cause for which he was soliciting was a local one—the *SLATE Supplement to the General Catalog*, an "unauthorized" publication that offered frank evaluations of the Berkeley faculty, and whose parent organization, the rabble-rousing left-wing student group SLATE, had had numerous run-ins with the administration.

The very day after he was suspended, several young members of the Congress of Racial Equality (CORE), Goines among them, set up a table on campus, again in direct violation of the university's policy. One of their number, a recent UC-Berkeley graduate named Jack Weinberg, began to pontificate against racial discrimination and institutional suppression. On cue, the police swarmed in to arrest Weinberg, who, taking a page right out of the civil-disobedience playbook, let his body go slack, forcing the cops to carry him off and bundle him into a waiting squad car. What the police didn't anticipate, though, was that dozens of CORE members and other student agitators would surround the car before it could pull away, staging an impromptu sit-in around the vehicle. One demonstrator stuck an apple in the car's tailpipe; Goines dug his thumbnail into the valve of the tire nearest him, letting the air out. As hundreds of people gathered to witness the protest or participate in it, another student and FSM firebrand, Mario Savio, climbed onto the roof of the marooned vehicle and announced that he was "publicly serving notice that we're going to continue direct action" until the university acceded to student demands. Savio's speech was followed by several more, including one by Goines. The demonstration stretched well into the following day; Weinberg spent a total of thirty-two hours inside the car.*

The Free Speech Movement, to that point a story with little resonance beyond the Bay Area, became national news when photographs of Savio atop the car appeared in the October 2 papers. It became a still bigger story on December 2, when some 1,500 Free Speechers, singing a rousing rendition of "We Shall Overcome" led by special guest protester Joan Baez, poured into Sproul Hall, the main administrative building on the Berkeley campus, taking over all four floors of the building and settling in for a prolonged sit-in. (Baez split early, but not before helping distribute peanut-butter sandwiches to the diehards.) By the wee hours of December 3, Governor Pat Brown had called in the California Highway Patrol to defuse the situation. When it was over, the police had arrested 800 demonstrators, the largest mass arrest in California history. Most of those arrested got off with probation, but Savio and Weinberg were each sentenced to 120 days in jail; Goines was sentenced to 60 days, which he served, for legal-wrangling reasons, in two separate installments, one in 1965 and one in 1967.

ALICE LOUISE WATERS didn't know Goines when both were undergraduates at UC-Berkeley, but he was precisely the kind of non–Ken doll she'd hoped to meet when, in January of 1964, she transferred—indeed, fled—up north from the University of California's Santa Barbara campus with three of her fellow disgruntled sisters at the Alpha Phi sorority. "The women we'd met in Santa Barbara were all lined up to get married when they were twenty-two," says Eleanor Bertino, who roomed with Waters on both campuses and also had been her classmate for one year at Van Nuys High School in Southern California. (Waters grew up in Chatham, New Jersey, but moved west with her family in 1961, her last year before college.) "We pledged the same sorority at Santa Barbara because it was the only way you could have a so-

---

*It was Weinberg who, in 1964, coined the phrase "Never trust anyone over thirty."

cial life," says Bertino. "Very shortly, there were four of us who were like 'Oh, my God—this is not for us.' There had to be something more exciting and interesting than living in a sorority. Halfway through our sophomore year, we all transferred to Berkeley. None of us were politically involved, but we just liked the fact that there was activity going on up there. I mean, we were nice girls, not radical at all. I remember going to see an English teacher of mine before I left Santa Barbara, and she said, 'I'll send you brownies in jail.' I had no idea what she was talking about."

But it didn't take long for the erstwhile sorority sisters to acclimate to Berkeley life. Sexually, the new campus was much more to their liking— "Without being outcasts, we didn't have to get married, and you could move in with your boyfriend, and you had the pill," says Bertino—and when the Free Speech Movement kicked in during their second semester there, they threw themselves into the cause, if not to the extent of getting arrested and incarcerated. "I loved the sense of community that flowed out of the Free Speech Movement and my little group of friends, and I knew I just wanted to be here," says Waters, who, apart from a junior year abroad in France and a prolonged overseas trip in 1967–68, has lived in Berkeley ever since.

Waters's first trip to France, the site of her culinary awakening, came in 1965, the year after her political awakening. "I went to Paris and to Brittany. And that's really what awakened me in a sensual way to food," she says. "I hadn't ever been enthusiastic or excited about food. My mother wasn't really a good cook; more of a health-food person, always giving us vitamins." Like Julia Child, Chuck Williams, and Judith Jones before her, Waters was struck that people in France "just *cared* about food—they cared about the buying of it and the cooking of it, no matter whether they ate at home or went to a restaurant. They bought the best bread and went to the farmers' market two times a day, 'cause they didn't want the produce that had come in in the morning for the dinner."

At one particular Breton restaurant, situated in a rustic stone house set by a stream and run by a husband-waiter and cook-wife, Waters experienced

the equivalent of Child's sole meunière moment in Rouen, watching, blissfully stunned, as her order of trout amandine came to fruition: the husband
went out back with a fishing pole, caught a fish, presented it to her in its
flopping, gasping state, and then hurried it back to the kitchen, where it soon
reemerged as a finished dish, served with vegetables picked from the restaurant's own garden. For the husband and wife, it was all in a day's work; for
Waters, it was the birth of an idée fixe: seasonal, local ingredients served in
the freshest state possible.

Not that she could return to Berkeley and implement this idea instantly; she was still a student with a few semesters to go. In 1966, while she
continued her studies, she volunteered to work on the congressional campaign of Robert Scheer, one of the editors of *Ramparts*, the leading magazine
of the New Left.* Scheer's campaign quickly ran aground, but not before it
provided the opportunity for Waters to meet Goines. Since getting suspended from school, Goines had found happy employment at the Berkeley
Free Press—the print shop where Scheer's campaign posters were being
produced—and was developing a side career as a graphic artist. Goines was
immediately smitten with the delicately pretty little Scheer volunteer who
regularly showed up at the print shop with the campaign's poster artwork. In
those pre-bandanna, pre-beret days, Waters wore her hair in an adorable
Mary Tyler Moore flip and looked, says Bertino, like a "pre-Raphaelite angel." Not long after they met, Waters and Goines moved in together in an
apartment on the corner of Grove Street (now Martin Luther King Jr. Way)
and Francisco Street, not far from the UC-Berkeley campus. When Goines
returned to prison in June of 1967 to serve out the remainder of his sentence, Waters visited him faithfully every weekend, and was there, in a borrowed car, to retrieve him upon his release.

The Goines-Waters apartment became something of a salon for FSM
veterans, all of whom were impressed by Waters's cooking, as unpracticed as

---

*Scheer later become a national correspondent for the *Los Angeles Times* and a prominent leftie
pundit, as well as the *Playboy* interviewer who extracted Jimmy Carter's infamous 1976 admission
that he had "committed adultery in [his] heart many times."

it was at the time. "I remember one time very distinctly that Alice made a béarnaise—which I, of course, had never heard of before—and the egg yolks curdled," says Goines. "And I was all for trying to save it and fix it. You know, because 'God! This is, like, real expensive!' And she just threw it away and started over again. I was real impressed by that. We certainly weren't a Stalinist cell, eating wretched food."

"At one dinner we had snails, and the dessert was chocolate mousse," says Bertino. "And David said, 'I hope you realize there's more protein in this chocolate mousse than the average Vietnamese gets in a week.' I just thought, 'God, how annoying, David! Just shut up and eat!' "

It *was* kind of an issue, how food fit into the revolution that the young left was fomenting. Waters was decidedly a sensualist and flavorist who had no truck with the puritanical types who saw nobility in deprivation or junky, pseudo-proletarian dietary choices. The yippie leader Jerry Rubin ran with the FSM crowd but insisted on eating bologna-and-white-bread sandwiches because that, allegedly, was what the masses, the *real* cogs of the revolution, ate. This sort of attitude exasperated Waters. "As Alice used to put it, 'Just because you're a revolutionary doesn't mean your idea of a good meal should be Chef Boyardee ravioli reheated in a dog dish,' " says Tom Luddy, another UC-Berkeley grad and member of the FSM circle, who ran the local art-house movie theater, the Telegraph Repertory Cinema. (During the marathon Sproul Hall sit-in, Luddy kept the troops entertained by carting in a projector and screening silent Charlie Chaplin shorts on a wall.) "Alice was the only one who kept insisting that the way we eat is political," says Luddy. "She would berate everyone in the movement, saying, 'It's not enough to liberate yourself politically, to liberate yourself sexually—you have to liber-ate *all* the senses.' She believed that eating together was a socially progressive act, one that was under threat from the fifties American-TV, frozen-food culture." This jibed with Waters's experiences in France, where she discov-ered that even impoverished students and intellectuals placed a premium on eating well, and devoted as much argumentative fervor to a discussion of what was for dinner that night as they did to the merits of bolshevism.

Yet Waters, for all her later advocacy of organic farming and healthy eating, was not aligned with the burgeoning mung-beans-and-tofu "natural foods" movement, either. Having grown up in a brown-rice household—where her mother equated drably prepared whole grains with healthfulness—the ascetic, deflavorized rabbit-food diet was, she says, "what I was trying to escape from."

Nevertheless, the Bay Area was crawling with young radicals who, like Waters, were reconsidering their relationship with food and, in so doing, were taking an increasing interest in health-food authorities they'd earlier ignored or dismissed as old crackpots—people like the lichen-munching naturalist Euell Gibbons, whose 1962 book, *Stalking the Wild Asparagus*, acquired new chic, and the magazine publisher Jerome Irving (J.I.) Rodale, who was the first person to use the term "organic" in an agricultural context, and whose quarter-century-old publication *Organic Farming and Gardening* suddenly enjoyed a huge spike in readership. As the author Warren Belasco notes in his wry, masterful work of culinary anthropology, *Appetite for Change: How the Counterculture Took on the Food Industry*, "White versus brown was a central contrast. White meant Wonder Bread, White Tower, Cool Whip, Minute Rice, instant mashed potatoes, peeled apples, White Tornadoes, white coats, white collar, whitewash, White House, white racism. Brown meant whole-wheat bread, unhulled rice, turbinado sugar, wildflower honey, unsulfured molasses, soy sauce, peasant yams, 'black is beautiful.' "

The young progenitors of the countercuisine, as Belasco calls it, saw food as a means to circumvent the military-industrial establishment and build an alternative system of nourishing the masses, mentally as well as physically. Across the Bay Bridge in San Francisco, where the Haight-Ashbury hippie scene was unfolding, an activist group known as the Diggers was attracting notice for its "feeds," in which its members distributed free food—much of it scavenged from restaurants and bakeries, or stolen—to the scraggly youths who swarmed the streets. But before they got their free grub, the kids were subjected to Digger harangues about the evils of industrialization and forced to accept mimeographed Digger literature. (The Diggers began as an outgrowth of the San Francisco Mime Troupe, an avant-garde guerrilla theater group that performed satirical plays and took their name from a seventeenth-century band of English antipoverty activists who planted vegetable crops in town commons and distributed the yield to the poor.) The Diggers advocated not only free food for all but, as one of their manifestoes put it, a "return to the land . . . to straighten our heads in a natural environment, to straighten our bodies with healthier foods and Pan's work, toe to toe with the physical world." To that end, a bunch of them convinced Lou Gottlieb, a former member of the folksinging group the Limeliters, to let them use his Sonoma County ranch as a farm-commune-ashram, which, predictably, degenerated within a year's time into a messy, chaotic refugee camp for zonked-out Haight hard cases.

Waters and Goines were not unsympathetic to a lot of the countercuisine notions that were in circulation at the time—the need for alternative food sources, the establishment of farming collectives, the virtues of little ethnic groceries vis-à-vis the evils of supermarkets—nor were they fans of processed food (though Bertino remembers her roommate, pre-France, merrily eating Wonder Bread in riposte to her mother's doctrinaire brownbreadism). But they were too pragmatic to go in for the phoofy "Pan's work" utopianism and agitprop histrionics of the San Franciscans. As their writer friend Greil Marcus, who graduated from UC-Berkeley the same year as Waters, sums up the Berkeley–San Francisco attitudinal divide, "We were thinkers; they were crazy."

Berkeley was developing its own, more accessible brand of culinary nonconformity, assaulting the "white food" status quo from a more cerebral, European angle by offering high-quality "gourmet" goods to the university community, which was full of worldly, educated people who had traveled abroad or actually were from abroad—the West Coast equivalents of the people with whom Julia and Paul Child circulated in Cambridge. In 1966, a cantankerous Dutchman named Alfred Peet opened a shop right near Waters and Goines's apartment, on the corner of Walnut and Vine Streets, called Peet's Coffee & Tea. Mr. Peet, as he was universally known, had grown up in the coffee business in Holland and worked as a tea trader in the East Indies, and proselytized to his clientele on the importance of using high-quality arabica beans rather than the cheaper, lower-grade robusta beans used by commercial producers like Folgers and Maxwell House. He quickly developed a loyal following among students and locals, who became addicted to his strong, deep-roasted, intensely flavorful coffee and carefully followed his precepts for re-creating his potent brew at home. (Goines remembers he and all his friends buying hourglass-shaped Chemex filter coffeemakers from Peet, who, with characteristic severity, insisted that his coffee *never* be percolated.) Among Peet's most devoted early converts was a recent University of San Francisco graduate named Jerry Baldwin, who, even after he moved to Seattle, ordered sacks of Peet's Coffee by mail so he could get his daily fix. In 1971, with Peet acting as their supplier and roaster, Baldwin and two of his Seattle buddies, Zev Siegl and Gordon Bowker, made a go of it with their own coffee company, Starbucks.

A year after Peet's opened, Sahag and Elizabeth Avedisian, a middle-aged couple who had met on an Israeli kibbutz, opened a shop a little farther up Vine Street called the Cheese Board. Well ahead of their time, the Avedisians offered a wide array of imported cheeses that were then hard to find, things like chèvre and Gruyère, and plied shoppers with free samples. Unlike Peet, who behaviorally remained true to the Old World, the Avedisians let their hair down and embraced Berkeley radicalism, transforming their privately owned shop into a worker's collective where every employee was an owner and earned the same wage. The Cheese Board collective was a monster success from the outset, proving that the countercuisine didn't have to be, by definition, budget-priced, low-cal, or ascetic.* The Cheese Board served as a model for all manner of collectives and cooperative groceries that popped up in the Bay Area in the late sixties and early seventies, though

---

*One original member of the Cheese Board collective, Darryl Henriques, a San Francisco Mime Troupe member, responded to customers' requests for recommendations with cheeky boomer humor: "If you like fat mixed with salt wrapped in polyvinyl chloride," he said, "then everything's good."

none would match its success and longevity, which, in a capitalism-wary town like Berkeley, caused some resentment and suspicion; as late as 1980, one disgruntled hard-liner took the Cheese Board to task in a letter to the *Bay Area Directory of Collectives* for "selling cheese to an endless stream of customers."

To Waters, the most important gourmet shop to open in Berkeley in this period was the Kitchen, on Channing Street, which was not a food store but a specialty kitchenwares shop, a sort of small-scale version of San Francisco's Williams-Sonoma. The Kitchen's owner, a faculty wife named Gene Opton, took pride in offering an eclectic array of cookbooks in addition to her impressive line of wire whisks, Scandinavian cheese planes, and T. G. Green mixing bowls imported from England. It was she who importuned Waters, one of her regulars, to check out the works of Elizabeth David, a star of English cookery who was then little known in America outside of food-establishment circles. (The hard-to-please Michael Field was a fan.)

David, like Waters, had felt no particular affinity for food until she went to France as a student—in her case in 1929, when, at sixteen, she was sent by her father, a Conservative member of the British Parliament, to spend a year at the Sorbonne in Paris, where she discovered that there was more to eating than the "nursery tapioca" and "appalling boiled cod" she'd experienced at home. David later traveled extensively, to India, Egypt, the Greek Islands, Italy, and throughout provincial France, picking up recipes and techniques along the way. In the 1950s, as British food was at its most postwar-scarce and monochromatic, she wrote a series of books on French and Italian country cooking that enchanted English readers with sun-dappled visions of "unknown cafés along the banks of the Burgundy canal, patronized by men who sail the great petrol and timber barges to and from Marseille" (from *French Country Cooking*, 1951) and farmers' markets brimming with "bunches of gaudy gold marrow-flowers [that] show off the elegance of pink and white marbled bean pods, primrose potatoes, green plums, green peas" (from *Italian Food*, 1954).

Though the critic Alexander Cockburn would later rather contemptuously describe David as a progenitor of the now ubiquitous "cookbook pastoral" voice, this sort of writing was all but unknown to Americans in the 1960s. In David, Waters had at last found a food person in the Anglophone world who was speaking her language, calling for an honest, straightforward cookery "carried out with care and skill, with due regard to the quality of the materials, but without extravagance or pretension," to quote from *French Provincial Cooking* (1960), the more substantial follow-up to the slender *French Country Cooking*. David's prose alone was intoxicatingly summery and transportive, but her recipes, so much simpler (if more vaguely articulated) than Child's labor-intensive *chaud-froid* sauces and boned birds served *en croûte*, made possible the reality of bringing the bounty of the rough-hewn Provençal farm table right to your flecked-Formica countertop: duck with figs, *ratatouille niçoise*, garlic soup, a classic *pissaladière* topped with olives, onions, and anchovies. Waters admired Julia Child, and was as enamored of *Mastering the Art of French Cooking* as any culinarily adventurous young woman in the sixties, but David touched her soul. Here was a representation of French cookery that offered a dream fusion of the countercuisine's pro-natural, anti–white food goals and Waters's own romance with the "little no-star restaurants and bistros and cafés" that she'd experienced in France.

Such was the impression that David made on Waters that when the opportunity arose in 1967 for Waters to go to England to earn a degree in Montessori education, she chose to do so in part because going to England might afford her the chance to meet her idol, who at the time was running a kitchenwares shop in London not unlike Opton's. And so, Waters moved to London for eight months, with Goines coming along to study calligraphy. She made her pilgrimage to David's Bourne Street shop and saw the great author in the flesh, but couldn't summon the nerve to introduce herself. (They wouldn't formally meet until years later, when David, making her first trip to the United States in the early 1980s, came to Chez Panisse as a guest of the *Gourmet* wine columnist Gerald Asher.)

After getting her Montessori certification, Waters bummed around Europe for a few more months before resuming her life with Goines and their

Grove Street dinner parties. One of the frequent guests at these dinners was Bob Novick, another ex–Sproul Hall arrestee, who, late in 1968, started up an alternative newspaper with a fellow FSM alum, Marvin Garson, called the *San Francisco Express Times*. Novick asked Waters to contribute a weekly cooking column for the paper, with Goines doing the artwork and calligraphy. The column, called "Alice's Restaurant" after the Arlo Guthrie song—which was itself about another countercuisine heroine, Guthrie's friend Alice Brock, who ran a hippie-friendly café in Stockbridge, Massachusetts—was Waters's first foray into being a public food person.

From the perspective of the early twenty-first century, the *Express Times* recipes—for things like vichyssoise, chicken breasts florentine, carrot bread, and "Russian beef borsch"—are, by Waters's later exacting standards, cursory, primitive, and not totally cool on the from-scratch front; she uses canned cherries for her cherries jubilee (!), and, for the crust of her cheese and onion pie, recommends a "store-bought pastry stick"(!!!).* But her disciplined pâté maison and chicken biryani were a far cry from the improvised, overseasoned hashes and stews that were popular in stoner circles at the time—"disgusting hippie crap," as Luddy remembers with a shudder—and she did make a point of urging readers to use a cream cheese "without gum" for the filling of her blueberry tart.

By the time she was seriously considering giving up her day job as a Montessori teacher to open a restaurant, Waters had amicably split up with Goines, and was living with Luddy. Her new boyfriend's connections in the film world broadened her social circle considerably. She got to know Francis and Eleanor Coppola, who had started up the American Zoetrope studio in

---

*In 1970, Goines packaged the *Express Times* recipes, with his gorgeous woodblock illustrations and offset print work, as a portfolio called *Thirty Recipes Suitable for Framing*—effectively Waters's first cookbook. Though it sold out regularly in Opton's shop and other local stores, Goines ceased publishing *Thirty Recipes* at Waters's request in 1978, by which time Chez Panisse had a national reputation and she considered the old recipes a "disgrace." Nevertheless, the proceeds from the first couple of printings alone were enough to enable Goines to buy the very print shop where he was an employee, and where he remains to this day.

an old San Francisco warehouse in 1969, and, with Luddy, she traveled to the island of Noirmoutier, France, to stay as a guest of the filmmaking couple Jacques Demy and Agnès Varda. While Luddy talked movies with his hosts— the directors, respectively, of *The Umbrellas of Cherbourg* and *Cleo from 5 to 7*— Waters hung back in the kitchen with Demy's mother, who prepared the sorts of gutsy, unpretentious French meals that Elizabeth David wrote about.

In Berkeley, Waters's dinner parties with Luddy were even more elaborate affairs than the ones she'd hosted with Goines, rich with culturati like Jean-Luc Godard and Susan Sontag and political activists like Abbie Hoffman and Huey Newton, the Black Panther leader. "It was radical chic, like Leonard Bernstein," says Bertino. "All these people would come through their modest little bungalow, Alice would cook this lovely dinner, then more people would come, and Tom would screen a film, and then Alice would serve Armagnac afterward, and there would be these group political discussions."

Luddy was also the one to turn Waters on to the films of Marcel Pagnol, in particular the director's Marseilles trilogy from the 1930s, which the couple took in at the Surf Theater in San Francisco. The three films, *Marius*, *Fanny*, and *César*, follow the intertwined lives of a group of Provençal characters from youth to late middle age. The setting dovetailed nicely with Waters's Elizabeth David obsession and affinity for all things Provençal, and she saw in the characters' vicissitudes and passions a reflection of her own tight-knit, argumentative Berkeley set; not for nothing did Waters, an incorrigible romantic, start dressing in 1920s and '30s period clothing—cloche hats, berets, and vintage dresses that made her look a bit like Orane Demazis, the actress who played Fanny, the trilogy's female protagonist. "We were all wearing vintage clothes then, because you could buy them for nothing," says Bertino. "It was more glamorous than hippie clothing. Alice would get these beautiful 1920s beaded dresses for $10 that would fall apart after she wore them four times, but it didn't matter because they barely cost anything."

Waters's favorite character in the Pagnol trilogy, or at least the one she grew mistiest over, was Panisse, a kindly, besotted sailmaker who offers to marry Fanny when she learns she's pregnant by another man, Marius, who has forsaken her for a life at sea. When Waters started casting about for names for her restaurant, Luddy suggested that she name it after Panisse.

It was another of Luddy's film buddies, a Berkeley junior professor and fledgling filmmaker named Paul Aratow, who provided the impetus for Chez Panisse to become a reality. Aratow had spent time in France and Italy on a Fulbright fellowship, was an even more accomplished home cook than Waters, *and* he was willing to put up some of his family's money to support the venture. "He had confidence up the kazoo, chutzpah, which Alice didn't have. He really helped get us off the ground," says Luddy. "He was very good in meetings, and would probably have made a greater impression on somebody loaning you money or equipment than Alice." Aratow was the one who cut a deal to buy a run-down house on Shattuck Avenue off Vine Street, not too far from the Cheese Board and Peet's, as the restaurant's site— "an ugly, squat, two-story, Hollywood-type stucco apartment house that I tore apart with four or five hippie carpenters," he says.

As 1970 turned into 1971, Aratow and the head carpenter, Kip Mesirow, hammered and sawed away, retrofitting the house with Mission-style woodwork and light fixtures, while Waters kept teaching at the Montessori school, planning menus at night. Victoria Kroyer, a former doctoral candidate in philosophy, was hired to be the chef, despite having zero professional cooking experience, because Aratow liked her confidence and the influences she cited: Michael Field, Elizabeth David, and Alice B. Toklas. "It was that impetuous—'You're hired!'—and I guess it was just my lucky day," says Victoria Wise, who now goes by her married name.

Waters's friend Lindsey Shere, who lived down the block from the apartment she'd shared with Goines, agreed to come on board as pastry chef. Goines agreed to design and letter the menus. And Waters herself was responsible for the front of the house, hostessing, coordinating with the kitchen, and making sure everything looked perfect, from the flowers to the (mismatched) flatware. "It was sort of like those Judy Garland and Mickey Rooney movies—'Hey, let's put on a show!' " says Goines. "Which seems kind of dorky, but that's exactly what happened. It had the same innocence, and what was lacking in skill and experience was made up for in enthusiasm and intent." To ensure that the staff could concentrate on getting the meal just right, there would be a set dinner menu every night of three or four courses, with no à la carte choices.

CHEZ PANISSE SERVED its first dinner on August 28, 1971: an appetizer of pâté *en croûte* (an un-Provençal nod to Julia Child, whose haute, buttery tendencies were mitigated, in Waters's mind, by her boosterism of French cookery and general wonderfulness), a main course of duck with olives, a salad, and Lindsey Shere's almond tart. Waters wore a vintage beige lace dress. The kitchen wasn't finished yet, there was insufficient silverware (Waters would return to the flea market several times that week for reinforcements), and the five waiters kept bumping into each other, because Aratow and Waters hadn't yet figured out that the smallish dining room required only two or three. But for all the naïveté and rank amateurism, Chez Panisse's principals knew they'd struck a nerve. "It was exactly the right historical moment for this to happen in Berkeley," says Wise, who somehow kept her bearings in the kitchen that night. "The educated clientele, the professors and students who had been to Europe, were waiting for a restaurant like this."

"We knew in a couple of days that we had something really hot," says Aratow. "The place was jammed. People were coming over from San Francisco to eat in Berkeley. I mean, that never happened." At the time, the most influential food writer in San Francisco was Jack Shelton, who published a dining-out newsletter with a circulation that hovered around 20,000. He reviewed Chez Panisse eight months into its existence and was hesitantly positive, calling the food and service uneven, but noting, by way of compliment, "I have never, ever been bored."

The fixed price the first few months was $3.95, which was both a terrific value for a four-course meal and suicidally inexpensive considering the restaurant's high overhead—the remodeling costs, Waters's insistence on the finest ingredients and floral arrangements, and her and Aratow's "come one, come all" approach to staffing, which meant that there were as many workers in the restaurant as there were customers in the dining room. But it was still pricey for young Bay Area counterculturists. "I went to dinner on opening night with Ronnie Davis, who started the San Francisco Mime Troupe," says Bertino, "and we thought it was outrageously expensive, and fancier food, richer food, than we were accustomed to eating."

To Bertino, Chez Panisse's opening marked a signal moment of retreat from the barricade-storming ethos of the sixties, of "backing away from politics and going into other things, food being one of them." Just two and a half years earlier, on April 20, 1969, many of these same diners had taken part in the seizure of a vacant plot of land that was owned by the university, planting vegetable gardens, installing park benches and playground equipment, and naming the usurped parcel People's Park. (Aptly for residents of a budding foodie mecca, the invaders celebrated into the night by drinking wine and dancing to the music of a hippie band called the Joy of Cooking.) Governor Ronald Reagan, who had defeated Pat Brown in 1966 in part on a pledge to "clean up the mess in Berkeley," sent in the National Guard to retake People's Park, resulting in the biggest Berkeley ruction since the Sproul Hall arrests—protesters rioted, tear-gas grenades were thrown, one young man was shot dead by deputies of the Alameda County Sheriff's Department, and another was blinded by buckshot while watching the proceedings from the roof of Luddy's cinema.

But the very week Chez Panisse opened, Bertino, Davis, and their pal Huey Newton were dismayed by the underwhelming attendance at an event that, in an earlier time, would have turned out masses of Berkeley radicals: the funeral of George Jackson, the imprisoned Black Panther leader who, eight days earlier, had been shot dead by guards while leading a breakout attempt at San Quentin. Few whites turned out for Jackson; Chez Panisse, on the other hand, kept packing 'em in, night after night.

It's common for detractors to remark today on the "irony" that a restaurant founded on principles of sixties idealism now caters mostly to an elite, moneyed clientele. But this gripe actually dates back to the oldest of the old days, when some Berkeleyites had a hard time coming to grips with Chez Panisse's instant popularity. The Cheese Board collective's members, despite their friendships with the Panisse staff, were particularly tortured about what their neighbor represented. Bob Waks, who expanded the collective's product line by baking rapturously received sourdough baguettes, was happy to bake *some* baguettes for Chez Panisse, but not enough to fulfill their demand, because he didn't want to be seen as a servant of the hoity-toity. Sahag Avedisian, the Cheese Board's founder, was more confrontational. Though willing to sell his cheeses to the restaurant, he railed against a Chez Panisse employee sent over to buy them for being a "capitalist villain," and, in one instance in the early seventies, instigated a very Diggers-like stunt: a "streak" through the restaurant in which several members of the collective, Avedisian included, ran into Chez Panisse stark naked, exposing their bottoms and genitalia to bemused customers.

But despite the concerns of people like Bertino and Avedisian, Chez Panisse wasn't a retreat from politics—it *was* politics, a representation of what American food could be if people weren't complacent about gassed, flavorless tomatoes and frozen TV dinners. The counterculture generated plenty of misbegotten movements and lysergically distorted belief systems that would later cause its members to feel disillusioned or embarrassed, but the fresh-food movement wasn't one of them. In fact, it might well be the counterculture's greatest and most lasting triumph.

AS IMMEDIATELY POPULAR as Chez Panisse was, it nearly didn't survive its first year, and for a very counterculturish reason: no one had any business sense. "Those of us who were working hard figured somebody had a handle on it, that the cash flow was being properly managed—and we were wrong," says Jerry Budrick, who was a waiter on opening night and remained on staff for seventeen years, becoming the headwaiter and in-house handyman in the process. "It turned out that nobody had any idea of how much was going out compared to what was coming in. The whole operation was sliding deeper into debt."

The absurdly optimistic initial plan was for the restaurant to serve breakfast, lunch, and dinner, "seven days a week, from 7 a.m. to two in the morning," says Waters. "That was foolishness." The breakfast was quickly phased out, and lunch became a rudimentary mix of soups, sandwiches, and the previous night's leftovers. But even with these cutbacks, the hours were still impossibly long for Waters, which put a strain on her health and her relationship with Luddy. "She was a total workaholic, and I was very impatient and angry with her much of the time," he says. "She had no time for anybody—just driven, driven, driven. I wanted her to take Sundays off and be more reasonable about her health. I remember once coming to the kitchen and seeing her sitting on an upturned pot, and I said, 'What are you doing?' She said that she couldn't see—she was blind. Her system had short-circuited, and she sat there maybe, like, an hour before her sight came back."

Luddy and Waters broke up, and Aratow, too, soon fell away, eager to devote his time to filmmaking and unable to reconcile his desire to make a buck with Waters's high ideals, spendthrift ways, and what he calls her "China-teacup personality." "I'd say, 'We've gotta put another four tables in or we're gonna go down!' " he says. "And she would say, 'No, it'll be too crowded!' She didn't really care about the money." Victoria Wise didn't last much more than a year, either, resigning as chef because she didn't like working nights and didn't like Waters's interference in planning menus. "There wasn't room in the kitchen for two bossy women, put it that way," she says.

Still, for all the volatility, the place had a certain lusty, Pagnol-esque joie de vivre that was precisely what Waters was after. When it was over between her and Luddy, she simply moved on to Budrick, a jolly, Falstaffian sort who was known for drinking prodigiously even as he waited on tables. "We never had any rules about drinking on duty," he says, "but we had an unwritten rule that you couldn't smoke marijuana, because you can't do a restaurant on marijuana." The restaurant's most skilled prep cook was an elfin but temperamental artist named Willy Bishop—"the only real beatnik I've ever known," says Budrick—who started out as a dishwasher but turned out to be a maestro with a chopping knife, and who specialized in unsellable psychosexual canvases: "these wild watercolors of guys jerking off and cum flying all over the place, with Mallarmé poetry written down the side. Or people sitting on toilets, you know, blowing themselves," Jeremiah Tower says.

The staff, Waters included, broke out the good wine and Armagnac every night once the last of the customers had left, and casual, drunken pairings were the norm after hours. Waters also made a point of maintaining warm relations with her exes. So Luddy, who'd moved on from the Telegraph Repertory Cinema to run the Pacific Film Archive, continued to bring in filmmakers like George Lucas, Nicholas Ray, Roberto Rossellini, Satyajit Ray, and Akira Kurosawa*; and Goines, in 1972, designed the first of his annual Chez Panisse posters, an Art Nouveau–evocative image of a red-haired lady sipping from an aperitif glass.

"I do want all three of them," Waters would say of Budrick, Luddy, and Goines in an early-eighties interview with *Savvy* magazine, when she wasn't yet a mother or the James Beard Foundation's Humanitarian of the Year, and therefore didn't present as carefully crafted a public persona as she later would. "I wonder about my selfishness. I just don't want to lose them. I'm not really jealous of their women, but I want them to want me most. You know, before I begin to cook, I have to touch the food. I'll hold the leg of lamb. Touch the tomatoes. It's the same as Jerry, Tom, or David—I want to go around and touch home base with them." (At the time of the interview, she was dating the much younger Todd Koons, then a cook at Chez Panisse,

---

*For a time, the Pacific Film Archive had its own café called the Swallow, a collectively run offshoot of the Cheese Board. Among its employee-members were Ruth Reichl, now the editor of *Gourmet*, and S. Irene Virbila, now the restaurant critic for the *Los Angeles Times*. The Swallow is no more, but visitors to the Archive can visit its replacement, Café Muse, which, in the Berkeley spirit, offers "innovative raw dishes that capture taste *and* nutritional value, as well as sandwiches and cooked specialties using sustainably grown ingredients."

later to achieve foodie fame as the founder of Epic Roots, the mâche-in-a-bag people.)

IN 1972, THOUGH, the fun-loving abandon was taking its toll financially, and the future didn't look good for Chez Panisse. With Wise about to leave and suppliers getting irritable about lack of payment, the restaurant seemed destined to be another failed let's-open-our-own-place fantasy, albeit a quirkier and more hirsute one than most. Chez Panisse received a stay of execution, though, when Gene Opton of the Kitchen, who was a little older than Waters and company and actually ran a profitable business, agreed to come on staff as manager, pumping some of her own money into the enterprise, too. "Alice just said, 'We really need some help,' " says Opton. "There was a little cottage in back of the house, and in the cottage there was a desk, and it had a drawer. I pulled open the drawer, and in it were stuck all these little bits of paper for their expenses. That was their record-keeping." Opton did her best to straighten out the finances, and, when Wise left, took on some of the cooking responsibilities, alternating with Waters as chef even as she continued to run her shop.

This arrangement saved the restaurant from oblivion, but it couldn't last, not least because the sensible, straightforward Opton was an ill fit with the freak parade, and, as Budrick says, "She wasn't Gallic. It was a French restaurant, and she was bringing influences that were more of a stern nature, Germanic stuff." Opton confirms that she cooked "some kind of braised beef, because I do have this Alsatian background, and, to go with it, a steamed pudding that included currants, and a lovely sweet-and-sour gravy to go over it. And Alice was not happy with that—it was a night that Tom Luddy brought Howard Hawks to dinner."

Bishop, the only kitchen staffer who consistently performed his duties with some measure of professionalism, frequently grew exasperated at the chaos and ever-changing personnel, and threatened to quit on a regular basis, casting off his apron theatrically. But he couldn't help but admire Waters's wiles in rallying people to her cause. "Whenever she got pressured, she'd turn into a little girl, make a little high voice, and everyone would just come and help her—involuntarily," he says. "She knew how to work that. She was like one of the Gish sisters—she dressed like that, she looked like that, she was innocent and weak. [*Mimicking pale, consumptive nineteenth-century heroine*] 'Oh, who's gonna help me? Who will peel the garlic?' And *bada-boom*! Here come the troops!" Indeed, the English-born Gerald Asher, when he was new to San Francisco and working in the wine trade as well as writing for *Gourmet*, recalls paying a visit to Chez Panisse and being pressed into service by its hostess-owner "to shave carrots or something" as he waited for his dinner to be cooked.

"What you had at that time was a bunch of people in the kitchen who could do one specific dish well—nobody was well-rounded," says Bishop. "When I did dinner with Alice, she would spend, like, two hours making a béarnaise, futzing around. Alice never had restaurant-cooking chops."

"I will give her credit, she's the best maker of salade composé I've ever seen," says Staggs, the former maître d'. "She really has a mastery of making salads of diverse ingredients. I remember the first time she made this pigeon salad, with little lettuces from somebody's garden up the hill and grilled pigeon, and warm vinaigrette made from the juices of the pigeon. I mean, she's great at that. But when she would have to work the line, when some cook didn't show up, she would be back there hacking a leg of lamb and get two orders out of it when a good cook could get seven or nine."

Chez Panisse had become a special place in Berkeley, and, on account of Luddy, a filmmakers' hangout and a rubbernecker's paradise for film geeks. But it couldn't go on functioning like this. And it certainly wasn't yet an important place culinarily. The wine writer Robert Finigan, who was working for the restaurant critic Jack Shelton in 1972 and soon thereafter took over his newsletter—and who would later have his own romantic dalliance with Waters (apparently during one of her hiatuses from Budrick)—characterizes the restaurant as he remembered it then as a "beef-stew and fruit-tart bistro for students and junior faculty. That's all it was. The presence of Jeremiah is what changed everything. Jeremiah really made the restaurant."

"JEREMIAH" IS, OF COURSE, the estimable Jeremiah Tower. In February 1973, though, Tower was a thirty-year-old gadabout with two Harvard degrees who'd never held a proper job and was down to his last twenty-five bucks. He was, in fact, merely Jerry Tower at the time. Only after he'd been hired, and Budrick had insisted that there could be just one Jerry at Chez Panisse, did he begin using his given name in its full regal splendor.

Stressed out and backed into a corner, Waters and Opton had resorted to placing an ad in the *San Francisco Chronicle* that sought out "an inspired and energetic chef who will plan and cook menus weekly for a single entrée five course dinner à la Elizabeth David and Fernand Point." Tower happened to be staying in San Francisco at the time, sleeping on the couches of his Harvard friends Michael Palmer, the poet, and John Sanger. The West Coast was something of a last resort for Tower, who, since his graduation from college in 1965, had lived an itinerant life, using his good looks, pansexual appeal, and gift for ingratiation to insinuate himself into artistic and wealthy circles like a real-life version of Patricia Highsmith's talented Mr. Tom Ripley.

He had traveled to Ireland and England, thinking, perhaps, that a career in the wine business might be in the offing, but, as he recalled in his 2003 memoir, *California Dish*, "My first visit to a wine company led only to the director's bed and the advice that I was too ambitious to settle for never being able to own this, his boss's family's company." Returning to the States, Tower journeyed to Carmel, California, where his grandmother lived, and borrowed her car to pay an unsolicited visit to the Big Sur home of the artist Emile Norman, who, scandalously for the time, was living openly with his male companion, Brooks Clement, in a mountaintop retreat where clothing was optional. Norman and Clement were only too happy to have the handsome young caller join them for a literal naked lunch, but California, at that time, offered Tower no ready job prospects. So he re-enrolled at Harvard, this time to get a master's degree in architecture, and took up for a period with Annie Meyer, the granddaughter of the late *Washington Post* owner Eugene Meyer and niece of the *Post*'s then matriarch, Katharine Graham.

Unlike Tom Ripley, Tower came from a reasonably well-to-do background and had a talent beyond oleaginous charm: he could cook up a storm. Though American-born, he was reared mostly in Australia and England, spending much of his childhood in pampered solitude in grand hotels and on ocean liners while his disengaged parents—Dad a peripatetic WASP business executive, Mom a kindly but alcoholic gardening enthusiast from a wealthy Irish Catholic family—attended to their professional and social obligations. This upbringing imbued him with both an ambiguous quasi-British accent and a precocious love of Escoffier-style *grande cuisine* as it was still practiced in the 1950s in places like London's Hyde Park Hotel and the kitchens of the *Queen Elizabeth*.

A true culinary-freak prodigy on the level of the young James Beard, the boy Tower feasted eagerly on *tête de veau*, calf's head, with *sauce gribiche*, the classic French mayonnaise made of hard-boiled eggs, vinegar, and parsley, and amused himself by splurging on treats from the food halls of Harrods and Fortnum & Mason. (Fortunately, he had the metabolism and athleticism to offset the constant gorging; Beard was not so lucky.) Unlike Waters, Tower had a culinarily savvy mother, and came to understand the value of fresh, seasonal ingredients by helping out with her garden in the English countryside, which yielded fantastic beans, herbs, and strawberries, not to mention the edible nasturtium flowers with which he would later adorn salads in America, kicking off one of the more ridiculous food trends of the 1980s. Tower learned to cook by observing his mother in the kitchen (she was a dab hand at the stove when she wasn't drinking too much), intuiting his own versions of what he'd eaten in fine restaurants, studying *Larousse gastronomique* and whatever cookbooks he could get his hands on, and following the recipes sent to him by his favorite relative, his mother's eldest sister, a flamboyant Auntie Mame type who lived in Washington, D.C., with her second husband, a rich Russian czarist who had fled during the Revolution and ran with a crowd of decadent, vodkaed-up aristo-exiles.

At Harvard, Tower's cooking chops attracted as much notice as his cheekbones and jawline. Underwritten by his father and the rich kids to whom he was naturally drawn, he spent prodigious sums on Château d'Yquem, the king of all Sauternes, and the finest cuts of beef, whipping up ever-more elaborate meals for his louche, too-cool-for-campus circle, whose members enjoyed not only his interpretations of classical cuisine but such inventions as "Consommé Marijuana" (made with chicken stock, fresh basil, sea salt, pepper, and "one packed cup marijuana stems and seeds"). Though he dabbled in student activism, Tower never came close to sharing the conviction of Waters and her crowd, declaring himself "annoyed by the crude fascism" of Students for a Democratic Society, the largest of the national student organizations. His idea of revolution was to prepare a feast for the prima ballerina Margot Fonteyn—who performed in Boston while he was at grad school and, to his delighted surprise, accepted his invitation to dinner—with a menu that consisted entirely of ingredients and vintage Lafites that his roommates had stolen from Cambridge shops.

But by New Year's Day of 1973, the jig was up. Tower was getting a bit old for the role of pretty boy at large, was unable to convince anyone of his architectural genius (he specialized in designing untenable underwater habitats), and, to his humiliation, was scratching out a subsistence living as a gardener for wealthy Bay Area homeowners. Fortunately, Palmer, his temporary host, saw Chez Panisse's want ad in the *Chronicle* and, mindful of his friend's cooking prowess at Harvard, suggested that Tower pay a call to the restaurant. Which Tower, in an uncharacteristic state of nervousness and supplication, did.

THE CIRCUMSTANCES OF Tower's hiring are a matter of debate. As he tells it, he went to Chez Panisse for a 6 p.m. interview, walked in, found the kitchen in a state of preparatory frenzy, and was received by a harried Waters, who pointed to a giant pot and said, "Do something to that soup"; Tower doctored the soup with salt, white wine, and cream; Waters tasted it, smiled, and shouted, "You're hired!" through the din of the kitchen; and thus began one of the most notorious stints by a chef in American culinary history.

"That is *so much* a fiction. That isn't how it happened at all," says Opton. In her recollection, Tower was one of several candidates who were asked to provide a week's worth of sample menus and cook an "audition" meal for the core staff: she, Waters, Budrick, and Tom Guernsey, who alternated with Budrick as headwaiter and cooked Sunday brunch. All the surviving principals save Tower support Opton's version (Guernsey died of AIDS-related illness in 1990), but agree that Tower was far and away the standout candidate. "We almost hired someone else before him," says Budrick, "but Jeremiah came and plopped down a *month's* worth of menus and cooked this incredible meal for us. We all just looked at one another and said, 'Well, if he really can do what he says he can do, then this is our guy.' "

It was a fortuitous case of mutual desperation—Chez Panisse needed a chef, and Tower needed a steady job, even one that paid all of $400 a month. He also signed on to join the new partnership that the restaurant's main players were forming in order keep Chez Panisse from unraveling financially. "We explained the dangers of being a general partner, that if the restaurant went under he'd be liable like the rest of us," says Budrick, "but he was instantly willing to sign anything. He was penniless and didn't care." Tower, Waters, Budrick, Guernsey, and Lindsey Shere (along with her husband, Charles, the music critic for the *Oakland Tribune*) were the general partners, investing their "sweat equity" in the place, since none of them had any money to speak of. In addition, four limited partners were brought in to kick in actual capital—among them Greil Marcus, who had already made a name for himself as an editor at *Rolling Stone* and as a rock critic for *Creem*—and to buy out Opton, who'd had enough of the craziness. The restaurant's new management company was cutely named Pagnol et Cie, French for Pagnol and Company.

Despite his inexperience, Tower brought an instant professionalism to the kitchen, his comfortably worn East Coast authoritarianism a welcome antidote to the antihierarchical guilt and collectivism of the Berkeley gang. Whereas Victoria Wise played Led Zeppelin and David Bowie on the kitchen's record player, Tower, in his pomp, took to blasting Marlene Dietrich and

Italian opera—Puccini, Bellini, Rossini, Verdi. Culinarily, though, he kept his flamboyance under wraps at first, sticking to Waters and Opton's prescribed bistro menus of quiche, French onion soup, *boeuf bourguignon*, and the like, so he could acclimate himself to the task of cooking for dozens of people rather than six or eight stoned dinner-party guests.

After a few months, however, when he realized that his encyclopedic knowledge of food far exceeded everyone else's there, Waters's included, Tower began dipping into his vast cookbook collection, drawing upon such golden oldies as Escoffier and Curnonsky, as well as the somewhat more recent works of the mid-century master Fernand Point. "The newspaper ad had asked for someone who was passionate about Elizabeth David and Fernand Point," Tower says. "So I was looking at Alice's historical record of two years of menus at Panisse. I just laughed to myself. Fernand Point? I mean, hardly. But since his *Ma gastronomie* was one of my favorite books and always had been, I started trying to do a couple of simple things, like *crème gratin*, or *quenelles Lyonnaise*, things like that." Before long, Berkeleyites were being served entrées like *truite jurascienne*, trout cooked in rosé wine with hollandaise sauce and buttered croutons, and *la brioche de ris de veau au champagne*, sweetbreads in brioche pastry with champagne sauce.

This wasn't quite what Waters had envisioned for her *haimish* little community bistro, but, initially, she and Tower co-existed happily. Both adored not only Elizabeth David but Richard Olney, a native Iowan who had emigrated to France in 1951, and whose cultishly popular *French Menu Cookbook*, published in 1970, was predicated on the very David-like dictum that "one can only eat marvelously by respecting the seasons"—though his recipes were much more challenging and Escoffier-steeped than David's. (Tellingly, whereas Waters had been too intimidated to introduce herself to David in London, Tower had no qualms about dashing off a fan letter to Olney. Even before he'd been hired at Chez Panisse, the cocky Harvard graduate had struck up an ongoing, friendly correspondence with the cookbook author.)

Both Waters and Tower obsessed over procuring the finest, freshest ingredients available, no matter what the cost or inconvenience, in an era when even the white-tablecloth French restaurants across the bay in San Francisco were using frozen steaks and pre-butchered poultry. Using Waters's geriatric Dodge Dart, Tower drove to San Francisco's Chinatown for whole ducks and fresh fish, and crossed back over the Bay Bridge into Oakland to visit a meatpacking warehouse whose Sicilian proprietor let him plunge his arms into the bloody organ buckets and pluck out the best calf livers and sweet-breads for himself. Tower found a wild-boar supplier in Carmel, a spot-prawn supplier in Monterey Bay, and, recalling a childhood trip with his father to the Garrapata Trout Farm near Big Sur, special-ordered fish from the farm, which were delivered, still swimming, in a tank on a flatbed truck.

Chez Panisse didn't have a full-time forager at this time—that wouldn't happen until 1983, when a former Chez Panisse cook named Sibella Kraus was given the position—but Waters complemented Tower's ingredient searches by seeking out and cultivating produce that the grocery stores didn't carry. Sometimes this meant literally foraging for wild fennel and mustard greens along railroad tracks and in vacant lots; Tower would use the fennel to perfume the pork loins and game birds he grilled, throwing the stalks and greens directly onto the mesquite coals that he imported from Mexico (when few people had heard of mesquite) and burned outdoors (in violation of Berkeley city code) in a makeshift grill fashioned from a wheelbarrow.

Though Tower was unquestionably the chef, Waters was the salad evangelist. She'd return from her periodic sorties to France with seeds for then exotic greens like sorrel, mâche, and radicchio, which she convinced friends to plant in their backyards and garden plots. It was possible to have a salad at Chez Panisse whose lettuces had been picked just hours earlier from some neighborhood hippie's little half-acre or quarter-acre lot—and, for that matter, to have a Meyer lemon tart whose lemons came from some univer-sity professor's tree. "You couldn't buy fresh herbs," says Tower, "so you had to grow them. And it didn't take long to exhaust everybody's little flower-pot full of thyme or something. It was like, 'Come to dinner and bring your tarragon!' "

As word got out that Waters and Tower preferred their provisioners to be as local as possible, some locals simply started showing up with their offerings to see if Chez Panisse was interested. "There was a lunatic who believed in what he called 'companion plants,' where he raised carrots with, let's say, ragweed, because if you grow this plant and this plant together, both turn out better, even though one is not an edible plant," says Goines, who was a constant presence at the restaurant and occasionally helped out in the kitchen. "But the carrots were fabulously good! And I remember that people would come with a basket of vegetables—you know, literally, *one basket* of vegetables: 'These are from my backyard, and I have more tomatoes than I can eat.' It's more organized now, because you can't really run a huge operation with people stumbling in saying 'Here's a squirrel I shot this morning.' You don't have, you know, gingham-clad six-year-olds showing up with baskets of eggs. That doesn't happen any longer. But it certainly did."

"People seemed to find their way there, with these little products that were sweet and cute," says Bishop. "Mainly it was little things that Alice liked—baby things. That's how she used to talk. [*Little-girl voice*] 'Little baby radish! Little baby lettuce!' You know, she never had a kid until years later. I think, at the time, her children were these little baby food things." ("It's not a compulsion!" Waters retorts. "I don't want anything that's small for small's sake. I like small because that's where the best taste is. And I like big old radishes for certain uses.")

Though Waters's baby-greens fetish would prove to be hugely influential in the long run, it was Tower's sophisticated cookery that had people talking in the Bay Area in 1973 and 1974. Emboldened by the positive response, he decided to up the ante. "We had Berkeley already," he says, "and I was after the national press." So he started planning entire dinners around specific classical chefs; or around contemporary masters like Elizabeth David and Richard Olney; or around specific French regions such as Brittany, Franche-Comté, and Provence; or around wines not normally drunk with each and every course, like champagne and Sauternes. Sometimes Tower even journeyed beyond France, doing a Moroccan regional dinner one night (with marijuana stems burning in the kitchen braziers for "atmosphere") and a Corsican dinner on another occasion. "It all came pouring out of him," says Budrick. "He never had a real job in his life before, so he had all this energy, years of pent-up desire to do something that was really fulfilling. Willy was his right-hand man, and you could feel the energy between them. It was contagious and infectious, and we all just went along with it."

"Generally, it worked," says Bishop. "And it worked because this guy, Jeremiah, was so manic and insane. If he was gonna make bouillabaisse, he'd go to Chinatown and come back with, like, a six-foot conger eel: 'Look what I got in Chinatown!' I was like, 'What the fuck is it?' " For the beatnik dishwasher turned sous-chef, nearing forty and accustomed to scraping by on society's edges as an artist and sometime drummer in jazz combos, cooking with Tower brought him the greatest rush of artistic fulfillment he'd ever felt in his life. What was most extraordinary about their partnership, Bishop says, is that Tower wrote out these elaborate, themed menus, a different one for each night of the week, and sent them off to Goines to be rendered in calligraphy, printed up, and posted for public viewing a few days before they'd be served . . . *without ever having cooked any of the dishes described.*

Which meant that every night, Tower and Bishop were essentially winging it, relying on Tower's instinctual gift for getting things to taste perfect and Bishop's telegraphic ability to instantly absorb and execute Tower's visions. "We'd be doing ninety or a hundred soufflés," Bishop says, "and we only had one oven behind us and two down below, and you gotta keep that door closed. For some reason, we were always able to pull that shit off. None of us, myself included, had the slightest idea of the chemistry, what food does when it does those things. It was kind of like World War I: give the guy a gun, send him out there—and fuck him!"

Tower is equally complimentary about Bishop's skills. "He couldn't taste anything," the chef says, "because he sucked on English mints and menthol cigarettes, so he had zero palate—but he knew the workings of the kitchen. I mean, my God, if you had ever seen Willy make a duxelle out of twenty pounds of mushrooms, that's my favorite image of him. Today, with young kids out of cooking schools, you can hear them chopping from a mile away. But Willy was a drummer, a musician. He would take two Chinese cleavers, dump the mushrooms out onto the six-foot butcher-block table, and he'd go around the table, wielding the two cleavers. Within ten minutes, you had perfect duxelle. And the cleaver would just barely touch the table."

If there was an air of naughtiness and decadence behind the scenes at Chez Panisse even before Tower's arrival, by the time he was firmly in charge of the kitchen, the atmosphere was positively Caligulan. "It was so outrageous when Jeremiah was there, almost like another plane," says Staggs, who was waiting tables at the time. "There were magnums of Sauternes, and champagne all the time, and he used to keep these nitrous-oxide canisters around for whipping the cream. The waiters would take a hit of nitrous oxide before delivering the entrées to the dining room." Tower tamped down his hangover every morning by raiding Shere's section of the fridge for crème anglaise, the thick, yolky dessert sauce, which he poured into a giant snifter and drank as his breakfast. He dates the start of his cocaine habit to the restaurant's third birthday, on August 28, 1974. With the turnout much greater than he'd anticipated, Tower found that his energy was flagging. As word of his bedraggled state got out, he recalls, a friend of one of the waiters came back into the kitchen with a "black-leather-coated accomplice" who whipped out a big bag of blow and started cutting lines on top of the chest freezer. Reenergized, Tower returned to his ovens, in which were baking individual-sized pizzas—California's first, so he claims.

Thereafter, Tower and Bishop were hooked. For the debauched but hyperambitious chef, cocaine actually enhanced his performance—"It was a party in the kitchen, but he controlled it, and was serious about the food," says Staggs—but Bishop was not so fortunate or self-disciplined. As dealers started showing up at the back door with regularity, he and some of his acquaintances got into increasingly harder stuff. "We were doing opium-stuffing," he says. "You stick it up your ass. Just a quarter of a gram, a little ball, and you bypass the alimentary canal—you don't get nauseous, you just absorb it." Bishop's drug problems intensified to the point where, some years later, after he'd left Chez Panisse, he was a suicidal, freebasing wreck. In an especially cruel twist of fate, given that he was revered in the kitchen for his nonpareil knife work, he wound up doing time for stabbing a man in an Oakland dive bar with his paring knife.* Thanks to the magnanimous intervention of Waters, who secured him the best legal representation possible, Bishop got off lightly, with eight months in jail plus three years of probation.

Waters frowned upon the drug scene, but she imbibed as freely as anyone and was fully involved in the Fleetwood Mac–like carnival of sexual entanglings and disentanglings. "It was absolutely predictable," says Staggs. "It's after work, the customers are gone, the drugs come out, everybody starts drinking, the tango music comes on. Alice would get drunk, her incisors would show, and she would attack some poor innocent person and bed him." Bishop claims he slept with both Waters *and* Tower, "though not at the same time." And, despite his general orientation, Tower had a few romantic episodes with Waters, even while she was ostensibly going with Budrick. As Tower wrote in his memoir, "Drugs were easier to organize than sex, unless it was casual, which usually meant with one another. Who else would put up with us?"

BY 1975, TOWER'S THEME dinners and ever-more outlandish flights of culinary fancy—like his Gertrude Stein–Alice B. Toklas dinner, composed of recipes from *The Alice B. Toklas Cookbook*, and his week of Salvador Dalí–inspired fare, such as *l'entre-plat drogue et sodomise*, a leg of lamb "drugged and sodomized" by a mixture of Madeira, brandy, and tangerine juice injected through a syringe—started attracting the press attention he craved. Herb Caen, the *San Francisco Chronicle* columnist and beloved local institution, wrote up the Stein-Toklas dinner, and James Beard, during one of his regular trips west to

---

*"Aww, God, I was insane," says the remorseful Bishop. "I had a knife. I was gonna go to a triple-X movie theater and stab myself. Not to kill myself, but to get attention. And then someone said the wrong thing in a bar—we were the only two white guys in a black bar—and said it again and again. And 'Artistry in Rhythm' by Stan Kenton was playing. And I was wasted."

teach cooking classes, paid a visit to Chez Panisse and mentioned it in his syndicated column as a "fascinating" new place to watch. "I don't know where it came from, but I have a very good instinct for PR," Tower says. "Basically, getting somebody to write about you is the same as getting them to sleep with you. And I'd had a lot of practice in that. I adored Richard Olney, but he wasn't any use. Jim Beard, I realized, was gonna be very useful to us, because he had a hundred newspapers or something syndicating him."

Tagging along with Beard's friend Cecilia Chiang, proprietor of the Mandarin restaurant in Ghirardelli Square in San Francisco, Tower met the master in his suite at the Stanford Court Hotel. "Cecilia took me up to the hotel," Tower says, "and it didn't hurt that he was receptive to my paying attention to him." Everything went as planned: Beard took a shine to Tower, and soon was inviting him up to the Stanford Court whenever he was in San Francisco, addressing the young chef as "darling" and "my dear" in the swishy manner he reserved for boys he fancied.

In October of 1975, *Gourmet* ran a rave review of Chez Panisse by Caroline Bates, the magazine's West Coast correspondent, hailing Tower for "joyously exploring *la vraie cuisine française* in all its vigor, freshness, and variety and ignoring those French dishes that turn up elsewhere with such monotonous regularity." The *Gourmet* review was crucial, its appearance the juncture at which Chez Panisse gained a national reputation, and at which people with unfamiliar area codes started calling for reservations. It was also a crossroads for Bishop, who, a few months after the review appeared, threw down his apron for good, unable to abide the onslaught of what he called "food weenies," some of whom dined with that issue of *Gourmet* open in their laps, hoping to find the dishes they'd read about re-created—a futile hope at Chez Panisse, where, at least in those days, no menu was ever served twice.

The question arises: Precisely what was Alice Waters, the person most readily identified with Chez Panisse, doing as all this dazzling culinary wizardry was transpiring? "Overbooking, mainly," says Bishop. "And then hiding in the kitchen when she overbooked, because we only had enough food for a certain number of people." In fairness, it should be noted that the front of the house, Waters's domain, also came in for copious praise in the *Gourmet* review, with Bates devoting her entire first paragraph to the atmosphere that Waters had so carefully cultivated: "It is warm with the honesty of natural wood . . . Just inside the main dining room a still-life table arrangement of flowers, unblemished fresh fruit, and glistening fruit tarts suggest that this is a restaurant more interested in art than in artifice." But the kitchen was very much Tower's show in those days, and as the restaurant grew more successful and Tower and Waters more famous, their relationship, always volatile, suffered more blowups.

There was a notorious episode in which Waters seated a party of four after 10 p.m. that included her then boyfriend Robert Finigan, the restaurant critic and wine writer, even though the group had no reservation. Tower was furious—the night's entrée, *gigot d'agneau*, leg of lamb, was almost sold out, and he didn't have enough for everyone. He offered to cook someone a steak instead, but was told by a waiter that Waters, who had sat down with the group, demanded that everyone be served the lamb. "So the other three people at the table had perfect lamb," says Finigan, "and my plate was so gristly that I couldn't eat it. And I—politely, I think—asked the waiter to take it back to the kitchen and say to the chef that he couldn't have intended that to be the case." The waiter complied, but Tower, growing angrier by the minute, replied, "Tough shit!" The waiter, inexperienced and terrified of further incurring Tower's wrath, returned to the table and announced, "The chef says to tell you, 'Tough shit.'" Moments later, Waters stormed into the kitchen, sobbing and screaming, "Jeremiah, how could you?"*

Asked for her own assessment of the Tower era, Waters says, "That was a period of time when I was very much on the foraging side and Jeremiah was very much on the cooking side, so we fit that together. I had always in-

---

*Finigan wrote about the incident with good humor in his newsletter, saying, "I might well have decorated the waiter with the *gigot rôti* and then set out for the kitchen, but instead I cooled my outrage with sips of the remarkable 1972 Mt. Eden Pinot Noir."

tended Chez Panisse to be a simple little place. Never wanted anything more, and I still don't want anything more. When Jeremiah came, he had a whole other vision of the food. It was just the kind of food that I . . . [*contemplative pause*] wasn't cooking. And I was fascinated by it at the time."

If there's a whiff of diplomatic evasiveness about these comments, it's because Tower's contribution to Chez Panisse remains a touchy subject, and the relationship between Tower and Waters remains rather tortured and complex. Tower, though he physically still looks like someone who should be "standing at the prow of a yacht," as the Chez Panisse busboy-turned-baker Steve Sullivan puts it, has withdrawn from the restaurant game and acquired the gossipy mien of the late-period Truman Capote; he's funny and unafraid to say whatever is on his mind, yet his wit and entertaining braggadocio can't mask an abiding bitterness—in his case, over Waters's "editing," as he puts it, of his role at the restaurant. Waters, on the other hand, has matured into a great doer of good, America's foremost champion of organic farming, sustainable agriculture, and healthily fed schoolchildren, beatified in a PBS *American Masters* special as the architect of a "delicious revolution." As such, she comports herself with the dignity and guard-up caution of a UN goodwill ambassador. Yet even she can't suppress a smirk and a roll of the eyes when a portion of Bates's *Gourmet* review is read aloud to her, a paragraph that praises a course of "quenelles of fresh fish, beef suet, and marrow with a lobster sauce."

"That was a baroque period," she says, smiling. "But that was *his* . . . his taste, his desire."

The paradox of the Tower period is that it put Chez Panisse on the map, but in many respects wasn't representative of what the restaurant, or Waters, stood for, before or after. Some Waters loyalists, like Tom Luddy and Greil Marcus, go so far as to label the Tower era a ghastly aberration. "If you read Jeremiah's menus from that time, they're incredibly pretentious," says Luddy. "They were going toward that Paris haute-cuisine thing that Chez Panisse later turned against. I'd go to Alice and say, 'I can't eat this—it's too rich. And then there's all this cheese coming.' " Marcus remembers going to

Chez Panisse for a New Year's Eve dinner in 1975 with his wife, Jenny, a fellow Pagnol et Cie board member, as they'd done every New Year's Eve since the restaurant opened. They arrived, Marcus says, to find the place bereft of their old Berkeley crowd and "packed with Jeremiah's cocaine-dealer friends. We took one look at the crowd, and the menu, which was full of all these haute, heavy courses we didn't want to eat, and left."

The price for that night's dinner, whose main course was "prime sirloin of beef with truffles, roasted and served with a truffled Madeira sauce," was an astounding $25 a person, not including wine—a long way from the convivial Francophile bistro that had arisen out of the Free Speech Movement. Yet those who actually were on the staff at the time say that Tower's transformative effect on the restaurant is indisputable. "Anybody who says that Jeremiah made it too fancy is whistling in the wind to me," says Jerry Budrick, the headwaiter. "All I know is we sold out every dinner. The more elegant Jeremiah made those dinners, the more the public responded. And it wasn't just the snobby elite."

"There are two camps," says Tower. "There's someone like Darrell Corti [the Sacramento wine expert and gourmet-foods-shop owner], who sent a Sicilian Mafia funeral wreath when I did the week of Escoffier menus, saying 'This is the end, Chez Panisse can never be greater than this.' And the other camp is, I destroyed the little Pagnol-movie neighborhood thing. And the truth is, you know, both."

BY 1976, BURNED OUT by the long hours and the tensions at Chez Panisse, Tower was trying to conjure an exit strategy. Beard suggested that Tower take over the kitchen of Maxwell's Plum, Warner LeRoy's upscale pub in New York. Tower rejected that idea, having grown too fond of the ingredients and open spaces that northern California afforded, but was intrigued by Beard's advice to "just stick with America." Beard had been proselytizing on behalf of American food for years, and had published his would-be masterwork, *American Cookery*, in 1972, but it wasn't until Tower was feeling stirrings of discontent that Beard's message reached him, that it occurred to him that a serious chef could, as he puts it, "use American ingredients for themselves rather than as substitutes for unobtainable French ones."

The epiphany occurred when Tower, as was his wont, was paging through an ancient cookbook for inspiration—in this case, *The Epicurean*, by Charles Ranhofer, the chef at Delmonico's, the great restaurant of New York's Gilded Age. One of Ranhofer's recipes was for *crème de maïs à la Mendocino*, a cream of corn soup. The town and county of Mendocino were just up the coast from Berkeley, due north of Sonoma. Tower remembers thinking, "What in the world was the chef of New York's most famous restaurant doing thinking about dishes local to small regions of California?" More to the point, he wondered, "Why fret any longer about the authenticity of 'French' ingredients for French regional food? Why not just go shopping in northern California and call that the region?"

On October 7, 1976, having exhausted nearly all the regions in France and nearly all the French cookbook authors whose recipes interested him, Tower unveiled his Northern California regional dinner at Chez Panisse, its menu entirely in English. The second course was "cream of fresh corn soup, Mendocino style, with crayfish butter." In another nod to Ranhofer's era, when restaurants often listed the provenance of the ingredients on the menu, Chez Panisse that night served, among other courses, "Spenger's Tomales Bay bluepoint oysters on ice," "Big Sur Garrapata Creek smoked trout steamed over California bay leaves," "Monterey Bay prawns sautéed with garlic, parsley, and butter," and "Preserved California geese from Sebastopol." The descriptions didn't yet have the intimacy of later years—apart from the mention of Spenger's, a Berkeley fish market, there was no nod by name to a supplier, à la "Bob's turnips" and "DeeAnn's garden greens"—but there would be no turning back. The notion of a "California cuisine" was afoot.

Within a couple of years, California cuisine would be seen as a bona fide culinary movement, though its base of operations would not be Berkeley but Los Angeles, the home of the young chefs Wolfgang Puck and Jonathan Waxman, the latter a Chez Panisse alum. In the meantime, Berkeley had its own mini-movement in the form of the "Gourmet Ghetto," as the area around Shattuck and Vine was coming to be known. The Cheese Board had moved directly across the street from Chez Panisse in 1975, in a space next door to the Pig-by-the-Tail Charcuterie, which had been opened two years earlier by Chez Panisse's first chef, Victoria Kroyer Wise. The opening in 1977 of yet another culinary shrine on the block, Alice Medrich's Cocolat, the dessert shop that kicked off the chocolate-truffle craze in America, "is what kind of cinched the whole Gourmet Ghetto thing," says Wise. Just as sleepy little Freeport, Maine, by virtue of being the home of L.L. Bean's outlet store, became Outlet Town, U.S.A., so was Berkeley, California, by virtue of Chez Panisse and its neighbors, becoming Gourmet Town, U.S.A.

AS 1977 APPROACHED, Tower was presented with an enticing short-term opportunity: Richard Olney had been asked by Time-Life to compile and edit another of its multivolume cookbook series, this one to be called *The Good Cook*, and he wanted Tower to join him in France and work on the project. Tower and Olney had finally met in person in 1973, when the latter came to San Francisco for a book signing at Williams-Sonoma, and they had subsequently become fast friends. On one of his vacations from Chez Panisse, Tower journeyed to Olney's home in Provence to learn the master's secrets, and, inevitably, go to bed with him.* He decided to take Olney up on the offer, telling Waters he would be gone by the end of the year. Tower toggled between the French and American idioms for the last three months of his tenure, signing off after one last New Year's Eve dinner, at which he served, in a final flourish of Toweresque decadence, a truffle soup.

Chez Panisse's kitchen was taken over by a committee led by Tower's sous-chef, Jean-Pierre Moullé, an actual Frenchman and the first employee of the restaurant to have authentic culinary training. Moullé's deputies were

---

*From Tower's memoir: "[Richard] was not beautiful, but the sight of him walking fully tanned around the vegetable garden in turquoise cotton briefs, a bottle of Krug chilling in an ice bucket under the grape arbor behind him, could be thrilling."

Mark Miller and Michel Troisgros, the nephew of the great French chef Jean Troisgros, who was so taken with Chez Panisse that he wanted one of his kin to experience its inner workings firsthand.

But as of 1977, the restaurant was indisputably Waters's. With Tower around, she had achieved recognition as a restaurateur, but had never been the go-to person when it came to food itself. Now she was planning the menus and calling herself the "chef," even though she was more of a kitchen overseer and Moullé the actual guy cooking. And, with Budrick's help, she was starting up a Chez Panisse garden on an expanse of property that Budrick owned in Amador County, northeast of Berkeley, with the hope that the restaurant would be able to grow its own unusual produce, planted and harvested to Waters's specifications.* With Tower's outsize presence no longer a factor, she was now the focus of articles about Chez Panisse, and would gradually emerge as the Waters that America would come to know: the farm-to-table lady in the beret, importuning us to think globally and eat locally.

Waters and Tower remained cordial enough for him to make a brief return engagement at the end of 1978, when she was going to be away and wanted someone she could trust to oversee Moullé and his staff. But in the aftermath of that stint, she would tell *New West* magazine that Chez Panisse, under her stewardship, was benefiting from a shift away from the "old conservative menus" (for "conservative," read "fancy") of the previous regime. Tower was wounded, telling a reporter that "In the beginning, Alice didn't know a little vegetable from a rotten one," and the skirmishes in the press would continue for at least a decade—most notably in 1982, when the first Chez Panisse cookbook, *Chez Panisse Menu Cookbook*, was published, and Tower felt his contributions weren't sufficiently acknowledged. Later, from

---

*Waters and the Coppolas, Francis and Eleanor, briefly entertained the idea of opening a restaurant-inn-farm on the old Inglenook Estate, a portion of which the Coppolas purchased as a weekend getaway in 1975, with the idea that all the restaurant's produce would come directly from the farm. This never amounted to anything more than a "pipe dream," Waters says, but the Coppolas continued to buy up portions of the Inglenook Estate, which is now the site of their Niebaum-Coppola Estate Winery.

his perch at Stars, the large, vibrant San Francisco restaurant he owned and ran in the 1980s and early 1990s, Tower would deploy the phrase "too Berkeley" as his favorite pejorative.

But even Tower can still admire Waters for sticking to her vision. "She deserves credit for being in love with food, being in love with the neighborhood bistro that should be part of everyone's life," he says. "Where you can just drop in, and you say 'Hi' to the bartender, and you have a glass of wine that's interesting and good and inexpensive. And just have a pizza or sit down and have a meal. That's a Pagnol vision, a European vision—that the bistro was the heart of the village. Her vision was incredibly strong and has never wavered, really, so she deserves credit for sticking by it. To have never given up that vision, and not to have done it another way, like Wolfgang Puck, with a $378 million a year gross income—it's almost unique in this part of our culinary history."

There's also much to be said for the environment Waters fostered, the excitement she generated that so many young countercuisinists wanted their share of. Steve Sullivan, the busboy and gofer who later established the rip-roaringly successful Acme Bread Company, recalls that his lonely graveyard shift at the restaurant was frequently interrupted by 4 a.m. telephone calls from "college students who wanted to work with Alice."

"I'd pick up the phone thinking it *was* Alice, telling me to get something else at the market," he says, "and it was some kid saying 'I've been reading about Chez Panisse and I really want to come to Berkeley and be an apprentice.'"

Among those pulled in by the Chez Panisse mystique, besides Sullivan, were Deborah Madison (or "Debbie," as she was then known), the lunch-time cook who opened the vegetarian restaurant Greens; Judy Rodgers, Madison's fellow lunch-shifter, later of Zuni Café; Mark Miller, the sous-chef later to be the Southwestern evangelist behind the Coyote Cafe; and Jonathan Waxman and Mark Peel, both of whom briefly passed through Chez Panisse's kitchen en route to stardom in LA. Waters, essentially, had a kitchen-staff equivalent of her friend Francis Coppola's cast for his 1983 film

The Outsiders, an assemblage of then unknowns and little knowns that included Tom Cruise, Matt Dillon, Emilio Estevez, Rob Lowe, and Patrick Swayze. And as many a Panisser has noted, her motley collection of ex-, current, and quasi-boyfriends was itself an amazing marshaling of disparate talents that she put to good use—Goines for his Art Deco–Art Nouveau graphics sensibility, Luddy for his pull in the film world, Budrick for his provisioning and Mr. Fix-it skills, Robert Finigan for his influence in the food press, the wine merchant Kermit Lynch for his oenological expertise.

"Alice was innocent and frail and weak, but at the same time, she was a bad motherfucker," says Bishop. "Her determination and her strength, hidden behind that frailty, made that place continue and continue and continue, no matter who left. And *everybody* left. But she didn't. She is the woman."

CHAPTER SIX

RIGHTEOUS AND CRUNCHY

Ten thousand flowers in spring, the moon in autumn, a cool breeze in summer, snow in winter. If your mind isn't clouded by unnecessary things, this is the best season of your life.

—medieval Chinese philosopher Wu Men . . .
as quoted on a box of Celestial Seasonings tea

IF CHEZ PANISSE AND ITS GOURMET GHETTO NEIGHBORS WERE A PERSUASIVE ARGU-ment for the joys of living in Berkeley, not everyone was buying it. Concurrent with the restaurant's rise in the early seventies was a migration north from the Bay Area by shaken and disillusioned activists. Marin, Sonoma, Mendocino, Humboldt—the counties up the California coast were verdant refuges from the bad vibes of the late sixties, the places to go if you'd been on the barricades, seen too much, and decided to chuck it all and go back to the land. "We were working to create alternative institutions and really were not feeling very good about the government," says Bill Niman of his circle of friends, which settled in Marin County. "We were quick to think that there was a conspiracy behind every event, and, certainly, the situations with Jack and Robert Kennedy were paramount in our minds."

But the rural stretches above Berkeley and San Francisco proved so fertile, both agriculturally and ideologically, that even these escape-minded back-to-the-landers ended up being part of the Bay Area's gourmet revolution. Not that this was necessarily by design. Niman's rise to foodie fame as a supplier of high-quality, humanely raised pork and beef was slow and gradual, his food career something he more or less stumbled into. Much the same could be said of Laura Chenel, a Sonoma County nature girl who became

PAGE 167: *Celestial Seasonings founder Mo Siegel enjoys a Rocky Mountain high, top; Moosewood nymph Mollie Katzen lolls in the grass, bottom.*

the nation's first commercial producer of goat cheese, and of Mary Keehn, a single mother of hippieish mien, who, way up in the Humboldt County town of McKinleyville, invented a delightfully original goat cheese which she named Humboldt Fog—chalky in the center and gooey around the edges—that eventually became a centerpiece of the "cheese course" frenzy that gripped American fine dining in the 1990s. Though it wasn't until the end of the twentieth century that the names of Niman, Chenel, and Keehn were familiar even to the East Coast food establishment, all three had been around for a while, products of the same sixties counterculture that gave birth to Chez Panisse.

Niman was a Minneapolis grocer's son who'd moved to California in 1968, the year he turned twenty-four, in a rush of altruism. The Elementary and Secondary Education Act of 1965, a cornerstone of President Lyndon Johnson's War on Poverty, specifically earmarked public money for poor school districts, and Niman, eager to do his part, got a job teaching middle-school kids in the rural San Joaquin valley, in the interior of central California. Thrilled with the experience but raw as a teacher, he moved on to Berkeley to get more formal educational training. But Berkeley "was already pretty dicey" by the time he joined its school system, he says, fraught with racial tension and "bad energy." Niman's sister lived in Marin County, just over the Golden Gate Bridge from San Francisco, and she told her brother about Bolinas, a progressive community that was looking for "a New Age kind of teacher."

Bolinas at that point was one of the most extraordinary places in the United States, its citizens bohemian but civic-minded, druggy but not to the point where they would let their town become a fetid, Haight-style free-for-all. The landscape was too gorgeous to sully: at once rural and coastal, with thick forests of cypress and eucalyptus and large tracts of open pastureland that rolled right out to the foggy Pacific. No town not anchored by a university had a greater concentration of poets. Among Bolinas's residents in the late sixties and early seventies were Ted Berrigan, Richard Brautigan, Jim Carroll, Robert Creeley, Lewis MacAdams, Alice Notley, and Aram Saroyan.

Niman wasn't as boho as this crowd—with his mustache and broad shoulders, he looked more like an electrician than a poet—but he knew he'd found the place where he wanted to spend the rest of his life.

Ranching wasn't originally part of his plan—he was a schoolteacher, after all. But Niman and his future wife, Amy, another teacher, scraped together enough money to buy an eleven-acre homestead, building their own little house and barn on the property. Though Niman's entrepreneurial future lay in beef and pork, he originally had no cattle and just a few pigs. Like other homesteaders in Marin and points north, Niman kept animals for the simple purpose of self-sufficiency. "It was about producing your own food," he says. "We had a lot of smart people in Bolinas, Ph.D.s and talented people, twenty- to thirty-year-olds who were very hip and active. And part of being in this community was making it self-reliant: raising our own food. Everybody was diddling in it and dabbing in it and had his own methods. That knowledge was being shared all around town. We would sell wiener pigs, little pigs, to somebody else for meat, and other people were doing vegetables, which they would sell to us."

It was no wonder that the members of this community were hungry. Among its early cooperative horticultural goals was the cultivation of the perfect marijuana. "There was breeding going on, and exchanging of seeds," says Niman. "Plantations of marijuana all over the area, in Bolinas, Sonoma, and Mendocino County. If you went to a party in Bolinas, there'd be a mound of big joints, made from the best pot. Everybody was openly smoking, everywhere."

Just about every homesteader, Niman included, kept a few goats around. Goats were the ultimate hippie livestock, both because they evoked the humble peasant cultures that the counterculture romanticized and because they were easy to care for.* They were small, they were cute, they were

---

*One of the Bolinas poets, Duncan McNaughton, chose to use a photograph of a billy goat as the cover for his 1979 collection of poems inspired by his life in the town. The book's title: *Shit on My Shoes*.

intelligent, they happily foraged on poor-quality land, and they required no special trailers or equipment to transport—a VW bus or Volvo station wagon would do the job fine. Female goats also happened to be prolific milk producers, and this milk could be used in a number of ways—as a beverage, to make cheese, and to nurse the other animals. In a happy convergence of zoology, animal husbandry, and hippie rhetoric, the goat was known as nature's "universal mother," its naturally homogenized milk palatable to humans, calves, piglets, and lambs, all of whom could digest it with no ill effects.

Up in Sonoma County, Laura Chenel was especially taken with goats. Having logged time in the early seventies at the University of California's two freakiest campuses, Berkeley and Santa Cruz, she was propelled by the back-to-the-land movement into the town of Sebastopol. Growing vegetables appealed to her well enough, but raising goats moved her in a way that she never expected. She felt an instant kinship with the animals—a feeling, she says, "that I belong to the goats, that I am in their tribe." When her goats started producing more milk than she knew what to do with, Chenel decided to try making cheese, holding down a waitressing job to underwrite her study. Making chèvre was a way of honoring her herd, something she needed to do, she says, "for the goats' sake, and for the sake of all the people who love goats." Still farther up, in Humboldt County, Mary Keehn's life traveled a similar path, starting when she caught a wild doe, as the female of the species is known, and named her Hazel. A few mating seasons later, Keehn, too, had a surplus of milk and was experimenting with goat-milk cultures in her kitchen.

In the seventies, there was still no commercial goat cheese produced in the United States; it was all imported from Europe and sold mostly in specialty shops to discerning customers. Outside of countercultural and Francophile gourmet circles, goats were unpopular, warily regarded as barnyardy, pungent, possibly unhygienic beasts. (It didn't help that the French word used to describe the little disks in which chèvre is often sold, *crottin*, literally translates as "animal turd.") So when Chenel decided to turn her cheese-making hobby into a business, she faced an uphill battle. She spent three months in France on a fact-finding mission, learning the ropes of goat-cheese production from local farmers whose families had been making chèvre for centuries. Upon her return, she found that the markets of the food-forward Bay Area were reasonably receptive to giving her *crottins* a chance, but usually on the condition that she "demo" her wares in-store.

This proved harrowing. "The word 'goat,' I'd say that was the first hurdle," she says. "I'd be standing in some supermarket with tasting samples, having people say 'What's that?' I'd say 'Goat cheese,' and they'd go '*Noooo!*' and back away in the opposite direction. There was a lot of rejection."

Fortunately, Alice Waters was more accepting. In 1980, her first full year of commercial production, Chenel showed up at Chez Panisse with *crottins* in tow. Waters was so impressed that she placed a standing order for Chenel's chèvre, the big break that freed Chenel from her waitressing job. Waters's salad of baby lettuces topped with vinaigrette and a baked disk of "Laura Chenel's Chèvre," as it was acknowledged on the menu, not only became a standby of Chez Panisse's menu but was widely imitated—so much so that Chenel's modest little garage operation would eventually grow into one that sells upward of a million pounds of cheese a year.

Mary Keehn's operation in McKinleyville, Cypress Grove Chèvre, took longer to catch on, but once it did, Keehn remained true to her counterculture roots, expanding her line to include a lavender-spiked goat cheese called Purple Haze and another product, a "cheese torta" interspersed with layers of pesto, tomatoes, and pine nuts, called Fromage à Trois. The latter's label features a *Joy of Sex*–style illustration (circa the original 1972 edition) of a bearded, naked fellow entangled with two equally clothesless ladies. Its slogan: "Fromage à Trois: You've always wanted to try it!"

IN BOLINAS, BILL NIMAN stuck to education and local politics for a long time before he got into the meat business. One of his best friends was Orville Schell, a China scholar who'd done graduate work at Berkeley before moving to Marin County. Frustrated, like Niman, with the slow rate of return on Lyndon Johnson's Great Society efforts to overhaul America's ills, Schell joined Niman in trying to effect social change at the local level. In 1971, the two young men helped instigate a recall election in Bolinas that put them in charge of the public utility board—a position of tremendous power in the unincorporated town, since anyone needing water permits for new buildings required the utility board's approval. Eager to preserve the rural character of the town, Niman, Schell, and their allies placed an immediate moratorium on giving out such permits, effectively putting a halt to further development of Bolinas.*

In due time, Schell also became involved in Niman's ranching operation, moving onto the homestead and using some of the proceeds from his successful writing career to underwrite their pig business. That it actually *was* a business was something of an unplanned development. By the mid-seventies, Niman was working primarily as a building contractor and Schell as a writer, his dispatches on China appearing regularly in *The New Yorker.* Initially, they sold their pork on an informal, ad hoc basis. But word got out in the region that their pigs were of superior quality, and soon enough, they had a list of regular customers who would buy whole sides of pork from them. In 1977, momentarily flush, Niman and Schell purchased the land where Niman Ranch now sits, a larger tract than the one that Niman had initially settled on with his wife, who was killed the previous year in a horseback-riding accident. They also had cattle on the property. A few years before her death, Amy Niman had tutored for an old ranching family in the

---

*Bolinas retains its natural loveliness and strict curbs on development, but its once-admirable iconoclasm has, in some cases, ossified into misanthropy and hippie-hangover derangement. Its residents have been known to tear down road signs that alert motorists to the town's existence, and, in 2003, they voted in favor of a stream-of-consciousness initiative known as Measure B, which officially adopted a policy that Bolinas be declared "a socially acknowledged nature-loving town because to like to drink the water out of the lakes to like to eat the blueberries to like the bears is not hatred to hotels and motor boats. Dakar. Temporary and way to save life, skunks and foxes (airplanes to go over the ocean) and to make it beautiful." Niman, a businessman and engaged citizen of the world, diplomatically rolls his eyes and keeps mum when this aspect of his adopted hometown is raised.

area, who offered the Nimans some excess Hereford calves they didn't need. Bill shepherded them back to his property in the front seat of his old 1956 Mercedes 220 S, each calf in a gunnysack, and thus was his career as a beef man launched.

Just as the Niman–Schell Ranch, as it was then called, was getting serious about its business, selling sides of beef to health-food stores, its next-door neighbor, Star Route Farms, overseen by Warren Weber, a Berkeley Ph.D. in English literature, was gaining recognition as California's first certified organic farm. Before long, Bolinas was known as much for its funky, alternative agriculture as it was for its literary community and ferocious zoning restrictions—a circumstance that the poets Ted Berrigan and Tom Clark found all too precious. Together, they wrote a book-length satire of the scene called *Bolinas Eyewash* that includes a moment in which a caricaturishly flaky Bolinas resident reacts to a fine levied on the town by the state, saying, "I don't have any money, but I'll be glad to give the Attorney General some of this here broccoli."

Niman and Schell kept forging ahead, though, applying the conviction they'd brought to Bolinas politics to food politics. Intuitively, and in keeping with the "organic" ethos of their community, they had always raised their cattle on a natural diet, letting the animals roam free and "finishing" them on a mix of grains. But as they became more serious about putting aside their other careers to focus on ranching, Niman and Schell researched the subject and discovered how profoundly out of whack commercial meat production had become in America, and how unwittingly radical their enterprise was. In the early eighties, Schell took a break from Chinese history to write *Modern Meat: Antibiotics, Hormones, and the Pharmaceutical Farm*, the most incriminating exposé of the beef industry since Upton Sinclair's 1906 novel *The Jungle*.

While today "grass-fed beef" is a luxury product that sells at a premium, pretty much all beef was grass-fed beef until the middle of the twentieth century. There were no feedlots where cattle ate in confinement, just pastures where they grazed. The taller and lusher the grass, the chubbier the animals became. As such, freshly killed and dressed beef was as seasonal as tomatoes and summer corn, because farmers chose to slaughter their cattle at their peak of fattiness. "Think about bears getting ready to hibernate, eating salmon, gorging themselves, getting fat, gaining hundreds of pounds," says Niman. With cattle, this fatty peak, before their bodies start consuming their own energy reserves, is dependent on the local climate and the life cycle of the grasses that they feed on. On a farm in old New England, the slaughtering time would have been in autumn, after the grass's summery zenith but before the first frost set in. On a farm in old Bolinas, where the grass grew highest with the rains of March and April, the slaughtering time fell around late May or early June.

The advent of the railroad changed things somewhat, as cattle could be moved reasonably long distances to urban processing centers, making for a more mobile, less seasonal beef supply. Improvements in refrigeration technology helped the industry, too, lengthening the shelf life of butchered beef. But none of these advances extended the period during which a live steer's muscle tissue was at its most lusciously marbled with fat. Not until after World War II did America truly enter the era of year-round, freshly slaughtered beef—a phenomenon largely attributable to postwar grain surpluses.

The surpluses were the result of a confluence of factors. Through the early part of the twentieth century, the most common sources of nitrogen, an essential element for plant growth, were natural: manure, compost, and so on. However, the war effort resulted in a huge investment in munitions plants that manufactured such substances as ammonium nitrate, a solid nitrogen product used to make explosives. After the war—and after it was observed that grass grew faster in the areas around munitions dumps—these munitions plants were rededicated to the purpose of making fertilizer for farming. In a similar act of repurposing, many factories that had been devoted to the manufacture of military vehicles during the war were given over to the manufacture of self-propelled grain combines (machines that harvest grain), tractors, and other heavy equipment that made grain farming more efficient.

The upshot of all this was that postwar America was verily flooded in grain. Cattle farmers took notice, as did cereal-crop farmers who suddenly decided to go into the cattle business. In the fifties, sixties, and seventies, these entrepreneurial farmers dedicated themselves to building enclosed feedlots where their animals, rather than relying on the vagaries of the grass-growing season, feasted on cheap corn and soybean through *all* the seasons. The result: a year-round supply of fattened-up, ready-for-slaughter animals.

The problem with this model is that cattle, as ruminants, are supposed to subsist for the first year of their lives on mother's milk and grass. Not until they are sixteen to eighteen months old have their gastrointestinal tracts "hardened," to use the industry term, to the point where they can digest grain with no ill effects. The commercial beef industry, however, had an economic imperative to get its animals to slaughter and its meat to market as soon as possible. As such, it became common practice for animals to be started on grain long before they were ready. This practice succeeded in fattening up the cattle and getting them to market weight in a mere twelve to sixteen months (rather than the two to three years it took for a grass-fed steer), but it also put serious stresses on the animals. Feeding on grain before they were fully capable of digesting it, the cattle often developed stomach abscesses, diarrhea, and bacterial infections. On top of this, the immune systems of the calves were weakened by the stress of being separated from their mothers and carted off to feedlots without proper weaning.

To stave off gastrointestinal-tract ailments, Schell explained in *Modern Meat*, commercial ranchers took to preemptively feeding their animals antibiotics. As the technology developed, cattle were also given "growth promotants"—hormones—to help them along to slaughtering size at the twelve-to-sixteen-month mark. And so the industry-standard beef steer was, and remains, a prematurely pumped-up, inhumanely raised adolescent animal that has an aggravated digestive system and drugs in its blood. And the more antibiotics these livestock were given, the faster their bodies developed populations of microbes resistant to the antibiotics—microbes that had the potential to get passed on to the human beings who processed and ate the meat from these animals. To top off the Orwellian wrongness of it all, the cultivation of the grain on which these animals fed was underwritten by U.S. government subsidies and abetted by environmentally detrimental chemical fertilizers and pesticides.

Equipped with this knowledge, Niman and Schell decided to revisit the ranching methodologies of the pre-grain era, throwing in some new touches of counterculture enlightenment. They set up a system in which calves were kept with their mothers for as long as they needed to nurse, and then gently weaned, placed in proximity to the mother cows but separated by a fence to keep them from charging for the teats. Only after sixteen to eighteen months, by which time the cattle's gastrointestinal tracts were sufficiently hardened, were the animals "finished" on feed, and even then, the feed was all-natural and mixed by the farmers themselves, a sort of Niman's Own munchie mix. The animals were market-ready at two years or so, double the industry standard, which meant higher production costs but no dependence on antibiotics, growth hormones, or subsidized grain.

Like "Laura Chenel's Chèvre," the phrase "Niman-Schell Beef" caught on in the 1980s as a mark of distinction on northern California menus, first at Cafe Beaujolais, a restaurant in Mendocino, and then at San Francisco's Stars and Zuni Café, and, inevitably, at Berkeley's Chez Panisse. Niman-Schell beef not only had the all-natural and local angles going for it but also a distinctive flavor profile—many old-timers said it tasted more like the beef they remembered eating as children—and the do-gooder cachet of having been prepared in humane, eco-friendly, small-farmer-supportive fashion. As chefs from other parts of the country visited the Bay Area and asked if they could get Niman-Schell products, the two men built up a network of ranchers around the country who raised cattle to their standards, thereby ensuring a year-round supply of their brand of beef.* It was a triumphal bridging of the "natural" and gourmet cultures.

---

*Schell officially left the partnership in 1999, after he'd returned to academia, becoming the dean of the graduate program in journalism at UC-Berkeley.

FOR THOSE BAY AREA gourmets for whom even humanely raised meat was inhumane, there was Greens, the vegetarian restaurant run under the auspices of the San Francisco Zen Center, with produce trucked in from the Zen Center's own spread in Marin County, Green Gulch Farm. Greens didn't open until 1979, but it, too, was a product of the sixties counterculture—in this case, as experienced by a young Zen Buddhist named Deborah Madison. A graduate of the University of California at Santa Cruz, where she had studied sociology and city planning, Madison moved into the Zen Center in 1969, another idealistic kid seeking refuge from the violence at the barricades.

The Zen Center kept a vegetarian kitchen. At the time of Madison's arrival there, the cooks were experimenting with macrobiotics, a movement that, like J. I. Rodale's organic philosophy, had been around for a while but hadn't received much attention in America until the hippies discovered it. The modern macrobiotic movement had been founded in the 1930s by a Japanese man, George Ohsawa (1893–1966), who borrowed from ancient Chinese philosophies (Taoism, Confucianism) and traditional East Asian dietary practices to devise a multidisciplinary nutritional and philosophical program that, above all, sought balance between the complementary dark and light forces of the universe—the proverbial yin and yang. Ohsawa placed special emphasis on whole grains such as brown rice as the most "balanced" of foods, while arguing that sugary foods, processed foods, and animal-based foods (meats, eggs, dairy products) were either "too yin" or "too yang," and were thus to be avoided. While his Asian disciples were able to fashion myriad flavorful dishes faithful to this philosophy, such as miso soups and vegetable stir-fries, in the United States, where Ohsawa's teachings were poorly understood in the sixties, "going macro" seemed to be mostly a matter of dutifully, mirthlessly eating brown rice to the exclusion of nearly everything else.

The Zen Center was an exception, Madison recalls, a place whose head

cook, Loring Palmer, "made macrobiotics what it could be, in terms of re-
alizing its great potential for balance and flavor." But even for Buddhists who
had forsworn material pleasures and outside diversions, Palmer's meals were
a bit scant, and many of the students used what little funds they had to duck
out to the coffee shop down the street. When her turn to run the kitchen
arrived, Madison aimed to woo back her fellow Buddhists, preparing crowd-
pleasers like waffles and pancakes and "bringing on the butter and the cream
and the cheese." It worked, but it wasn't especially healthful fare, and Madison realized that she had a lot to learn about vegetarian cooking, and cooking in general.

The early seventies were a good time to go down this path. In 1971, a
Berkeley woman named Frances Moore Lappé published a vegetarian manifesto called *Diet for a Small Planet* that became a surprise best seller. A bible
of the burgeoning ecology movement, Lappé's book argued not only that a
perfectly healthful, protein-rich diet could be had without any reliance on
meat but that a nationwide switch to vegetarianism would ease world
hunger. Having put aside her graduate studies at the University of California
in the sixties in order to research the root causes of famine and poverty,
Lappé came to the conclusion that the issue was not one of food scarcity but
of misbegotten policies: America was investing more than half of its grain in
the feeding of its livestock, an inefficient use of resources. If people ate this
grain themselves and left the animals alone, they would get all the nutrition
they needed and have plenty of food left to give to disadvantaged peoples.

Lappé's outlook might have been politically naïve, but she presented
her argument in a measured, non-crackpot tone that was persuasive to a lot
of readers.* She became a counterculture heroine, and her book sold nearly
two million copies in the seventies, earning her mainstream press recognition as the "Julia Child of the Soybean Circuit." The same year *Diet for a*

---

*In a sense, Lappé wasn't worlds apart from Niman and Schell, in that both parties agreed that
America had set up a huge, wasteful infrastructure for the dubious purpose of feeding grain to animals. Perhaps if all beef were raised according to Niman Ranch methods, the "diet for a small
planet" might include the occasional steak.

Small Planet came out, *The New York Times* seized the opportunity to harness the zeitgeist by publishing *The New York Times Natural Foods Cookbook.* The *Times's* book was written not by Craig Claiborne but by another food writer, Jean Hewitt, who compiled its recipes from those the paper had received from readers more interested in lentil stews and tabbouleh salad than in *filet de boeuf braisé Prince Albert.*

Even the Zen Center had its own culinary star of sorts, Ed Brown, author of *The Tassajara Bread Book* (1970). Brown was a monk in training at the Tassajara Zen Mountain Center, the organization's monastery located in Monterey County, inland from Big Sur. A gentle soul who had endured a difficult childhood, losing his mother at age three and spending much of his early life in an orphanage, Brown found in Shunryu Suzuki, the Zen Center's founder and abbot, the loving authority figure he'd long sought. Eager to do something to demonstrate his gratitude to Suzuki and the other monks, Brown took up baking bread. He turned out to be very good at it. The book of recipes he compiled, appealingly packaged in a folksy cover of rough brown paper decorated with exotic typography and pleasant line drawings—the food journalist Ann Hodgman wrote in 2003 that the volume looked like something that "should be sitting on a butcher-block kitchen counter 30 years ago, next to an avocado pit that someone's trying to sprout in a jar of water"—became another left-field publishing phenomenon, selling 750,000 copies and establishing itself as a fixture on the hippie cook's shelf.

Baking bread was an especially popular activity among vegetarians and back-to-the-landers, redolent of self-sufficiency and independence from the nefarious corporate chemists who foisted rubbery presliced Wonder Bread upon the masses. Even James Beard got in on the act, writing *Beard on Bread* in his debut as a Knopf author. The late sixties had been something of a literary fallow period for the Big Buddha, who had coasted on reputation and not sold many books. But Judith Jones believed that the old-timer had plenty of worthwhile work left in him, and she lassoed him into her stable of cookbook stars.

Beard on Bread was something of a commercial comeback, winning great reviews and doing brisk bookstore business upon its 1973 publication. Jones had shrewdly packaged it in earth tones, its type set in dark brown, its illustrations done in light brown, its cover a scrawly pen-and-ink illustration of a yeasty country loaf on a wheat-beige background; whether by accident or design, the book looked like a Yankee cousin of *The Tassajara Bread Book*. With lots of whole-grain bread recipes and a dedication at the front of the book to that simple-life sensualist Elizabeth David (who was at work on her own baking masterpiece, *English Bread and Yeast Cookery*), *Beard on Bread* connected its author to a whole new generation of readers who might have otherwise regarded him as a jolly, fat anachronism.

But as the saying goes, man cannot live on bread alone. Vegetarianism remained a tricky business in the early seventies, its culinary potential often obscured by nut-ball ascetics who advocated chewing each mouthful of brown rice in meditative silence for ten minutes (Fletcherizing redux!) and overcompensatory mad-scientist cooks who believed in meat-substitute "nut loaves" fashioned of cashews, sunflower seeds, cream cheese, curry powder, carrot shavings, eggs, raisins, and dried apricots. Even a credible text like *Diet for a Small Planet* made meatless eating sound like an arduous if redeeming chore. Lappé was so concerned with nutritional credibility that she advocated complex meal-planning prescriptions in which foods with low amino-acid counts needed to be combined with foods with high amino-acid counts in order to satisfy the body's protein requirements.*

Madison, for her part, just wanted to figure out a way to make vegetarian meals as flavorful and rich in variety as the stuff that Julia Child cooked. While studying and cooking at the Zen Center and at Green Gulch Farm, she indulged in an active fantasy life about food, subscribing to *Gourmet* ("I'm sure I'm the only Zen student who did") and devouring any reports she could get her hands on about the burgeoning Bay Area scene,

---

*Lappé later realized the folly of this approach. "In combating the myth that meat is the only way to get high-quality protein, I reinforced another myth," she said. "I gave the impression that in order to get enough protein without meat, considerable care was needed in choosing foods. Actually, it is much easier than I thought."

whose restaurants she couldn't afford to visit on her tiny stipend. "I would read reviews that Caroline Bates wrote about California restaurants, and I had no idea what she was describing," Madison says. "It was like hearing about an orgasm when you're ten years old and you can't possibly understand what it might be. She was describing all these veloutés and textures, and it just sounded like the most wonderful thing in the world—this absolutely over-the-top thing that could be had for nothing. I mean, it was *legal*—you just needed money."

Fate intervened when, one day in 1977, Alice Waters and Lindsey Shere paid a visit to Green Gulch Farm to see what it was all about, and Madison was assigned the task of showing them around. "I just started asking them questions," Madison says. "Have you ever heard of Richard Olney or Elizabeth David? Oh, you *know* Elizabeth David?! Do you—do you make tarte tatin?" The amused Waters and Shere were enchanted by the overeager Zen student and invited her to dine at their restaurant some time as their guest. Madison took them up on their offer the very next evening, arriving at Chez Panisse's doorstep with her then husband, a fellow student at the Zen Center.

"It was just the most memorable meal," Madison says, "because the sensibility of food that I'd kind of gained through reading but had never really experienced—there it was! Jean-Pierre Moullé was cooking, and he made this beautiful little shellfish ragout with mussels and clams and scallops. We had a lamb course of little lamb chops and turnip puree. Of course, there was a little salad. And then there was a cheese course. My husband and I had goat cheese for the first time ever and just, like, went ballistic. Then we had little fruit tarts. And we also went through two baskets of bread, and lots of butter."

Flush with food, wine, animal fats, and excitement, Madison returned late to Green Gulch Farm and noticed that the abbot's light was still on. "I knocked on the door and I went up," she says. "And I said, 'I've just been to Chez Panisse, and *I have to work there!*' You didn't do that at Zen Center. You didn't announce what you *wanted* to do. It was a very hierarchical situation where you were told, 'You're going to go to Tassajara,' or 'You're gonna be on the board,' or 'You're not gonna be on the board.' "

The abbot, Richard Baker, who succeeded Suzuki upon the latter's death in 1971, was an intimidating figure who didn't brook uppitiness among his students.* But it was Madison's good fortune that Baker was almost as food-obsessed as she. Not only had he, too, dined at Chez Panisse; he had privately been mulling the idea of opening a restaurant in conjunction with the Zen Center, and was only too happy to let one of his students apprentice with Alice.

Madison was immediately thrown into the Chez Panisse whirl as the deputy to Lindsey Shere, the pastry chef, and took over desserts completely for a couple of months when Shere went away for the summer. The following year, she joined Waters and several other members of the Chez Panisse staff on a culinary tour of France. While overseas, Madison collected seeds for all manner of salad greens and vegetables—radicchio, borage, chicories, different varieties of cucumbers—that were relatively unknown in America at the time, and handed them over to the head gardener at Green Gulch Farm. In one fell swoop, she introduced a whole mess of new options to the Bay Area salad mix.

By 1979, Madison was seasoned enough as a cook to open Greens, a San Francisco restaurant that magically reconciled the precepts of austere Zen Buddhism and hedonistic Chez Panisse–ism. "Attention to detail is such a big thing in Buddhism," she says. "I've always felt that there was a strong element of that in the Chez Panisse kitchen. There could be opera playing, there could be zydeco music, there could be hustle and bustle, but in terms of real focus, the level of concentration was phenomenal. It was a beautiful example of what Buddhist practice might bring to a similar situation."

As lofty and New Agey as this statement might sound to skeptical ears,

---

*Baker was eventually ousted from the San Francisco Zen Center in an ugly, highly publicized 1984 scandal in which he was accused of sexual harassment and inordinate flashiness, particularly where his white BMW was concerned.

it sums up the achievement of the post–Jeremiah Tower Chez Panisse. Waters could be derided for not having "restaurant chops" as a cook—a charge that was also leveled with some frequency at Beard, Child, and Claiborne—but she was exacting in her vision. Even as her restaurant went through its carousel of chefs of different influences, from the traditionally French Moullé to the Southwestern-minded Mark Miller to the savory-Italian Paul Bertolli (whose hearty, gloppy, slow-cooked preparations of short ribs and pork shoulder were called "swamp cuisine" by the waitstaff), Chez Panisse retained the indelible Waters mark: seasonal, local, fresh, composed, everything just so.

In embracing this philosophy for Greens, Madison lapped the vegetarian competition and put to shame the drab, brown-rice hippie-hangover feedlots that still dotted San Francisco. Madison believed in bright purees of multicolored summer tomatoes, elegantly composed salads, and upscale borrowings from ethnic cuisines. She served polenta with gorgonzola and braised greens, made crepes out of masa, the dough used by Mexicans to make corn tortillas, and offered goat-milk panna cotta for dessert. She furthermore rejected the "fake meat" approach of some veggie outlets—she detested soy cutlets almost as much as she did the word "veggie"—and the overcompensatory school of vegetarian cooking that demanded sixteen ingredients in every dish.

IN A SENSE, GREENS was the culmination of a move away from joyless vegetarianism that had begun in the early seventies with such places as the Moosewood Restaurant, a utopian hangout in Ithaca, New York, that opened in 1973. The Moosewood, distant as it was from California, was yet another countercuisine shrine with Bay Area roots. Its original head cook—"chef" seems too high-flown a word—was Mollie Katzen, an East Coast girl who had soaked up the patchouli funk of the West Coast while studying at the San Francisco Art Institute and taking folk-dancing classes in Berkeley.

A native of Rochester, New York, Katzen was something of a reluctant counterculturist. She had originally enrolled at Cornell University in Ithaca, but her matriculation there coincided with the most tumultuous period in the school's history. The student body shut down the campus twice for long stretches—in 1969, in the cause of the Vietnam Moratorium, a massive antiwar protest, and in 1970, in protest against the U.S. invasion of Cambodia and the subsequent murder by National Guardsmen of four student protesters at Kent State University. "I just kind of wanted to go to school," she says. "Everyone was like, 'Nixon invaded Cambodia, so we shouldn't go to school!' I was thinking, 'I don't completely see the connection.' I'd been studying to be a painter at Cornell, so I left and went to the San Francisco Art Institute to finish my degree."

The move to the Bay Area proved crucial, for Katzen, who'd always enjoyed puttering around in the kitchen, took a job working at a now forgotten San Francisco vegetarian restaurant called the Shandygaff to help pay her tuition. Having served brief stints as a kitchen worker in soul-crushingly pious macrobiotic restaurants in Ithaca that were, in her estimation, "monochromatic, everything a certain shade of beige, from the chairs to the tables to the dishes to the food, which I called 'remorse cuisine,'" Katzen was stunned by the chirpy California sunniness of her new place of employment. "It was *colorful!*" she says. "Healthy, movie stars and tennis players, California lifestyle. Avocados. A lot of ferns hanging. And the food was excellent, really the first time I'd seen a bridge between macrobiotic and gourmet."

The Shandygaff took advantage of its proximity to excellent produce by making simple yet flavorful concoctions that Katzen had until then never heard of, such as pesto sauce and fruit smoothies. More important, the restaurant's cooks, while true to the hippie propensity for dabbling in ethnic cuisines, managed not to botch their preparations through overseasoning or stoner sloppiness. At the Shandygaff, Katzen learned how to make baba ghanoush, the Middle Eastern eggplant puree, and spanakopita, the Greek spinach pie, for the first time, as well as a lot of Indian-inspired dishes, such as a vegetable curry "with bright yellow sauce and turmeric, with bright red peppers poking out," that she would more or less re-create ingredient for ingredient at Moosewood.

The Moosewood opportunity came about while Katzen, twenty-two years old and just out of the Art Institute, was back east, visiting her brother, a Cornell graduate, and some of his buddies in Ithaca. In the hippie spirit, this group of friends was renovating a space in an old school building with an eye toward opening a progressive restaurant. But no one in this group had any restaurant experience or a sense of what the menu should include. Aware of Katzen's tour of duty at the Shandygaff, they drafted her as a sort of culinary director, and the Moosewood opened on January 3, 1973, with a single main course of moussaka, offered with a filling of either ground lamb or mushrooms. (The strictly vegetarian policy didn't go into effect until a year later.)

Katzen's cuisine was a homey amalgam of the Shandygaff's pepped-up California vegetarian fare (as reinterpreted with East Coast ingredients), her own evocations of the Jewish food she grew up with (a noodle kugel was among the Moosewood's most popular offerings), and the ethnic dishes that she had learned about in Bay Area counterculture circles (attending a party after her folk-dancing class in Berkeley, she ate something "with eggplant and a white sauce and a tomato sauce that tasted wonderful"—the moussaka that became Moosewood's opening-night dish). The Moosewood's food was not nearly as polished as what Greens would later offer, being much more "crunchy," to use a favorite word of Katzen's, and occasionally guilty of super-caloric, multi-ingredient overkill. Its broccoli-mushroom noodle casserole, for example, called for three eggs, one cup of sour cream, one cup of grated cheddar, two tablespoons of butter, and three cups (!) of cottage cheese.

"I wasn't thinking about fat or calories or anything," says Katzen, who, like Lappé and Madison, was initially naïve about the ability of vegetables themselves to deliver adequate dietary allotments of protein. (She would later drastically modify and simplify her cooking.) Katzen was also playing up the butter and cream, she says, to win over the Julia Child–loving moms of the crunchy kids, "thinking they would want to know what to cook for their sons and daughters who were vegetarians."

Like Chez Panisse, the Moosewood Restaurant was an almost immediate local hit despite its staff's inexperience and borderline incompetence. As a national institution, in fact, the Moosewood caught on earlier than Chez Panisse, its very name becoming a byword in the late seventies for a Birkenstock-and-backpack way of life. "I liken it to birds eating berries and then scattering the seeds," says Katzen. "Because of the nomadic nature of the counterculture, the way people hitchhiked across the country, there was a fluidity between places like Ithaca, Ann Arbor, Cambridge, Berkeley, Madison, Seattle, maybe a little bit in Austin. The word got out."

Katzen discovered the power of this informal countercultural network after putting together the original version of *The Moosewood Cookbook*, an un-bylined, spiral-bound booklet of her recipes that was sold exclusively at an independent bookstore in Ithaca called McBooks.* To her surprise, she started getting letters from people in university towns like Cambridge, Massachusetts, and Madison, Wisconsin, who had seen their friends' copies of the book and wanted their own. By the time she'd mailed off some 5,000 copies, it was evident to Katzen that, she says, "This really was a *book*." Spurning offers from major New York publishers, she signed a deal with the Berkeley-based Ten Speed Press, which in 1977 turned out the version of *The Moosewood Cookbook* familiar to crunchy families from Martha's Vineyard to Mendocino, its recipes rendered entirely in Katzen's twinkly hand and adorned with her pen-and-ink illustrations of chubby cherubs and asparagus spears in repose. By 1981, the book had sold more than 250,000 copies, and Katzen had a hit sequel on the way, *The Enchanted Broccoli Forest*.†

---

*McBooks, too, branched out into the publishing business, forming McBooks Press in 1980. Its first title was *Vegetarian Baby*, a primer for raising young children on a meatless diet.

†Never a dogged ideologue, Katzen was unhappy when her fellow Moosewood partners took action to turn the restaurant, originally a corporation, into a Cheese Board–style collective. She departed around the time the Ten Speed Press version of *The Moosewood Cookbook* was published, with an agreement that she would retain the rights to the book while the collective would keep the rights to the Moosewood name. She relocated to Berkeley, where she remains a Ten Speed author. The Moosewood Collective continues to operate the restaurant and publishes its own line of brisk-selling cookbooks.

ANOTHER COUNTERCUISINE NOMAD, Odessa Piper, was self-conscious enough about her wanderlust to rechristen herself in homage to Homer's famous voyager, Odysseus. Born Karen Piper in the coastal town of Portsmouth, New Hampshire, she got swept up in political and personal romance, quit high school, "fell in love with a Dartmouth boy who protested against the ROTC a little too vigorously," joined a commune with said Dartmouth boy, and changed her name. The commune, located on a farm in Canaan, New Hampshire, and populated mostly by other Dartmouth students booted from campus for their protest activities, turned out to be a passing fancy for the teenage girl—"I wanted to gentrify, to have indoor plumbing and hot show-ers," she says—but it gave Piper a crash course in farming, which proved use-ful when she found her bliss in Wisconsin, America's dairy land.

Piper's wanderings away from the East Coast took her initially to Chicago, where her sister was in college and where she fell under the sway of an older woman named JoAnna Guthrie. Guthrie was a cultured, worldly, proper lady who, despite her past as TV weathercaster and former gal Friday for the millionaire Winthrop Rockefeller, was embraced as a role model by young countercultural types. This was because of her relatively late-in-life embrace of theosophy, a murky, mystical belief system that championed the "ancient wisdom" of Tibetan Buddhists, Zoroastrians, Hindus, and Cabalists. Guthrie lectured frequently for Chicago university audiences, and as sideshow-ish as some of these public appearances were—she considered her-self a clairvoyant and performed "readings" of her followers—she used her quirky outlook for good.

"She was telling us not to tear down society. She saw an opportunity to point out the achievements of Old World cultures and find in them the seeds of a new culture that could be cultivated," says Piper. "Specifically, she was looking at agriculture and cooking." Possessed of a noble sense of com-munity and an Alice Waters–ish urgency to reestablish the connection be-tween rural and urban peoples, Guthrie purchased a farm in Wisconsin's

Kickapoo River Valley and a building in Madison, Wisconsin, in the late sixties. In the building, she opened a restaurant called the Ovens of Brittany in 1972. The farm—staffed, like the restaurant, with Guthrie's young followers—supplied the Ovens of Brittany with organically raised produce. "We were doing farm-to-table when it was just a gleam in Berkeley's eye," Piper says. "It was lettuces from the farm and freshly made, unlicensed, probably highly illegal chèvre from local goats."

Like Chez Panisse, the Ovens of Brittany skewed more French country than crunchy, with *poulet Parisienne* and liver pâtés with cornichons and exquisitely arranged salads of local ingredients. "We were not the granola-lentil tribe," says Piper, who recalls the staff consulting the works of Beard and Child as they felt their way toward a vernacular French-Wisconsin hybrid. Some of Guthrie's policies bordered on the daft and New Agey—female workers recall her forbidding them to part their hair because such an action somehow upset the "energy flow" of the kitchen—but this didn't stop the Ovens of Brittany from being ecstatically embraced by the city of Madison. The restaurant thrived to the point where it eventually became a minichain, with nine locations throughout the state, but, just a few years after its initial success, Guthrie's mystical dynamism deteriorated into erratic, delusional behavior. "She kind of went away, and things got hard at the restaurant, so I decided to move on," says Piper. (Guthrie was eventually diagnosed as a schizophrenic and wound up living in an Ohio nursing home, where she died in 2000.)

In 1976, when she was still only twenty-three, Piper opened up her own place in Madison, L'Etoile, which was, if anything, an even greater triumph than the Ovens of Brittany, its dedication to local foods inspiring the food press to posit Piper as a Midwestern analogue to Alice Waters. Whereas the Chez Panisse logo depicted a freshly dug radish with its green top and spindly root tip intact, Piper embraced the local hickory nut as her calling card. "I'm wary of sounding preachy," she says, "but as a sort of heartfelt welcome to each diner, I sent out a little canapé of a thin wafer cracker topped with some local chèvre and a perfectly toasted hickory nut, and I called it a 'hickory-nut shaman.' A shaman is a teacher. It's just the idea that this beautiful tree is teaching us all about regionality and local history. It's very much the kind of idea that JoAnna Guthrie would have put out there."

AS POST-HIPPIE FOODIE enterprises popped up like chanterelle mushrooms across the country, a sort of nationwide mutual admiration society developed; the disparate members of the countercuisine intelligentsia *got* one another and fed off one another's good vibes. As far apart as the Moosewood and the Boulder, Colorado–based Celestial Seasonings tea company were geographically, they quickly spotted each other across the crowded landscape. Celestial Seasonings was the brainchild of a long-haired kid in his early twenties, Morris (Mo) Siegel, who, since 1969, had been foraging in the Rocky Mountain foothills for wild herbs and mixing them into a blend he called Mo's 24. By 1972, Siegel's operation had become a real-deal enterprise, its bottom line bolstered by the boffo sales of his latest trippy blend, Red Zinger, a mix of hibiscus flowers, rose hips, and lemongrass that produced a citric, arrestingly crimson brew. The look, ethos, and taste of Celestial Seasonings teas—whose psychedelic packaging suggested a cross between Beatrix Potter and Hieronymus Bosch—jibed perfectly with the crunchy, gnomy, "aware" tenor of the Moosewood, where Katzen had been using chamomile tea imported from Switzerland. The restaurant became the fast-growing Colorado tea company's first East Coast account—a strategic hippie-business alliance.

For some hardcore Marxists, it was unconscionable that Siegel was so baldly entrepreneurial, that, by the late seventies, he had turned Celestial Seasonings into a $9 million a year business. But as the lines between "natural" and "gourmet" and "veggie" and "local" got blurred, the hallmark of the countercuisine wasn't so much a commitment to revolution or healthfulness as a general sense of belonging, of being part of a new foodie paradigm that had nothing to do with Henri Soulé (whoever he was) and your uptight mom's crown roast of lamb with paper tassels. If your menu was written out in multicolored chalk on a blackboard (like the Moosewood's), or if your café's logo looked like it had been designed by the cartoonist R. Crumb or the Haight-Ashbury poster artist Rick Griffin, you were slyly acknowledging that you were "with it," as were your customers.

For some reason, maverick young manufacturers of premium ice cream did especially well in this context. In-the-know kids thronged Steve's Ice Cream, a modest storefront operation in Somerville, Massachusetts, that was launched in 1973 by Steve Herrell, a jovial twenty-nine-year-old ex-schoolteacher who had altered a conventional commercial-batch ice-cream machine so it would produce a dense, high-butterfat dessert with less air in it than ordinary supermarket ice cream. Herrell further upped the ante by inventing what he called "mix-ins" or "smoosh-ins," unholy concoctions of ice cream with nuts, dried fruits, and such sugary treats as Heath Bars and Oreos crumbled in.

Warren Belasco speculates that mix-in mania, along with the subsequent emergence of rococo ice-cream flavors in the premium section of the supermarket freezer, derived from the stoner penchant for mixing any old shit together to see if it tasted good. "It was no coincidence," he writes in his book *Appetite for Change*, "that some of today's superpremium ice cream moguls started out as hip restaurateurs serving zonked customers attuned to strange blends of thick fresh cream, tropical fruits, and crushed candy bars." Among Herrell's most flagrant imitators were Ben Cohen and Jerry Greenfield, two fur-faced Vermont Deadheads who frequently pilgrimaged to Steve's and didn't bother to hide their intentions, snapping photos of the Somerville shop and parking themselves outside the store's front window, where they could study the mechanical workings of Herrell's retrofitted ice-cream machine as it churned. In 1978, they opened the first Ben & Jerry's in a converted gas station in Burlington, luring customers out in northern Vermont's wintry weather by knocking a penny off the price of a cone for every degree below freezing it was on the thermometer.

But even such butterfat-peddling, unabashedly for-profit countercuisine enterprises as Steve's and Ben & Jerry's offered a measure of do-gooder solace to their consumers, proudly proclaiming their commitment to natural ingredients and local dairies. Ben & Jerry's went still further, adopting policies that it would donate 7.5 percent of its pretax profits to charity and that its highest-paid executives would never make more than seven times the salary of its bottom wage earners (a pledge that was rescinded in 1994, when the company realized it needed a proper white-collar CEO to handle its expansion plans). While Ben & Jerry's tactics sometimes came off as cloyingly self-congratulatory, the notion of a "halo effect," of being nourished morally by doing business with a socially conscious company, proved to be a powerful marketing idea in the gourmet world.

Among the growing ranks of specialty coffee companies—such as Starbucks in Washington, the Coffee Connection in Massachusetts, Green Mountain Coffee in Vermont, and Thanksgiving Coffee in California—socially conscious initiatives became especially popular. Coffee and activism were a good fit: most coffee beans came from Third World countries where poverty and human-rights violations were problems, and many specialty coffee drinkers were college students who were eager to be politically engaged.

So when the specialty roasters started working on what would come to be known as fair-trade issues—ensuring that their coffee beans came from growers who treated their workers humanely and compensated them appropriately; paying their suppliers a guaranteed minimum price for their beans as a hedge against market fluctuations; and educating their growers about ecologically sustainable farming methods—these roasters acquired a certain cachet among young customers. Specialty coffee wasn't just delicious; it was righteous and cool. No coffee company mined this vein of sentiment more astutely than Starbucks, which somehow managed to maintain an image as a hip, enlightened company even as it expanded with a zeal and rapaciousness to rival McDonald's. By 2005, the company was taking out full-page ads in newspapers and magazines that focused less on its product line than on its socially conscious practices, which readers were invited to learn more about on a specially created Web site called whatmakescoffeegood.com.

LESS WITTINGLY, BILL NIMAN learned of his own brand's halo effect when he entered into an agreement in 2001 to sell his pork to Chipotle, a burrito chain. Chipotle, based in Denver, was founded in 1993 by Steve Ells, a trained chef and alumnus of Jeremiah Tower's Stars. By the time Niman became one of its suppliers, though, the Chipotle chain was 90 percent owned by the great McSatan itself, McDonald's. Nevertheless, Ells continued to run the company with a great deal of autonomy, and if it was Niman Ranch pork he wanted, it was Niman Ranch pork he got—even though, to recoup the extra expense of buying Niman's boutique meat, Chipotle had to raise the cost of its carnitas burritos and tacos by a significant margin, from $4.65 a serving to $5.50.

Instead of low-keying the switch to a more expensive brand of pork, Chipotle hyped it. The chain launched a print advertising campaign that celebrated the Niman Ranch network of pig farmers with such headlines as EAT A BURRITO. HELP A FAMILY FARM and WELCOME TO PORKUTOPIA. The accompanying text enumerated the animal-, farmer-, environment-, and consumer-friendly virtues of Niman Ranch's product and concluded, "We think it's the best-tasting pork available." Niman was as surprised as anyone when the unit sales of Chipotle's carnitas meals quickly shot up 250 percent, even with the steep price increase. "It kind of blew the mind of everybody at Oak Brook, the McDonald's headquarters in Illinois," he says. It was even more mind-blowing that America's greatest symbol of cultural imperialism, beset by image problems, was suddenly eager to bask in the reflective glow of a company founded by Bolinas radicals.

CHAPTER SEVEN

THE NEW SUN-DRIED
LIFESTYLE

You're all mixed up, like pasta primavera.

—Beastie Boys, "What Comes Around"

THE INTERTWINING OF THE GOURMET AND NATURAL-FOODS WORLDS PROCEEDED APACE
in the seventies, with the spartan, sloganeering health-food stores of yore sup-
planted by colorful, bountiful markets with organically grown produce, fresh
baked goods, and the finest in Norwegian flatbreads and Swiss mueslis. Some
of these new-breed emporiums, like Bread & Circus in Brookline, Massachusetts (established in 1975), and Mrs. Gooch's Natural Foods Market in West
Los Angeles (established in 1977), found success so quickly that they rapidly
expanded into regional chains. Down in Austin, Texas, the epicenter of Lone
Star State counterculture, a young man named John Mackey had even bigger
plans for the natural-gourmet crossover genre. In 1980, he merged operations
of his two-year-old store, Safer Way Natural Foods, with those of a market
called Clarksville Natural Grocery, and built an 11,000-square-foot superstore that he named Whole Foods Market. For crunchy Austinites, the aisles
upon aisles of filbert butter and hibiscus tea proved too much to resist—
Whole Foods was a sensation, and Mackey swiftly opened a second Austin
store and new locations in Houston and Dallas. By the mid-nineties, Mackey
had taken Whole Foods nationwide, in part by gobbling up other natural-
foods retailers, Bread & Circus and Mrs. Gooch's among them.

But well before the Whole Foods juggernaut, in the food-fertile seventies, the gourmet movement was turning into a formidable market force
beyond the "natural" arena. It wasn't just the crunchies who discovered the
selling power of upscale, high-quality food; it was also the next-generation

PAGE 195: *Joel Dean and Giorgio DeLuca man their shop—and foster a million
yuppies' dreams, 1981.*

Italian greengrocers and Jewish deli men who saw a world beyond the niche markets of their fathers—people like Andy Balducci and Eli Zabar, both scions of beloved New York ethnic markets that bore their family name, both believers in the idea that if they applied their parents' standards of excellence to a wider variety of goods, they would attract a wider variety of customers. Even some conventional supermarkets were getting hip to so-called specialty foods, again thanks to the agitation of second-generation guys who sensed a change in the air—guys like Rob Kaufelt and Glenn Rosengarten, both supermarket-chain princelings of the New York metro area, Kaufelt from a family that owned several Foodtown stores in New Jersey, Rosengarten from the family that founded the Westchester County chain Shopwell. "Glenn and I talked about what was happening a lot in the city with Balducci's and places like that," says Kaufelt. "We talked about how sterile our families' stores were compared to Balducci's, and what could be done about it."

The more ambitious Rosengarten created his own line of upscale supermarkets under the Food Emporium brand—in Manhattan, no less—to fill a niche between budget-price chains like ShopRite and specialty shops like Balducci's and Zabar's.* Kaufelt convinced his family to let him jazz up their existing shops with such fancy-for-the-seventies products as warm croissants—"bought frozen, but proofed and baked in-store"—and orange juice freshly squeezed on the premises. Each successful innovation begat another, to the point where, by the early eighties, Kaufelt remembers, the family's Fort Lee supermarket had moved into the brave new world of "big Lucite self-serve bins of nuts, candies, and dried fruits, with the beginnings of grains and lentils."

But no gourmet innovator of the seventies was more zealous than Giorgio DeLuca. He, too, was the son of a food man. His father was an importer of specialty Italian products in New York's old Washington Market, a bustling mercantile district on the city's lower west side that existed from the

---

*Food Emporium was bought out in 1986 by A&P, which turned the chain's stores into more conventional supermarkets.

1770s until the 1960s, when it was condemned to make way for the World Trade Center. As a child in the fifties, Giorgio frequently accompanied his father on his rounds, riding along, he says, "as my dad delivered stuff from the back of his car, which smelled of cheese all the time." The senior DeLuca sold his wares—olive oil, dried figs, chocolates, parmigiano-reggiano cheese, the Christmas cakes known as panettone, the hard sausages known as soppresatta—to wholesalers, who in turn sold these goods to specialty shops in Italian American enclaves. Still, Giorgio took no particular pride in the fact that the sandwiches that he brought to school were filled with caponata, the Sicilian tomato-eggplant relish, while other kids were eating cream cheese and jelly; Italian foods, no matter how *autentico*, were considered "low-end," he says, "and just for a limited market."

DeLuca was not a romantic. Born in 1944, two years after Martin Scorsese, he viewed life bleakly, through a grimy lens very much the one that trailed Harvey Keitel in Scorsese's seminal film *Mean Streets* (1973)—a movie whose narrative the director has described as the struggle of its protagonist, a young Italian American New Yorker, to make sense of life while "essentially living in a feudal society, structured by organized crime, family, and church."

"Growing up, personally and generally, it was tough times," DeLuca says. "It was a dark, grim world. We had the Korean War, we had the end of the Second World War, we had the holdover clouds from the Depression." Outwardly, DeLuca was charming and charismatic enough to be elected president of his class at Richmond Hill High School in Queens, but inwardly, he was a mess, subject to paralyzing anxiety attacks. These he traced to his uncertainty of where he fit in—was he destined to live out his existence in his feudal, outer-borough Italian American community, or would he somehow make his way into the wider world, and doing what? "I was asking myself, 'How do you find some degree of security in this fuckin' world?' " DeLuca says.

The one guiding principle that he took with him from his mixed-up school days was something he was told by his advance-placement history teacher at Richmond Hill High, Jack Estrin. "We were talking about aesthetics," DeLuca says. "He tried to tell us that beauty and truth are not *subjective*, they're *objective*. All us kids went, 'No, no! Art is not objective, it's a matter of opinion, a matter of what you like.' Estrin said we didn't know what we were talking about."

What this peculiar classroom exchange meant in practical terms, DeLuca couldn't yet fathom. After graduating, he took a stopgap job at a pharmacy, attended classes noncommittally at City College, smoked a lot of marijuana, and found a studio apartment in the basement of a town house on West Twelfth Street in Greenwich Village. In his comings and goings from the building, he became friendly with the gay couple who lived in the floor-through apartment on the second floor, Joel Dean and Jack Ceglic. Dean, a soft-spoken Michigan native thirteen years DeLuca's senior, was a publishing executive at Simon and Schuster. Ceglic was a fashion illustrator and painter. Raw and uncultured, DeLuca regarded these worldly, contented men with awe, and jumped at the chance to socialize with them.

"I wasn't a loner, but I felt distanced from society—pathologically distant. And that left me more malleable, amenable, and hungry to find something or someone to connect to," DeLuca says. "When I first walked into Dean's apartment, I was thunderstruck. I'd never seen a more beautiful place. They made a complete work of art out of their little apartment. Dean was this bright guy who wrote music and played the piano and had a master's degree in literature from Columbia. Steady as a rock—just the opposite of me. We got to talking, and I told him what Jack Estrin had told me. Dean was the first person to say to me, 'That guy knew what he was talking about. Art *is* objective. Beauty *is* objective. Otherwise, you couldn't agree on who all the great artists were through the ages.' "

Dean's cultured way of life seemed to be a validation of Estrin's outlook. "I learned that you could learn to see better, hear better, *taste* better," says DeLuca. With Ceglic, Dean educated DeLuca in the ways of opera, art, and, most consequentially, good eating. Ceglic, the son of a Brooklyn grocer, was a fine amateur cook and devoted Julia Child fan who, like lots of aspirational sixties adults, enjoyed taking on the recipes in *Mastering the Art of French Cooking*. "Joel and I liked a certain style of living," Ceglic says, "and we shopped and ate and did things a certain way. Giorgio seemed to fit right in with what we did."

As the three men started dining together regularly, DeLuca began to recognize the purity and virtues of the "low-end" things his father imported; pridefully, he'd bring Dean and Ceglic tins of briny Sicilian olives and yard-long soppresattas to slice up for antipasti. Somewhere along the way, the notion developed in DeLuca's mind to open a cheese shop, selling the kinds of pungent, flavorful imports that he'd tasted at the Washington Market: Italian gorgonzola and taleggio, French chèvre. Why not cheese? Cheese was something about which one could certainly make an objective judgment: it was good or it was bad. The writer Clifton Fadiman once described cheese as "milk's leap into immortality." Whatever cheese had inspired Fadiman to write such words, this was the kind of cheese that DeLuca wanted to sell in his shop.

That DeLuca eventually opened his shop on Prince Street, in the neighborhood south of Greenwich Village that had only recently come to be known as SoHo (south of Houston Street), was attributable to Dean and Ceglic. In 1970, the couple moved from the West Twelfth Street town house to a loft on SoHo's Wooster Street, where Ceglic could keep a studio in his own home. DeLuca, though he continued to live in the Village, became infatuated with his friends' new neighborhood.

The early seventies were New York City's shabbiest hour, a time of collapsing infrastructure, hard drugs, high crime rates, and *Kojak* tableaus of needle parks and graffitied subway cars. SoHo was an exception, "one of the few growth communities, one of the bright spots," DeLuca says. For an aesthete in training like him, the neighborhood was a refuge, a place where, among the stark industrial buildings and clean, bright interior spaces, one could shake off the stink of the city. For a time, SoHo, too, had been a part of New York's decline, a fading no-man's-land of printing plants and small factories sliding into insolvency. But like many a struggling urban neighborhood before it and since, SoHo owed its deliverance from decrepitude to struggling artists. As the industrial businesses closed up in the sixties, the artists trickled in, enthralled by the cheap rents and extraordinary allotments of square footage. By 1970, the year in which it actually became legal to live in SoHo (previously, the area had been zoned strictly for manufacturing and light industry), enough artists had moved in to constitute a full-blown bohemian community.

SoHo's bohemianism was of a different breed than the shaggy, tie-dyed, let-it-all-hang-out brand that prevailed out West in the same period. "It wasn't hippies," says DeLuca. "All the hippies [in New York] had decided that urban life was corrupt, and they needed to move to the ashram and the country life." In SoHo, the aesthetic was minimalist: urban renewal that began, figuratively and literally, with a clean slate. The artists left their concrete floors uncarpeted, their brick walls exposed, and their lightbulbs unshaded. Their principal meeting place was a cheap restaurant at the corner of Prince and Wooster Streets that a bunch of them had founded as a collective. It was called, simply, in accordance with the neighborhood's prevailing ethos of utilitarian chic, Food.

In 1973, after an unfulfilling stretch as a substitute teacher in the New York public school system and a happier, briefer stint working at Balducci's to learn the ropes of retail, DeLuca at last opened his cheese store. It was called, in compliance with SoHo's minimalist dictates, the Cheese Store. And it afforded DeLuca the chance to put Estrin's theory into practice: beauty, art, truth, taste—objective, not subjective.

"A lot of this was in reaction to the processed food that America was starting to live on," DeLuca says. "The Swanson's TV dinners, the Tang, the fucking WisPride cheddar in a crock—Americans were losing their ability to taste. I wanted to show that some things are *better* than others. Americans are taught just the opposite: 'Whatever makes you happy. You like Coca-Cola and this guy likes fine Burgundies? You can't say one is better than the other!' Can you imagine the absurdity of that? But that's the underlying philosophy that Americans are brainwashed into."

It wasn't a stretch for DeLuca to conflate his role with that of the artists who had repopulated and revived SoHo. He was an unabashed elitist and Europhile, there to provoke and reveal. A small, wiry, handsome man given to wearing Lacoste shirts, he looked like a European sophisticate, but his skittery demeanor and Noo Yawky dropped *r*'s were totally early-period Scorsese. The cheese-buying public had never seen anything like him. "I didn't want to just play the nice gentle thing," he says. "I wanted to make 'em lock onto me. I wanted to grab their attention. I would get confrontational about Jarlsberg. People would ask for it, and I would scorn them. *Scathingly* put 'em down. But then, then I would take 'em under my wing and say, 'C'mere— let me show you the possibilities. Let me show you real Emmenthaler.' "

Sometimes DeLuca took a more positive, proactive approach toward his Cheese Store customers, proffering samples to the uptowners who were starting to visit SoHo as gallery gawkers. "I used to give the blue-haired ladies a taste of the fresh chèvre from France," he says. "I remember putting olive oil on it and fresh thyme, then giving 'em a taste. Then I'd have some, too, and say 'Boy, that—that's like angel cum!' Just to freak 'em out. Then I'd pretend I didn't care—and let them come back after me. Which they usually did. I was trying to show people things. An artist shows people things that they can't see themselves."

FOUR MILES NORTH of the scene of DeLuca's performance-art salesmanship. Eli Zabar was dishing out even rougher treatment to his customers at E.A.T., the fancy-foods shop and café that he opened on Madison Avenue in 1973, the same year as the Cheese Store's debut. E.A.T. was a fantasy of culinary exquisiteness, stocked with imported specialty foods, breads and pastries from the city bakeries that Zabar had deemed worthy of his vision, and the proprietor's own prepared dishes and European-style loaves—all combined in one smart-looking shop with stainless-steel shelving and a checkerboard linoleum floor.

Zabar believed his products were the absolute best that Manhattan had to offer, and if you disagreed, or complained about the eyebrow-raising prices he charged for his croissants and preserves, he would unhesitatingly show you the door, heckling you with profanity as you exited. "In my earlier days, I was imperious," he says. "My wife tells a story from before we were married, that she came in to ask about my croissants. She was making her own, and she hadn't been so successful, and she thought maybe I could give her a hint. Instead, apparently, I was very . . . *not nice*, and threw her out."

A self-described "product of affluence," Zabar was the cosseted baby son of the family that owned the Upper West Side's greatest Jewish-foods emporium, Zabar's. His father, Louis, had emigrated from the Ukraine in the early twenties and a decade later founded what Eli describes as "what was called an 'appetizing store'—not a delicatessen. An appetizing store carried a lot of cheeses, lots of kinds of smoked fish. It smelled of coffee and spices and teas. It was all counter service, everyone in white aprons, running around. The clientele was exclusively immigrant Jewish."

In 1950, when Eli was seven years old, Louis Zabar died, leaving the business in the hands of Eli's brothers Saul and Stanley, fifteen and eleven years his senior, respectively. (They later took on a third partner, Murray Klein.) Saul and Stanley broadened the mandate of Zabar's somewhat, roasting their own coffee, offering myriad cold cuts, and carrying soft French cheeses like brie, but Zabar's remained a Jewish store in idiom.

Eli never quite felt a part of the family operation. He'd gone to a different prep school than his brothers—they'd attended Horace Mann, "where every Jew who had made his fortune sent his children," while he was sent to Fieldston, which was "more arty, and they expected more poets than accountants"—and he possessed a querulousness and independent streak that precluded him from respecting any authority figure, whether a boss, a teacher, or even an older brother. In the sixties, he worked unhappily as a night manager at Zabar's, uncertain of his future. The only thing he was sure of was that he didn't want to go to Vietnam—a fate he deflected by attending Columbia University's business school and then, when that no longer exempted him from the draft, by becoming a teacher in the New York City public school system. (DeLuca, though he, too, had been a teacher, got his military service over with before that, enlisting in the Army National Guard.) In these wilderness years, Zabar, like Deborah Madison at her Zen retreat, found escapist relief in the pages of *Gourmet* magazine. Finally, in 1970, he bundled himself off to Europe with a few hundred dollars and a Michelin guide, eager to see what he'd been missing. Oddly enough, Zabar found his inspiration not in Paris or Tuscany but in London, where a fancy-foods shop called Justin De Blanc Provisions caught his eye. "At the counter, they had the prettiest English girls with milkmaid skin," he says. "They carried smoked salmon and stuff like that, but also a lot of homemade goods. I thought, 'That's exactly what I want to do.'"

Upon returning to New York, Zabar took it upon himself to learn how to bake bread, working from cookbooks to perfect his favorite, the finger-width French loaf known as ficelle, browned to the cusp of being burned. Zabar found an empty storefront on Madison at East Eightieth Street, due east of his brothers' shop and in an altogether more refined, snooty New York neighborhood, the Upper East Side. He chose this location, Zabar says, because "I loved the way women looked and smelled on Madison." Unlike his brothers, he wasn't aiming for a Jewish audience but for a willing congregation of culinary aesthetes who would gladly pay top dollar for top foods. His anger over the deadening of the American palate rivaled DeLuca's. As the building contractors readied E.A.T. for its 1973 opening, Zabar papered its windows with a "manifesto" he'd written himself. "It started off by saying, 'What's going on here?'" Zabar recalls. "And then it said, 'Soon there will be no more bakers; there will be no more decent produce; there will be no more whatever. And what I'm gonna do is seek all this out and sell it here.'"

E.A.T. was an audacious leap forward for the gourmet shop, reinterpreting homey staples like fresh bread and chicken salad as prestigious "artisanal" goods, and causing sticker shock among customers who nevertheless paid up and came back. "I was charging three dollars for a brownie when other people were charging sixty cents, and it became this easy handle for the press, 'the most expensive food per ounce in Manhattan,' " Zabar says. "But it wasn't just a *brownie*—it was the philosophy, the effort. Because I did it myself, I had a very high value on my own efforts, on my own sense of self."

It was this proprietary outlook, Zabar says, that compelled him to boot DeLuca from his shop when the downtown cheese merchant paid a visit to E.A.T. early in its run. "I used to have shelves along the wall of the merchandise that I used to import from everywhere—mustards, jams, spices— and DeLuca was looking at the merchandise, writing down where it came from," Zabar says. "I threw him out—physically. I didn't want him copying me. He came back with a policeman. The policeman came in and said, 'This isn't a dispute that I'm gonna get involved in,' and he left."

DeLuca, unsurprisingly, remembers the incident differently. "I came in with a date to sit down, and Zabar thought I was doing espionage," he says. "He was flattering himself to the max, man! Like I would want to copy him! He was mashing up Schaller & Weber liverwurst, smooshing in currants and pouring in brandy, and calling it some kind of foie gras!"

REGARDLESS OF WHO was the nuttier food evangelist, the fact was that DeLuca and Zabar had both hit on the same big idea: the reeducation of the American palate. Having chosen their shop locations strategically, in areas where they hoped to benefit from heavy foot traffic, they found their expectations surpassed: both stores became destinations in themselves.

In SoHo, the artist-driven model of urban renewal had unfolded according to plan: the artists attracted an in-the-know crowd of bourgeois hipsters; these hipsters attracted moneyed uptown folk who wanted to buy art and reporters who wanted a story; and the newspaper and magazine reports attracted tourists and suburbanite day-trippers sniffing for authentic urban adventure. By 1975, SoHo was, as *The New York Times* announced in a discomfiting attempt at period vernacular, "a neighborhood really on the make. It's hip, with it, Madison Avenue's replacement as the in place for a Saturday stroll in new Earth Shoes."

If you were the sort of upper-middlebrow dabbler who followed the lead of the *Times* Weekend section, your typical SoHo itinerary entailed a gallery hop—from, say, Andre Emmerich to Ileana Sonnabend to OK Harris—followed by a stop at Poster Originals to buy a $15 reproduction of a Rauschenberg or Lichtenstein for the den, followed by a late lunch at a local "artist's hang" like Food, followed by a visit to the Cheese Store for a little something stinky to take back to Teaneck. It was a form of cultural nourishment, the SoHo dabble, a visit to the cutting edge, a glimpse of the sleek, arty future the eighties promised.

Joel Dean was by this point "bored to death" at Simon and Schuster, he recalled, "and I decided I ought to open a pot-and-pan store in SoHo, 'cause there really wasn't anything like that around." But when the large space across from DeLuca's Cheese Store, at 121 Prince, became available, Dean and DeLuca decided to go into business together and create a new-paradigm food store that would surpass Balducci's, Zabar's, E.A.T., and every other nosheteria New York had ever known. For all of Dean's Midwestern equanimity—"All my aunts and uncles are 300-pounders for the most part, basically farmers in Michigan and Ohio," he said in an interview before his death in 2004—he matched DeLuca in the fierceness of his food ideals and was not easily pleased. He and Ceglic, together since the 1950s,* had logged plenty of time in the great specialty food shops of Europe: Fauchon in Paris, Dallmayr in Munich, Fortnum & Mason and the enormous food hall of Harrods in London. While he, Ceglic, and DeLuca were modeling their new store, to a degree, on these places—and, to a lesser extent, on the Harrods-imitative fancy-foods departments of Macy's and Bloomingdale's uptown—Dean found even these models wanting. "A lot of what Fauchon sold was mediocre," he said. "You'd say to yourself, 'Why is everything in aspic?' and it was in aspic because that was the only way you could display something for twelve days without its going rotten. And why were all the Fortnum & Mason jams so insipid? Because they just weren't paying attention."

---

*"Their story is, they double-dated with two girls, and then they met each other, and then they ditched the girls," says DeLuca.

One of the new store's central missions was to revive a notion that had been lost in America's rush toward assimilation: that, in Dean's words, "New York was a port, and had always been a port, where everything was available." There would be imported pots and pans hanging from ceiling-mounted racks, and cheeses liberated from their refrigerated cases so that customers could appreciate them in all their odoriferous glory, and open sacks of coffee near the entrance as a sort of aromatic greeting. Dean handled the business end and the kitchenwares, DeLuca took care of the food and the marketing, and Ceglic created the store's SoHo-contextual, industrial-chic design, everything in gray and white.* "And we all tasted everything and became totally engrossed in our tastings," Dean said. "Because the whole point of our store was editing. We didn't take whole lines of food, we only took the products we thought were the best, like the Little Scarlet strawberry preserves from Tiptree."

The store opened in 1977, calling itself Dean & DeLuca. "Giorgio asked, 'Why is "Dean" first?' " Dean said. "And basically, I told him I didn't want it to sound like an Italian store, which at that point, everyone expected it to be. And 'Dean & DeLuca,' just the name itself, sounded so right." (Ceglic, though a partner in Dean & DeLuca, graciously opted out of naming privileges, knowing that his surname—pronounced che-GLICK—would baffle customers and mess up the alliteration.)

Just as DeLuca had entrusted his cultural betterment to Dean and Ceglic, so did he and his partners expect their customers to look to them for guidance. "The thing that we established fast was that you could trust us," Dean said. "What we ate was what we sold, what we sold was what we ate. The store looked like our loft. Basically, it was establishing a lifestyle that involved, in this case, food."

The weekend crowd embraced the Dean & DeLuca lifestyle so readily that it was sometimes more than the store's founders could handle. Their original counterman, the expert cheesemonger Steven Jenkins—who claims he was the first to apply the word "artisanal" to cheese—recalls a busy

---

*DeLuca converted the old Cheese Store into a sandwich shop called, inevitably, Sandwiches.

Saturday in the early years when a few staffers failed to show up, forcing a furious DeLuca to join Jenkins behind the counter. "It was total chaos, and Giorgio was slicing some preservative-free bacon, and he lopped off the tip of his thumb," Jenkins says. "He started cursing and rushed off to the clinic on Spring Street. Once he was gone, I decided to merchandise the piece of thumb, which still had fingernail on it. I put it on a little piece of marble in the display case with some rosemary and thyme and put up a sign that said 'Gaetano Crudo' "—*crudo* meaning "raw" in Italian, Gaetano being DeLuca's middle name. Fortunately, no one asked to taste the product, though Jenkins says a few people inquired as to "what the hell it was."

"WHAT DEAN & DeLUCA DID was give the food market a clean artistry that made it very now, very tied into the moment when SoHo was being noticed," says Florence Fabricant, the *New York Times* food-beat scoopmeister, who wrote about the store nearly from its inception. "Jack Ceglic was responsible for a lot of that, the industrial look. And Giorgio and Joel were really fanatic about ferreting out product. It all tied together. And the other important thing they tapped into was the need for prepared foods."

Indeed, the time had at last arrived when it was socially and economically acceptable for young professionals—and even harried moms in the suburbs—to take home freshly prepared entrées, along with salads and sides purchased by the pound. In an earlier era, prepared foods were problematic: they seemed too fancy and expensive (as Jean Vergnes found out during his brief experiment with Stop & Shop in the sixties), and, for women, they seemed a cop-out, a betrayal of their domestic duties. But with more women in the professional workforce and more people amenable to the general idea of "gourmet" eating, especially if it had the imprimatur of a prestigious shop like Dean & DeLuca or E.A.T., prepared foods started to take off—Rob Kaufelt, who grew up in the supermarket business and now runs Murray's, the beloved New York cheese store, calls the rise of prepared foods "the biggest change in the grocery-store business over the last thirty years."

Dean & DeLuca's secret weapon in this regard was Felipe Rojas-Lombardi, who for a time was a partner in the store with the namesake owners and Ceglic. Peruvian by birth, Rojas-Lombardi had come to Dean & DeLuca by way of the James Beard Cooking School, where he'd risen up through the ranks to become the master's right-hand man in the kitchen.* Rojas-Lombardi had also worked as *New York* magazine's in-house chef, their go-to man for testing recipes. This pedigree proved helpful not only in eliciting constant plugs for the store in Beard's syndicated column and in *New York* but in the fact that Rojas-Lombardi was a skilled, inventive cook: he roasted chickens tandoori-style, grilled salmon on cedar planks, and went out on a limb with such oddball entrées as elk steak and his notorious rabbit with forty cloves of garlic. "Felipe did some of the first pasta salads that people had ever seen," says Ceglic. "He did everything with the products we sold, and people cottoned to it."

"The idea was that if you didn't know what a sun-dried tomato was, well, here it was, in a pasta salad," said Dean.

The third point in New York's prepared-foods triangle, with Dean & DeLuca downtown and E.A.T. serving the Upper East Side, was the Silver Palate, a tiny shop on the Upper West Side, on what was then a drab stretch of Columbus Avenue. The Silver Palate's genesis lay in a mid-seventies catering company called The Other Woman, a single-person operation run by Sheila Lukins, a young mother of two who cooked out of her apartment on Central Park West. As her company's name and slogan ("So discreet, so delicious, and I deliver") suggested, Lukins's clientele was mostly male: profes-

---

*Beard's biographer, Robert Clark, suggests that Beard and Rojas-Lombardi had an intimate, if nonsexual, relationship: "Bearded, wavy-haired, and endowed with the sunny, angelic looks of a Latin shepherd boy, Rojas-Lombardi was as ambitious and willing as he was beautiful, and he absorbed every instruction that passed from James's lips and shadowed every movement of his hands . . . They blossomed for each other, Felipe absorbing the accumulated wisdom of his mentor and James losing twenty pounds, smartening up his wardrobe, and [temporarily] giving up liquor at his protégé's behest." More succinctly, Joel Dean recalled, "Felipe said that Jim used to say to him, 'I'm the king, you're the prince.' " Rojas-Lombardi died in 1991, when he was only forty-six.

sional men who wanted their dinner parties catered but not in an inordinately fussy, Edith Whartonian fashion.

Lukins was a self-taught cook, more or less—she had taken a course at the London Cordon Bleu while she and her husband lived there, but "it was the dilettante course," she says. Her greatest inspiration was not Child and company's *Mastering the Art of French Cooking* but the more practical, less labor-intensive recipes of Craig Claiborne's *New York Times* cookbooks and his Sunday pieces for the *Times Magazine*. Lukins's cooking was eclectic but somehow all of a piece—aspirational comfort food: moussaka, lasagna, ratatouille, stuffed grape leaves, and the quintessential Lukins dish, Chicken Marbella, the quartered bird baked after a long soak in a Mediterranean-style marinade of oil, vinegar, garlic, prunes, olives, and capers.

While running The Other Woman Catering Company, Lukins became acquainted with Julee Rosso, a young professional who worked in the advertising division of Burlington Mills, the textile company. Rosso had attended many events catered by Lukins, and was so impressed that one day, she hit up Lukins with a proposal. "She said, 'So many *women* are working late now. What if we opened up a shop for them?' " Lukins remembers. The two went into business as the Silver Palate in the summer of 1977, with Lukins as the cook—carting food over from her apartment several times a day to the then kitchenless store—and Rosso as the marketer and frontwoman.*

"It was a big deal for two women to go into business together in 1977," says Lukins, who thinks this angle helped the shop get press coverage almost as fawning and widespread as Dean & DeLuca's. Zabar was the odd man out where press was concerned. E.A.T. was flourishing, and it offered an even more extensive and dazzling line of prepared foods than the Silver Palate, but the proprietor's truculence precluded him from ever being a press favorite, a circumstance that only got worse in the eighties, when he let loose on the writer Julie Baumgold, the wife of *New York*'s then editor Edward Kosner,

---

*It was the *Times*' Florence Fabricant who suggested the shop's name.

for trying to return some item she'd purchased. ("I told her to go fuck herself, 'cause there was nothing wrong with it," Zabar says.)

"Eli's a great merchandiser, and his shop was always spectacular, but I don't think he liked us at all," says Lukins. "I think he thought we copied him—and we didn't. I mean, we were one tiny corner of his shop! But we got the publicity and the good reviews." Within a year of its opening, the Silver Palate was selling its own product line at Saks Fifth Avenue, including such items as winter fruit compote, Damson plums in brandy, and blueberry vinegar.

Four years later, *The Silver Palate Cookbook* was published by Workman and became *the* cookbook of the eighties, not just in Manhattan but throughout the United States. More disciplined and earthbound than *The Moosewood Cookbook*, yet less intimidating and grown-up than the two volumes of *Mastering the Art of French Cooking*, Lukins and Rosso's book was perfect for have-it-all, multitasking baby boomers who wanted to cook well but not all the time. Its introduction recalled the state of affairs that led the two ladies to their decision to open their shop: a new era in which women found themselves juggling "school schedules, business appointments, political activities, art projects, sculpting classes, movie going, exercising, theater, chamber music concerts, tennis, squash, weekends in the country or at the beach, friends, family, fund raisers, books to read, [and] shopping," and yet were still compelled "to prepare creative, well-balanced meals and the occasional dinner party at home." The Silver Palate lifestyle offered two solutions: you could use Lukins and Rosso's recipes, or buy their products and prepared foods.

The very emergence of the word "lifestyle" in the late seventies signaled a progression in America's food culture. Stylish living wasn't just for wealthy boulevardiers anymore, but for anyone who considered himself upwardly mobile—and eating, cooking, and food-shopping were about as lifestylish as things got. In 1976, when *The New York Times* expanded from two to four sections a day, introducing a new daily business section and a rotating fourth section devoted to soft news and service journalism, the first two "fourth sections" to appear were Weekend (on Fridays) and the Living section (on Wednesdays), both of which had a heavy food component. The Weekend section carried the restaurant-review column, which ran longer and held greater weight than it had when Claiborne introduced the column in the early sixties. Whereas Claiborne's early columns were often roundups, devoting just a blurb or a short paragraph to each restaurant, the new version evaluated no more than two restaurants at a time, with much more intimate, first-person critiques by the *Times'* new reviewer, Mimi Sheraton.

The Living section was even more gastronomically inclined, with shopping news and product evaluations from Florence Fabricant; a wine column by Frank Prial (a metro-desk reporter who happened to be an oenophile); health and nutrition news from Jane Brody; recipes, essays, and travelogues from Claiborne; and a new column by Pierre Franey, bylined at last, called "60-Minute Gourmet." Arthur Gelb, who was put in charge of the new culture sections by the paper's executive editor, Abe Rosenthal, had wanted to appeal to time-strapped upwardly mobile home cooks by running a column called "30-Minute Gourmet"; Gelb and his wife, Barbara, had been impressed by Franey's ability to whip up quick, simple, delicious meals in the Hamptons—flounder in a butter sauce, say, or pork chops with capers—after a long day of fishing.

But Franey was still too much of a purist to limit himself to thirty minutes. (Like a lot of chefs, he was also made queasy by the word "gourmet" and preferred the title "60-Minute Chef," but he yielded to Gelb on that matter.) The first "60-Minute Gourmet" column featured a recipe for *crevettes "margarita"*—an invention of Franey's that called for shrimp to be cooked in a sauce of tequila, shallots, and cream, with avocado slices tossed in at the end—and began with a statement of intent (written by Claiborne) that declared, "With inventiveness and a little planning, there is no reason why a working wife, a bachelor, or a husband who likes to cook cannot prepare an elegant meal in under an hour."

The *Times* and *New York* magazine were the brand leaders in chic food journalism, steering it away from the mumsy casseroles and layer cakes of *McCall's* and *Redbook* and into the seductive "lifestyle" format that appealed to men and women alike. Sheraton, in her memoir, *Eating My Words*, explained the allure of this format, saying, "I remain convinced that there are more people interested in knowing where to buy the best bagel than about the latest act of political or corporate corruption, primarily because they personally can do something about the bagel but feel powerless against the Enrons of the world." Sheraton had come to the *Times* from *New York*, whose founder, Clay Felker, was the dean of what Gelb admiringly terms "high-class consumerism," and she was among the first to recognize a sea change in the way the middle class felt about restaurant dining—whereas it had long been regarded as an extravagance, by the mid-seventies, she told the culinary scholar Mitchell Davis, "[people] were beginning to entertain by going out."

Sheraton was the first *Times* restaurant reviewer since Claiborne to have staying power. After Claiborne had burned out on reviewing in 1972, he was replaced by Raymond Sokolov, a former *Newsweek* reporter, who lasted just two years in the job, though he later distinguished himself as the author of several good food books and as the culinary correspondent for *The Wall Street Journal*. Sokolov was followed as restaurant critic by John L. Hess, the *Times* Paris correspondent, and John Canaday, the paper's art critic, who served even shorter stints on the restaurant beat than Sokolov. It was a perverse measure of Claiborne's achievements that, nearly twenty years after he had to pester Jane Nickerson about the legitimacy of his candidacy, as a man, to be the paper's food editor, now the *Times* management had decided that only men were worthy of the position. Sheraton had campaigned for the job in 1972 and gotten nowhere, prompting her to send a vitriolic letter expressing her umbrage to the paper's publisher and several of its editors. But by 1976, the *Times* saw the virtue in going with someone who, like Claiborne, knew how to cook and had a track record in food reporting, and the feisty Sheraton assumed the post.

Like Gael Greene, Sheraton believed in reviewing incognito in order to better gauge the experience of the average diner—"It's not what a chef *can* do, it's what he *will* do," she declared. But she wrote with none of Greene's *Laugh-In* frothiness, nor did she seek out friendships with chefs, as

Claiborne did. Reviewing was serious business, consumer advocacy, and she wasn't going to mince words or cuddle up to maître d's. In his memoir, *City Room*, Gelb asserts that "Mimi's power was such that when she liked a new restaurant, she could put it on the map overnight, but when a restaurant displeased her, the ruthlessness of her review could put it out of business." Sheraton was also imposing in person. A large woman during her stint at the *Times*,* she admits in *Eating My Words* "to having subliminally felt a sense of power that went along with being heavy, as though the more mass I had, the more space I occupied and so controlled." While some *Times* people faulted Claiborne for being occasionally prickly, they *feared* Sheraton.

Claiborne actually spent two years away from the *Times* in the early seventies, giving up not only his review column in 1972 but his job and benefits. In a pattern that would be repeated by many a name food writer, he grew restive in mid-career and wondered if there wasn't more to life than his high-profile perch, if there wasn't some opportunity out there for him to be *in charge* of something. He had also grown frustrated with the *Times* policy against co-bylines and Franey's consequent anonymity as his unsung collaborator. With these issues in mind, he and Franey rounded up some investors, pumped in considerable sums of their own money, and started up *The Craig Claiborne Journal*, a biweekly newsletter devoted to food news, restaurant reviews, recipes, product testing, and insider scuttlebutt about the food world. A prescient mix of the technique lessons and consumer journalism of *Cook's Illustrated* and the first-class-cabin luxe-life posturing of *Wine Spectator* and *Cigar Aficionado*, *The Craig Claiborne Journal* was well-executed but too far ahead of its time. In less than two years, Claiborne and Franey found themselves undersubscribed and deeply in debt.

Gelb had rued the day that Claiborne left and seized the moment to woo back the prodigal food guru. Early in 1974, the *Times* put an ad in the

---

*Sheraton topped out at 205 pounds, but managed to shed sixty pounds after quitting the *Times* in 1983. "Upon seeing the thinner me, several magazine editors asked me to write about my experience, but they all backed out when they heard it had taken three years," she wrote in her memoir. "'Couldn't you get it down to three weeks?' was the gist of their suggestions."

paper heralding Claiborne's return, a photograph of the writer peering mischievously over his trademark half-glasses, overlaid with the headline HE SOMETIMES BITES THE HAND THAT FEEDS HIM. Claiborne came back on the conditions that he no longer would have to review restaurants; that he could file his stories from his house in East Hampton, sparing him the agita of living in the city; and that Franey would receive byline credit for his work. The *Times* also paid off Claiborne's and Franey's debts, making an arrangement for the two men to repay the paper with earnings from their books.

Claiborne relievedly resumed writing for the paper, and Franey flourished in his new, late-in-life role as a public figure. But an incident on the eve of Claiborne's return foreshadowed the dark turn that his life would take. The day that he and Franey had closed the last issue of *The Craig Claiborne Journal*, they treated their small staff to "a champagne lunch of striped bass with *sauce gribiche*," preceded by Bloody Marys. After the staff and Franey had filed out of his home, Claiborne, alone, sozzled, and depressed, drove over to Bobby Van's, a writer's haunt in the neighboring town of Bridgehampton. There, at the bar, he happened upon Willie Morris, the writer and former boy-wonder editor of *Harper's* magazine. Morris was a fellow Mississippian, and, even more so than Claiborne, one of New York's professional literary Southerners.* Claiborne settled in for a scotch and soda and some rote suth'n-boy talk—"through William Faulkner for the hundred and eleventh time," he later recalled—and switched to dry martinis when Morris asked him to stay on at the restaurant for dinner. Swerving and swooping his way home that cold winter night, Claiborne was pulled over by the East Hampton police for drunk driving and thrown into a jail cell. With the one phone call allowed him, he woke up Gelb at 2 a.m., pleading for help.

Gelb found a lawyer for Claiborne and sweet-talked the desk officer into driving the writer home. Claiborne got off with probation and a six-

---

*Morris seemed to be channeling Claiborne when he told a reporter in 1979, "If there is anything that makes southerners distinctive from the main body of Americans, it is a certain burden of memory and a burden of history . . . I think sensitive southerners have this in their bones, this profound awareness of the past."

month suspension of his driver's license, but his drinking grew ever more pronounced as the years went on—as did his impertinent outbursts of potty talk and fits of embarrassing behavior. During Claiborne's second go-round at the *Times*, Gelb remembers him making sloppy advances on the decidedly heterosexual novelist Joseph Heller—"And Joe, of course, being a very macho guy, would say, 'C'mon, c'mon, that's enough,'" Gelb says—and another incident in which the Gelbs and Claiborne were invited by Turner Catledge's elegant widow, Abby, to dinner at the starchy Cosmopolitan Club. Claiborne, soused again, broke a lull in the conversation by suddenly blurting out, "When I die and they autopsy my brain, do you know what they'll find?" After a nervous silence, he answered his own question: "Pubic hair!" Mrs. Catledge was not amused. Claiborne still had plenty of good journalism left in him, but his return to the *Times* marked the beginning of his decline.

WHO BETTER TO ARTICULATE the ascent of the "lifestyle" ethos than Woody Allen, who in the late seventies was at the peak of his popularity as an adorable icon of upper-middlebrow cosmopolitanism? Tellingly, Allen used Dean & DeLuca as a setting for a scene in *Manhattan* (1979), his most boosterish, seductive, I ♥ NY movie, the one that began with fireworks over Central Park and Gershwin's *Rhapsody in Blue*. For those who actually shopped at the store, the *Manhattan* scene was a status-conferring event, a validation of their raffish urbanity. At the film's end, Allen lies in repose on a couch and voices into a tape recorder his list of things that make life worth living, among them "Groucho Marx . . . Willie Mays . . . the second movement of the *Jupiter Symphony* . . . Louis Armstrong's recording of 'Potato Head Blues' . . . *Sentimental Education* by Flaubert . . . those incredible apples and pears by Cézanne . . ." Joan Didion, writing in *The New York Review of Books*, declared this list to be Allen's "ultimate consumer report," arguing that "the extent to which it has been quoted approvingly suggests a new class in America, a subworld of people rigid with apprehension that they will die wearing the wrong sneaker, naming the wrong symphony, preferring *Madame Bovary.*"

Didion was being inordinately doomy and apocalyptic, as was her wont, but she correctly deduced that a new class of status- and lifestyle-conscious Americans was taking shape, even if no one was yet calling them yuppies or aging boomers or chardonnay-swilling brie-eaters. Dean & DeLuca was a culinary manifestation of this phenomenon: status food and status kitchenwares in an aspirational setting. Allen's celebratory list might well have been amended to include balsamic vinegar, sun-dried tomatoes, and extra-virgin olive oil, three ingredients that came to symbolize a whole way of life, and that Dean & DeLuca had a huge hand in popularizing.

For all of Joel Dean's wariness of the "Italian market" pigeonhole, the Italian products that Giorgio DeLuca imported turned out to be the store's biggest sellers and greatest status-generators in its early days—a preview, in effect, of the ascension in the eighties of Italian food, northern Italian especially. It's probable that no one played a larger role in making balsamic vinegar ubiquitous than DeLuca, though he wasn't the first to sell it in America. Chuck Williams, whose success in San Francisco had prompted him to start a Williams-Sonoma mail-order catalog in 1971 and a second store on Rodeo Drive in Beverly Hills in 1973, was offering small bottles of aged *aceto balsamico* by Fini, a producer in Modena, as early as the mid-seventies. Marcella Hazan claims it was she who prompted Williams to do so. "I asked him, 'Chuck, why's everything French in your catalog?' and he looked at me and said, 'What is Italy?' Not the right thing, to tell me that," she says. "I had a little bottle of real *aceto balsamico* in the kitchen, and I say, 'Taste it,' and he starts asking me all these questions. Anyway, a little later, we receive the catalog, and there was *aceto balsamico.*"

Williams, for his part, recalls discovering balsamic vinegar entirely on his own, on one of his sorties to Rome in search of new products. In the food hall of a department store, he remembers seeing "these hexagonal bottles that were frosted, with '*aceto balsamico*' on them. I didn't know what it was. I'd look at it, and I'd think it looked more like hair tonic than anything else. I just sort of passed it up for a couple of years, until I asked one of the girls in the department what it was, and she told me that it was very special, how it was made and so forth. We got it in the catalog right away. It became very popular with the upscale group of customers, especially the ladies who wanted to be careful about how they eat and keep their figures. This was perfect, because you didn't need any oil with it: half of an avocado, and fill the center with balsamic."

DeLuca, too, was intrigued by the possibilities of pitching balsamic vinegar as a sort of new-wave health food. Using his father's connections, he was able to import a cheaper, lower-grade balsamic vinegar by Monari Federzoni in 1978, but he was required to buy 150 cases, a massive order; he would have preferred to take just five.

"Dean's looking at me, like 'What are you doing with 150 cases of vinegar?' " he says. "And so I called *The New York Times*, and I told 'em, 'I got balsamic vinegar, it's considered one of the finest vinegars in the world, and it's sweet, you don't need oil with it.' " The *Times* reporter, Ann Barry, dutifully wrote a four-column article about DeLuca's new featured product in the Living section (LA DOLCE VINEGAR, RICH AND ROBUST) and noted that "Its flavor, a mellow harmony of sour and sweet, is so robust that it may be used as a salad dressing in itself—a bonus for the diet-conscious."

After the *Times* article came out, Dean & DeLuca was thronged, and DeLuca's importer wanted to take back some of the Monari Federzoni cases to sell to other commercial customers. "I said, 'No way, I paid for it,' " DeLuca says. "I had a lock on something. I realized, 'I'm shopping for all these other guys'—because then, people from other stores started trying to sell what we had." DeLuca set up his own import and distribution business, serving not only Dean & DeLuca but stores and restaurants throughout the country, as well as other New York–based importing companies. In so doing, he helped broaden the reach not only of balsamic vinegar but of such Italian products as extra-virgin olive oil, the purest, richest, most labor-intensive, and lowest-acidity of olive oils. DeLuca secured an exclusive deal to represent the olive oil operations of Antinori, the Florentine wine estate.

"I was demoing Antinori olive oil in Charlotte, North Carolina," he says, "and I asked this woman if she'd ever had extra-virgin olive oil on asparagus. She said she didn't think so—because she didn't think she'd ever had asparagus. I thought, 'Oh, my God—this has gotta be a crusade!' "

The Italian food manufacturers, long accustomed to being second-class citizens to the French in the eyes of American gourmets, were so delighted with their newfound chic that DeLuca found himself being stuffed like a foie gras goose whenever he visited Italy on one of his tasting tours; everyone wanted to be the next Monari Federzoni, Antinori, or Badia a Coltibuono, another winemaker whose extra-virgin olive oil DeLuca was importing. "You'd need two assholes to keep up with how much they were feeding us for lunch, two alimentary canals," he says. "Before lunch was over, they were talking about dinner."

While in Milan, DeLuca came across some olives he liked that came in an attractive tin. Excited, he asked to be put in touch with the producer right away, so that he might secure a distribution exclusive for his importing company. A phone call was placed, and the olives' producer, Livio Crespi, agreed to meet with DeLuca as soon as he could make it to Crespi's farm, north of San Remo. That it was beginning to rain, and that the farm was reachable only via a winding, perilous drive through the mountains above the Italian Riviera, didn't deter DeLuca—he hopped into a car, drove for hours in lashing rain in the dark, and, at midnight, found Crespi standing atop a hill under an umbrella, waiting with a flashlight.

"He was this earnest man, more monkish than entrepreneur," DeLuca says. "We start to talk olives, and he says, 'I got *la bomba*. Taste these: sundried tomatoes.' He was using his olive oil to help cure and preserve them."

DeLuca, despite his Italian American background, had never heard of sun-dried tomatoes. *Pomodori secchi*, as they were known in Italy, had been around for centuries, a vestige of the days before modern canning and refrigeration, when farmers and gardeners (mostly in the south, not in Crespi's native Liguria), anticipating the winter months, would slit fresh tomatoes, dry them on roof tiles, and pack them in olive oil for later use. DeLuca was so bowled over by the flavor of the tomatoes that he made a deal with Crespi on the spot to import and distribute them in the United States.

"Giorgio brought back those San Remo sun-dried tomatoes, and Felipe Rojas-Lombardi said, 'Oh, I know those tomatoes, I had them in Italy and they're disgusting,' " says Ceglic. "But he tried Giorgio's and thought they were fabulous." The shriveled, concentrated little slices, sweet and chewy like dried fruit but with a coppery saline zing, proved to be as big a sensation in New York as balsamic vinegar. In the imitative world of food retail, it wasn't long before other stores had set up their own deals to carry particular brands of sun-dried tomatoes, balsamic vinegars, extra-virgin olive oils, and imported cheeses—and not only in New York, where Balducci's, Zabar's, and the department stores started carrying product lines similar to Dean & DeLuca's. (For a short time, Hazan had her own boutique in the Bloomingdale's food hall called Marcella Hazan's Italian Kitchen.)

In Akron, Ohio, Russ Vernon, a bespectacled, Orville Redenbacher-ish homespun second-generation grocer, reinvented the city's West Point Market—which had been founded in 1936 by his father, Slim, and two partners—as a specialty-foods wonderland. He kept a close eye on what the fancy-food shops in New York were doing, and often went beyond them in showmanship, establishing, for example, what was surely Ohio's first-ever olive-oil tasting station. In Napa Valley, the winemaker Joseph Phelps purchased the Oakville Grocery, a general store nearly a hundred years old, and made it over as a West Coast answer to Dean & DeLuca, with a similar line of imported goods to complement its local wines and cheeses.

Just as Whole Foods provided an evolutionary model for hippie food stores looking for a footing in the future, so did Dean & DeLuca and the Oakville Grocery show a way forward for outmoded greengrocers, delis, and supermarkets. Even stores whose launches postdated Dean & DeLuca—like Zingerman's, a hip Jewish deli in Ann Arbor, Michigan, that opened in 1982—essentially morphed into variations on Dean & DeLuca as they grew, with the requisite signature roast coffee, strung-up prosciuttos and Parma hams, bakery shelves groaning with artisanal breads, expansive lines of top-quality olive oils and balsamic vinegars, and super-duper cheese counters presided over by curatorial cheesemongers who wrote up fulsome descriptions of each cheese on pronged signs that were stuck directly into the cheeses displayed.

The sudden popularity of balsamic vinegar and sun-dried tomatoes in America caused a wrinkle in the cultural space-time continuum, surprising and taking aback the Italians, to whom these products were small-batch regional delicacies, not widely known even within Italy. It had never occurred to Italian people to top their pizzas with sun-dried tomatoes, or to put slivers of them in chicken-basil sausage. Authentic balsamic vinegar was used sparingly and ceremonially, not splashed indiscriminately on salads like something from a Good Seasons carafe, or used as a glazing agent on chicken and fish. The vinegar, made for centuries by wealthy families in the towns of Modena and Reggio, in the Emilia-Romagna region, was painstakingly refined and aged in a series of progressively smaller barrels, until it reached a viscous, syrupy consistency. Kept in small vials, *aceto balsamico* was doled out in eyedropper amounts, as a condiment or seasoning.*

DeLuca's balsamic vinegar from Monari Federzoni wasn't the long-aged, rarefied stuff of Modenese lore (which the company did offer at a much higher price), but it was still the real thing, aged in wood and made from trebbiano grapes. But the trendiness of balsamic vinegar in America upended the balsamic-vinegar industry in Italy, to the point where Gianni Federzoni—whose grandmother, Elena Monari Federzoni, had first started selling vinegar made according to the family's secret formula in 1912—responded to demand by building a factory in the early eighties to produce balsamic vinegar in industrial quantities, using new technologies to accelerate the process.

Other Italian companies were less scrupulous in their drive to meet consumer demand. "If you go to a restaurant now and ask for olive oil and

---

*In the old days, balsamic vinegar was even thought to have curative properties—its name derives from *balsamum*, the Latin word for the balsam tree, whose aromatic resin was used as a healing agent—and was considered so precious that vials of it were often included in the dowries of Modena brides.

balsamic vinegar for your salad, what they give you is not balsamic vinegar," says Hazan. "It's vinegar that they make with red-wine vinegar plus caramel. Balsamic vinegar, you need at least thirty, forty years to make. In Italy, only a small part of Emilia-Romagna, something like less than thirty kilometers, or twenty miles radius, knew about *aceto balsamico*. The rest of Italy didn't know. But because the Italians like to copy Americans very much, now they put it in the salads, too."

Even Hazan wasn't purist enough for Claiborne and Franey's friend Ed Giobbi, the artist and virtuoso amateur Italian cook, who cringed at her use of extra-virgin olive oil in recipes for meatballs and pan-fried steaks in her later books. "Marcella doesn't come from an olive-oil tradition," he says. "She comes from Emilia-Romagna, which is known for using lard, pork fat, butter. You shouldn't cook with the extra-virgin because it's expensive, it's too intense and fruity for sautéing, and when you heat it, it begins to deteriorate. You should use it raw, to garnish vegetables and *bollito misto*, the mixed boiled meats."

Giobbi and Claiborne had enjoyed extra-virgin olive oil in precisely this fashion when they were served a special meal of *bollito misto* at Le Cirque, the restaurant opened in 1974 by Sirio Maccioni, the former maître d' at the Colony. Maccioni had recently traveled to his native Tuscany and brought back some extra-virgin olive oil whose color Giobbi remembers as a "poisonous, beautiful green. You could see the color came just from the skin. They'd barely squeezed it." At Giobbi and Maccioni's urging, Claiborne drizzled the oil on the boiled meats in lieu of sauce, adding a little salt and pepper. "It was just divine, and Craig got it," says Giobbi.

The son of immigrants from the Marche region of Italy, on the Adriatic coast, Giobbi had grown up eating an appetizer called *pinzimonio*, which his mother prepared by simply serving raw fennel and celery stalks to be dipped in extra-virgin olive oil, salt, and ground pepper. "It was country-style eating," he says. "So was the idea of dipping bread in olive oil. When I came home from school, my mother gave me a piece of bread in olive oil. They did it that way in Italy, too, but never in restaurants." Maccioni, causing another wrinkle in the Italian culinary tradition, repurposed extra-virgin olive oil as a part of the theater of fine dining, brought out in a handsome bottle and drizzled into a shallow dish—at first only for the delectation of his favorite customers, but later as a part of every customer's dining experience. With his Tuscan connections, Maccioni always had the best oil, but, between Le Cirque and shops like Dean & DeLuca, the phrase "extra-virgin olive oil" acquired a name-drop cachet that led to the same kind of labeling abuses that bedeviled balsamic vinegar; sleazy companies started selling inferior olive oil, sometimes even blended with other vegetable oils, as "extra-virgin."

If Giobbi is especially sensitive to issues of purism and authenticity where Italian cuisine is concerned, it's because he was a central player in the pasta primavera craze that began to spread through the United States in the late seventies. "Pasta primavera, I don't know what it is anymore," he says, shaking his head in disgust. "It's junk food in this country."

Giobbi's initial connection to Maccioni was Le Cirque's original chef, Jean Vergnes—like Maccioni, a graduate of the Colony—who the artist had gotten to know from their frequent marathon cooking sessions with Franey, Jacques Pépin, and Roger Fessaguet at Claiborne's East Hampton house. Vergnes, a middle-aged Frenchman of the old school, and Maccioni, suaver, younger, slicker, and *molto Italiano*, were poorly matched partners from the get-go. One of the issues that they fought over was Maccioni's insistence that there be a pasta dish on Le Cirque's otherwise Francocentric menu. As Giobbi tells the story, Vergnes and Maccioni paid a visit to his rustic kitchen in a rural section of Katonah, New York, to feel him out on ideas for a pasta recipe that would work at Le Cirque.

"I made about three or four different pasta recipes, and one was pasta primavera, which I used to eat in Florence when I was a student," Giobbi says. " 'Primavera' means 'springtime.' It was a strictly seasonal dish. You got it in May and June, when the first tomatoes came in in late spring. It was made with chopped raw tomatoes, chopped garlic, basil, and extra-virgin olive oil, served on spaghettini. That was it. I made it at home, but I pureed it and made it into a sauce. I served that to Sirio and Jean, and they loved it." Giobbi recalls that initially, Maccioni simply asked that pignoli, or pine nuts, be added to his recipe, and it became an off-menu special at Le Cirque. But pasta primavera mutated rapidly and caused great controversy in Vergnes's French kitchen, which makes the truth about its origins difficult to divine. Vergnes confirms that he and Maccioni ventured out to Katonah to taste Giobbi's recipe, but he remembers chunks of vegetables in the sauce, "asparagus and everything."

"I tasted it and got to thinking, in Provence they have fresh vegetables in the spring, too," he says. Working with his Franco-Italian sous-chef, Jean-Louis Todeschini, Vergnes recalls "putting in a bit of mushroom, a bit of peas, string beans, broccoli, and, for Sirio, the pignoli. And I called it not 'pasta primavera' but 'spaghetti *au premier Provençal*'—'*au premier*' meaning the first new vegetables of spring, in the style of Provence. Later, I started to put in a little bit of cream, but just a little, to make the texture much more smooth. And I put in a little bit of Gruyère, but not that much. And Sirio, he said, 'No, no, no, *tsk, tsk, tsk*, no Gruyère—Parmesan cheese!' "

Maccioni, meanwhile, tells an elaborate story of a springtime trip to Canada in the mid-seventies that he took with his wife, Egidiana, and Vergnes, Claiborne, and the Franeys. The group was staying in a remote Nova Scotia estate borrowed from a rich Italian of Maccioni's acquaintance. One cold day, Maccioni maintains, Egidiana threw together a pasta meal based on what was in the cupboards and the freezer, using frozen peas, mushrooms, garlic, a tomato, cream, and Parmesan, with no olive oil whatsoever. "When I came back to New York," he writes in his memoir, *Sirio*, "we worked on the recipe a bit, but not very much, and we served it in the restaurant. It was not on the menu, but people liked it, and it took off."

Maccioni maintains that Vergnes and the French chefs who followed him were so contemptuous of the idea of pasta in their kitchens that he prepared the dish himself, abetted by his waitstaff. "We put a pan of hot water in the corridor and cooked the pasta there and finished it in the dining room," he says. The New York chef Geoffrey Zakarian, who worked at Le Cirque early in his career, lent some credibility to Maccioni's version in an interview for Maccioni's memoir, recalling that Vergnes and his successor, Alain Sailhac, loathed pasta primavera, and that "We had to prep it in this dingy back part of that awful kitchen, and then it was all put together in the dining room."

Whatever the truth was, "spaghetti primavera," as it was then called, became Le Cirque's most talked-about, widely imitated menu item. In October of 1977, Maccioni and Vergnes made nice for the benefit of Claiborne and Franey's recipe column in *The New York Times Magazine*, preparing the dish together in Claiborne's East Hampton kitchen and posing, all smiles, for the paper's photographer. In his write-up, Claiborne described spaghetti primavera as "an inspired blend of pasta and crisp, tender vegetables, such as zucchini and mushrooms and broccoli and green beans, plus cheese, cream, and toasted pine nuts. These are tossed hot and crowned with a delicate fresh tomato sauce." The recipe that followed called not only for these ingredients but also for chopped chilies, basil leaves, asparagus, and chicken broth.

Just a few weeks earlier, Mimi Sheraton had devastated Maccioni and Vergnes by subtracting one and a half stars from the two-and-a-half-star rating that John Canaday had given Le Cirque shortly after its opening. In her review, Sheraton cited spaghetti primavera confusion as one of the reasons for the demotion. "Spaghetti primavera, not on the menu, but one of the best house specials . . . is another dish that varies," she wrote. "One night the spaghetti, though slightly undersalted, came with a satiny rich sauce of consommé, cream, and cheese that bound bits of vegetables such as zucchini, mushrooms, flowerets of broccoli, peas, string beans, and lightly sautéed diced tomatoes together, all with a few pignoli nuts included for a bit of crunch. But at lunch, we detected neither cream nor cheese—just butter and consommé, although the management insisted the sauce was made as always."

Claiborne and Franey's column might well have been conceived in riposte to Sheraton's review. "Craig hated Mimi Sheraton, and she hated him," says Gelb. "There was constant friction. I had my hands full trying to work out the animosities between them."

Giobbi, for his part, was more miffed than anything that Sheraton would presume to be an authority on spaghetti primavera. "Mimi Sheraton was physically very unattractive, and Sirio was this handsome, elegant man, and she just had it in for him and Le Cirque," he says. "Sirio told me, 'She was leaving the restaurant Monday, she had pasta primavera, and as she walked out she said, "You didn't put enough cream in the pasta primavera sauce." ' Like she knew what the original recipe was supposed to be!"

"There was another incident," Giobbi says, "where Jane Brody wrote a book where she had pasta primavera. She told a story about how she went home from work and didn't know what to cook, so she opened up the vegetable bin in her refrigerator and found all the different vegetables—a little bit of cabbage, a little bit of this—and made the best pasta primavera sauce she ever tasted. The point is, these people didn't do their homework. I think it's fine to be inventive with a recipe, but I hate it when they don't take the trouble to find out what the original recipe is."

STILL, THE VERY FACT that a pasta dish could get attention at a French restaurant, and that Americans were willing to veer away from their old red-sauce preconceptions of spaghetti, augured well for Italian cooking in the United States. For too long, non-Italians had been constricted by the misperception of "Italian food" as an oversauced bowl of spaghetti with a giant meatball on top. This, in fact, was not Italian food but Sicilian immigrant food, concocted on American shores. It wasn't even representative of the best kitchens in Sicily; whereas a great many Frenchmen immigrated to New York for the express purpose of working in restaurant kitchens, the Sicilians who came over to New York in large numbers in the late nineteenth and early twentieth centuries were by and large poor laborers and tradesmen who were making do with the cheap ingredients available to them.

"It wasn't all bad, pizzas and macaroni and eggplant Parmesan," says Giorgio DeLuca, "but Americans didn't know about the aristocratic jewels of Italian cuisine, like fine balsamic vinegar, white truffles, porcini mushrooms. We were helping people realize the potential of Italian food." Le Cirque further contributed to this cause by introducing New York to radicchio, a beautiful, carefully cultivated variety of chicory with wine-red leaves and white veins. Maccioni started importing radicchio from Treviso, in the northeastern region of Italy called Veneto, in the mid-seventies. He was so pleased with his first batch that he took to displaying the red bunches of leaves, still in their shipping crates, in the dining room. "Within six months," says Giobbi, "every three- and four-star restaurant in New York had radicchio on the menu."

Within a few years, radicchio was making its way down and across the interstates. "I think the most impressed I ever was by the filtering-down effect was when I went to Atlantic City, because they always had the worst food there," said Dean. "I went to this hotel restaurant about five years after we opened, and they had radicchio in their salad. I was like, '*Jesus Christ!* I don't believe it!' "

With its slightly bitter taste and brilliant color, radicchio was excellent simply grilled and anointed with a drop of *aceto balsamico*. It was also wonderful raw in a salad, especially as a complement and counterpoint to another leafy vegetable popular in Italy, *ruchetta*, a peppery-tasting green with small, rounded leaves. *Ruchetta* was familiar to the surprisingly salad-forward English as rocket, but in the United States, where bland iceberg lettuce had long held sway, the green was variously described by excited seventies food writers as rucola, roquette, and rugola before a consensus emerged that "arugula" would be the standard designation. Arugula was a labor-intensive green, grown in loamy, gritty soil that took several washings to get off its leaves, but American chefs fell in love with its piquancy. It soon became de rigueur for any Italian restaurant with serious aspirations to offer a "tricolore salad" that, in homage to the flag of Italy, mixed arugula not only with radicchio, but with white spears of Belgian endive.

As the popularity of such exotic produce as Treviso radicchio and French mâche boomed, it dawned on Dean, DeLuca, and Ceglic that they could probably save a lot of money, and make a lot of money, by cultivating these greens in the United States. "We smuggled in some radicchio seeds from Italy and gave 'em to this farmer in Pennsylvania," said Dean. "And it all came up green." The Dean & DeLuca farming operation didn't work out, but other Europhile seed smugglers, from Deborah Madison to Ed Giobbi (who had been growing radicchio for his own personal use since the sixties), were cultivating these plants with success. "Radicchio *does* come up tall and green the first time you plant it, and the leaves are quite bitter once they're big," Giobbi explains. "But then a second growth comes up in late February. See, you have to give the plant a chance to establish a tap root. Then, after the root is set up the first year, it produces the bud, and you harvest the bud before it opens. Every year, I clear away the snow in late winter to find that all these beautiful purple buds have come up. Unfortunately, the damned woodchucks ate all of it last year."

THE BREADTH AND VARIETY of the Italian foodstuffs that Americans were getting excited about gave lie to the very idea of "Italian food," which turned out to be something of a phony construct. Italy, in truth, was a country predicated more on regional identities than a national one—people, and cuisines, were Bolognese, or Tuscan, or Neapolitan. It was a credit to Marcella Hazan that her book *The Classic Italian Cook Book* and its 1978 sequel, *More Classic Italian Cooking*, managed not only to expose Americans to a world beyond spaghetti and meatballs and Mama Leone's–style tourist-trap restaurants ("I hate when they say '*Mangia, mangia!*'" Hazan says) but also to assimilate these regional cuisines into a coherent, user-friendly body of work.

As the "Julia Child of Italian cooking," Hazan became quite friendly with the real Julia, who, with Paul Child, visited Hazan and her husband, Victor, at the cooking school the Hazans operated for part of the year in Bologna, servicing a mostly American clientele. But Hazan maintains that Child was uneasy with the new reverence for Italian cooking, considering it simply not as worthy of respect as France's. "I heard Julia say, 'That is enough to read about pasta,'" Hazan says, alluding to Child's response to her books.

But then, Hazan is every bit as prejudiced in favor of Italian food, especially where adaptability to American tastes is concerned. "I think the Italian food is not so complicated, like the French is," she says. "I remember, once I did a [French] recipe with Julia, some kind of lamb. It took me all morning—'Add this and this and this.' The Italians, we don't have many recipes like this. You can make a meal in half an hour if you want to. And it's food that you eat with pleasure, without thinking too much. You don't have to analyze it, you just enjoy that it's so. It's *easy*."

CHAPTER EIGHT

CALIFORNIA
NOUVELLE

These days, the focal point of culinary innovation in California has shifted from San Francisco to Los Angeles, where foods are combined with wild abandon.

—Marian Burros, *The New York Times*, 1984

IN A SLOW NEWS PERIOD IN THE SUMMER OF 1975, *NEWSWEEK* DECIDED TO TAKE stock of all the fun and ferment in the American food world with a cover story entitled "Food: The New Wave." A prime example of the burgeoning "lifestyle" genre of journalism—indeed, the magazine ran the story under the rubric "Life/Style"—the article declared, "In a burst of new interest in food, U.S. chefs and home cooks are grappling with today's mounting concern for health, lower calories, and higher nutrition. Americans are demanding—and paying for—the freshest and least chemically treated products available. The new gusto for experimenting with food . . . stretches from the back-to-basics passion for organically grown vegetables to a boom in arcane $190 food processors, from a surge in restaurants stressing regional Yankee cookery to cooking schools of every conceivable ethnic persuasion."

The article noted that the Culinary Institute of America, which had relocated in 1972 from New Haven, Connecticut, to Hyde Park, New York, had seen a dramatic upsurge in enrollment, with 3,430 students in 1975, compared to just 1,590 students five years earlier. Also mentioned was a fast-growing kitchenwares and home-furnishings chain in the Chicago area called Crate and Barrel, whose owner, Gordon Segal, sensed an "increased seriousness about food" among his customers, and a bustling midtown Manhattan restaurant called La Potagerie that was devoted exclusively to soups—

PAGE 231: *Wolfgang Puck (center) trades the toque for a baseball cap at his new restaurant, Spago, in 1983.*

though *Newsweek* didn't note that La Potagerie's chef-owner was Jacques Pépin,* who had emerged from Pierre Franey's shadow to become one of America's most in-demand cooking teachers; nor was the magazine aware of the imminent publication of Pépin's *La Technique*, a groundbreaking, photo-illustrated book in which the author taught his readers the fundamentals of professional kitchen methodology, from how to hold a chopping knife to how to tie a roast.

As for those "arcane" food processors, they were anything but. Earlier that year, in *The New York Times Magazine*, Craig Claiborne and Pierre Franey had hailed the advent of the Cuisinart, the brand name by which these machines went, as an invention that, "in the minds of serious cooks, ranks with that of the printing press, cotton gin, steamboat, paper clips, Kleenex, wastebaskets, contour sheets, and disposable diapers." Though its price was steep, the Cuisinart caused elbows-out battles among customers in the first two shops that carried it, Bloomingdale's in New York and Williams-Sonoma in San Francisco. Chuck Williams admits that he didn't initially realize the food processor's potential as a home appliance. At a European kitchenwares expo in the early seventies, he'd seen a sophisticated industrial blender called Le Magimix that could slice and puree vegetables with dispatch. "It would've needed a whole new electrical underwiring system to work in this country, and a whole new motor, too, so I never thought there was anything we could do about it," he says. However, a retired, MIT-educated engineer and cook-ing enthusiast named Carl Sontheimer was at the same expo. An inveterate tinkerer, he purchased a Magimix, took it back to his Connecticut home, and made precisely the adjustments that Williams describes. He obtained a license from the machine's manufacturer, a French company called Robot Coupe, to sell the modified machines under the name Cuisinart.

The media-savvy Sontheimer demonstrated his machine for James

---

*Years ahead of Al Yeganeh, the irritable maestro immortalized in *Seinfeld*'s "Soup Nazi" episode, Pépin was dishing out dazzlingly inventive soups-as-meals, among them a creamy veal goulash with spaetzle, a bouillabaisse with saffron, and even a breakfast soup made from oatmeal, chicken stock, leeks, and bacon crumblings.

Beard, who put Sontheimer in touch with Williams and other retailers. With the gushing endorsements of Beard, Claiborne, and Franey—the latter two of whom marveled in the *Times Magazine* over the Cuisinart's ability to make "a devastatingly good guacamole" (using Diana Kennedy's recipe from *The Cuisines of Mexico*); to shred "50 pounds of cabbage into the base for sauerkraut, one of the most tedious of things to do, in what could be reckoned in minutes"; and to "grind to a fine purée fish such as salmon, pike, or sole for such dishes as mousse of fish or pike quenelles," a task that used to require Franey to "pound the fish fine, then laboriously push it through a hair sieve"—the upwardly mobile home cook needed little persuading to buy the contraption. Like Italian balsamic vinegar and sun-dried tomatoes, the French-designed food processor became far more popular in the United States than in its land of origin, where chefs and *mamans* remained wary of violating kitchen traditions with *électronique* equipment. Even in earth-toned Berkeley, Gene Opton found that Cuisinarts flew out of her little shop, the Kitchen. "The Birkenstock trade were horrified at something over a hundred dollars," she says, "but it was probably the first time that people were enthusiastic over something not only because it was a useful piece of equipment but because it was a gleam-in-your-eye kind of thing. Like the Sub-Zero fridge is now, but not quite as foolish."

Newsweek may have been heralding a "new wave" in American appreciation of food, but its cover subject, in his toque and whites, with pots, pans, and strung-up lobsters surrounding him, looked for all the world like a central-casting French chef—which, in a sense, he was. Paul Bocuse, then forty-nine years old, had apprenticed under Fernand Point at La Pyramide and was now running his own eponymous restaurant, rated three stars in *Le guide Michelin*, in a small town just north of Lyons. Tall and calculatedly imposing—he modeled himself on Point, who he admiringly described as "a little mean," and dismissed the notion of women in professional kitchens by saying, "The only place for them is in bed"—Bocuse was the great and feared Oz to gourmets, "indisputably the most famous chef in the world," as Claiborne wrote. Yet he was at the forefront of a progressive movement that, in some intellectual quarters of France, was regarded as the culinary analogue to the French New Wave film movement that produced the directors François Truffaut, Jean-Luc Godard, and Eric Rohmer. He was the face of nouvelle cuisine.

In 1969, with France still in the grips of the revolutionary spirit fomented by the previous year's student riots and corresponding labor strikes, the journalists Henri Gault and Christian Millau founded a magazine called *Le nouveau guide*—a *Cahiers du cinéma* for insurgent foodies—whose debut issue featured the cover line MICHELIN: DON'T FORGET THESE 48 STARS! The "stars" in question were relatively unknown chefs who didn't warrant the attention of the "establishment" restaurant guide, which the tire company Michelin had been publishing for seven decades. The idea was that Michelin awarded *its* stars to stodgy places that hewed closely to Escoffier and masked the flavors of meat, fish, and vegetables with heavy sauces and overcooking. Bocuse, who had been running his own restaurant since 1962, was as highly Michelin-rated as chefs came, but, like Point, he regarded his classicist training as a springboard from which to invent, not an orthodoxy to which he had to rigidly adhere. He told *Newsweek* that he had admired the way Point violated traditionalist code by barely cooking his green beans, serving them crunchy "because his instinct told him they were better that way."

Gault and Millau lionized Bocuse and such contemporaries as Roger Vergé, Michel Guérard, Alain Chapel, Georges Blanc, Louis Outhier, and the brothers Jean and Pierre Troisgros as avatars of France's new, improved restaurant cookery. In 1972, *Le nouveau guide* ran a manifesto, immodestly entitled "The Ten Commandments of Nouvelle Cuisine," in which Gault and Millau set out to codify what they were talking about. The first commandment was "Reject unnecessarily complex preparations," and the second was "Reduce cooking times." Like any dogmatists, Gault and Millau made up some rules that bordered on the nonsensical; Commandment Five, for example, forbade marinades and the hanging of game, on the grounds that "marinating meat hides its taste," and that "if game is hung at all it should only be for a very short time, otherwise its flavor is altered and an undesirable fermentation begins"—never mind that this fermentation is precisely what many game aficionados are after. But the two men played an important role in bringing attention to these chefs, and, indeed, in making them aware of one another—all the more so when the crusading journalists spun off an annual guidebook from their magazine called *Le guide Gault-Millau*, a pithier, wackier, more descriptive reference than *Le guide Michelin*.*

In the years since the early seventies, nouvelle cuisine's identity has been so distorted and misunderstood that to many in the food community, the movement is a joke. Nora Ephron calls it a phony trend fabricated by Yanou Collart, Bocuse's and Vergé's aggressive Frenchwoman publicist, who became chummy with Claiborne and arranged junkets in which American food writers such as Ephron and *Town & Country*'s James Villas were whisked from one elaborate Gault-Millau-ratified meal to another. Bocuse himself has cracked that even he has no idea what the term "nouvelle cuisine" really means. But in the movement's early years, at least, the term was genuinely useful in describing the cookery of French chefs who, while not outright rejecting the precepts of Escoffier, had the temerity to lighten their recipes, flash-cook fish, use more vegetable juices and stocks, and plan menus according to season rather than to the dictates of grand-hotel dining tradition.

Contrary to widespread popular belief, nouvelle cuisine was not dietetic and low-cal, except in the case of Guérard's *cuisine minceur*, which was explicitly conceived as a slimming cuisine (*minceur* means "leanness"), since Guérard operated his restaurant out of a spa in the Pyrenees called Les Prés et les Sources d'Eugénie. While Guérard was experimenting with fat-free offerings like aubergine puree infused with saffron steam, Bocuse's signature

---

*Gault and Millau's 1981 *Guide to New York*, their first foray into the New World, intended for the eyes of their countrymen and written in French, reads like absurdist comic literature. New York, they wrote, is "beautiful and hideous, tender and violent, generous and greedy, fascinating and horrifying." Visiting it, they promised their fellow Frenchmen, will be "more than a simple tourist trip, it will be a decisive stage in your maturation." Grazing their way around town, Gault and Millau had high praise for the Four Seasons and Lutèce, but were disappointed by the famous hamburger at P. J. Clarke's, which they pronounced "both cooked to death and cold and even an English dog would not want to eat it."

dish was *loup de mer en croûte*, fish stuffed with lobster mousse, encased in a labor-intensive pastry shell that visually reproduced the fish's scales, and served with Choron sauce, essentially a hollandaise tinted pink by the addition of pureed tomato. Bocuse justified this dish's nouvelle-ness to *Newsweek* by noting that the fish itself had been cooked for just two minutes under high heat rather than slow-braised.

Culinarily, nouvelle cuisine's most significant across-the-board departure was its general avoidance of flour as a binding agent for sauces. Flour, and not butter, was what gave the white béchamel and brown *espagnole* sauces of Carême and Escoffier their opaque quality and heavy texture. The nouvelle crew, with their emphasis on "letting the ingredients taste like what they are," were more inclined to deglaze a pan in which meat had been cooked with some liquid (such as water, wine, or vegetable stock), and then swirl in some butter or cream, resulting in a light sauce that complemented, rather than masked, the flavor of the main ingredient. Julia Child, in a curious comment in the *Newsweek* article, said that the French chefs had "finally gotten it through their thick heads that there are some people who don't want to be stuffed full of fat and truffles," but she rather missed the point.* The nouvelle-ists were not against calories or decadence per se—Bocuse was also famous for his truffle soup, which Jeremiah Tower, America's Mr. Extravagance, re-created for one of his New Year's bashes at Chez Panisse—but against a French cuisine they felt had grown leaden, gloopy, and uninspired.

The excitement over nouvelle cuisine reverberated well beyond the circles of traveling businessmen who could afford $300 meals, inspiring many a young American and European to seek out the opportunity to *stage* in the kitchens of Gault and Millau's favorite chefs. By the eighties, when these youngsters came of age and assumed command of their own kitchens, Americans began to feel the full force of the nouvelle movement. Hubert Keller

---

*Child's "thick heads" comment was all the more strange since she was more responsible than anyone else for the propensity among status-seeking Americans to stuff themselves full of fat and truffles. Perhaps this was her way of expressing her disdain for Bocuse, whose sexism and roving eye she deplored.

(of San Francisco's Fleur de Lys) and Daniel Boulud (of New York's Le Cirque and then his own Daniel), both Frenchmen, trained under Vergé in the seventies at his Le Moulin de Mougins restaurant on the Côte d'Azur, as did David Bouley (of Montrachet and then Bouley), a son of Rhode Island; Keller and Bouley also logged time working in Bocuse's kitchen. Larry Forgione (of New York's River Café and An American Place) was slated to work for Guérard in the mid-seventies but was rebuffed by the French government "because by that point," he says, "there was a big crackdown on non–French apprentices. French apprentices were complaining that they couldn't get work in the better kitchens because there were so many Americans and Japanese."* Forgione settled for a *stage* in London's Connaught hotel, whose kitchen, he says, was then going through a "borderline nouvelle cuisine" phase.

Judy Rodgers, on the other hand, the future star of San Francisco's Zuni Café, ended up spending her senior year of high school living in the Hôtel Troisgros in Roanne—home to the three-star Les Frères Troisgros restaurant—through sheer happenstance. In 1973, a businessman neighbor of her family's in St. Louis who frequently lodged at chez Troisgros when his work took him to France—"like you'd stay in Hampton Suites," she says—mentioned to Rodgers's parents that Jean Troisgros was interested in sending his teenage daughter to America to learn English in an exchange program. Rodgers ended up being the other half of the exchange. An indifferent eater up to that point, Rodgers was transformed into a food person by

---

*Daniel Boulud credits the Japanese with creating a market for lucrative consultancy positions for name French chefs. "In the seventies," he says, "the biggest group we had, in terms of wanting to learn the movement of France, was the Japanese. Every kitchen had two or three Japanese cooks inside, and Bocuse and other big chefs were spending a lot of time in cooking schools in Japan. It was very interesting and very strange." Indeed, Bocuse supplemented his income handsomely by teaching at a hotel school in Osaka, and in the early seventies was already a partner in Tokyo's Renga-Ya restaurant. The crucial difference between the Japanese and American apprentices, Boulud says, is that "the Japanese learned, went home, and then replicated the French cooking, whereas I think for the Americans it was more about getting an understanding and then creating their own thing."

her long hours in the company of her host dad, Jean Troisgros, who christened his sixteen-year-old guest Mata Hari, and, in Henry Higgins fashion, educated the young lady about fresh ingredients, the glory of simplicity, and the *batterie de cuisine*.*

"The first thing I ever tried to cook, the summer after I got home from France, was Jean's little salad of green beans," Rodgers says. "Just little velvety green beans coated with a little crème fraîche, and he would put little ribbons of champignons de Paris [button mushrooms] in it. It was one of my favorite things at Troisgros, an absolute home run with the bases loaded. I thought, 'Heck, I can make this.' But I found out that I wasn't gonna find these ingredients in St. Louis in 1974. The green beans in the supermarket in St. Louis were like Lincoln Logs. And I made the salad, and it was just dreadful. I'd heard all year at Troisgros, 'It's the ingredients, it's the ingredients'—and I'd violated that."

But in Los Angeles, where quality ingredients were easier to come by, the nouvelle ethos took hold much earlier. Among its early champions was the chef Jean Bertranou, who ran two of the best French restaurants in the city, La Chaumière, which opened in 1965, and his masterwork, L'Ermitage, which he opened a decade later. Bertranou is something of a forgotten figure now, having died of a brain tumor in 1980, when he was only fifty years old, but he is the unsung hero of the LA restaurant scene, the man who pushed the city toward gastronomic credibility. The food journalist Colman Andrews, eulogizing Bertranou in *New West* magazine a few weeks after his death, credited the chef with fostering "the beginnings of a whole new restaurant community, French and otherwise."

Though his early career in the United States saw him cooking in places where the quality of the food was an afterthought—he seemed to be following Frank Sinatra's restaurant-going trajectory, working at El Morocco in

---

*The Troisgros brothers were the nouvelle chefs hippest to the possibilities of American food. Not only did Pierre send his son Michel to work at Chez Panisse, but Rodgers recalls that Jean adored McDonald's french fries "back when they were cooked in beef tallow."

New York, followed by the Hollywood hangout Ciro's, followed by the Sultan's Table at the Dunes hotel in Las Vegas—Bertranou kept abreast of what was going on in his native France and was inspired to rescue LA from its gastronomic hick-town status. "It's still cowboy country," he complained to *Los Angeles* magazine in 1972. "Everybody wants the duckling crisp, like plywood. Duck should be moist, and pink inside." Sounding downright Beardian, Bertranou lamented the obliviousness of Angelenos to the excellent seafood they had right under their noses: "There's good fish here. Fresh salmon from the northwest, sand dabs, corvina, and Pacific lobster which is in season from the fifteenth of September to the fifteenth of March."

In 1975, Bertranou launched L'Ermitage, which, despite its location on a trafficked stretch of La Cienega Boulevard, he likened to Vergé's Le Moulin de Mougins.* His operative words were "light" and "clean." There were lots of fish entrées in flourless sauces, such as poached salmon covered in a mousseline of sole (a fish sauce with whipped cream beaten into it to lighten the texture) and complemented by a beurre rouge that was nothing more than a reduction of vinegar, red wine, butter, and herbs. Bertranou even reconceived the most colon-punishing of Escoffier classics, veal chops Prince Orloff, as a lighter dish, forgoing the traditional heavy Mornay sauce and mountains of truffles in favor of a thin layer of duxelles and a restrained soubise of cream and pureed onions.

Among Bertranou's friends and admirers in his L'Ermitage days were two young fellows on the make in the LA restaurant scene: an Austrian named Wolfgang Puck, and a rich kid from Westchester County in New York named Michael McCarty. Both were indebted to Bertranou for his cooking guidance and his sourcing of ingredients. With McCarty, who went on to open the Santa Monica restaurant Michael's in 1979, Bertranou even formed a partnership to raise ducks he called "mullards," lean, flavorful hybrids of the Pekin and Muscovy breeds. "We had an enormous duck farm in

---

*Vergé's restaurant was so named—*moulin* means "mill"—because it was on the site of a sixteenth-century olive-oil mill.

Acton, California, which was known as the crystal-meth capital," says Mc-Carty. "There were lilacs, there was our duck farm, and then there were, every so often, in the far desert, these little explosions."

As for Puck, he arrived in Los Angeles in 1975, right at the moment when L'Ermitage was taking off—a circumstance that gave him hope just as he was beginning to doubt the wisdom of his move to the United States. The Austrian had come to New York in 1973, when he was twenty-four years old, after stints at L'Oustau de Baumanière, a resort in Provence, and the famous Maxim's in Paris. He bounded into Manhattan with high hopes and a promise, through the French-chef grapevine, that a good job awaited him in the big city. But this job turned out to be at La Goulue, the ladies-who-lunch bistro on Madison Avenue. Puck, affronted, rejected the assignment. "I hadn't gone to France and worked in all these great restaurants to do bistro food," he says.

He next tried to secure a position at La Grenouille. The restaurant's owner, Charles Masson, had no openings, but he took pity on Puck, and, through a friend of a friend, found an opening at an upscale French restaurant in Indianapolis. Puck, who adored auto racing, was naïve enough to expect that the city, since it was the home of the Indy 500, would be somewhat like Monte Carlo, where he had also worked. After a restless, lonely period in Hoosierland, Puck agitated for and got a job at a middling French restaurant in downtown Los Angeles that was owned by Davre, the same company as the Indianapolis place.

That Puck had even willed himself to LA was an index of how far he'd come from his unhappy childhood in Austria. His parents divorced when he was two, and when he was fourteen, he was put on a train from his hometown of Klagenfurt to another town where he was to apprentice in a hotel kitchen. The petrified, diminutive Puck, who looked even younger than he was, had been working at the hotel a few days, peeling potatoes and chopping onions, when the chef told him to beat it. In a form of verbal abuse evidently endemic to Austria, the chef belittled young Wolf as a girlie-man, telling him, "You'd better go home to your mother so she can breast-feed you for another year." It was a form of hazing, more of a test than an order, but the sensitive Puck was devastated and spent several hours that day on a bridge in the town, gloomily contemplating jumping off.

Yet Puck realized that he enjoyed cooking, if not authoritarian Austrian chefs. He persevered, moving to France to begin his apprenticeship in earnest. Compared to his teen years, the situation in Los Angeles was not so dire, and when he learned that a restaurateur named Patrick Terrail was looking for a chef at his West Hollywood bistro Ma Maison, Puck saw it as a ripe opportunity. Terrail, a tall, dapper man with a chipmunk face and a carnation in his lapel, came from restaurant royalty. His uncle Claude was the proprietor of La Tour d'Argent, the fine-dining palace on the banks of the Seine, and his great-grandfather, Claudius Burdel, ran the Café Anglais, among the poshest of Paris's nineteenth-century restaurants. But Ma Maison was not remotely in his forebears' league—it was a homely place in a stucco house on a dingy commercial stretch of Melrose Avenue that had only just begun to revive under the aegis of pioneering gallery owners and gay men who were opening up boutiques and antique shops.

Terrail had bounced from job to job in the hospitality industry, working for a time under Joe Baum at Restaurant Associates in New York—"I started out as assistant receiving steward, which meant I was counting eggs," he says—and then running hotels in Africa and Tahiti. He finally settled on Los Angeles as his home and opened Ma Maison with seed money from Hollywood people, including Gene Kelly, who had dined at his uncle's place while filming *An American in Paris*. But Terrail's budget was skimpy—Kelly's contribution was a mere $5,000—and the thrift-shop tables were set with secondhand china and silverware. The outdoor patio's famous Astroturf carpeting, which became an emblem of Ma Maison's reverse chic, was a simple matter of budgetary expediency. "It was a question of recementing the whole floor, which I couldn't afford, or going out and buying $600 worth of Astroturf," says Terrail. "Then we realized there was something good about the Astroturf—it absorbed sound, and you could hose it down. Though we did change it every August."

Ma Maison opened in 1973 to what Terrail calls "the most terrible reviews in the history of the restaurant business." After two years of struggle, he realized that the bistro menu wasn't going to cut it, and he contacted an acquaintance at Maxim's in Paris to see if he had any chef recommendations. The acquaintance recommended two ex-Maxim's staffers, Puck and another cook, Guy Leroy, who were both working in the same Los Angeles restaurant. Terrail hired both Puck and Leroy, though it was the former who emerged as the star. "One day, at the other place where I was working, the manager wrote out a new menu and told me to cook it, and I gave him my apron," says Puck. "I said, 'You know what? If you write the menu, why don't you just cook it, too?' I knew at Ma Maison I could do whatever I wanted, cooking-wise. It looked like a dump, but I could cook exactly the way I wanted."

Right away, Puck unleashed his French training on Ma Maison. In homage to Terrail's heritage, he served *canard Tour d'Argent*, the Paris restaurant's famous duck served in two courses: first, the breast covered in a sauce *au sang*, thickened with the bird's blood, and then, the duck's legs, simply broiled. In homage to Paul Bocuse, Puck served fish *en croûte*.

"It was an interesting contrast," Puck says, "because the quality of the food was as good as anywhere, but you had plastic chairs and Astroturf, and artists like Bob Rauschenberg and David Hockney coming in from across the street with paint all over their shoes." He reckons that the lunchtime business nearly tripled over his first three months at Ma Maison. Before long, the movie and TV people started to come. Orson Welles installed himself at a table in the back, where he could be found almost daily until the end of his life, and Ma Maison became a regular haunt of the establishment players—Michael Caine; David Janssen, Jack Lemmon, Ed McMahon, Bob Newhart; the agent Greg Bautzer; the studio executives Sherry Lansing and David Begelman—as well as the body-wave glamour gals of the *Knots Landing* era, among them Loni Anderson, Jacqueline Bisset, Joan Collins, Morgan Fairchild, Donna Mills, Suzanne Somers, and Alana Stewart.

Terrail, a born showman, fussed over the star clientele and had his valets park the flashiest cars—the Rolls-Royces and Bentleys—in the spaces directly in front of the restaurant, rather than in a lot around the corner. Ostensibly, this was so his staff could keep an eye on the expensive cars, but really, it was Robin Leach–style public relations for Ma Maison (where, indeed, the assaultively loud *Lifestyles of the Rich and Famous* host was among the most loyal customers). Ma Maison also introduced the concept of the coveted unlisted phone number, though Terrail insists this came about by accident. *People* magazine, he says, was supposed to run a story on the restaurant just as he was leaving for a vacation; not wanting to overburden his staff with the excessive call volume that the article's publication would surely bring, he had Ma Maison's number removed from the phone-company directory. But the article was delayed, and Terrail forgot to have the listing reinstated, inadvertently making knowledge of the number (for the record, it was 213-655-1991) an insiderist status symbol among LA's showbiz kids.

Terrail further embraced two terms that made more skeptical food people recoil, "California cuisine," which he'd heard in reference to Chez Panisse, and the ubiquitous "nouvelle cuisine." Combining the two, he declared Ma Maison to be "California nouvelle." "I thought, 'What the hell, why not?'" he says. "Because we're using California ingredients, but we're also doing a version of the cuisine of the sun, *la cuisine du soleil*, which is what Roger Vergé was calling his cooking in Provence. I strongly believed in the phrase and promoted it."

Terrail also claims to have been the pioneer in popularizing that most Californian of beverage trends, bottled water. "We were the first people to serve Perrier water—in California, anyway," he says. "Flat water was not the first popular water, Perrier was. Because of the health-conscious attitude of Californians, it became kind of fashionable to say, 'Gimme a Perrier and lemon,' or 'Gimme a Perrier spritzer,' which was really just Perrier with a little bit of white wine for flavor. From the restaurant's standpoint, it was kind of cool, because we were selling it for $3.95 a bottle."*

---

*Perrier, based in France, started selling to the American market in 1976. By 1988, it accounted for 80 percent of the imported water sold in the United States, but its market share suffered significantly two years later, when traces of benzene, a carcinogen, were found in bottles of its water, prompting a massive recall. One result of the recall was an uptick in the popularity of a rival sparkling water, San Pellegrino, from the Italian Alps. Since the 1990s, both Perrier and San Pellegrino have been owned by Nestlé.

The food press rallied around Ma Maison, too, retracting its earlier condemnations, with the *Los Angeles Times* going so far as to proclaim, "Ma Maison not only has found its way to go, but has gone further than intended . . . Patrick Terrail's destiny caught up with him in the person of his chef, Wolfgang Puck." But the ambitious Puck and the vain Terrail were not destined to co-exist for long. "In a way, Patrick never trusted me," says Puck. "He never let me sign the checks—he got all nervous about it, because one time, he went away on vacation, and I thought, 'I can't serve food on this old, gray, secondhand china,' so I ordered new china. Also, I was looking around at what was happening in Napa, San Francisco, Berkeley, and I thought we had to change our approach and do more in the style of Italy and Nice—where we'd have some raviolis, maybe some pizzas."

Terrail balked at Puck's suggestions, so the chef started laying the groundwork for his own place, which he was going to call Spago. Puck chose an Italian word—*spago* means "string" and is Neapolitan slang for "spaghetti"—because he wanted to incorporate Italian elements into his cookery. Though he was exasperated by Ma Maison's secondhand flatware and cheap decor ("I thought maybe we could get rid of the Astroturf and get a brick floor or something"), he was intrigued by the restaurant's mix of high and low: the way his customers were a mix of people in jeans and suits, and the corresponding lack of strictures on what defined fine and casual dining, and even what defined French cuisine.

"In New York, they were completely boxed into French or Italian, but here, there was no tradition," he says. "And *I* didn't have the tradition, because I wasn't from France. Jean Bertranou had very good food, but L'Ermitage was very formal. Somehow, I saw the whole picture of California being relaxed and casual, but still with really good food." Puck found a location in a terraced building perched just above Sunset Strip that used to house a Russian restaurant called Kavkaz, and, before that, had been the Café Gala, a Hollywood high-life supper club where the young Bobby Short played the piano in the forties. With funding from Giorgio Moroder, the electro-pop composer known for his *Midnight Express* soundtrack and slinky disco hits for Donna Summer, Puck secured the space in 1981.

Puck had been to Berkeley and was duly impressed by what Alice Waters had done in 1980 with the upstairs area of the building that housed Chez Panisse, converting it into a lower-priced café with an à la carte menu and its own wood-burning pizza oven. On Waters's recommendation, he hired the same German artisan who had built Chez Panisse's oven to do Spago's. He announced that he and his chef, Mark Peel, would prepare the pizzas right in front of the customers in an open kitchen. He also hired Ed LaDou, an actual experienced pizza maker who had worked at various restaurants in San Francisco and made a minor name for himself as a bold pizza experimentalist, stealing ingredients from the pasta stations in the restaurants where he worked—chopped garlic, eggplant, clams—and adding them to his pies. This practice did not endear him to his bosses, but LaDou developed a small following, and Puck hired him after venturing up to the enfant terrible's last pre-LA employer, Prego, and eating a LaDou pizza topped with ricotta cheese, red peppers, pâté, and mustard.

At the dawn of the eighties, it was considered bizarre for an acclaimed chef to want to make pizza. Even now, Terrail says, "I think Spago was a step down, if anything." The LA fooderati covered the run-up to Spago's opening with hedged expectations, with *Los Angeles* magazine noting that Puck planned to use, in lieu of tomato sauce, "vine-ripened tomatoes, thinly sliced and marinated for one or two days in olive oil with a hint of basil" and then "strained and layered on the crust." When the magazine asked Puck if this posed the risk of alienating "those diehards who feel that dodging quantities of sauce as it slides off a slice is what pizza eating is all about," he responded cheerfully, "They'll adapt."

Puck's serenity and good humor were frequently noted by his fellow chefs and the food press. Perhaps as a consequence of the rough treatment he'd received at the hands of that brute chef back in Austria, he never became a screamer or a bully, even as he ascended to the top of the kitchen brigade. Still, in the chaotic, unpredictable restaurant business, it was helpful to have a fearless, mouthy "bad cop" to look out for you, and this role was ably filled by the redoubtable Barbara Lazaroff, Puck's girlfriend, and, as of

1984, his wife. A human tornado with curtains of dark hair, a Funkadelic wardrobe, and the sexpot body and tough-chick mien of the protagonist in a women's-prison exploitation movie, Lazaroff was the id that Puck never dared unleash. "Wolfgang would never have gotten anywhere without Barbara—she was the catalyst who made him what he is," says Terrail. "I'm not gonna go into that conversation, except to say that she was the reason that Wolf and I split. Otherwise, we'd still be together."

Lazaroff—who memorably made her entrance in an early-eighties *People* profile "poured into a sequined bodysuit, with streamers floating from her waist and a pet cockatiel perched on her head"—is unapologetic about stoking Puck's ambition. "If it was up to Wolf in the beginning, he probably would have had one restaurant—*maybe*," she says. "You know what? It *was* the good cop, bad cop thing. Basically, if there was something that had to get done that he didn't want to do, he would say [*comic Austrian accent*], '*Baba-waa!*' He'd tell me to do it."

Puck is as wary of being typecast as the gifted naïf steered to fame and prosperity by his force-of-nature scorpion woman as Lazaroff is of being known to posterity as Wolfgang Puck's other half. ("She used to say, 'They always just talk about you,' " Puck says. "We used to go to a shrink just because of that.") But though their marriage ultimately foundered—they were finalizing their divorce as this book was being prepared—Puck grants that they had a combustive chemistry that helped them build what has become an empire of restaurants, cafés, supermarket products, and cookware bearing his name. "It was a very complex relationship," he says. "She was ambitious, I was ambitious. Maybe being the yin and the yang is what made it work. She was the loud one, out in front, yelling at everybody about everything. The thing she forgets is, she yelled at me the same way."

Puck and Lazaroff met at an LA club in 1979, when he was licking the wounds from his failed first marriage to a waitress from Ma Maison. In the *People* profile, he described being struck by Lazaroff as "a challenge, an original. She was crazy, dancing wild and falling out of her clothes." Lazaroff hates this oft-told tale, "because it makes me sound like some sort of idiot child," she says. "I was premed! I was studying to be a physician!" As Lazaroff remembers it, she was trying to fend off the advances of some creep in the club, and did so by asking the guy next to the creep if he wanted to dance— "and it was Wolf." The cherubic little Austrian with the snub nose and the self-described "Jewish broad from the Bronx" hit it off, and before long, she was helping him write his first cookbook and serving as his de facto press agent, using her connections to land him his first television appearance, on *Hour Magazine*, a syndicated infotainment program hosted by Gary Collins.

As Puck nurtured his dream of leaving Ma Maison to open Spago, Lazaroff emerged as his expert navigator of building codes, contractors, and bureaucratic red tape, using her battering-ram personality to accomplish in hours or minutes what took other would-be restaurateurs months. When Puck first articulated to Lazaroff his dream of building an open kitchen with a wood-burning pizza oven, he almost immediately cast doubt on the practicality of the idea, worrying that the fire department would never approve such a setup. "So I picked up the phone and called the fire marshal," Lazaroff says. "It was four o'clock in the afternoon. I remember that because we were in bed. We were always in bed between lunch and dinner—that was the only time for sex. I had to rearrange my entire life around him, basically, my classes, everything. I called it 'The World According to Puck,' instead of Garp. *Anyway.* So I got a fire marshal on the phone and I explained to him what the idea was. I said, 'We'll build a counter in front of the oven, and the customers won't be able to get to it. It'll be like a fireplace.' This was just churning around in my head, and it came out of my mouth. And the guy said, 'Sounds okay to me, lady.' Next thing you know, we were trying to raise money for Spago."

Spago, which opened in early 1982, won over the skeptics so fast that Puck still shudders at the memory of keeping the food coming. "It was a nightmare," he says. "I'd look out the window and think, 'How am I gonna manage this restaurant? Everybody's screaming at me; everybody wants a table.' I've never seen a restaurant get as crazy as that one was the first six months."

"We all looked at each other after the first day and went, 'Whoa, what just happened? Two hundred people just walked through the door,'" says Nancy Silverton, Spago's original pastry chef, who had trained in France under the brilliant Gaston Lenôtre, the nouvelle cuisine gang's token *pâtissier* (an honorific akin to being Joey Bishop in the Rat Pack).

The foodie intelligentsia couldn't contain their curiosity over Spago's fancy-chef-does-pizza angle. *California* magazine's star restaurant critic, Ruth Reichl, sat at the bar by the open kitchen on the restaurant's third night of operation and received a blast not of heat from the pizza oven but of admonishment from a tired, pissed-off cook. "Why are you all here so *early*?" the cook said to Reichl, pointing out two other critics in the room. "It's not fair to judge us now."

Lazaroff had further ratcheted up anticipation for Spago by taking over its design planning, even though she had no experience in that realm. Puck's pipe dream of a willfully dingy "comfortable neighborhood restaurant," in his words, turned into a gleaming, Hockneyesque theater of California-casual event dining. Out went the "red-checkered tablecloths, sawdust on the floor, and a musician playing in the corner," as Silverton remembers Puck's original plan, and in came the white tablecloths, Christofle silverware, and huge sprays of gladiola. If it was glamour that Lazaroff was after, it was glamour that she got. Spago was thronged by both the older Hollywood crowd that had frequented Ma Maison—led by the director Billy Wilder, Puck's fellow expatriate Austrian—and a younger, groovier constituency. Warren Beatty and Jack Nicholson were regulars, as was David Bowie. Before long, the talent agent Swifty Lazar was renting out the whole place for his annual invitation-only Oscar-night party, effectively making Spago a byword for celebrity infestation.

"We had so little money for design, and one of the very few nice things I could have was the French tile I imported for the bathroom counters—and inside a week, the tiles had all these little cuts in them," says Lazaroff. "I was beside myself, screaming, '*What are these cuts doing in my tile?*' And the busboys and the waiters and waitresses were giggling, and they had to take me

aside and explain about the customers coming out of the bathroom with little white mustaches. They were messing up my tile to cut up coke!"
(Lazaroff credits Michael McCarty with getting off the best line about the
frenetic tenor of early Spago: that it was "an ego emergency room.")

But it was the exotic pizzas, more than the celebrity scene or toilet
tootling, that truly put Spago and Puck on the map. "If people thought the
celebrated chef who made nouvelle cuisine *the* thing to eat in Hollywood
wouldn't know how to produce a pizza, they were dead wrong," Reichl
wrote. "He may serve them on thirteen-inch Villeroy & Boch plates, but it
soon becomes clear that they belong there."

Deviating from the traditionalist Italian American portfolio of pepper-
oni, sausage, onions, and peppers, Puck topped his pizzas with everything
that seemed palatable to him: fresh Santa Barbara prawns, prosciutto, scallops,
Sonoma goat cheese from Laura Chenel, artichokes, eggplant, zucchini flowers. For LaDou, whom Puck permitted to cherry-pick whatever fresh ingredients the chef had procured from the markets that day, "It was like being an
artist who'd worked with ten colors all his life and then got to use three hundred." When Puck *did* top pizzas with sausage, he used duck or lamb sausage
that he himself had made on the premises. Most famously, he served a pizza
adorned with thin slices of smoked salmon, caviar, red onion, and dill-
flecked crème fraîche—a tip of the hat to the Jewish breakfast of bagels and
lox that many industry *machers* enjoyed on Sunday mornings.

As the ecstatic critics noted, Spago served many other dishes besides
pizza.* A born assimilationist, Puck soaked up whatever regional and na-

---

*The only serious reservations about Spago came from Caroline Bates, *Gourmet*'s intrepid California correspondent, who tut-tutted that, having enjoyed the "fugal complexities of Puck's dishes at
Ma Maison," she was "just a little disappointed to find him composing the culinary equivalent of
one- and two-part inventions, which must be real child's play for someone of his abilities." Still,
she couldn't help but rave over dishes "so honest and pleasurable and admirably mated to the
Southern California climate and spirit," and presciently predicted that "at age thirty-three, Puck
surely hasn't reached his pinnacle with pizza." Indeed, the current incarnation of Spago in Beverly
Hills, which opened in 1997 (concurrent with the shuttering of the original Sunset Boulevard location), more adeptly balances haute complexity and California simplicity under the direction of
Puck, who still cooks there when he isn't traveling, and his executive chef, Lee Hefter.

tional culinary traditions he encountered in polyglot Los Angeles, making Spago, in a sense, the ultimate American restaurant—as conceived by an Austrian with French training. Puck bought his fish at the Japanese markets in downtown LA ("when there was no white guy who did that," he says), and he served sashimi-quality tuna raw—sliced thick, marinated in basil-infused olive oil, and set on a bed of radicchio, with an accompaniment of sliced local avocado and rings of sweet onions flown in from Maui: Pacific Rim with a touch of Italy. In a nod of sorts to his home turf, he marinated squabs in sweet Auslese wine from Germany and served the birds grilled. In acknowledgment of his friends and forebears upstate, he composed salads of Panissean bravado, from the expected arugula-and-radicchio (accompanied, in Spago's case, by goat cheese roasted in a savory herb butter) to a bed of greens topped by striped bass, yellow summer squash, and the fresh Oregon girolles, or chanterelles, that André Soltner had struggled to get his hands on a decade earlier. Puck also splurged on not one but two wood-burning ovens, the second for roasting meats, which enabled him and Peel to pull off such showpieces as suckling pig and whole roasted lamb.

A few months into Spago's existence, a group of Japanese men visited the restaurant, taking measurements of the kitchen and clinically photographing the facility from every angle. Puck, by then used to the media onslaught, assumed his visitors were from a magazine and didn't give their presence much thought. "Little did I know that they were restaurant people," says Puck. "Then they came to me and said 'We want to open Spago in Tokyo.' I said, 'No, this is crazy.' But they basically told me, 'We will do it with you or without you.' So we became partners with them and went to Japan. They had it all laid out, exactly like our kitchen was and everything, except a little smaller." And so, in 1983, Spago found itself with a Japanese clone, Spago Tokyo—Puck's first, if inadvertent, step toward creating a multirestaurant empire.

His second Los Angeles restaurant and first proper branch-out, Chinois on Main, in Santa Monica, opened later in 1983. Emboldened by the fast success of Spago, Puck decided to conceive a restaurant based on his take on Chinese food, with no specifics in mind other than that Chinois would feature . . . his take on Chinese food. "I knew what I wanted, but I somehow couldn't explain it," he says. This would prove to be Puck's surprisingly effective modus operandi in expanding his empire: an intuitive, felt-out approach that would madden and frenzy his staff but somehow coalesce into a coherent vision by the time opening day rolled around.

He knew that Silverton's crème brûlées were popular at Spago, so he decided that Chinois would feature "Chinese" riffs on the dessert and came up with a trio of brûlées flavored with ginger, mint, and mandarin orange, served in little sake cups (never mind that sake is Japanese). He created a chopped chicken salad that simultaneously harkened back to the Cobb salad invented by Bob Cobb of Hollywood's Brown Derby restaurant in 1937 and evoked the comfort of leftover Chinese takeout eaten straight from its white carton with the refrigerator door open; the salad was made of shredded chicken breast and chopped Asian vegetables, and topped with crispy wonton noodles and a honey-mustard dressing. Smitten with the golden-brown smoked ducks that hung in the windows of LA's Chinatown shops, Puck bought his own smoker to play with, "but I could not make them right," he says. Instead, he struck a deal with Nelson Moy, a poultry wholesaler in Chinatown, to smoke the ducks for him, but only after Puck had rubbed and filled the ducks with his own blend of spices. The result—a Sino-French fusion before the word fusion was used in relation to cuisines—so pleased Puck that, only half in jest, he told Reichl on the eve of the new restaurant's opening that "At Chinois, we will cook food the Chinese will be eating thirty years from now."

While Puck fashioned his own new culinary vernacular for Chinois, Lazaroff let loose her every whim on the design of both the restaurant and the waiters' uniforms, dictating that the dining room's support columns be painted different colors—pink, celadon, black—and filling the room with undulating curves and, in what would become her signature touch as she and Puck opened more and more restaurants; hundreds of shiny, colorful, irregularly shaped handmade tiles. "She worked really hard at designing the places," Puck says. "Some of them I really loved, and some of them I really hated. We had fights about it. Like the Wolfgang Puck Cafés, with all these crazy mosaic tiles. Oh, in the beginning, they were all full of tiles! It used to drive me crazy. The café in Sunset Plaza looked like it was inside a bathroom. Now, some people found that beautiful. But for me, with my name on it, I couldn't stand it."

For her part, Lazaroff recalls the nerve-fraying pressure of having to rush her grand plans on account of Puck's insanely optimistic forecasts of when his restaurants would be ready to open. "Chinois was nowhere near ready, and then he tells me he'd promised an anniversary party for David and Gladyce Begelman," she says. "I said, '*Are you effin' kidding me?*' I slept two to four hours a night for fifteen years. I mean, the crazy things he made me do—I wanted to just strangle him most of the time."

WITH HIS BRAVADO, her wackiness, and their very public, spirited bickering, Puck and Lazaroff made for terrific copy, and Reichl was on the scene to capture it all in print. Her "process piece" about the making of Chinois was a vibrant, detail-stuffed feature that evoked Gael Greene's and Nora Ephron's articles for *New York* (Reichl on Lazaroff's demeanor at the work site: "Like a geyser, she explodes at least once a day"). From her perch in Berkeley, Reichl was also well-positioned to thoroughly chronicle Chez Panisse and its ever-growing sphere of influence. *California* magazine had gotten its start in 1977 under the name *New West,* founded by none other than Clay Felker, the visionary behind *New York* and "lifestyle" journalism, who had moved to the Golden State in the mid-seventies. As the California food scene became an ever-bigger deal, the West Coast developed its own group of gifted writers to compare with Claiborne, Greene, Sheraton, *Town & Country's* James Villas, and *Esquire's* John Mariani on the East Coast.

The dean of the West Coast crew was the *New West/California* food editor Colman Andrews, a suave, Francophilic food-and-wine know-it-all who cockily declared in a 1979 article that "this state has, arguably, the best French restaurants in the United States"—pointedly distinguishing French food from "Continental" food, which he derided as a "mongrelized cuisine, in which most things are stuffed, most things are heavily sauced, and many things have cheese melted over them." In a screwball-comedy twist, Andrews and Reichl were a secret couple, enjoying romantic trysts (Reichl was then married to another man) while they covered the birth of California cuisine.* Among the other writers in Andrews's stable were two veterans of *Rolling Stone*'s early, druggy, San Francisco–based incarnation, Merrill Shindler and Charles Perry, both of whom brought a bit of gonzo sensibility to the magazine's food coverage.† LA's other heavy hitters were Lois Dwan of the *Los Angeles Times*, Bruce David Colen of *Los Angeles* magazine, and *Gourmet*'s Caroline Bates, though Bates had the whole of California to roam.

FOUR YEARS BEFORE she wrote her making-of piece about Chinois, Reichl did a similar article about another soon-to-be paradigmatic Los Angeles restaurant, Michael's. Michael McCarty was a real-life Bret Easton Ellis character, a precociously poised and natty twenty-five-year-old who wore suits, slicked his hair back, went to private schools, and comported himself like a big shot. "I didn't really like him," says Puck. "He's completely different now, but he had too much of a big mouth at the time. He was so arrogant."

The well-to-do son of a General Electric executive, McCarty fell in

---

*In a screwball twist on the screwball twist, Reichl and Andrews, long after they'd broken up, ended up editing rival magazines in the late nineties, with Reichl taking the helm of *Gourmet* and Andrews running *Saveur*.

†Shindler later achieved fame as the best-known radio food critic in Los Angeles, while Perry not only writes for the *Los Angeles Times* but is America's leading expert on medieval Arabic cookery. The latter's articles about his attempts to re-create *murri* and *kâmakh ahmar*, medieval condiments made from rotted barley, are small masterpieces of out-there food journalism. Following procedures from the tenth and thirteenth centuries, Perry systematically let barley rot on his porch for weeks in Los Angeles, discovering that "*kâmakh ahmar* has the sharp aroma of a blue cheese (in the beginning, of a very strong blue cheese; I have emptied rooms by opening a container of it)."

love with French food and culture while spending his junior year of high school living with a family in Brittany. "They were a large Catholic family with a beach house and a little château that was nine hundred years old, but they had no money," he says. "The count, the head of the family, had polio and was in really bad shape, and he made his money repairing TVs and radios. It was really madcap. But the way they kept their château was that they had six farmers who were sharecroppers. And when it came to events, which they had all the time, they knew how to party. It was a continuation of my parents' life, the joy of people getting together, having a great time. So I thought that I wanted to run an operation that could provide that."

Audaciously for a boarding-school product (he attended the Hill School in Pottstown, Pennsylvania), McCarty dropped out of college after just nine months and made his way back to France, devising his own curriculum for becoming a restaurant owner, which took the form of a whistle-stop tour of Paris's hospitality schools. In short order, he attended L'École Hôtelière de Paris, L'Académie du Vin, and the Cordon Bleu. "I lived in Paris during the first half of the seventies, which was a very timely thing, because that was right in the middle of the nouvelle cuisine revolution," he says. "Right in front of your eyes, you could see the French changing their years of reliance on Escoffier. I knew both Troisgros brothers, Bocuse, Michel Guérard, and then the guys who were just a little older than I was, like Guy Savoy and Michel Rostaing."

Upon his return, McCarty took a summer course at Cornell University's hotel school—"which, if you were a graduate of a hotel school in Europe, was like a little Americanization refresher course," he says. He spent a few years in Colorado before he followed his parents out to their new home in Malibu, where he lived while devising his plan for the ultimate French-informed American restaurant. It was during this period that he attached himself to Jean Bertranou, learning the L'Ermitage chef's tricks and going into the duck-breeding business with him. McCarty also busied himself with trips back to Europe, where he performed such essential "research" as repeatedly visiting the eponymous restaurant of Frédy Girardet, a Swiss chef and adjunct member of the nouvelle crew who had taken over his father's modest bistro in a suburb of Lausanne and turned it into what many connoisseurs considered the best restaurant in the world.* "I'd go to Girardet for a whole week," McCarty says. "I wouldn't work in the kitchen, I'd eat. Lunch, dinner; lunch, dinner; lunch, dinner; lunch, dinner. And through that process, I learned the restaurant business."

In 1978, McCarty fell in love with a thirties-era residential building on Third Street in Santa Monica, on the west side of Los Angeles, that happened to have a huge backyard—ideal for putting in a garden. Approaching bank after bank, he finally found a loan officer who happened to be a foodie and enjoyed McCarty's spiels about cooking—"He said, 'I got a piece of swordfish at home; tell me about that sauce?' and I knew that I had him hooked"—and he was on his way.

"Michael really had his act together—I think the term wunderkind is not inappropriate," says Jonathan Waxman, who was one of McCarty's first hires. As word got out among California's restaurant community that some flashy kid was opening up a nouvelle cuisine–inspired restaurant, talented young chefs from all over started showing up at his Third Street door like wolfhounds drawn to a poodle in heat. One of them was Ken Frank, who was even more of a wunderkind than McCarty. In 1977, when he was just twenty-one, Frank had been the chef of a small restaurant called La Guillotine that spectacularly crashed and burned. It had only been open a short time when the LA critics discovered it, rhapsodizing over Frank's langoustines in mustard sauce and sweetbreads with morel mushrooms. This inspired the foodie herds to converge on the place. La Guillotine's owner responded to the rush by cramming in more seats and taking more reservations than the restaurant could handle, causing Frank to quit in frustration and the *Los Angeles Times*' Lois Dwan to take the extraordinary step of re-

---

*Wayne Nish, who owns the restaurant March in New York, was so blown away by the meal he and his wife had at Girardet during their 1980 honeymoon that he made a decision then and there to sell his successful printing business and start his training to be a chef.

tracting her earlier rave. "Restaurants should understand their own abilities and not be flattered into accepting commitments they cannot fulfill," she wrote in a re-review that, she later conceded, helped put the restaurant out of business.

Frank made no secret of his desire to open his own place in the old location of La Guillotine. "He was biding his time," McCarty says, "and he said, 'I'm gonna open my own restaurant. Can I come to work for you for three, four, five months?' And I thought it would be good to have Ken, because he knew all the purveyors in town." Frank effectively served as the restaurant's rocket booster, helping propel Michael's into orbit before falling away to do his own thing; he left as planned and founded his own place in LA, La Toque, a version of which he operates to this day in Napa Valley. Waxman, who grew up in the Berkeley area, was the steadying force at Michael's, someone who had gone to cooking school in Paris and worked at Chez Panisse during its immediate post–Jeremiah Tower era, when Jean-Pierre Moullé was running the kitchen.

At twenty-eight, Waxman was, incredibly, the oldest guy in the kitchen at Michael's, the granddaddy of a group that also included Billy Pflug, a nutty young graduate of the Culinary Institute of America who had worked at the Boston restaurant Dodin-Bouffant; Jimmy Brinkley, who had been Bertranou's pastry chef at L'Ermitage; and Mark Peel, who had trained under Puck at Ma Maison. (Peel followed the reverse track of Waxman, going to work at Chez Panisse *after* his time at Michael's. Momentarily considering an alternative life to chefdom, he moved north to Davis, California, to pursue a degree in agricultural economics and worked at Chez Panisse part-time. In 1981, Peel was lured back to Los Angeles by Puck to be the chef at Spago. It was during the frenzied run-up to Spago's opening that Peel and Spago's pastry chef, Nancy Silverton, who had worked at Michael's as Brinkley's assistant, fell in love and got married.)

"In the photograph the restaurant's PR agent circulated to the press, Michael looks more like the lead singer for a surly new rock group called The Chefs than a serious cook," wrote Reichl in *New West*, having sniffed out the story of the incredible new joint in the works in Santa Monica, which finally opened for business in the spring of 1979. She was right: Waxman, with his wavy mane and beard, looked like the missing Doobie Brother (he had indeed been a rock musician, playing in a band called Lynx), while Frank, with his skinny build and longish, center-parted hair, could have been Jackson Browne's kid brother. Reichl asked their frontman, McCarty, why such gifted cooks would roll the dice on a place whose leader was so untested. "Because I'm not a fifty-year-old Frenchman who owns the restaurant and is mean," he replied. "They've all been working with these crusty old bastards who treat them like assholes and don't let them do anything creative. If you were a second or third chef in Bertranou's kitchen and you wanted to do something, do you think he'd let you? Never. We're doing something different here. There's tons of room for creativity. I want to do the weirdest things."

Looking back on this statement, McCarty says his goal was nothing less than to upend the time-tested apprentice system that old-timers like Pierre Franey and Roger Fessaguet held dear, which he found barbaric. "How brutal was the system of learning how to be a chef in France?" he says. "It was, take an unruly bunch of fifteen-year-olds, and the only way to discipline 'em is to beat 'em with spoons and shit like that. Or punish them by giving them fifty pounds of potatoes to peel. One of the things I did for the restaurant business in America was change all that."

Indeed, the gathered cooks couldn't believe their good fortune, even if their young boss was occasionally given to bouts of flakiness and imperiousness. "There was a lot of ego around, but it was more about how exciting it was than a we-can-do-no-wrong sort of thing," says Waxman, who was delighted to be asked to join McCarty on one of his "research" trips to Frédy Girardet in Switzerland. With Frank there only temporarily, Waxman would have a chance to be the star for the first time, and within a couple of years was living in Malibu and commuting to work every day in his Alfa Romeo—until he bought his Ferrari.

The whole Michael's package was seductive. The exterior and interior walls of the 1930s house were done up in pale shades and mostly stripped of adornment—Lois Dwan thought the restaurant looked "Moorish, Bauhaus, Southern California." The waiters wore pink prepster shirts. The paintings on the walls were by Jasper Johns, David Hockney, and Richard Diebenkorn. The silverware was by Christofle, and the plates were gigantic and white (which soon became standard practice at all fancy restaurants with "nouvelle" or "California" pretensions). The wine list, compiled by *New West*'s former wine writer, Phil Reich, was heavy on California vineyards, no small feat in 1979, when the state's wines were only just coming into their own.* Even more astonishingly for the era, the list was distributed to customers as a computer printout that offered an up-to-date reckoning of the cellar's inventory.

All that aside, plenty of early reviewers were put off by what they perceived to be McCarty's rich-kid snottiness. Bruce David Colen gave the place a reaming in *Los Angeles* (in an article headlined MICHAEL, THROW THE GLOAT ASHORE), expressing disgust that, when he asked McCarty if his party might be seated at an unoccupied corner table, the proprietor responded, "Oh, no, that's reserved for some very special friends of mine." "Repeating the exact words cannot, however, capture the smiling condescension with which they were uttered," Colen added. Sandra Rosenzweig, in *New West*, made fun of McCarty's "more-perfect-than-the-French French" and wrote, "Someone has to teach the rudiments of hospitality to these very bright but rebellious teenagers."

But there was no getting around the fact that amazing things were coming out of the kitchen: slices of charcoal-broiled lamb painted with a red currant sauce; a salad of boned, grilled squab served warm over endive and spinach with a raspberry vinaigrette; seared hot scallops served on baby

---

*The watershed moment for California wines came in 1976, when the young English wineshop owner Steven Spurrier arranged a blind tasting of French and California wines in Paris. To the shock and evident dismay of the nine judges, all of whom were French, they selected a Napa Valley Chardonnay as the best of the whites and a Napa Cabernet Sauvignon as the best of the reds. It would be another decade, though, before a wide selection of California wines were available outside of California.

greens, with the warmth of the scallops wilting the tender leaves underneath; a grilled chicken breast stuffed with the livers of McCarty-Bertranou "mullard" ducks and covered with morels; a simple but perfectly executed crisp-skinned, juicy-inside grilled chicken, served with watercress and french fries.

"There was a French-nouvelle base, but all the barbecuing and grilling of things, that was an American sensibility," says Waxman, for whom the grilled chicken would become a culinary signature, toted from restaurant to restaurant over the next twenty-odd years. ("That was actually a dish Michael got from Bertranou, *poulet et pommes frites*, just a traditional bistro thing," he says.) Most of this grilling was done on charcoal made from mesquite, a hardwood native to Mexico that California chefs liked because it burned hotter than regular charcoal and imparted a sweet, slightly acidic flavor to the foods cooked over it.*

Like Chez Panisse, Michael's put an emphasis on procuring the best possible ingredients and not getting in their way. But Waxman, a veteran of both places, differentiates between the two restaurants by saying "Alice's approach was more intellectual, delving into old recipes and French tradition. Whereas Michael was more about the dynamic of the present, looking forward, and more American in outlook." McCarty seconds this assessment, calling his place "a modern American restaurant" in comparison to Waters's "nostalgic, literature, south-of-France thing."

Among the most impressed visitors to Michael's was Jeremiah Tower, who recalls being "choked up by seeing and sitting in the future." He loved Waxman's grilled chicken—"the perfect spirit of French cooking, but better than most in France could do it"—and the fact that "the waiters, the umbrellas in the open garden, the curtains, the walls, the tablecloths, were all the color of Michael's suit—off-white toward cream." Never a fan of Berke-

---

*The only drawback of mesquite in those days, says Jeremiah Tower, was that sometimes, prankster Mexican baggers would slip unspent .22 bullets into the charcoal pieces, resulting in potentially lethal explosions.

ley's mud-brown aesthetic to begin with, Tower was further dazzled by two other blanched, spare LA restaurants in this new vein, the West Beach Café in Venice, a sort of Spago-by-the-sea overseen by the young chef Bruce Marder, and Trumps in West Hollywood, the creation of a rising culinary star named Michael Roberts, whose bright ideas, like a "guacamole" made from pureed green peas, outweighed his ridiculous ideas, like a lobster salad made with pickled watermelon.

Another new booster of the LA scene was none other than Julia Child, who, reclaiming her Pasadena heritage, compared the Bay Area scene unfavorably to that of "her" Southern California. "We're adventurous," she told *The New York Times* in 1984. "They are a bit self-satisfied. We don't have to worry about standards as much."

The reporter who elicited this quote from Child, Marian Burros, didn't take a side in the northern-versus-southern debate, but, in the same article, she attempted to codify California cuisine as she understood it, and her definition sounded more Spago-Michael's than Chez Panisse. The cuisine's primary characteristics, Burros wrote, were "Grilling, especially with mesquite; combining cuisines that scarcely had a nodding acquaintance before, such as Japanese and French; replacing stock-based sauces with compound butters or no sauce at all; using baby vegetables to garnish almost every plate; serving fish, chicken, squab, and quail rather than red meat; [and] elevating country food to the status usually reserved for truffles and caviar."

WHICHEVER WAY YOU LOOKED at California, the truth was that its most celebrated restaurants were perpetuating their own family trees just as Henri Soulé's Le Pavillon had begotten an entire generation (or two) of great French restaurants. "He worked under Wolf"—or, alternately, "He worked under Alice"—became the new "He worked under Soulé." The ascent of California was a mixed blessing for James Beard. On the one hand, the shift it augured toward trend-chasing and compulsive dining out ran counter to his embrace of good ol' home cookin' and America's foodways. The chef and winemaker David Page—who lifted the name of his New York restaurant, Home, from the Beard aphorism "American food is anything you eat at home"—makes the case that Beard's slow-selling would-be masterwork, the breadbox-sized *James Beard's American Cookery* (1972), suffered from coming along at the wrong time. "He wrote this beautiful tome on American cookery, drawing together all of these different ideas from every region of the country," Page says, "and it got ignored because everyone was obsessed with Provence and nouvelle cuisine. It was a missed opportunity for American cuisine, and one that's only been righted in the last ten years."

But on the other hand, what was California cuisine, despite its French overlay, if not "modern American" food, as McCarty puts it? Beard, a born West Coaster, was pleased to find young chefs interested in native fish and produce, and, unlike many a skeptical food critic, he did not mind the new penchant for Asian-inspired flourishes, since, from his dress code to his childhood adoration of his family's Chinese cook, Jue-Let, Beard was himself full of Asian-inspired flourishes. (He is even said to have had a half-Chinese half brother, the product of an affair between his father and a mistress in Portland's Chinatown.)

Furthermore, the shift in the food press's attention toward California occasioned more trips west for Beard, who increasingly preferred his roost in San Francisco's Stanford Court hotel to the chaos of his latest, biggest New York town house, at 167 West Twelfth Street, which always seemed to be in the grips of repair work and the internecine squabbles within his ever-expanding retinue, which included his alcoholic, depressive amanuensis José Wilson (who committed suicide in 1980), an assistant named Richard Nimmo who also drank too much, and the annoying hanger-on Gino Cofacci. "Jim moved from Tenth Street partly to find space for Gino to have cooking facilities," says John Ferrone. "But it was a great mistake, because it took a great deal of money to put the Twelfth Street place in shape. It was very terribly run-down. He always regretted having moved, because the Tenth Street house was his favorite. It was much smaller in scale, but Jim always seemed to defy space anyway."

In San Francisco, Beard reveled in the generosity of the hotelier James Nassikas, who had gutted and renovated an old apartment house on Nob Hill and reopened it in 1972 as the Stanford Court. During one of his early stays at the hotel, Beard had mentioned to Nassikas that he was thinking of teaching classes in San Francisco. "And like a bolt of lightning, it occurred to me that our restaurant in the hotel, Fournou's Ovens, was vacant all day," Nassikas says. "I said, 'Jim, I have a perfect setting for you,' and he said, 'Indeed, you do.' And we got Chuck Williams involved, because he saw it as a great opportunity to promote his kitchen utensils." Starting in 1974, Beard taught classes at the Stanford Court for stretches that lasted weeks and sometimes even months. Nassikas never charged him for his suite or for use of the restaurant. "It was good exposure for the hotel, certainly, but Jim was just a wonderful guy and I enjoyed knowing him," he says. "I think that in New York, where he was into so many people's lives, you begin sharing their burdens—the Gino Cofaccis and so forth. You wake up one day and say, 'I've gotta get outta here!' That's what I think San Francisco meant to him."

In his seventh-floor suite at the Stanford Court, Beard presided over a foodie salon of sorts, "sitting on a sofa with no clothes on, just a robe that barely covered him," Nassikas says. "You know, it was Jeremiah Tower, Alice Waters, Mark Miller, a steady flow of them." Another regular was Clark Wolf, a new protégé, a young man who ran a little cheese shop at the base of Nob Hill that opened in 1976. "One day I was alone in the shop, and the door darkens—I mean, truly *darkens*—and I look up, and there is this huge person with a floor-to-sky black-leather trench coat," Wolf remembers. "He lumbers into this 500-square-foot, tiny cheese shop, with the wooden floors creaking, and he says, '*My doctor says I'm not to have any of this! How's your Morbier? Do you have some Saint-Nectaire? Do you have any good Appenzeller?*'" Supplying Beard with his furtive cheese fix, Wolf endeared himself to the master, and they became close friends late in Beard's life, especially after Wolf, who also logged time at the Oakville Grocery, moved to New York to become a restaurant consultant. "That's what a big piece of the connection between the California and New York food worlds was," says Wolf.

"It was James Beard living in the Village *and* at the top of Nob Hill in San Francisco."

One of the most important California–New York connections that Beard facilitated was between his editor in the late seventies, Judith Jones of Knopf, and another of his protégés, a middle-aged woman from the San Francisco suburb of Walnut Creek, Marion Cunningham. Cunningham was a late bloomer, having endured something of a grim first chapter of her life. The daughter of homebound, invalid parents, she grew up in the Southern California town of Glendale, got married when she was just twenty-one, managed a gas station for a while in the forties, and developed a serious drinking habit. One of her few solaces was cooking, an activity she took great pleasure in—though even this was something of a solitary exercise, since her lawyer-husband, Robert, seldom ate her food, preferring a diet of "burned beef and bourbon," she says. But in 1972, when she was fifty-one and sober, Cunningham ventured out of California—for the first time in her life—to stay in Gearhart, Oregon, where Beard, her favorite cookbook author, was teaching a cooking course in the resort town of his childhood. In Gearhart, Cunningham so impressed Beard that he asked her to return the following year as his assistant. "I actually thought he made a mistake and thought I was somebody else, but I certainly wasn't gonna call his attention to it," she says. "Then the classes moved down to Fournou's Ovens in the Stanford Court, and that's when it all began for me."

Though she was raised in poverty and was one-quarter Italian (it was her Italian grandmother, in fact, who cultivated her zeal for cooking), Cunningham, with her patrician beauty and blond-going-white hair pulled back like an equestrienne's, looked like the ultimate Yankee kitchen authority. Her no-nonsense approach to cooking complemented the look: she was adamantly traditionalist, populist, and home-centered, wary of all that was nouvelle and flamboyant—a trait that Jeremiah Tower says Beard ridiculed behind her back, referring to her as "Cookie" in allusion to her penchant for mumsy biscuit-baking. But it was this very straightforwardness that made Cunningham the ideal candidate, in Beard's eyes, to fulfill an assignment that

Judith Jones had mentioned to him: Who might be a good person to do a wholesale revision of *The Fannie Farmer Cookbook*?

"The candy company up in Boston that owned the rights to the cookbook wanted to see me about doing a new version, but I didn't want to touch it if we couldn't revise it from head to toe," says Jones. "It had become a collection of anonymous home-ec recipes, with nobody there." The heirs of Farmer—who died in 1915, and, though she subscribed to the home-ec lunacies of her era, at least had a good palate—had steadily desecrated the cookbook over the decades, introducing more and more frozen and canned ingredients and adding nasty recipes for gelatin molds and a guacamole made with ketchup. With the guidance of Beard and Jones, Cunningham painstakingly tested recipes for nearly five years, straining out the gelatin gloop of the older editions and acknowledging that the newfangled food processor was a good mechanism for, say, pureeing chestnuts for Fannie's cream of chestnut soup. Cunningham also added some new, non-Fannie recipes from her own experience as a lifelong Californian—for tacos, enchiladas, and two dishes indigenous to San Francisco, cioppino, the tomato-based fish stew created by the city's Italian immigrants, and Little Joes, a humble, pan-cooked hash of ground beef, eggs, and spinach. Adamantly unsnobbish and seemingly oblivious to food fashions, Cunningham even spoke up for things that most foodies considered anathema, like the iceberg lettuce wedge, whose layered crunch she found pleasurable, baby arugula be damned.*

The twelfth edition of *The Fannie Farmer Cookbook*, bearing Cunningham's name, came out in 1979 and was the fastest-selling edition in the

*But this didn't mean that Cunningham was aligning herself with such kitsch enthusiasts as Jane and Michael Stern, a married couple who started their own cottage industry in 1977 with the first edition of *Roadfood*, a brilliant book that flew in the face of foodie orthodoxy by celebrating, state by state, the nation's best greasy spoons, drive-ins, and truck stops. Cunningham told an interviewer that "greasy hamburgers" were a "sad reality about American life," while the Sterns, to quote Beard's biographer, Robert Clark, "fawned with Warholesque camp enthusiasm over dishes that members of the food establishment considered beyond the pale, lavishing on unpretentious and unassuming juke joints the same fevered attentions that gourmets once reserved for Le Pavillon."

book's history—nearly 400,000 copies in its first year alone. In a sense, Cunningham's *Fannie Farmer* succeeded at the dawn of the eighties in being what *James Beard's American Cookery* had failed to be less than a decade earlier, the definitive big, fat, friendly, popular, all-American cookbook. As seemingly untrendy as it was, the new *Fannie Farmer* was a product of its time, its reclamation of fresh ingredients and rejection of commercial-food corruption very much in tune with what its author's fellow Californians were preaching. Alice Waters was a fan, and she and Cunningham—a belated entrant into the food firmament—became the best of friends.

CHAPTER NINE

LAND OF THE
FREE-RANGE

The eighties were America's culinary adolescence. We could drive our food car, and we wanted to show off. We wanted to eat every single thing. There was a period of time when they had *snail roe*—they were gonna make caviar out of snail pellets. I mean, it was just, "How far can we go?" Shoulder pads as food.

—Clark Wolf, restaurant consultant

"MY REACQUAINTANCE WITH THE POST HOUSE COULD NOT HAVE COME AT A MORE PRO-pitious moment: just after a trip to northern California, where I was confronted with such ghastly combinations as sweetbreads with orange sections and red snapper with blueberries," wrote Bryan Miller in the summer of 1988, his fifth as the *New York Times* restaurant critic. "From Kennedy Airport, I went straight to this eight-year-old East Side steakhouse craving meat and potatoes."

The owners of the Post House were so pleased with Miller's review that, for several years afterward, they bought full-page ads in the paper that simply reprinted the review, complete with its indictment of California cuisine run amok. By the late eighties, the backlash was in effect: combining fruits with meats and sweets with savories was fine if you had the palate and training of a Wolfgang Puck or a Jonathan Waxman, but in the hands of lesser imitators, the results were nasty. "What happened was, the craziness occurred—every chef in America tried to get thirty-eight ingredients in one dish," says Michael McCarty. "Modern American California cuisine backfired: raspberries on everything, kiwi on everything."

PAGE 267: *Farmers' market pioneer Barry Benepe demonstrates the possibilities of local foods, mid-1980s.*

Indeed, the phrase "California cuisine," like "nouvelle cuisine" before it, came to be so misunderstood that its original practitioners recoiled from it, unwilling to take the fall for some Delaware chef's kiwi–halibut kebabs or Thai-spiced lamb chops adorned with squeeze-bottle squiggles of boysenberry coulis. The kiwi fruit in particular, a brown, fuzzy, egg-shaped oddity that, when cut open, revealed a jewel-green, food-stylist-ready interior, became a symbol of culinary tackiness, the mark of a clueless chef or restaurateur trying too hard to be chic.*

But at the beginning of the eighties, food people exulted in the possibilities that California represented. If that state could produce its own cuisine, why couldn't all the other regions of the United States? Larry Forgione, the chef at the River Café in Brooklyn from 1979 to 1983, considered this question more carefully than most. Until his arrival, the River Café, housed in a barge permanently docked along the East River, was a big-ticket tourist place that traded on its views of the water and lower Manhattan, with an afterthought menu devoted to infernal continental cuisine ("from a continent yet unknown," Craig Claiborne cracked). But the restaurant's owner, Michael "Buzzy" O'Keeffe, was feeling frisky at the end of the seventies and was eager to try something new. Soon, the duck à l'orange and chateaubriand were consigned to the dustbin, replaced, Gael Greene later recalled in *New York* magazine, with "a menu [that] mimicked a Rand McNally road map: Peconic bay scallops, Smithfield ham, morel mushrooms

---

*As baffled as anyone by the kiwi's sudden popularity was the woman who introduced it to America, a Los Angeles exotic-produce supplier named Frieda Caplan. She had started importing the fruit in the early sixties from New Zealand, when it was known as the Chinese gooseberry, and it was her company that suggested to New Zealand's growers that they rename the fruit after their country's flightless national bird, which it vaguely resembles. Over the course of the sixties and seventies, the try-anything Caplan successfully established other exotic items as supermarket staples—such as fresh mushrooms, papayas, mangoes, horseradish roots, spaghetti squash, "burpless" cucumbers, and Jerusalem artichokes (which Caplan's company, Frieda's, successfully rebranded as "sunchokes")—but it wasn't until the early eighties that the kiwi unaccountably took off, earning Caplan the epithet "Queen of Kiwi Fruit" in the supermarket trade press.

and wild huckleberries and farmed buffalo from Michigan, fresh shrimp from Key West, Belon oysters and periwinkles from Maine."

A member of the Culinary Institute of America's class of 1974 (the first class to go through the CIA's entire program on its new Hyde Park campus), Forgione landed his first big job at Regine's, the New York branch of the Eurotrash Paris nightclub, which opened in 1976. Michel Guérard, the inventor of *cuisine minceur*, was the official consultant on the menu at Regine's, but he liked Forgione and allowed him plenty of leeway in procuring his supplies. Gentle, bearded, and soft-spoken, Forgione seemed more like a scholar than a chef, and his scholarly bent compelled him to start studying old cookbooks and foodways to learn about the American culinary past.

"I had worked at the Connaught in London before Regine's," he says, "and, while their menu was mostly French, they always had these British traditional foods as specials, as trolley items—steak and kidney pudding, boiled silverside, chicken curry. It was a very nice thing for me to learn, how the past and the future worked in tandem. The other thing that happened was that the chef got a shipment of *poulets de Bresse*, the famous chickens, and it was almost ceremonial. I remember tasting one of the chickens and thinking, 'Geez, this tastes just like chickens from my grandmother's farm!' All of a sudden, it clicked: that America has the great resources to produce quality ingredients. In Europe, I saw the difference: that farmers grew for chefs, and the everyday shoppers, the consumers, got to use the same products. Whereas in America, it was reversed: everybody was growing for the consumer, and the chef was stuck using the same products. I realized that that had to change. We had to get back to dealing with farmers."

While at Regine's, Forgione began building up a network of small-time farmers that he worked with himself, with no middlemen involved. He found a quail farmer in Griggstown, New Jersey, and a fellow in eastern Long Island who was willing to sell Forgione wild ducks killed on his hunting preserve. Forgione took up mycology, the study of fungi, and, through mycological circles, found a woman who educated him not only about wild mushrooms but about "wild edible plants like purslane and lamb's-quarters, which is a variety of wild spinach."

When O'Keeffe hired him to take over the kitchen of the River Café in 1979, Forgione, aware that he would be performing on a bigger stage, sought the imprimatur of James Beard. "I needed as much help as I could get, and I thought, 'Who's the greatest resource on American cooking?' It was obvious who it was," he says. Forgione, still relatively unknown, courted Beard by sending goodie baskets to the master's West Twelfth Street town house filled with whatever indigenous ingredients he'd gotten his hands on: fresh morel mushrooms, wild tarragon, an antique strain of apple that the commercial growers weren't bothering with anymore.

It worked. "He gave me a call, and came over to the restaurant and had dinner," says Forgione. "From there, we became great friends, and I spent a great deal of time talking to him and being pointed in the right direction on things. Like, if you talked to him about butter, he could tell you about butter from Wisconsin and butter from Illinois and so on, and, because of his incredible recall, he could tell you exactly what each one of them tasted like. Julia Child, when you talked to her, would say, 'Well, just buy butter from Brittany, it's the best butter in the world.' At the time, it probably was. But Jim was always focusing on America."

Forgione's greatest triumph in sourcing an ingredient, though, came entirely through his own industriousness. The flavor of that *poulet de Bresse* he'd eaten in London stayed with him, reminding him of the flavorful, undeniably *chickeny*-tasting chickens he'd eaten on his Italian grandmother's farm in Port Jefferson, an old shipbuilding village on the north shore of Long Island. The potency of the farmstead taste memory shouldn't be discounted; two great chefs who would come along in Forgione's wake, David Bouley and Emeril Lagasse, also grew up with farms in their extended families, alerting them early on to flavor ideals that kids raised on supermarket foods didn't know about.

Foremost in Forgione's memory, after the way his grandmother's chickens tasted, was how they left the coop each morning to roam a yard "where they could go out and scratch and peck for different insects and so on," he says. "I just wanted chickens raised that way." Finding such chickens proved a challenge, though, in the age of Tyson and Perdue, massive, high-volume operations whose pen-raised chickens, like San Fernando Valley porn, offered consistency and enormous breasts but little in the way of lasting satisfaction.

But one day in 1980, the piano player at the River Café brought in a basket of multicolored, Easter-hued eggs that piqued Forgione's interest. The piano player explained that the eggs came from a neighbor of his in Warwick, New York, a town just above the north Jersey border, who was raising Araucana chickens, an uncommon breed known for laying eggs with blue and green shells. "I figured if this guy's crazy enough to raise Araucana chickens for Easter eggs, he might be willing to do this chicken project for me," Forgione says.

The Araucana-chicken man turned out to be microbiologist and hobby farmer Paul Kaiser. Kaiser gamely agreed to take on the project, working with Forgione on trying out different mixes of breeds until they came up with the perfect roasting chicken. "I made a commitment with Paul that we would buy a certain amount of chickens from him every week—whether good, bad, or indifferent, we would take them," Forgione says. "And in the beginning, they were terrible—tough, with concave breasts, and the meat not distributed properly. But if they were no good, we'd use them to make soup, or staff meals, or make a terrine out of 'em. The thing that made it successful for us was that there was a great deal of trust between the person buying the ingredients and the person that was taking the chance on the ingredient."

After nearly a year of experimentation, Forgione and Kaiser found poultry nirvana in a large bird that was a cross between the Rhode Island Red and Plymouth Rock breeds, with ample breasts and a thick layer of subcutaneous fat that gushed flavor when melted by heat. Kaiser fed these birds an all-natural blend of grains he mixed himself, and, true to Forgione's memory of his grandmother's little farm, he allowed the chickens to wander his property, scratching and pecking for whatever they might find.

Forgione puzzled over what to call his special chickens on his menu, because, he says, "Back then, 'natural' didn't really mean anything, 'farm-fresh' didn't mean anything, and 'farm-raised' didn't mean anything, because all of the big producers were using that terminology as well." In his historical research on chickens, though, he'd become enchanted with a description of a wild native American breed known as the prairie chicken. "It was in, like, *The History of Chicken*, or some ridiculous book like that," he says. "It said in the description that the prairie chicken always stayed around the edges of a forest, for the protection and for the grasslands. It said that the chicken 'freely ranged' from this section to that section. So I just said, 'Okay, well, how about "free-range"?' "

The Kaiser-Forgione chickens were received so orgiastically by the River Café's customers and the New York food press that "free-range chicken" entered the gourmet lexicon—though, contrary to popular belief, it is not an official designation of the United States Department of Agriculture. When Murray's Chickens, an all-natural poultry company, inquired as to what the protocol was for using the term "free-range" in its labeling, their head of sales, Steve Gold, reported to Forgione, "The government told us it's whatever Larry Forgione says it is."

FORGIONE WAS THE EIGHTIES' most celebrated proponent of American ingredients, but even the French were getting in on the act. In the new decade, up-start chefs like Jean-Louis Palladin of Jean-Louis in Washington, D.C., and Gilbert Le Coze of Le Bernardin in New York were fervent in their desire to refute what the New York restaurateur Drew Nieporent calls "the everything's-better-in-France bullshit." Nieporent, who in 1985 opened his first restaurant, Montrachet, in response to his experiences working at such hidebound places as La Reserve, remembers dealing with a pervasive mentality of "the butter's better in France, the fish is better in France, the oysters are better in France, everything is better in France—the endless importing of Dover sole, foie gras in a fucking can, Perigord truffles in a bottle." Then, he says, "Gilbert Le Coze showed up, went to the Fulton Fish Market, served you local fish that were five dollars a pound, and proved that, if well-treated and prepared, that stuff tasted as good as anything you'll find in France."

"Le Coze was the one who really helped me out," says Jean-Georges

Vongerichten, who came to New York in 1986 to cook at the Lafayette in the Drake Hotel after an itinerant training period at the various Southeast Asian hotel restaurants where his mentor, the French nouvelle cuisine star Louis Outhier, had consultancy contracts. (Outhier was also the consultant at the Drake.) "The hotel was buying me fish from a middleman, where they went to the market, bought the fish, took it to New Jersey, cleaned it up over there, kept it on ice for a couple days, and *then* sold it to the hotel," Vongerichten says. "I introduced myself to Gilbert and said, 'Listen, I know you have the best fish in town. Help me out here.' He said, 'You want to see it? Come with me at five tomorrow morning to the fish market.' "

Daniel Boulud, who arrived in the United States in 1980 to cook at the European Commission in Washington, D.C., was also eager to make use of what America offered. When he moved to New York two years later to run the kitchen of the Polo Restaurant in the Westbury Hotel, he was shocked at how classicist and unresourceful the old-line French restaurants were. "Coming from France and having spent ten years with the greatest chefs in the new movement, it was like a time warp, twenty years behind," he says. "It was still done in a very continental way. La Côte Basque and La Caravelle were stuck in the sixties and seventies. I wanted to be more creative than that."*

Working first at the Polo and later on the bigger stage of Le Cirque—where, from 1986 to 1992, he endured a tempestuous but mutually beneficial relationship with Sirio Maccioni—Boulud let the American marketplace dictate how he would apply his nouvelle training. "Frédy Girardet had done a *rouge*, a red mullet, covered in scales of sliced zucchini, and Paul Bocuse did it with little scalloped potatoes," he says. "At Le Cirque, I thought, 'Well, I like that, but I don't like the fact that you have to have a cook spending five hours putting those little scales on it.' For me, it was too much. And I had these huge, beautiful Idaho potatoes that you can't even find in France, about

---

*David Bouley, though American, had spent so much time training under Roger Vergé in France that he had much the same experience as Boulud when he came back to the United States. "I worked at several restaurants, La Côte Basque, Le Périgord, Le Cirque, and I couldn't find any place to fit my training already," he says. "There was completely a generation gap."

a pound each. So I sliced them lengthwise, because I wanted to do a sort of bandage around the fish. Wrapped it around some sea bass, and bingo!—the dish was made, an instant classic. It will be on my tombstone: the paupiette of sea bass, potato-wrapped."

OUT ON THE West Coast, the restaurateurs of the Bay Area in California were intensifying their long-running campaign to support small farmers. For all of Alice Waters's ambition, there were still very few "farm to table" relationships, to use the lyrical phrase, that put farmers in direct contact with chefs. Waters and Jerry Budrick had hoped to at least partially address this problem in the late seventies by *being* the farmers, growing their own produce on Budrick's property in Amador County—mesclun greens, baby carrots, and the like—"but it turned out to be too far away, and too hot," says Budrick.

To a large degree, Chez Panisse and other restaurants of its ilk were still relying on an inefficient, ad hoc approach of getting some ingredients from local gardeners, some from wholesalers, and, occasionally, some from the producers themselves via jerry-rigged transportation arrangements. Laura Chenel's goat cheese, for example, traveled from Sonoma in the cargo hold of a Greyhound bus bound for Oakland; at the bus depot, someone from Chez Panisse would personally pick up the cheese order, like it was an unaccompanied minor.

Help arrived in the early eighties in the form of Sibella Kraus, an Australian free spirit who had studied dance, lived in communes, moved to Berkeley, and, inevitably, found work as a cook in the Chez Panisse kitchen—in her case, upstairs at the café, where she started in 1981. While working at Chez Panisse, Kraus went back to school at Berkeley to study agricultural economics, and in 1983, shortly after attending an ecological farming conference, came up with the idea of something she called the Farm-Restaurant Project: an effort to band together restaurateurs as a bloc to buy specialty produce from small farms, thereby streamlining distribution and making it worth the farmers' while to grow better, noncommercial stuff.

"At the farm conference, I met farmers who were growing eight kinds of heirloom Japanese eggplant, but for themselves, just as an experiment," Kraus says. As someone who'd spent time at Chez Panisse "taking a romaine that weighed two pounds and paring it down to five ounces to get the little leaves inside, and then throwing the rest away," Kraus figured that if the farmers became aware of exactly what the chefs were after (lettuces picked tiny!) and if the chefs became aware of the fun stuff the farmers weren't showing to wholesalers (heirloom eggplants and tomatoes!), maybe her plan would work.

She enlisted six Bay Area restaurants, among them Judy Rodgers's Zuni Café, Michael Wild's Bay Wolf in Oakland, and Patty Unterman's Hayes Street Grill in San Francisco, to chip in money. "People got these lists," Kraus says, "and on this list, it'd say, 'Here's what these dozen farmers have, and if you order this on Tuesday, you can get it on Friday.' And in the course of the Farm-Restaurant Project, most things were delivered directly from the farmer"—usually by Kraus herself, who schlepped fruits and vegetables from Sonoma and Marin over the Golden Gate Bridge in her car. The Farm-Restaurant Project begat an annual event called the Tasting of Summer Produce, in which farmers, chefs, and other agricultural professionals meet face-to-face every summer to break bread and exchange ideas. More important, it led to a position for Kraus at GreenLeaf Produce, a progressive San Francisco wholesaler that had the trucks, warehouse space, and distribution know-how to make her ideas work on a larger scale.

In the nineties, Kraus became the director of the Center for Urban Education about Sustainable Agriculture, the organization that established San Francisco's Ferry Plaza Farmers Market, one of America's most glorious. But oddly, given its pioneer role in so many food trends, the Bay Area was not the trailblazer in the modern farmers' market movement. Seattle probably claims that title on the basis of the Pike Place Market, which dates back to 1907 and became a cause célèbre for foodie progressivists and city activists when it was threatened with extinction in the sixties.

Launched on a trial basis by the city in the Teddy Roosevelt years, when Seattle citizens were in an uproar about the high cost of onions—which were marked up in price by unscrupulous wholesalers who bought them from poor immigrant farmers from Italy, Germany, China, Japan, and the Philippines—the Pike Place Market was an immediate financial success: an opportunity for face-to-face interaction between farmers and customers, a money-saver for consumers, and a sprawling, chaotic slice of life for anyone who relished salty, multicultural urban adventure.

But the market fell into steep decline in the fifties and sixties as customers moved to the suburbs, took to shopping in supermarkets, and started buying long-haul goods delivered on refrigerated trucks from warm-weather states rather than their own local goods. The market became seedy and blighted, a trawling ground for prostitutes in search of randy mariners; in due course, the sixties urban planners descended like vultures, with their usual talk of condemning the market to make way for parking lots and office towers. But local activists, led by the preservationist and architect Victor Steinbrueck, who designed the city's famous Space Needle, formed an organization called the Friends of the Market that doggedly fought to save Pike Place Market; Steinbrueck's son Peter, who grew up to be a Seattle city councilman, recalled that his father's effort "wasn't so much about saving the buildings but about preserving a way of life, especially the presence of local farmers." (Another Seattle architect, Fred Bassetti, one of Steinbrueck's colleagues in the Friends of the Market, memorably championed Pike Place as "an honest place in a phony time.") After years of skirmishing between the city and the Friends of the Market, Seattle voters approved a ballot initiative in 1971 to preserve and improve the market, initiating its revival. The shoppers, chastened by the flavorless, ethylene-gassed produce they'd been buying in the supermarkets, returned to Pike Place in force, and today, the market, with its cod-tossing fishmongers and Art Deco PUBLIC MARKET CENTER sign, is the most recognizable symbol of Seattle after the Space Needle and the Starbucks logo.

New York's equivalent of Victor Steinbrueck was Barry Benepe—like Steinbrueck, an architect with an interest in city planning. But Benepe wasn't so much a preservationist as an agitator, someone fed up with the fact that, as he says, "In August, when Long Island peaches were great, you'd go to a New York City supermarket and find hard, green nuggets for peaches, with no juice and no flavor. It was an insult." His planning work took him in the mid-seventies to upstate New York, where he saw foundering family farms all around him. A lot of these farmers, their operations too small to compete with the agribusiness big boys, were giving up and selling their land to developers. At first, Benepe hatched a scheme to win over the developers by urging them to preserve the area's orchards as they built their planned communities, turning the proximity of farms and apple trees into a quality-of-life selling point to home buyers.

But when this idea failed to achieve traction, Benepe and another planner, Bob Lewis, set their sites on establishing farmers' markets in New York City. They founded an organization called Greenmarket, and in July 1976, after a year's worth of nudging city agencies and hustling up funding and permits, opened their first market in a city-owned lot on the corner of Second Avenue and Fifty-ninth Street. By later on that summer, Greenmarket was operating at two more locations, one in Union Square, the other in the Fort Greene section of Brooklyn.

It was an exhausting process, full of red tape and resistance from wholesalers and grocers, who initially feared unfair competition from vendors who were paying no rent. "They relaxed once they saw we were serious about selling strictly locally grown farm food, which they didn't see as competitive," says Benepe. "They were selling California and Florida stuff, which they considered superior." Benepe credits the fiery food iconoclast John L. Hess as his inspiration in fighting the good fight, "the instigator, the godfather of Greenmarket," he says. "He wrote so passionately about farmers' markets and the loss of local cheeses, things like that."

Hess, the shortest-lived of the short-term *New York Times* critics who filled the restaurant-reviewer role between Craig Claiborne and Mimi Sheraton, was an unlikely white knight, given his acrimonious relationship with the American food establishment. With his wife, the food historian Karen Hess, he had published a book-length polemic in 1977 called *The Taste of*

America that showered the establishment's leading lights with spittle-laced invective, the worst of it reserved for Claiborne and Julia Child.

The Hesses, who had lived in Paris while John was the *Times* correspondent there, blasted Claiborne and Child as phonies who not only didn't understand French cuisine but were responsible for misinforming Americans about French techniques and corrupting American foodways by perpetrating a "Gourmet Plague" of overwrought aspirational cooking. Repeating and amplifying these charges in a 1997 essay in *The Nation* entitled "Icon Flambé," the Hesses wrote, "To the extent that [Child] had any practical influence, she may have helped to bury American cookery by urging viewers who (like herself not long before) could not scramble eggs, to do quiches and soufflés instead."

While Karen Hess's scholarly work on early Americans' cooking and marketing habits is invaluable, and while many of the Hesses' complaints about American eating habits were valid—the rise of processed foods, the increasing percentage of junk foods in the American diet, the sundering of connections between farmers and consumers—the couple's default argumentative position of irate-granddad apoplexy severely compromised their credibility. In *The Taste of America*'s first chapter, entitled, with characteristic restraint, "The Rape of the Palate," they stated at the outset that "Our most respected authorities on cookery are poseurs," and favorably quoted from a recently published, apropos-of-nothing letter to the *Times* in which an eighty-nine-year-old woman complained, "What a rotten world we are handing down to our grandchildren," citing "violence and football on TV" and "screaming records on the radio and adulterated foods to eat" as her grievances.*

---

*In *The Taste of America*'s second chapter, entitled "Onward and Downward," the Hesses offered a grouchier take on Giorgio DeLuca's rejection of subjectivism and relativism: " '*De gustibus non disputandum est*' (there's no arguing about taste) is a notion that we shall dispute to our dying breath. It implies that we cannot maintain that Bach is better than the latest noise on the Hit Parade, that Tolstoy is better than Herman Wouk, that homemade bread with Jersey butter is better than Wonder Bread with margarine." Were they not accursed with such tin ears vis-à-vis popular culture, the Hesses might have jettisoned their put-downs of the talented Mr. Wouk and rock music and still made their point about Wonder Bread.

The Hesses also had a bizarre disdain for spicy foods (Szechuan, Mexican) that belied their worldly multiculturalism, and a propensity for cheap-shot, nyah-nyah put-downs that is even more acute in person. In an interview for this book, Karen Hess (whose husband died in January 2005) referred to Child as a "dithering idiot," Mimi Sheraton as "stupid," Alice Waters as "*so* stupid," Claiborne as "disgusting," and Franey, most preposterously, as "what the French call *routinier*, merely ordinary; a hack."

But the one section of *The Taste of America* that steered clear of vitriol was John Hess's account of the farmers' market in Syracuse, New York, which he adapted from articles he'd written for the *Times* and other publications. As Hess wrote in his original *Times* dispatch from 1973, Syracuse had bollixed up its thriving downtown in the 1960s in much the same way as other cities had, by bulldozing the old blocks at the heart of the city and putting in highways, thereby encouraging white flight to the suburbs and turning vibrant urban centers into grim ghost towns.

Recognizing the error of their ways in the seventies, Syracuse's civic leaders took the radical step in 1972 of closing off a city block to traffic once a week to make way for a European-style open-air market in which farmers could sell their wares directly to consumers. The resulting bustle pleased not only the farmers and their customers but the surrounding downtown stores, which noted an appreciable uptick in business on market days. One local lettuce farmer, doing brisk sales, told Hess, "Our stuff is number-one quality, but the commercial buyers will not take it if it's spotted or dirty—we'd get maybe nine cents a head. We're getting twenty-five cents here. In the supermarket, it'd be maybe forty-nine cents, and not picked this morning, either."

This was the scenario that motivated Benepe, who was so inspired by Hess's report, he says, that "We originally modeled Greenmarket on Syracuse." The effect was the same. While Benepe and a handful of farmers were setting up at the original Greenmarket location on Fifty-ninth and Second, in a fenced-in lot where the police used to keep their unmarked cars, Benepe noticed customers "lined up at the gate, waiting to get in. I felt like a general reviewing the troops." Similar models were being tested out in other communities, with the same salutary effect. Nina Planck, who would grow up to be one of the nation's leading advocates of farmers' markets and local foods, remembers vividly from her childhood the day in 1980 when her parents, vegetable farmers in northern Virginia, drove with their cukes, corn, beans, beets, chard, tomatoes, and squash to a fledgling farmers' market in the parking lot of the Arlington courthouse, just outside of Washington, D.C. "We got to market an hour late, and it was *packed*—as if customers had waited all their lives for farmers to come to town and put their tailgates down," she says.

The Union Square Greenmarket in New York was slower to take off, mainly on account of the square's reputation in the late seventies as a drug dealers' bazaar, "more famous for needles than nettles," as the restaurateur Danny Meyer puts it. Just a block east of the third location of Delmonico's, where Charles Ranhofer had prepared an elaborate banquet in honor of a visiting Charles Dickens in 1868, Union Square had by the early 1970s become a scary place, with the closing of S. Klein's, the department store on the southeast corner, seeming to be the final nail in its coffin.* "A dealer in the park came up to me with concern," says Benepe, "and literally told me, 'You don't want to come in here, it's not safe.'"

But, as in Syracuse, an unassuming farmers' market proved to be a catalyst for urban renewal. Meyer, a travel agent's son from St. Louis, had been nurturing a dream of opening a casual restaurant that would serve an American version of the type of food he'd enjoyed in trattorias on his college-age trips to Rome. "I was determined to offer excellent value," he says, "and I knew that I would have to be in an emerging neighborhood to do that. Given the fact that Union Square had the Greenmarket, it was a slam dunk." In 1985, when he was twenty-seven, Meyer opened the Union Square Cafe

---

*For a good view of Union Square at its most decrepit, watch the climactic scene of the 1974 film *The Taking of Pelham One Two Three*, the ultimate cinematic depiction of New York's darkest hour. The film's plot concerns a band of criminals that hijacks a subway car.

half a block west of the square, quickly developing relationships with the farmers who sold at the Greenmarket. Within five years, with Meyer's restaurant as the anchor tenant, the whole complexion of the neighborhood had changed—lofts, playgrounds, commerce that was actually legal—and the Union Square Greenmarket was the city's most celebrated.

For Larry Forgione, the advent of farmers' markets was a complement to his own network, "another way that we went back to dealing with suppliers." It meant that the philosophy of "fresh, local, seasonal" was not exclusive to California, and that California cuisine was morphing into something called New American cuisine.

"For me, it was always an absurd association, of 'California foods' being fresh food," says Thomas Keller, who would nevertheless come to represent the apotheosis of Californian brilliance at the French Laundry, the pull-out-all-the-stops country restaurant he opened in Napa Valley in 1994. In the early eighties, Keller, who grew up in Florida, was working at high-end restaurants in New York City and upstate, "and in the kind of restaurants I was working in," he says, "the food was always fresh. It wasn't about a certain geographical place, but a certain standard. I always dismissed the whole California thing. That was just propaganda."

IN 1983, FORGIONE was ready to leave Buzzy O'Keeffe's employ to open his own restaurant, where he would take his indigenous-ingredient sourcing even further: the goal was nothing less than to open an all-American fine-dining restaurant that had no French airs about it whatsoever (though Forgione was taking over the Lexington Avenue town house previously inhabited by a renowned French restaurant called Le Plaisir). James Beard, with whom Forgione was now enjoying hour-long telephone conversations nearly every morning, suggested the name: An American Place, after the gallery that the photographer Alfred Stieglitz had opened in 1929 for the then radical purpose of highlighting the works of young American artists.

The pull of American tradition was evident on the menu, but the preparations were progressive enough, and the prices high enough, to dissuade anyone from mistaking An American Place for a Colonial Williamsburg theme-food trap, or, as *Town & Country*'s James Villas put it, "a chicken pot-pie place." It was Villas who had seven years earlier called for a "formal codification" of American cuisine in his bicentennial-celebrating article "From the Abundant Land: At Last, a Table of Our Own," and though he now concedes that this was an absurd idea—"That was a long time ago, and I was young," he shrugs—he credits Forgione for being "the only person to stick to his guns on that, to try to be exploiting so many regions of American food in this country that it'd make you blow your mind out."

Forgione's spoon-bread griddlecakes and cornmeal pancakes were straight out of Amelia Simmons's *American Cookery*, but his accompaniments to them—respectively, duck sausage and spicy roast duck with cilantro—bore traces of Wolfgang Puck. The cream biscuits in his berry shortcake were made according to one of Mary Beard's old recipes, and the after-dinner cheeses were proudly declared to be from "independent American cheese producers," which, in 1983, was really saying something. "We served a lot of things in American cooking that you might have heard about but never tried," says Forgione. "Like, we were the first ones to serve buffalo in probably fifty years. It was fresh buffalo from a farmer in northern Michigan who had the largest herd east of the Mississippi. And then just little things, like fried whitebait."

MEANWHILE, JONATHAN WAXMAN was itching to get out of California. For years, even before Michael's, he'd had a "New York jones," a desire to run his own place someday in the Big Apple. Way back in 1980, when Michael McCarty told him that he'd found an ideal location for a New York Michael's—an old Italian restaurant in midtown that actually had a back garden space, just like the Santa Monica Michael's—Waxman thought his ship had come in, and mentally started preparing for a move east. But the real-estate deal fell through at the last second, and McCarty wasn't interested in any other Manhattan space; every other year, he called the Italian restaurant's elderly owner, fruitlessly, to see if he was willing to reconsider.

By 1983, Waxman had grown tired of waiting for McCarty's New York opportunity and decided to create his own. (The old Italian man finally relented in 1989, selling the property on West Fifty-fifth Street to McCarty, whose New York version of Michael's instantly become a lunchtime haunt for publishing and media folk.) Waxman quit his job at Michael's and found a business partner, Melvyn Master, an effervescent Englishman and expert schmoozer who had done public relations for Paul Bocuse, run his own wine-importing business, and helped launch Sonoma County's Jordan Winery in 1980. The two men spent much of the summer of 1983 tooling around France in Waxman's Ferrari, discussing their grand plans for a New York restaurant.

The result, in 1984, was a new restaurant on the Upper East Side called Jams, an acronym for Jonathan and Melvyn's. "Melvyn actually coined it," says Waxman, "because there's a phrase in French that means, 'Life is not worth living without jam.' And 'jam' also means 'money' in Aix-en-Provence dialect." The basic philosophy of the restaurant was that Waxman would adapt his signature dishes from Michael's "but be as seasonable as possible, as market-driven as possible, even more so than Michael's." Given the agricultural limitations of New York vis-à-vis Southern California this was a tall order, but Waxman leaned heavily on Forgione, who was so generous with his sources that Waxman's running joke was that Jams should have been called Another American Place.

More surprisingly, Waxman even received the blessing and sourcing help of the greatest working French chef in New York, Lutèce's André Soltner, who did not wholeheartedly embrace the press's gush over all things American. Over the course of modern culinary history, Soltner says, "It happens that the French cuisine was the best. You cannot go against that. We don't say we are the best to go to the moon. But in cooking, we are the best. You Americans, for a long time, seemed to me a little bit frustrated that it was the French, you know? So when the young American chefs came— Alice Waters and so on—you were so happy that you went a little bit overboard." Still, Waxman recalls that "André was like my uncle. He was very respectful of me, for some reason. Maybe because I sought him out; maybe because I spoke French."*

The first *New York Times* review of Jams, written by food correspondent Marian Burros in the interregnum between the reigns of Mimi Sheraton and Bryan Miller, made clear the degree to which New York's interest in California had been piqued. "Cognoscenti and would-be cognoscenti have been flocking to Jams on the Upper East Side for the last six weeks, eager to be among the first to sample the California cuisine they have heard so much about," wrote Burros. "For the untutored, New York's first restaurant to offer this minimalist style of cooking in a minimalist setting may come as something of a shock. At $25 for a small piece of fish and some vegetables, New Yorkers expect something more elaborate, but in many ways the simplicity of the dishes is even more exacting than haute cuisine."

Decor-wise, Jams's debts to Michael's and Spago were obvious. Orville Schell, moonlighting as *California* magazine's reviewer of New York restaurants—a telling reversal of publishing norms—observed with amusement, "Terrazzo tile, black-and-white linoleum, clean white walls with gaudy but not too interesting modern art . . . all proclaim to a Californian that he is home-away-from-home. Guests can watch chefs clad in white in the open, very clean kitchen laboring energetically over their work, like a crack surgical team in an operating theater. After coming in off the streets of New York, it's as if one were viewing a diorama of contemporary California life in the Museum of Natural History."

The simplest yet most celebrated (and most celebratedly expensive) of

*In her introduction to *Chez Panisse Vegetables* (1996), Alice Waters tells a story that has entered foodie lore as the greatest example of the Frenchified old guard's wariness of the California-fresh upstarts. "Not long after Chez Panisse began to acquire a national reputation," she writes, "we were invited to prepare one course of a charitable benefit banquet in New York City. We flew to the East Coast with boxes and boxes of absolutely fresh, organic, hand-picked seasonal greens from which we prepared a simple salad. One famous chef looked at our contribution and remarked, with mock censure and perhaps a little envy, 'That's not cooking, that's shopping!' " In a similar outburst, the irrepressibly Gallic Christian Millau ridiculed the New American culinary idiom as "*la grande folie*" (the great folly), cracking, "Americans not only search for their roots, they eat them."

Waxman's dishes was his mesquite-grilled half chicken, an update of the one he'd been doing at Michael's. "I think maybe New York restaurants thought chicken was mundane, and it was sort of relegated to the back of the menu," says Waxman. But these weren't just any chickens; they were the jumbo free-rangers raised by Paul Kaiser, Forgione's guy upstate. "The chickens that Michael had were more like the equivalent of Bell and Evans chickens—which are nice chickens," Waxman says. "But they weren't these massive, free-range, gnarly birds that Paul Kaiser had. He delivered them, basically, warm from the Chinese butcher up there, and they were fantastic. The first time I put them on the grill, the skin started to cook under that intense, perfect heat of the mesquite wood, and the fat started bubbling, and the skin got crispy—wonderful! At Jams, I cooked everything to order, so people had to wait the thirty-five or forty minutes for half a chicken to cook. But once they got it, with those french fries, I think it was kind of orgasmic for them. People flipped out."

At $23 per order, in 1984 dollars, no less, there was no way Waxman's grilled chicken could afford *not* to be orgasmic. "The chickens cost me a lot of money in those days, eight or nine bucks, almost as expensive as the chickens I buy now," says Waxman. "But let's face it: it's like charging a lot for a good wine. If you believe in your product and you want to make money, you've got to charge a lot for it. So I became notorious for charging that much money for chicken. Some people thought I was arrogant, some people knew the story. But I think it helped build the spin on it."

"You can't find a chicken like that anywhere in New York today—I still remember the taste of it, and I'm gonna tell you what it tasted like," says Bobby Flay, literally licking his lips at the memory. "It tasted like the crispiest, juiciest, and most perfectly, simply seasoned chicken you ever tasted." Years before he was a Food Network star and the owner of the quasi-Mexican Mesa Grill, among other restaurants, Flay was a wet-behind-the-ears protégé of Waxman's. A native New Yorker, he grew up around restaurants; his father was the business partner of Joe Allen, the restaurateur behind the theater-district standbys Joe Allen and Orso. But those places served unexceptional if reliable food to hurried diners with an eight o'clock curtain to catch, whereas Jams and the two other New York restaurants that Waxman and Master opened in rapid succession—Bud's in 1985, and Hulot's in 1986—were kaleidoscopically mind-blowing to the young Flay. He took a cooking job at Bud's in 1985 and served tours of duty at each of the three Waxman-Master restaurants.

"Jonathan's influence is still prevalent in my cooking," Flay says. "I do stuff at Mesa Grill today that we were doing at Bud's. You know, shucking fresh corn and making a relish out of it with fresh lime juice. And chilies and cilantro. And using avocados to make relishes with the chili peppers. Blue cornmeal. Roasted poblano peppers to flavor things. He was the first person to introduce me to that kind of stuff. I didn't know anything about that then. No one on this coast did."

"The West Coast was seminal at that time, and the young New York chefs picked up on it—it took the California phenomenon to open their eyes," says Bryan Miller, whose tenure as the *Times* restaurant critic began in 1984, just as the Waxman-led Californification of New York was unfolding. "It was exciting. I loved it—grill, grill, grill. There wasn't much grilling in New York up to then. And the side dishes: the composed salads, just the beautiful ingredients that you didn't have before. It took a while, but then, all of a sudden, it was also happening in Chicago, Boston, Atlanta. It was a blast."

MILLER'S ASCENT COINCIDED all too neatly with Claiborne's decline. The former had been contributing to the *Times* food section on a freelance basis for a few years when, suddenly, he was thrust into the position of collaborating with Franey on the "60-Minute Gourmet" column after Franey and Claiborne had a massive falling-out.

Recalling the beginning of the end of his friendship with Claiborne, Franey wrote in his memoir, "I felt the need to cut back on the seven-day cooking weeks, which is what they had now become. I wanted to spend more time with my family in leisure activities, and to go fishing and hunting. My children needed me more, I felt. So I told Craig I wasn't going to work weekends anymore . . . and that I really meant it, although I would still certainly work with him on other days."

Claiborne didn't absorb this news well, interpreting it as an outright rejection. The churning psychological torment that Claiborne had long kept at bay with a busy work schedule, and an even busier social schedule, bubbled up to the surface and erupted. "Craig got a load on one night and told off Pierre's wife, Betty," Miller says.

James Villas, who lived near both men in East Hampton and received a play-by-play account of the fracas from the involved parties, recalls, "Craig was demanding more and more and more of Pierre's time. And I can certainly understand Betty's position. Craig was screaming and hollering and really trying to get Pierre to work, and he got particularly drunk. I can't *tell* you what Craig was like when he was drunk! Oh, the times he crashed into my trees and didn't know where he was going! He was a *bad* drunk. And he blew up and let Betty have it, and she gave it right back to him. From that moment on, the schism really was established between Pierre and Craig."

Looking back, Villas believes that "at the very beginning, at least, Craig was in love with Pierre. And I think Betty always thought that was true, and that got to be ugly." Miller confirms that "a lot of people thought that Craig and Pierre were an item. I think it bothered Pierre a little bit. Back then, you would see Craig Claiborne and Pierre Franey together, and, you know, half the food writers were gay, so people just made that assumption. I can't tell you how many times I had to disabuse people of that."

Betty Franey will only say that her husband "was glad to get away from Craig, to tell you the truth, because he was so cranky. When the *Times* said, 'Okay, let Bryan do the byline,' that was a big relief." Franey continued to do the "60-Minute Gourmet" column all the way until 1994, and in his sixties, by which time his hair had turned all white, he emerged as a cuddly, telegenic PBS chef, starring in a cooking program called *Cuisine Rapide*, which yielded a best-selling tie-in book written with Miller.

"Pierre was the most completely content, happy man," says Miller. "He started out cooking when he was fourteen, and his life was to serve others. When he got behind the stove, something happened to him. He whistled—he always whistled when he was cooking. He loved his métier, he loved the people in the business, and I never heard anyone ever say an ill word about him."

Alas, Claiborne's descent into lonely, inebriated misery in the eighties was tragic—a descent exacerbated by the auto-crash death in 1986 of his sort-of companion, Henry Creel, and the poor sales and reception of his memoir, *A Feast Made for Laughter*. Published in 1982, a good decade before frank confessionals and psychosexual drama became the norm in contemporary nonfiction, the book laid out his memories of his nocturnal "explorations" of his father's body and his simmering contempt for his mother—and then, in the back, there were recipes for grapefruit sherbet and Jean Vergnes's seafood crepes. "People were interested in him food-wise; they didn't want to hear all that family business," says Betty Franey. "That was a mistake. Pierre felt bad about that."

His palate shot to hell by booze, his stamina reduced by bypass surgery, Claiborne was no longer the inexhaustibly curious culinary adventurer of yore, "and his writing deteriorated terribly," says Miller. "It got so bad that the desk wrote it. It was like staccato notes. Very sad, very sad." In a replay of the events of 1972, Claiborne also became consumed by the notion that the world hadn't given him his due, and that the *Times* had somehow done wrong by him.

"There was a hairpin turn into bitterness," Arthur Gelb recalls, and Claiborne huffily severed relations with the paper in 1988. He continued to accept assignments from other publications, notably *Food Arts*, a high-end publication founded in 1989 by Michael and Ariane Batterberry (the same urbane New York couple who, eleven years earlier, had founded *Food & Wine* magazine), but his output was meager, and his capabilities were limited. In a depressing letter to the chef Barry Wine of the acclaimed restaurant Quilted Giraffe, Claiborne requested an interview for *Food Arts* but cautioned, "To do this, for better or for worse, it would be necessary for you to come into my home for the talk. Because of an arthritic thumb, I cannot write in longhand."

Drew Nieporent remembers that in 1986, shortly after he'd opened Montrachet with the chef David Bouley, he received a call from Michael Tong of Shun Lee Palace, an innovative Chinese restaurant that Claiborne had championed. "He said, 'Craig's in the hospital, he's gonna be having some operation, and he would really love you guys to cook for him one night,'" Nieporent says. "So David Bouley and I collaborated on a menu. And the day that we were doing this, there was a blizzard. It was so bad that we actually closed the restaurant—and yet David and I still showed up for work. I said to David, 'Should we do this for Craig Claiborne?' And he said, 'I can do it if you can get the food to him.' So we did this beautiful meal. I somehow got a cab. The hospital was all the way uptown, and I remember climbing over snowdrifts with all this food and beautiful silverware. I knocked on Craig's door, and he said, 'You can put the food right over there.' We chatted for a little bit, and then he said, 'Well, I'm not feeling very well, so I'm gonna ask you to leave.' So I went out into the hallway, and, while I was waiting for the elevator to come, I looked over, and there was Craig Claiborne with the tray in his hands. And he turned to a nurse and said [*Southern accent*], 'Ah can't eat this shit! Can you get rid of this shit?'"

Claiborne somehow hung on all the way to the year 2000, though by then he had long been confined to a wheelchair and was behaving irascibly even toward the most loyal members of his dwindling circle of friends, which included Jacques Pépin, Ed Giobbi, and Villas. In the early nineties, Villas stopped by Claiborne's home, he says, "just to make sure he was alive." Finding no one there, he left a note saying he'd stopped by. A few days later, Villas received a pissy letter from Claiborne explaining that he'd been away. "Why don't you telephone me before you stop by?" Claiborne wrote. "It would be much more practical for both of us. Jean Stafford once had a note posted outside her kitchen and living room doors which said to the effect, 'Anyone who stops by here without prior notice will be humiliated.'"

"That hurt me terribly," says Villas. "But then I thought about it and realized, 'He's not himself.' " In Claiborne's last days, Villas wheeled America's preeminent food journalist to one of the few restaurants he cared to eat in anymore: the Fifty-seventh Street location of the Planet Hollywood chain, which was near his Manhattan apartment. Claiborne liked the club sandwich there.

Franey actually predeceased Claiborne by almost four years, but his final decade was much fuller and happier. His *Cuisine Rapide* success begat still more PBS series, *Pierre Franey's Cooking in America* and *Pierre Franey's Cooking in France*, and he never tired of teaching. Well into his seventies, he still got a kick from doing cooking demonstrations, for the fun of it as much as for the money. He had just finished doing one such demonstration, aboard the *Queen Elizabeth 2*, when he suffered the stroke that took his life in 1996.

"Their relationship was absolutely symbiotic—they needed each other," says Villas of Franey and Claiborne. "God, the days that I sat there and saw the entire scenario: Pierre, probably the greatest cook in my lifetime, over at the stove, and Craig, sitting at the typewriter with his half-glasses on, with a certain angst about him. I can hear him now: 'How many cups? No, not *about* how many, *exactly* how many?' And Pierre, never, ever getting fazed. I don't think I was really aware of what I was seeing there, and how important it was. Cooking and dining and eating values were being created as I was watching. Because it would all go into *The New York Times*."

THE DRAWN-OUT DENOUEMENT of Claiborne's life served him poorly for posterity. By the time he passed on, few people under the age of fifty had any sense of his mammoth contribution to America's eating habits, or even of who he was. James Beard, on the other hand, was an exalted figure until the day he died, in January of 1985, at the age of eighty-one. Certainly, his final decade was not without its unsavory aspects. He developed crushes on unattainable or exploitative young men. He had a mirror installed above the bed in his salmon-walled boudoir, and relished the opportunities his circulatory problems gave him to have young men kneeling at his feet, binding his lower legs with bandages while his robe fell open. He had a penchant for setting various members of his court against one another, taking wicked delight in watching, say, the sharp-taloned New Yorker Barbara Kafka ("a very difficult bitch," says Michael McCarty, admiringly) run roughshod over the timorous, self-effacing Marion Cunningham. Most painfully for Beard personally, he became involved in 1983 in a plagiarism scandal when a book to which he'd given a promotional blurb, *Richard Nelson's American Cooking*, by a Portland cooking teacher with whom he'd worked, was found to contain recipes lifted almost verbatim from other cookbooks, most notably Richard Olney's *Simple French Food*. (Olney took legal action and settled with Nelson, but he never forgave Beard.)

But Beard died a beloved, wanted man, surrounded by friends and protégés keen to perpetuate his legacy. As he lay on his deathbed in New York Hospital in early 1985, finally succumbing to all those years of animal fats and Glenlivet, he was attended to by his various devotees in the food world, among them Kafka, Forgione, Clark Wolf, John Ferrone, Judith Jones, Paul Kovi and Tom Margittai (the managing partners of the Four Seasons at the time), and the cooking teacher Peter Kump.* When Beard died, it was Kump who arranged the purchase of the West Twelfth Street town house from Beard's main beneficiary, Reed College of Oregon,† for the newly formed James Beard Foundation, of which he was the founding president.

---

*Like Michael Field, Kump initially made his name in another realm, having risen to the rank of educational director of the Evelyn Wood speed-reading school, a position that found him teaching this skill to members of the Nixon administration, among them John Dean, John Ehrlichman, Jeb Magruder, Rose Mary Woods, and Ron Ziegler. But after taking cooking classes with Beard, Simone Beck (at Beard's house), Diana Kennedy, and Marcella Hazan, Kump decided to run his own shop. With Beard's blessing, Kump was by the late seventies running the most prestigious cooking school in New York.

†Beard attended Reed College in 1920–21 but was expelled midway through his second semester. His biographer, Robert Clark, says that there is no official explanation on record for the expulsion, but notes that Beard had quickly established himself as a flamboyant campus celebrity, given to Jazz Age high jinks and flapdoodlery, and that "at some point [he] became lovers with one or more male students and a professor."

"Jim very much believed that he'd rather die at eighty and eat everything he wanted than live to ninety not having salt and sugar and desserts and Scotch," says Forgione, who was the last visitor to see Beard alive, and whose friendship with Beard was perhaps the most purely food-oriented, with no undercurrent of lust or exchanges of vicious food-world gossip. "Jim was just this warm, wonderful guy, and we wanted to keep him happy," Forgione says. "Everybody knew that the Four Seasons was doing his dinners in the hospital, and I'm certainly guilty of having sneaked Glenlivet to him."

Beard would go on to enjoy a fulfilling, sanitized afterlife as the patron saint of American culinary values—an oft-quoted, reverently invoked folk deity like Will Rogers or Vince Lombardi. But the West Twelfth Street town house, which Beard never cared for in the first place, couldn't shake off its bad karma, not even after the death in 1990 of its unwanted tenant, Gino Cofacci. The Beard Foundation was, from the get-go, amorphous of intent, with Kump proclaiming that its goal was "to gain recognition for the culinary arts as a bona fide art form." In practical terms, no one was quite sure what this meant. The foundation charged steep membership fees and hosted lavish events at the town house (now officially known as Beard House) in which acclaimed chefs cooked multicourse showcase meals for members and their guests. The members paid a hefty per-meal fee on top of their annual dues—as much as $150 a head—and the chefs donated their services and food, the idea being that the sacrifice was worth it for the invaluable New York exposure and the good works of the foundation. Anthony Bourdain, the gadfly chef-author, famously referred to Beard House as "a benevolent shakedown operation."

But even though Beard House packed them in, with its members dutifully putting their names on waiting lists to attend dinners prepared by whichever chef happened to be in town when a seat opened up, the foundation itself was as administratively inept as Beard himself had been. Under Kump, who died of cancer in 1995, the incompetence was benign, a matter of a cooking teacher being in over his head as an administrator.

But under Kump's successor, Len Pickell, the fogginess of the foundation's mission and its shoddy accounting practices became a criminal matter. The Beard Foundation had chartered itself as a nonprofit, tax-exempt organization, on the grounds that its revenue went toward such charitable purposes as a scholarship program for aspiring culinary professionals. But an audit of the 2003 fiscal year revealed that only $29,000 of the foundation's $4 million plus operating fund had gone toward scholarships. Pickell, though he had an authentic zeal for good food and wine, turned out to be a con man who falsely claimed to be an independently wealthy certified public accountant. In fact, he was not a CPA, had been unemployed before taking the unsalaried Beard Foundation position, lived with his wife in a middle-class New Jersey split-level, and had been financing his lavish trips, meals, and lifestyle with money stolen from the foundation. Pickell ended up going to prison in 2005 after pleading guilty to second-degree grand larceny, and the entire board of trustees was forced to resign.

Still, the Beard Foundation survives, rededicated to being an organization whose purpose is to "celebrate, preserve, and nurture America's culinary heritage and diversity in order to elevate the appreciation of our culinary excellence," to quote its mission statement—and, just as important, to not be just a "wine and dine society," in the derisive words of the new head of the new board of trustees, Dorothy Cann Hamilton, who also founded New York's French Culinary Institute. The annual James Beard Foundation Awards ceremony lives on, too, promulgating awareness not only of America's best chefs and most promising up-and-comers but of Beard himself, whose baldheaded, bow-tied likeness adorns the medallion bestowed upon winners.

A bigger character and better aphorist than the cranky Claiborne ever was, Beard left behind enough prophecies and aperçus to keep his name in food-world circulation in perpetuity. In 1982, he said, "We are now in a new epoch of gastronomic excellence that, with a liberal seasoning of common sense, will draw on the best of old American cookery as well as on the technological advances of the new." In late 2005, this declaration was repurposed as a fund-raising appeal, appearing atop a letter that was sent out to

Beard Foundation members as the organization sought to recover from the Pickell scandal. Below the quotation was a little box for a contributor to check and the sentence, "YES, I want to support the chefs, culinary students, and other people responsible for bringing about a new epoch in gastronomic excellence."

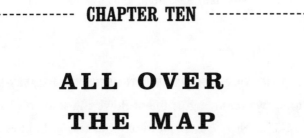

CHAPTER TEN

ALL OVER
THE MAP

Let's go get sushi and not pay.

—Duke, *Repo Man*, 1984

JAMES BEARD WENT TO HIS GRAVE AN OPTIMISTIC MAN BECAUSE HIS PET CAUSE, American food, was enjoying its fullest flowering since his barbecuing days of the 1950s. The New American idiom was taking hold as the alumni of the seminal California restaurants fanned out. "I absolutely remember the day I heard 'New American food' instead of 'California cuisine' or 'nouvelle cuisine'—the first time I heard the word 'new' instead of 'nouvelle,'" says Judy Rodgers. It was in 1980, when, after she'd left Chez Panisse but before she took over Zuni Café, she was recommended by Marion Cunningham for a job at the Union Hotel in Benicia, a quaint little town on the San Francisco Bay. Given a mandate by the hotel's owner to make the menu "American," Rodgers embarked on a Larry Forgione–like exhumation of forgotten cookbooks and Junior League fund-raising booklets. She opened shop with a menu that included fried chicken, quail with wild rice, celery soup, pickled beets and eggs, homemade plum jam, and Mississippi mud cake. "Opening night, Marion brought James Beard and Barbara Kafka, for God's sake!" Rodgers remembers. "Three days later, his nationally syndicated column is all over the United States, talking about the great Union Hotel."

A year before that, Mark Miller, at his wit's end at Chez Panisse, where he felt restricted by what he calls Alice Waters's "French Provençal 1928" menu dictates, left to open the Southwestern-inflected Fourth Street Grill in the faded maritime district of Berkeley, then known mostly for its lumberyards and the vestigial presence of Spenger's, an old seafood market and

PAGE 297: *Mexican-food guru Rick Bayless (left) and Japanese visionary Nobu Matsuhisa do kitchen prep in their pre-entrepreneurial days of the 1980s.*

restaurant of "Ar, matey" ambiance. The Fourth Street Grill's success was so lightning-quick that he soon opened another American restaurant in another dicey Berkeley locale, the Santa Fe Bar and Grill (in the derelict Santa Fe Southern railroad station). Like farmers' markets, good restaurants were turning into agents of gentrification; the very presence of the Fourth Street Grill triggered a renaissance for Fourth Street itself, which eventually out-gourmeted even Shattuck Avenue in its number of restaurants, food shops, and kitchenwares retailers.

In LA, Susan Feniger and Mary Sue Milliken, Midwesterners who'd cooked together in Chicago before becoming part of Puck's Ma Maison team, opened up the City Café in 1981, cooking "whatever we wanted to eat," says Milliken. "The menu would be, you know, salad with confit of duck, goat cheese, and lentils, and then shrimp and Pernod with pasta, and then beef carpaccio. And a vegetarian plate that had eggplant-spinach curry, raita, a chutney, and pickled tomatoes. It was all good, but it didn't really go together. But the thing is, *everyone loved it!* One of my favorite dishes we did from my Chicago days was lamb kidneys with fried spinach, which we'd sell maybe one a month in Chicago. Suddenly, we couldn't even get enough of 'em! I remember thinking, 'I'm so thankful to these people in this period of LA, 'cause they'll order anything we cook!' "

Less successful was the nine-month stint of Mark Peel and Nancy Silverton, the sweethearts of Spago, at Maxwell's Plum, the famous New York City swingles-scene place that had opened in 1966, laying the ground-work for the "fern bar" craze of the seventies. By the mid-eighties, the restaurant and its eclectic pub-grub menu had grown stale, and its flamboy-ant impresario, Warner LeRoy, who also ran the Tavern on the Green in Central Park, imported Peel and Silverton to New York in a high-profile, George Steinbrenner–style bid to outright purchase the Spago magic. The New York foodies were thrilled, but Peel and Silverton, an uncommonly at-tractive, photogenic couple who seemed to embody the exposed-brick yup-pie dream, chafed under LeRoy's dated, Tiffany-lamp tackiness and his failure to follow through on his promises to let them have free rein with the menu.* Still, their flight from New York and return to Los Angeles set the stage for Peel and Silverton's own triumphs of New Americanism: the rustic-Italian-by-way-of-California restaurant Campanile and the "artisanal" juggernaut that was the La Brea Bakery.

It wasn't just people from the Chez Panisse–Spago–Michael's orbit who were making the case for New American, either. Barry Wine, the self-taught chef behind the most celebrated of the *New York Times* four-star restaurants of the eighties, the Quilted Giraffe, was downright chauvinistic about what he was doing. "We used to have a saying that if you didn't know who Howdy Doody was, you couldn't cook at the Quilted Giraffe," says Wine. "In my perspective, the Quilted Giraffe was the first restaurant with serious ambitions, run by Americans, that looked to be the equivalent of the Michelin three-star-chef restaurant. We were out to compete with, and beat, the Lutèces of the world."

A securities lawyer who caught the cooking bug in the days of *The French Chef* and *The Galloping Gourmet*, Wine, with his wife, Susan, opened the original Quilted Giraffe in 1975 in the exurban town of New Paltz, New York, ninety miles up the thruway from the big city. In New Paltz, Wine was cooking "right out of Julia Child," he says; the early print ads for the Quilted Giraffe explicitly described it as "An Elegant French Restaurant."

But shortly after he and Susan moved their operation to Manhattan in 1979, Wine became as obsessed as Forgione with all-American sourcing, even if, unlike Forgione, he often used French culinary paradigms to inspire his dishes. "If Michel Guérard had leg of lamb baked in hay," he says, "we had leg of lamb baked in local corn husks." If the Quilted Giraffe was serving foie

---

*In the late nineties, David Bouley would also extricate himself from an agreement turned sour with LeRoy. Bouley had hoped that LeRoy would underwrite an elaborate complex in Tribeca's Mohawk building in which the chef would run a cooking school, a research center, a food shop, a bakery, and a restaurant. But the financing fell apart, and Bouley feels that the Tavern on the Green impresario was abusing his good name to generate excitement about other LeRoy projects that Bouley had little or nothing to do with—such as LeRoy's ill-fated plan to revive the venerable Russian Tea Room on West Fifty-seventh Street.

gras, it wasn't imported, like everyone else's, but from ducks raised near the Wines' New Paltz home by Michael Ginor and Izzy Yanay, two young men who were starting up an operation called Hudson Valley Foie Gras. The American sourcing didn't stop Wine from charging French-restaurant prices, though, nor did it prevent him from serving Russian caviar in his famous "beggar's purses," little crepes filled with beluga eggs and crème fraîche and knotted shut with chive strings. Among those paying attention to the show was Charlie Trotter, a young kid from the Chicago suburbs who bluffed his way into the Quilted Giraffe's kitchen to meet Wine, and who recalls the restaurant as "definitively, the most sophisticated New American cuisine restaurant in the country"—that is, until Trotter opened his own place in 1987.

Down in New Orleans, twenty-six-year-old tyro Emeril Lagasse was creating similar waves at Commander's Palace, a century-old landmark in the city's Garden District that had been purchased in 1974 by the siblings Ella and Dick Brennan. Under the Brennans' ownership, Commander's Palace had become famous for its "Haute Creole" cookery, a spruced-up rendering of such traditional regional dishes as shrimp remoulade, seafood gumbo, and trout amandine. But by 1983, the Brennans decided to freshen up the menu, controversially tapping the non-native Lagasse, a self-described "street guy from Fall River, Mass.," who had graduated from the Johnson and Wales culinary school in Providence, Rhode Island.

As "street" as Lagasse was, with his stevedore's build and honking locutions, he knew his stuff. "In the seventies, the kitchens in New York City were predominantly run by either the French, the Swiss, or the Germans," he says, "so here comes a cocky young American kid, and they laughed at me. They were like, 'What do you know about food? You're an American— you just know about hamburgers and hot dogs.' "

So Lagasse packed off to France, *staging* in restaurants in Lyons and Paris, including La Tour d'Argent. He also kept a close eye on the progress of Forgione. "I would chase restaurants back then, check 'em out, and I'd been chasing Larry since the River Café," Lagasse says. "In my early years at

Commander's, every time I would come to New York City, which was often, An American Place was the first restaurant I'd go see."

Inspired by Forgione's New Americanisms, Lagasse decided to attempt nothing less than what he deemed a "New New Orleans" cuisine. "I went to Ella Brennan and said, 'Have you ever run lamb here?' and she said, 'It's impossible, it'll never sell—New Orleanians hate lamb,' " Lagasse says. "So I asked her to at least let me try it as a special: rack of lamb with Creole mustard crust, apple mint relish, and rosemary mashed potatoes. And we sold out the first night. I ran it again the following week, and it sold out again. A couple of weeks go by, and I got Ella coming to me saying, 'You know, Dick and I decided we're gonna give you this right-hand side of the menu. Be creative, but don't be out there.' "

Meanwhile, Lagasse's predecessor at Commander's Palace, the roly-poly Cajun chef Paul Prudhomme, was gaining national attention at his new restaurant in New Orleans, K-Paul's, for initiating the eighties' most absurd food trend, although, in his hands, it actually tasted good: blackened redfish. More of a project for a smithy shop than a kitchen, Prudhomme's cayenne- and black-pepper-spiced preparation of the Gulf fish, also known as red drum, required him to dip the fillets in clarified butter and then sear them in iron skillets heated up to near moltenness—a bit of nouvelle flash-cooking technique wedded to his Acadian heritage. Prudhomme was such an adept self-promoter, appearing on all the morning talk shows and pushing his "Magic Seasoning Blends," that by 1987, his provisioners could barely keep up with the demand for redfish, especially with imitative chefs across the country demanding redfish of their own to blacken. By decade's end, the redfish population of the Gulf of Mexico was so depleted that regulatory action was required to protect the species, whose numbers would only return to pre-Prudhomme levels at the turn of the twenty-first century.

IN MAY OF 1983 came a signal moment in the evolution of the New American movement. The Stanford Court hotel, James Beard's home away from home in San Francisco, hosted the first major benefit for the American Institute of

Wine and Food (AIWF), an organization founded two years earlier by Julia Child and the Napa Valley winemaker Robert Mondavi to promote the appreciation of food and wine within the United States. A summit of sorts for America's emerging indigenous star chefs, it was where many of them met for the first time.

Michael McCarty and Jonathan Waxman teamed up to prepare red-pepper pasta with grilled scallops. Forgione did his signature terrine of three smoked fishes—salmon, whitefish, and sturgeon—attractively layered and garnished with their respective caviars. Alice Waters, naturally, handled the garden salad,* and Wolfgang Puck and Mark Peel, naturally, served Spago pizzas. Mark Miller prepared a course of marinated grilled quail with poblano chili, cilantro, and lime sauce. Jimmy Schmidt, of the London Chop House in Detroit, collaborated with a young Michigan-born chef who was working at the American Restaurant in Kansas City, Bradley Ogden, on a gratin of wild root vegetables, fiddlehead ferns, and cattail sprouts. Jeremiah Tower, temporarily employed at the Santa Fe Bar and Grill while he waited for his Stars financing to come together, made a dessert of pecan puff pastry with chocolate and sabayon sauces. And all the way from K-Paul's in New Orleans came Paul Prudhomme to do his blackened redfish. The Stanford Court's Jim Nassikas, fearful of alarms and sprinklers going off, to say nothing of the damage that Prudhomme's plumes of peppery black smoke might do to his hotel, exiled the hefty Cajun and his skillets to the fire escape.

It was an auspicious kickoff for both the AIWF and the New American movement. The assembled chefs, journalists, and hospitality professionals exchanged phone numbers and ideas, and there were even some business deals struck. Bill Wilkinson, the general manager of the Campton Place hotel near San Francisco's Union Square, was so impressed with Odgen that he hired him away from Kansas City, beginning the California phase of Ogden's life

---

*James Beard couldn't resist zinging the la-di-da tone of Waters's first proper cookbook, *The Chez Panisse Menu Cookbook* (1982), whose contents included "A Menu for the Zinfandel Festival" and "A Special Event to Celebrate Allium Satvium, Film, Music, and the Vernal Equinox." Leafing through the book with a smirk on his face, Beard told the Stanford Court's Jim Nassikas, "Jim, this is Alice in Food Wonderland!"

that would culminate in his opening of the Lark Creek Inn in Marin County. Before long, such gatherings of chefs were unremarkable. (In their frequency, that is; culinarily and socially, they were often Caligulan bacchanals.) The eighties marked the advent of the enormo-benefit for a good cause—whether it was fighting hunger, homelessness, AIDS, or Alzheimer's—and few food professionals ever turned down such organizations as Meals on Wheels, City Harvest, amfAR, and Share Our Strength.

"We're the most fuckin' charitable people on the planet!" says Drew Nieporent of Montrachet. "You should see the requests we get every day. We're the easiest marks in the world!" The do-good aspect certainly appealed to the chefs and restaurateurs, but working the benefits also afforded them a new opportunity to function as a community and to gain the kind of nation-wide exposure that the likes of Pierre Franey and André Soltner never enjoyed.

"I think it was the golden age of American cooking—Larry Forgione doing his thing, Alice, on the West Coast, doing her thing, and American chefs finally coming out from behind the stove," says Tom Colicchio, who made the rounds of New York's most progressive American-run kitchens of the eighties, working for Wine at the Quilted Giraffe, for Thomas Keller at Rakel, and for Alfred Portale at Gotham Bar and Grill before getting his own three-star perch at the short-lived Mondrian in 1988. "It was more exciting than what happened in the nineties because it was all brand-new. Maybe it was like it was back in the twenties and thirties in Harlem, when these jazz greats were all playing at the same time, all knowing each other, riffing off each other, supporting each other."*

---

*Many of New York's younger chefs of the eighties regularly networked and caroused as members of an informal club that called itself Chefs from Hell, Unicyclists, and Acrobats, and was organized by the wine writer and consultant Gerry Dawes. "We had stupid bylaws and everything, but it was really just an excuse to have a party," says Thomas Keller. "Gerry would bring the wines, and each month one of us would host a lunch." Colicchio remembers "sitting between [the chefs] Tom Valenti and Waldy Malouf and laughing so much I actually threw up."

IN 1985, TWO YEARS after the seminal AIWF gathering, Prudhomme, Tower, Waters, Waxman, Schmidt, Ogden, Wine, and Forgione were all quoted or mentioned in a celebratory *Time* cover story, written by Mimi Sheraton, that broadcast THE FUN OF AMERICAN FOOD and listed local produce, goat cheese, wild mushrooms, blue cornmeal, and game as all-the-rage ingredients. Sheraton has since become one of the prime critics of the food press's tendencies toward hype—"I am still at least as contentious in 2006 as I was back then, maybe more," she says—but even she believes that, in the mid-eighties, "It was a big development to have American cooking proudly expressed."

"There were a lot of forces at work to make Americans want to believe in American food," says Judy Rodgers. "Think about it: Reagan became president in 1981. Suddenly there was this real interest in 'proud to be American.' The stage was set, and who knows how much that influenced the media. I remember *Food & Wine* had a cover with a cake in the shape of the stars and stripes."

If the marriage between freaky-foodie chefs and "Morning in America" conservative pride was a strange one, then so was the wedding of the tortilla and the lobster. Down in Texas, a restaurant consultant named Anne Lindsay Greer got so miffed by the food press's focus on California and New York and its ignorance of her state that, in 1983, she consciously sought to launch her own regional food movement, which she called Southwestern cuisine. Rounding up three promising young Dallas-based chefs, Dean Fearing, Stephan Pyles, and Avner Samuel, and one Houston chef, Robert Del Grande, Greer urged them to dissuade the nation of the premise that Texas cooking meant "dirty Mexican food," and to prove that chilies, salsas, tortillas, cilantro, and the like could be the basis of a sophisticated, wonderful, region-specific cuisine.

The four chefs plus Greer—who came to be known as the "Gang of Five," a nickname assigned them by a Dallas food writer—met regularly to cook together and toss around ideas, one of which was that each come up with a media-friendly signature dish. For Del Grande, for example, it was the crab tostada he served at his Cafe Annie; for Fearing, it was the lobster taco he served at the Mansion on Turtle Creek; and for Pyles, the sole native Texan of the group, it was the ritzy lobster enchilada he served at Routh Street Café, essentially a classic *homard à l'américaine* preparation updated with Tex-Mex seasonings and tucked inside a tortilla.

As transparent as the Gang of Five's members were in their ploy, it worked. "Along comes a full-blown cuisine, complete with handsome guys that could talk!" Ruth Reichl told *The Dallas Morning News* in 2003, recalling the lime-juice-spritzed excitement of the Southwestern dawn. (Fearing, in particular, resembled a soap-opera heartthrob, or at least a six o'clock anchorman in a mid-market city.) Later on, the chefs admitted that, initially, they had no idea where they were headed. Fearing recalled wondering, "How are you going to sell this as five-star food for these prices when people can get tortillas and chilies down the street for $1.99?" He felt that he "had to throw pheasant or lobster in everything to keep people from seeing this as Tex-Mex." Fortunately, the Gang of Five chefs were talented enough to overcome the cynical origins of their plan and find their way to authentic culinary transcendence.

Still, the hype and the growing press obsession with innovation and "new cuisines" marked the beginning of American food's silly season, the Ascent of the Kiwi. The silliness wasn't limited to what was on the plate, either. If the good news for aspiring chefs was that telling your parents that you wanted to spend your career in the kitchen no longer meant automatic disownment,* the bad news was that many chefs of the eighties got so full of

---

*For me, in the late seventies, it was definitely kind of a fuck-you to your parents to say, 'I'm gonna be a chef,' " says Mary Sue Milliken. "It was like saying, 'I'm gonna be an auto mechanic,' or 'I'm gonna be a pipe fitter.' My cooking school was at a trade school on the South Side of Chicago, with plumbers, pipe fitters, auto mechanics, wallpaper hangers. They were learning a trade, and I was learning a trade. And none of us got any respect." Likewise, Emeril Lagasse, a promising drummer in his teens, recalls, "My mom was devastated when I told her I wanted to be a chef, because I turned down a full scholarship to the New England Conservatory of Music to take a job at a restaurant in Philadelphia to pay for cooking school. That went over like a lead balloon."

themselves, between the fawning media attention, the gush from the socialite benefit-goers, their own mutual-admiration societies, and the high-quality cocaine in which many of them indulged, that it was nearly their undoing. "They roll into town like rock stars, roadies in their wake," wrote the ever-attuned Reichl in the mid-eighties, by then the restaurant critic for the *Los Angeles Times*, in a report on a Meals on Wheels benefit in LA. "They stay in the best hotels, are wined and dined in the finest restaurants, and when show time finally comes, they are interviewed, photographed, and besieged by autograph hunters. They are The Celebrity Chefs."

"Everybody was doing way too much blow," says McCarty. "That's when 'rehab' became a word, and the money thing was getting completely out of hand, and people were buying their first Mercedes." As Jeremiah Tower had discovered earlier, cocaine was, in the short-term, a chef's best friend, the ideal way to keep one's energy from flagging while turning out 120 meals in a restaurant and another 200 at a benefit at the home of the so-cialite Denise Hale. "There are many chefs I know who worked eighteen-hour days and did brilliant stuff on cocaine, and then calmed down with a little glass of *Quelle heure est-il?*" says Clark Wolf.

But cocaine also fueled hubris, which in turn fueled conspicuous con-sumption, regrettable behavior, and poorly considered expansion plans. "There was a lot of *Behind the Music* stuff going on, put it that way," says Bobby Flay. "I would say the eighties restaurant scene was self-destructive. It was a fun scene, but a bad scene."

By the end of the decade, Flay's mentor, Waxman, came to signify the downside of the eighties as much as he had once signified its mesquite-infused promise. The prices at Jams were too high, customers and critics complained, and the door scene was haughty and nightclub-like. What's more, the chef was out on the town too much, checking out his buddies' restaurants. Either that, or he was in London, where he'd opened up another Jams in 1987. By 1990, the jig was up: the money ran out, and Waxman had lost all of his restaurants. He sold his Ferrari for $65,000 and moved back to California for a while, living on the proceeds of the car sale. Waxman maintains that it was disastrous business planning and the fallout from the 1987 stock-market crash that did him in, not drugs. "I was a rock and roller in the seventies, I grew up in Berkeley, and I started smoking pot when I was sixteen years old!" he says. "It was an occupational hazard, but I don't think it was something that destroyed my career. I mean, we're allowed our failures. Everybody's had their failures. Mine are louder than most."

The star-spangled promise of a definable "American cuisine" faded away, too. Forgione's approach succeeded as a personalized take on the nation's culinary heritage, but it wasn't something that other chefs picked up on. For Judy Rodgers, "This idea of 'it's gotta have an American hook' was putting me in a ghetto. I started thinking, 'I should just do good food.'" The most sensible way forward, Rodgers concluded, was not to worry how "American" one's cooking was, but to operate "more in a general sense of doing '*not* French classical food.'"

FEW PEOPLE COULD have cared less about French classicism—or fealty to any Old World cuisine, for that matter—than Mark Miller. "When they talk about Plymouth Rock in 1620—well, Santa Fe was founded in 1590, thirty years earlier, and Cortes was in Mexico City in 1521," he says. "The Spanish were here a hundred years before the Western Europeans were here. When we talk about America, we should always talk about the Spanish part as being the home of the original settlers. It is *not* Jamestown, Virginia. This is part of the pissiness that I get into."

The straight arrow of the Chez Panisse scene, Miller recused himself from the Berkeley gang's chemical excesses, deriving his kicks instead from studying Chinese art (eleventh-century Sung Dynasty paintings, to be precise) and Guatemalan weavings. The product of an academic family in Massachusetts, Miller had been working as an assistant professor in UC-Berkeley's anthropology department when he got sucked into the Panisse vortex. He switched gears from academia to cooking, but he never really stopped being an anthropologist.

Indeed, it was his aversion to Chez Panisse's party atmosphere and his inveterate explorations of New World culinary traditions that led to his decision to leave the restaurant. On the first count, he explains, "Both my parents are psychiatrists, and I grew up in a culture of hospitals and patients and substance abuse. I saw, early on, what that could do to people and their homes and families. So I was very worried." On the second count, he says, "Alice's underlying philosophy for thirty-odd years has been *la cuisine de bonne femme*, the French cuisine of the woman, and it will remain that philosophy. It's a very different philosophy than Jeremiah's philosophy, and it's a very different philosophy than mine. And it did not allow me to do dishes or create the flavors that I had come to love and understand in terms of my anthropology. Even if we did an ethnic dish, it was always in some way a lie."

Ferociously intellectual and not afraid to let you know it—in the course of a conversation, he will tell you, "I have two years of Zen gardening," and "I read Heinrich Schliemann's *Troy and Its Remains* when I was eight or nine years old," and "I started collecting primitive art when I was twelve"— Miller felt limited even by his Berkeley restaurants, the Fourth Street Grill and the Santa Fe Bar and Grill. Finally, in 1985, he settled in the *real* Santa Fe, the one in New Mexico. There, far from the highly developed but Eurocentric food scene of Berkeley, he felt free at last to explore the foodways of the American Southwest, where Native American, Hispanic, Mexican, Tex-Mex, and even Cajun and Creole cuisines bumped up against each other.

Miller's timing was good, for in the mid-eighties, America's palate was growing more accustomed to the flavors of such cultures. Twenty years earlier, Congress passed the Immigration Act of 1965, which abolished the discriminatory national-origins quota system that had favored white Western European immigrants over brown ones from undeveloped countries. The result was a boon not just to poor Mexicans looking for a better life but to the state of Mexican food in the United States. As the Mexican American population grew—between 1965 and 1977, one-third of all immigrants to the United States from the Western Hemisphere were Mexicans—so did the availability of the ingredients used in south-of-the-border cooking. In 1986, the Mexican-food authority Diana Kennedy felt compelled to revise her book *The Cuisines of Mexico*, noting that "phenomenal changes have taken place in the food world in general since the book was published fourteen years ago . . . Large food chains and specialty food stores have also contributed their part by making new and exotic ingredients available to a much wider public. This bounty has been particularly notable in the case of Mexican foods and produce—no doubt spurred on as well by the large Mexican immigration. Cilantro, tomatillos, Mexican-type cheeses, and *many* types of chilies are now routinely available throughout much of the country."

Kennedy wasn't thrilled about the custom in Mexican American restaurants of serving premeal chips and salsa—real Mexicans did no such thing, and she felt that the chips would fill up a diner while the salsa would dull his palate, rendering him unable to fully enjoy the food to come. But the very fact that Americans were growing amenable to salsas, fresher and less glutinous and salty than the commercial ketchups, mustards, and steak sauces that had long dominated the condiment market, was an indication that the American public was less intractable in its tastes than it was thought to be. David Pace, a Texan who, in 1947, founded what would become America's largest salsa manufacturer, Pace Foods, in the back of his San Antonio liquor store, marveled in 1992 that "in the seventies, the business exploded when the hippies came along. No question, this health stuff made the whole category explode, and it just tickles me to see these people take the ball and run with it."

For Miller, this was his moment to further the work of the Gang of Five, with whom he was friendly, and to help Americans achieve a deeper, richer understanding of Mexican-influenced food—which, to his chagrin, was too often thought of as *muy picante* jalapeño nachos or Gerberish combo plates of tacos, enchiladas, rice, and beans with shredded cheese on top. "With chilies, it was interesting, because here was a common spice that was really vastly misunderstood," he says. "Everybody just thought of them as *hot*—as part of the interruptiveness of the Western palate, this thing that spices something up. When I worked with chilies, I saw them as shadings and variegations, like the weave of a textile, in terms of the ability to be expressive and be used as an aesthetic tool within the cuisine."

It's debatable whether or not his diners grasped his lofty anthropological lessons, but there's no doubt that Miller's Coyote Cafe, which he finally opened in 1987, was a remarkably successful assimilation of cultures into a coherent whole, rather like Santa Fe itself. His wild-morel tamales, based on a recipe from pre-Columbian times, sat comfortably on the menu alongside his own inventions, such as quail in a hibiscus-blossom marinade (inspired by the purple hibiscus water sold as a thirst-quencher in Mexican markets) and tamarind barbecued ribs.* In his educational zeal, Miller also convinced Berkeley's Ten Speed Press to print his "Great Chile Poster," featuring photographs of chilies of different sizes, shapes, and degrees of heat, attractively arranged in botanical-guide fashion. Released in 1989, the poster was to food-mad yuppies what the Farrah Fawcett poster had been to adolescent boys a decade earlier, and it earned Miller a small fortune.

Perhaps there was something about Mexico's mystery and untapped complexity that drew intense, questing types, for the Chicago-based restaurateur Rick Bayless made even Miller look like a laid-back, Bermuda-shorted tourist. Originally from Oklahoma City, Bayless was, like Miller, a child of preternatural precocity—his parents, who ran a down-home barbecue restaurant, were alarmed when, at age ten or eleven, their boy got into the habit

---

*A couple of years before Miller opened the Coyote Cafe, Susan Feniger and Mary Sue Milliken moved their City Café in Los Angeles to a larger location, rechristening it City Restaurant. In the café's old location, they opened a restaurant called Border Grill, whose menu they based on the street food they'd eaten "while tooling around in Mexico in a VW Bug," Milliken says. While not as anthropologically ambitious as the Coyote Cafe, the Border Grill offered a similar smart-gringo take on Mexican food and wound up outlasting City Restaurant; it persists to this day at yet another location, in Santa Monica. In 1999, flush with TV success as the "Too Hot Tamales" on the Food Network program of the same title, Feniger and Milliken opened a second Border Grill in Las Vegas. "They've kind of regionalized the idea of LA Mexican food," says Miller of Feniger and Milliken. "I don't know their importance in the development of Mexican food, but I think that they made it approachable. Sort of like what Emeril does."

of watching *The French Chef*, taking notes, and immediately trying to reproduce Child's recipes in his mother's kitchen, "making things like the classic napoleons, with all the puff pastry made from scratch." Obsessed with travel, the young Bayless set his sights on Mexico as "the closest foreign country that spoke another language," and, at age fourteen, mapped out a Mexican vacation for his family, which his compliant parents dutifully went on with him. "When I got there, I felt totally at home, and I loved it," he says.

Like Miller, Bayless chose to study anthropology (forsaking cooking for a time in his teens "because of peer pressure"), and, like Miller, he eventually put aside his promising academic career to pursue a culinary career. In 1978, when he was twenty-five and teaching cooking classes, Bayless benefited from a stroke of luck when he heard that a small, student-run public-TV station in Bowling Green, Ohio, had planned a series on Mexican cooking, "and that the person who was gonna do it had bailed on them at the very last second. They were actually looking for a host for a public-television series on Mexican cooking!" Bayless seized the opportunity to win the job, and, though the TV program was only on for two years, he and his wife, Deann, ended up living in Mexico for almost five years in the early 1980s.

Bayless's goal at the time was to come up with a great, usable cookbook that showed Mexican cuisine for what it was, rather than for what it was misperceived as—usually as Tex-Mex, which, he says, is to authentic Mexican "like what Vietnamese food is to Thai food, about that closely related," or as Cal-Mex, which Bayless deemed "Chicano food, really not very Mexican."* He wanted to introduce people to *posoles*, the rich soup-stews made with hominy, and to the seven moles of Oaxaca, the delightful cooked sauces that came in black, green, yellow, two versions of red, one gravy-like version called *chichilo*, and a mild, fruit-flavored sauce called *manchamanteles*. The ob-

---

*Before there was a Bayless, a Mark Miller, or a Gang of Five, Jane Butel was publishing books on Tex-Mex and Southwestern food in the seventies. Though Bayless doesn't take her seriously, Butel, a smiley, charismatic character given to wearing fringed dresses and chunky Navajo jewelry, still runs a successful cooking school in Albuquerque, New Mexico.

vious hurdle was that Diana Kennedy had already been down this route. "I didn't want to just rewrite one of her books," Bayless says. "Then I realized that I'm a restaurant person, and she's a home cook. That's one of the big differences between the way we approach things: a lot of my recipes come from people who actually are preparing food for sale, and she is looking for the one person in the community that makes the very special whatever."

Bayless had mixed feelings about Kennedy. He found her books to be "overly complex in one way, and yet they don't give you enough information in another," but he still appreciated the fact that she'd blazed the trail for him. Early on in his time in Mexico, he felt it only appropriate to track her down so he could pay homage and perhaps soak up some knowledge. "But Diana's very difficult," he says. "She did everything but just chew me up and spit me out. I'd never been so poorly treated by any person. She said, 'This is over, I think we're done,' and kicked me out of her car and left me on a road. I had to walk back to town."

"The thing was this," says Kennedy in response. "I had just bought some land but not yet built a house, and he sort of trailed me there, and the day he arrived, somebody had cut down two trees on the land that I'd just bought, and I was furious. And then, you know, being young, he was sort of damned opinionated, and he kept saying things like, 'Well, why didn't you translate the Spanish titles in the tortilla book?' I said, 'Well, *for goodness' sake!*' He was being very brash, and I was getting annoyed, so that was it: I gave him the bum's rush."

In any event, Bayless recovered from this episode to emerge triumphant in 1987. That year, he and his wife came out with their first cookbook, *Authentic Mexican: Regional Cooking from the Heart of Mexico*—whose foreword contained a sly dig at Kennedy, promising readers a respite from other Mexican cookbooks "with peculiarly 'authentic' preparations and incomplete directions"—and their first restaurant, Frontera Grill, which they set up in Chicago because Deann's family was there.

"The first customers who walked through our door got up from the table and walked out, telling us, 'You will never make it. This isn't Mexican food,' " Bayless says. "They wanted burritos and nachos, and we didn't have either one of them on the menu." For a few months, Bayless sought to lure diners in with more Miller-ish, Gang of Five–ish Southwestern fare— "grilled fish with, you know, mango salsa," he says—but such diversions soon proved unnecessary. Marian Burros of *The New York Times* reported in May of 1987 that Frontera Grill was "packed" within weeks of its opening, and her article resulted in the restaurant being still more packed. Burros even elicited a faint-praise quote about Bayless from Kennedy: "He has certainly done his research. To me, it doesn't demonstrate that he has a real grass-roots knowledge of the different cuisines of Mexico. But at least he does something valid."

RIGHT ABOUT THE TIME that the Frontera Grill and the Coyote Cafe were awakening diners to sophisticated culinary experiences outside the bounds of Eurocentrism—urging them, as Miller puts it, to "look at flavors as a perceptual cultural system"—Nobu Matsuhisa was setting up shop in a little dive spot on La Cienega Boulevard at the edge of Beverly Hills. It didn't take long for LA's ever vigilant foodie clique to discover that this modest place, simply named Matsuhisa, wasn't just a sushi bar, but, as Caroline Bates wrote in *Gourmet* in 1988, "the only Japanese restaurant in Los Angeles that cooks with a Peruvian accent." After enduring the requisite apprenticeship for sushi chefs in his native Japan in the 1960s—novices aren't even allowed to handle the fish the first two years—Matsuhisa logged time at various sushi bars in Tokyo before he decided to visit a friend in Peru, a country with a large Japanese population and a fantastic variety of fish off its shore. Matsuhisa was so bedazzled by this latter circumstance that he decided to stay, taking a job at a sushi bar in Lima in 1974, when he was only twenty-three years old.

"The first time I ever ate ceviche was in Peru," Matsuhisa says. "I loved it, but I wanted to apply Japanese technique." In Latin countries, ceviche was traditionally prepared by marinating pieces of raw fish in citrus juices and chopped onion, "cooking" them for several hours until the acids in the juices had turned the translucent fish cubes opaque. But Matsuhisa, already California-nouvelle in spirit, preferred to essentially flash-"cook" his ceviche, drizzling his fish pieces in citric acid at the last minute and using yuzu, an especially sour Japanese citrus fruit—"not like Sunkist lemon, which is too sweet," he says—to achieve greater piquancy. Expanding on this idea, Matsuhisa also fooled around with a Peruvian-Japanese preparation called *tiradito*, in which thin slices of sashimi-grade fish are aesthetically fanned out like petals and dotted with a spicy chili sauce—a compositionally gorgeous mix of coolness and heat.

While Matsuhisa was in Peru, sushi chefs in America were already fiddling with tried-and-true formulas, adapting to the ingredients that America had on offer. The starting point of sushi in America was the Little Tokyo section of downtown Los Angeles, near the city's municipal government buildings. There, the first sushi restaurant in the United States opened in 1960, a tiny six-seat bar called Kawafuka, followed in short order by two more places, Eikiku and the larger Tokyo Kaikan, an American sibling of a Tokyo restaurant. It is Tokyo Kaikan's two sushi chefs in the sixties, Ichiro Mashita and Teruo Imaizumi, who are usually credited with creating the first cross-cultural sushi concoction, the California roll. "It wasn't because we were trying to make something more palatable for Americans, but because of the poor variety of fish back then," says Imaizumi (speaking in Japanese, with his daughter, Nana, translating). "The tuna was just a seasonal thing in LA, available in the summertime, and so we were thinking 'What else can we use? What else can we look for?' "

What Mashita and Imaizumi found in 1964 were avocados, which grew plentifully in California and were available in the grocery store right next door to their restaurant. Cut into little cubes, ripe avocado flesh had an unctuousness that approximated the texture of fatty fish, and the two sushi chefs combined it with king crab, cucumber, and ginger, serving their creation as a hand roll. Their Japanese diners were wary, Imaizumi recalls, "because there wasn't raw fish in there. They were going 'What is this?!' " But as Tokyo Kaikan started to attract more Caucasian diners—executives and financiers who had business with Japanese companies, and fearless diners emboldened by the new spirit of ethnic adventure afoot in the seventies—the California roll was popular precisely *because* it didn't contain raw fish. (Tokyo Kaikan also claimed to be where the inside-out roll was invented, to placate round-eye customers who didn't like the texture of the seaweed wrap, but Imaizumi, a purist, doesn't make them in his current Little Tokyo restaurant, Sushi Imai.)

For Caucasians, the California roll proved to be an ideal gateway drug to the hard stuff; once you got over the weirdness of a cold piece of something-or-other brushed with wasabi and rolled in vinegar-seasoned rice and seaweed, it wasn't so crazy to try sushi made with uncooked scallops or slices of velvety, high-quality raw tuna. In the early seventies, *Gourmet* still considered sushi and sashimi to be sufficiently exotic that both words were italicized in the magazine's pages, denoting their foreignness, but the magazine's New York critic at the time, Jay Jacobs, wrote, "With Japanese restaurants proliferating apace, New Yorkers are learning to knock back raw fish with the equanimity of so many gannets and to brandish a pair of chopsticks as if to the manner born." In 1980, the popularity of sushi received an unanticipated boost when tens of millions of Americans tuned in to the TV miniseries *Shogun*, based on the James Clavell novel and starring Richard Chamberlain, which spurred a faddist mania for all things Japanese.

The eighties were the time in which Japanese food came of age in the United States, with diet-conscious Americans warming to sushi as "pure, clean, healthy, something that goes with organic," as Clark Wolf puts it,* and status-conscious Americans eating raw fish just because it was cool to do so; it was a mark of the hipness of Alex Cox's dystopian LA comedy *Repo Man*, one of the signature cult films of the decade, that one of its street hoodlums

---

*In his capacity as a restaurant consultant, Wolf was astounded to discover, in the stressful months after the 9/11 terrorist attacks, that Americans were "turning to sushi as a comfort food." While he correctly anticipated the popularity in that time of such straightforward fare as roast chicken with mashed potatoes, he admits he understated the degree to which sushi was now accepted as a staple of American dining out.

uttered the improbable line "Let's go get sushi and not pay." Jean-Georges Vongerichten remembers eating sushi for the first time in New York City at the surprisingly late date (for a well-traveled chef) of 1985.

"It was mind-boggling to me," he says. "I had worked all this time in Southeast Asia, but I had never been to Japan." Though his own cross-cultural experimentation would borrow more from the flavors of Thailand—ginger, lemongrass, Thai basil, curry paste—Vongerichten loved the possibilities that the new American embrace of Japanese food suggested. "Everything felt so wide open," he says. "I thought, 'Wow, everything I experienced in Thailand, in Asia—let's push it.' "

Likewise, Barry Wine was so overcome by his first trip to Japan in 1985, that as the eighties progressed into the nineties, the Quilted Giraffe evolved from a defiantly American place into New York's fanciest Japanese American fusion restaurant, serving yellowtail sashimi, Kobe beef, a Wolf-gang Puckish ricotta cheese and wasabi pizza, and a $135 version of the rit-ualized Kaiseki tea ceremony. "I realized that what we called nouvelle cuisine was, in fact, very Japanese," he told Gael Greene. "The small portions on big plates, the emphasis on what's fresh in the market, the taste of food un-masked."

Appropriately enough, it was in Los Angeles, always at the vanguard of American sushi culture, that sushi made its greatest strides forward. Mat-suhisa made his way to the city in 1979, licking his wounds after an awful experience in Anchorage, Alaska, where he'd finally opened a restaurant of his own, called Kioi, only for it to burn to the ground fifty days into its ex-istence. After nearly nine years of working at a traditional sushi bar in West Hollywood as a mere employee, Matsuhisa finally had the money to open his place on La Cienega in 1987—conveniently located just north of Wilshire Boulevard, where the Hollywood agents worked.

As Ma Maison had proved, the movie-industry people loved nothing more than to be in the know about some grubby little place where the food was fantastic, and Matsuhisa, with its plain storefront disguising wondrously transcendent sushi and innovative Peruvian Japanese fusion within, was just the ticket. One of the restaurant's earliest regulars was Michael Ovitz, the founder of Creative Artists Agency, who was then regarded as the most powerful man in Hollywood. "Mike Ovitz used to bring in a lot of clients, because he say, 'Power lunch at Matsuhisa,'" says Matsuhisa. "He bring in producers, directors, Bob De Niro, Tom Cruise. And *then* people start talking about my restaurant."

For his high-profile clientele, Matsuhisa unleashed all his creative powers, offering not only some of the best raw fish in town but *tiraditos*; ceviches; broiled black cod marinated in sake and miso; "new-style sashimi" seared for a micro-moment in hot oil; squid sliced and scored to look like rigatoni, and served in a garlic sauce; and a plate of rock shrimp in a creamy sauce of mayonnaise, chili peppers, garlic, and onions that packed a wallop but visually resembled nothing so much as Kraft's Deluxe Macaroni & Cheese Dinner.

As the Nippophile Ovitz rose to the peak of his power, secretly negotiating the sales of Columbia Pictures and MCA-Universal to Japanese companies—Sony and Matsushita, respectively, in 1989 and 1990—so rose the popularity of Matsuhisa. It was only a matter of time before a group of investors, led by "Bob" De Niro, would encourage the modest Nobu Matsuhisa, who insisted he was really happy just to break even in his one little restaurant, to open a branch in New York.

CHAPTER ELEVEN

THE MAGIC
OF THINKING BIG

At Bouley, one of New York City's top restaurants, the most sensuous dish isn't the honey-glazed duck or halibut in thyme oil, but the hazel-eyed genius in the kitchen, chef David Bouley.

—*People* magazine, "The 50 Most
Beautiful People in the World," 1994

IN 1997, FOUR YEARS AFTER DAVID PAGE AND BARBARA SHINN HAD OPENED HOME, A much-beloved, postage-stamp-sized restaurant in New York's Greenwich Village, they were presiding over the grand opening of their second restaurant in the Village, Drover's Tap Room, a bigger, fuller realization of the farmhouse-cuisine vision they shared. "We were celebrating with family, drinking champagne, eating hors d'oeuvres, hanging out, just enjoying the night," Page says. "And then, a few people, one after another, came up and asked me what I was going to do next. *On opening night.*"*

The nineties were when the entrepreneurial spirit took hold of the food world, even before the words "dot-com" and "Internet" were on anyone's lips. They were the years when an interloper named Martha Stewart swooped in and showed the veterans a thing or two about building a brand. A Connecticut caterer and former stockbroker of middle-class, Polish American origins (birth name: Martha Kostyra), Stewart made her first foray into public life in 1982, with her debut book, *Entertaining*, a gracious-living primer that

---

*Though Page and Shinn briefly succumbed to New York City expansionism, opening a catering company and a takeout shop on top of their two restaurants, with plans for three more takeout shops, they chucked everything but their original restaurant, Home, in 1999, to become winemakers on Long Island's North Fork.

PAGE 3 1 9: *Promotional photo for NBC's ill-fated 2001 sitcom* Emeril.

combined James Beard's and Larry Forgione's love of culinary Americana with Ralph Lauren's jodhpur-fantasy approach to dress, table arrangements, and home decor. In the nineties, the unrelenting Stewart broadened her portfolio to include a magazine, many more books, TV programs, and various product lines, all collected, as of 1997, under the aptly omnivorous-sounding corporate title Martha Stewart Living Omnimedia.

Stewart wasn't strictly a food person, but the chefs and cookbook people paid close attention to her—figures from Emeril Lagasse to Julia Child to Mario Batali appeared on her television programs—and took note of how eagerly middle-class Americans latched on to Stewart, trusting her as an all-around arbiter of taste, personal shopper, gardening adviser, and kitchen sage. (Noting the resentment and contempt that the chilly, blond Stewart aroused in some people, Child said, "It's the haute bourgeoisie who have a problem with her—they're jealous of her. For what? That she manages everything so perfectly, I suppose. But the masses love her.") If this *caterer* could construct a multimedia empire, why not an accredited chef like Emeril?

Lagasse makes no bones about it: he wanted to become a big deal, and he primed himself for the decade by reading motivational books like *The Magic of Thinking Big*, by David Schwartz, and *In Search of Excellence*, by Thomas Peters and Robert Waterman. "In essence, the books say that everybody has a certain amount of smarts and drive and motivation inside of 'em, but you really gotta drive it up," he says. In 1990, Lagasse left Commander's Palace to start his own place, Emeril's, and, two years later, opened a second restaurant in New Orleans, NOLA. It would be on the strength of having nine restaurants, six of them outside of New Orleans, that he was able to find work for most of his employees in the aftermath of Hurricane Katrina.

Even more aggressive was Howard Schultz, a Brooklyn native who, in the early eighties, had made his living as the U.S. point man for a Swedish housewares manufacturer. In 1982, Schultz moved to Seattle to take a job as the director of retail operations for Starbucks—"and neither of us has been the same since," as he immodestly put it in his memoir, *Pour Your Heart into It*. In a complex series of transactions, Starbucks acquired Peet's Coffee, from whence it had sprung, and later split into two separate, unaffiliated companies. Jerry Baldwin, whose interests tilted more toward coffee roasting than running cafés, moved back to San Francisco, where he had attended college and pilgrimaged over the Bay Bridge to learn at the feet of Alfred Peet himself, to run Peet's as a regional chain. Schultz, in 1987, bought out the interests of Baldwin and Starbucks' other remaining co-founder, Gordon Bowker. As the CEO of what was now called Starbucks Corp., Schultz pushed into other cities, venturing beyond Seattle to open cafés in Chicago, Vancouver, and Portland, Oregon, in the late eighties. But it was in the nineties that he truly went on an expansionist tear, taking the whole shebang national; whereas there were only eighty-four Starbucks locations in America in 1990, by the year 2000, there were more than three thousand.

While some members of the food world had always envisioned running an empire—Drew Nieporent, modeling himself on Joe Baum and Restaurant Associates, named his company Myriad Restaurant Group because "myriad" implied "endless, countless, as many places as I could handle," he says—others found themselves blindsided by the development. Says Danny Meyer, "When I got into the business at Union Square Cafe, if you wanted to be taken seriously, you wanted to emulate André Soltner. Which is, 'I've got one restaurant. I live upstairs, and it's only open when I'm there, and if I need a vacation, I'm gonna close the restaurant.' "

Meyer sounds sheepish in acknowledging that he now runs a company called Union Square Hospitality Group, which, as of this writing, has seven restaurants in its portfolio. Whereas nine years passed between the opening of Union Square Cafe and Meyer's second place, Gramercy Tavern—"and I was kind of dragged, kicking and screaming, into opening that one," he says—he has since launched a further five restaurants; and compared to Nobu Matsuhisa (twelve restaurants as this book was going to press) and Jean-Georges Vongerichten (fifteen restaurants), he's a laggard.

Americans have come to follow restaurants, chefs, and their activities "like a spectator sport," Meyer says, citing the flurry of activity that's going on around him as he sits down to be interviewed in his office. His staff is scrambling to furnish *The New York Times* with information about his latest restaurant, the Modern, because it is to be reviewed the following week by the paper's current critic, Frank Bruni. At the same time, Meyer's public relations person is trying to help Bruni with an article he is preparing about the state of restrooms in restaurants, "right down to what the timing is of the automatic flushing system!" Meyer exclaims. "That's why I start talking about it being a spectator sport. Since when do people have time to be *thinking* about these kinds of things?"

But it's a very different world than the one that Meyer entered as a young man in 1985—just as the eclectic Union Square Cafe was very different from Le Pavillon, La Caravelle, and the other restaurants from which it then seemed a radical departure. (Meyer remembers an old-time restaurant consultant telling him, "This'll never fly. When New Yorkers go out to eat, they want to go out and eat French, or they want go to out and eat Chinese, or they want to go out and eat Italian.") The gears of food history turned more slowly in the forties, fifties, sixties, and seventies. But since then, it's been warp-drive.

Nearly every big-name fine-dining chef in the New York–LA–Bay Area triangle has more than one restaurant, a presence in Las Vegas, and some kind of line of retail products. Bobby Flay, Mario Batali, Rick Bayless, and Todd English compete against one another and the clock in the Food Network's *Iron Chef* program. The smoulderingly dreamy English and the brooding David Bouley made *People*'s "50 Most Beautiful People" list in different years, while the cherubic Rocco DiSpirito went them one better by making the magazine's "Sexiest Men Alive" list. Anthony Bourdain, the chef at a middling steak frites place in New York called Les Halles, got laypeople interested in the surly, druggy, foul-tempered backstage of restaurant life with his best seller *Kitchen Confidential* (2000), while, less wittingly, DiSpirito did the same thing in the NBC reality TV show *The Restaurant* (2003), letting viewers peek in as he (temporarily) torpedoed his own promising career.

The idea of chefs as *literal* entertainers may be a step too far at this point. Lagasse's 2001 attempt at an NBC sitcom, *Emeril*, died a quick death, as did Fox's hopes in the autumn of 2005 for a hit with their TV-series version of *Kitchen Confidential*. And the renowned director James L. Brooks's cinematic homage to the French Laundry's Thomas Keller, *Spanglish*, starring Adam Sandler as a gifted New American chef, stiffed in 2004. (Keller was listed in the credits as the film's "culinary consultant.")*

But none of this has stopped the food people from pursuing crossover success. As this book was being prepared, HBO announced that it was developing a TV series based on Ruth Reichl's memoirs *Comfort Me with Apples* and *Garlic and Sapphires*. And Wolfgang Puck, always two steps ahead of everyone else in terms of synergy and business acumen, had not only signed on for a recurring role as himself in the NBC drama *Las Vegas* but "opened" a new place in the show's fictional Montecito Resort and Casino—a fully operational soundstage restaurant that serves as an excellent promotional tool for his six real Vegas restaurants. If James Beard were alive now, he'd be giving Philip Seymour Hoffman tips on how to play him.

"I think chefs and restaurants became what they are today because when people finally woke up from the cocaine buzz of the eighties, they had to find another form of entertainment," says Tom Colicchio, who collaborated with Meyer on Gramercy Tavern before establishing his own restaurant group under the Craft name. "The club scene was dying out, and restaurants became the new entertainment, the new opiate."

Nina and Tim Zagat were coming to the same conclusion at the dawn of the nineties. A lawyer couple, they had cultivated a taste for dining out when they lived in Paris in the late sixties, and had gotten tremendous response from their American friends when they circulated a mimeographed roundup of their favorite places to eat there. Returning to New York, the Zagats decided, as a hobby, to launch a formal survey of New York's restaurants that allowed consumers—at the beginning, Tim and Nina's urban-professional acquaintances—to rate and comment upon the city's restaurants. In 1979, the Zagats distributed their debut "1980 NYC Restaurant

---

*It must be said that Nobu Matsuhisa was actually quite good as Mr. Roboto in *Austin Powers in Goldmember* (2002).

Survey" of "over 100 people" on two sides of a legal-size piece of paper, with homely, handwritten block lettering on the top and a spreadsheet-style layout that recorded numerical scores for the food, decor, service, and cleanliness of each rated restaurant, plus one short line of written commentary. (It verged on the salty in the early days; Charley O's was succinctly described as "Bar for middle lvl execs trying to lay their secretaries.") In November 1982, the Zagats self-published their first for-profit, booklet-length survey, with the now familiar burgundy cover. But it wasn't until 1990 that both Tim and Nina quit their law practices to become full-time food-guide people. The tipping point for Nina came "when people would call me in the office and say they had a big, important question for me," she says. "I'd think that they were having some legal problem—and they were trying to decide where to have dinner."

AS THE ZAGATS broadened their mandate in the nineties, publishing guidebooks for other cities and states, the standard-bearers in their surveys were Charlie Trotter's in Chicago, Bouley in New York, and the French Laundry in the little Napa Valley town of Yountville. The three chefs behind these three places—Trotter, Bouley, and Keller, respectively—weren't so much expansionists or exhibitionists, as some of their colleagues were, but lone-wolf perfectionists, less inclined than most chefs to *par-tay* into the wee hours with their colleagues.

Their ascent was a measure of how far American cookery, American ingredients, and American drive had come. All three men were American-born and never went to cooking school, yet all three willed themselves over to France to get work experience in the kitchens of Michelin three-star restaurants. And all three men decided, upon getting their main chance in America, to shoot the works. Trotter was inspired mostly by Frédy Girardet and La Pyramide, Fernand Point's old place; Keller, too, upheld La Pyramide as his model; and Bouley wanted to emulate Le Moulin de Mougins, the flagship restaurant of his mentor, Roger Vergé. The quest they had in common was to create in the United States the kind of European-style restaurant where you came in, sat down, stayed for three or four hours, and ate a multiple-course degustation, or tasting, menu of the best food you'd ever eaten in your life.

Trotter and Bouley opened their restaurants within months of each other in 1987 and both hit their stride in the early nineties, but otherwise, they had little in common. Trotter, baby-faced but preternaturally self-assured, came from the wealthy Chicago suburb of Wilmette—a preppie John Hughes–movie character come to life. Working at forty restaurants in four years—not counting the Monastery, where he earned money as a waiter while an undergraduate at the University of Wisconsin, "where we actually had to dress as monks," he says—he pronounced himself ready at age twenty-seven to run his own place.

Bouley, by contrast, was a handsome but haunted little fellow with a furtive, Ratso Rizzo–like demeanor. He rode motorcycles and was old enough to have experienced the terror of having a low draft number during the denouement of the Vietnam War, which played a significant role in his wanting to get over to France in the mid-seventies. (His family's French an-cestry qualified him for a French passport.) He opened Bouley after bolting Montrachet a mere thirteen months into its existence, finding himself unable to co-exist with the owner-frontman, Drew Nieporent. Bouley won't com-ment on the reasons for the split from Montrachet, but Nieporent, with whom the chef has since patched things up, says it was simply a matter of stub-bornness. "Like, for example, we opened one time on Mother's Day, and he refused to cook eggs," Nieporent says. "He says, 'I don't do eggs.' I said, 'Paul Bocuse does eggs! An egg is a culinary miracle! What the fuck is this about you don't want to make an egg?' And so the first omelet that goes out, goes to a friend of mine. I looked at it. You couldn't find a worse omelet at a diner! I go in the kitchen, I'm like an umpire, I'm up in his face: '*If one more fuckin' omelet comes out like that, I'm closing the fuckin' restaurant!*'"

At Bouley, the food was a fantastic synthesis of the chef's Vergé train-ing and American-market influences, but it was his way or the highway. If you didn't finish the rabbit terrine course on the tasting menu, the waiter would warily take your plate back to the kitchen and return moments later, asking, "The chef wants to know why you didn't finish this."

Though he's mellowed since those days, Bouley is unrepentant about his "the customer is always wrong" approach. "An old customer just reminded me of the time I stood up to his mother," he says. "I had real wild salmon, which we'd walk around the dining room whole to show people what a wild salmon looks like. The meat's so beautiful, and when you cook it, it doesn't turn white, like it does with farmed salmon. Good wild salmon stays red. And this guy's mother said it wasn't cooked, and she wanted it cooked white, no color. And the captain explained to her that this is wild salmon, it's different, it doesn't pale out. She said, 'No, I want my salmon cooked.' And so, nothing happened for ten minutes. I wasn't gonna corrupt that salmon. I sent out the captain to tell her to choose another dish."

It was at Bouley that the term "dayboat fish" entered the menu lexicon. As much as this term is lampooned as the height of culinary pretension—rather like calling a trout "line-caught" or a cheese "farmstead"—Bouley insists it was a matter of pride, an emphasis on the lengths to which he went to get the freshest fish possible. Growing up in Rhode Island, he spent his summers in Cape Cod and got to know the fishing families there, even working for them sometimes as a deckhand. For Bouley, the restaurant, he went back to Cape Cod to make good on these connections.

"In those days, most of the fish you ate was on a boat out to sea for many, many days," Bouley says. "They had ice machines on the boat to keep the fish cold. Then it came in and sat a day. And then, by the time it got to the restaurant, that fish was well over a week out of the water. The Bouley fish, particularly from April to December, was from the fishing boats, mostly out of Chatham, that would go out at four thirty in the morning and come back with their catch by one o'clock. My waiters and captains took turns driving up to the Cape. We'd have fish in the restaurant twelve, thirteen hours after it was killed." Pointedly, affrontedly, Bouley practically spits out his conclusion: "There was a *huge* difference with the dayboat catch! The people that *mocked* us, thinking it was a *gimmick*, had *no clue*."

Trotter was capable of being every bit as fearsome a character as Bouley, but more in the way of a formidable Fortune 500 boss than a hunched, mercurial street tough. A natural CEO, he recommended Ayn Rand's *The Fountainhead* to his staff, used the Michael Jordan–led Chicago Bulls teams of the nineties as a model of teamwork (with a benevolent dictator in charge, of course), and embraced the corporate credo of "the pursuit of excellence." Whereas Lagasse read books on excellence by motivational gurus, Trotter *wrote* a couple (with co-authors), *Lessons in Excellence from Charlie Trotter* and *Lessons in Service from Charlie Trotter*. Some of Trotter's lessons within the books were upbeat, such as "Be a Cheerleader and Recognize Employees"; as a pastry chef struggled to keep ice cream from sliding off a warm fig turnover, Trotter told her, "Stick with it, you're doing great!" and then, addressing the whole kitchen, shouted, "Let's see some energy, people. Help your teammate! What do they need? Figure it out!" But in a more eyebrow-raising lesson entitled "Don't Be Afraid to Fire Customers," Trotter explained, "It's not that I don't appreciate our customers, but sometimes it's better for me to take care of those who really understand this type of dining and not to worry about trying to satisfy everybody. We have deliberately, definitively cut off more and more segments of our customer base."

Trotter is not unaware of how strangely this comes off in relation to the eco-hippie-crunchy ethos that still pervades much of the American food world, but he doesn't care, either. "*Chicago* magazine did a list several years ago of the Ten Meanest Chicagoans, and I came in at number two, after Michael Jordan," he says. "Their definition of 'mean' was just being intense—like, Michael Jordan playing harder on the rookies in practice sessions than he would play against, you know, Charles Barkley during the game. I told my staff"—and here, you sense Trotter isn't speaking entirely in jest—" 'This is unacceptable. I am not accustomed to being number two. *At anything.*' "

"I'm a free-market advocate and a staunch libertarian," he says. "I don't feel like I'm part of the New American cuisine movement. I have no tolerance for the left-wing embrace of food politics and things like that. I think you can support farmers' markets and that you don't have to do it with a Berkeley sensibility. Don't get me wrong—I'm not on the other end of the spectrum. But everybody who's against genetically modified foods and against big corporate food production, I think they could be a little more open-minded in how they look at all these things."

And yet, there was no chef more masterful with vegetables in this country, both in terms of creativity and just making them taste good—complementing grilled Treviso radicchio with spicy, cinnamony, autumnal matsutake mushrooms, or mixing asparagus and basil to surprising effect in a chilled soup. "Fish and meat are kind of unidimensional in their texture and flavor, whereas I've always felt vegetables were the most interesting part of what's on a plate," Trotter says. "You don't need ten ounces of meat. You could have two ounces of meat and all these wonderful support components." Trotter was the first chef to offer an all-vegetarian tasting menu, and, what's more, one that a carnivore could enjoy without missing meat.

Trotter's interest in vegetables played a big role, in fact, in the success of the Chef's Garden, what is now the largest boutique farm in the Midwest, run by an Ohio family, the Joneses, who had lost their property to foreclosure in the early eighties, another set of victims of big agribusiness. Starting over on a modest six-acre plot, with the elder Farmer and Mrs. Jones moving in with their son, Lee, because they'd lost their house along with the farm, the family made a go of selling vegetables in Cleveland's farmers' markets, "mudding the license plates over, because they were invalid and we couldn't afford the registrations," Lee Jones says.

One day, Iris Bailin, the food editor of the *Cleveland Plain Dealer*, asked the Joneses if, since they were selling zucchinis, they would sell her zucchini blossoms. "I was nineteen years old, wet behind the ears, and I was embarrassed at this lady's stupidity," Lee says. "But she kept bugging me every week for these zucchini blooms, and I finally brought 'em down one week. I sort of sheepishly had them hidden underneath the counter and wanted her to kind of quietly come around to the back, 'cause I didn't want any other farmers to accuse me of being, you know, a flower-pushing farmer. So I got her to come around, and, well, what does she do? She starts screaming in the middle of this farmers' market, '*Oh, my God! I haven't seen these since Paris, France! Do you realize what these are?! I've gotta introduce you to a chef!*' Next thing you know, there's about eight people swarmed around her, and I am beet-red embarrassed."

Like a hunky Iowa rube come east to pose for a Calvin Klein underwear ad, the Joneses thought the city folks' requests to be bizarre and against their better judgment, but they needed the money. "The other farmers at the market were more established and comfortable," Lee says, "but we were willing to do things like pick lettuces when they were just three inches high because we were desperate to survive." Eventually, in the late eighties, the Joneses realized they could make a go of selling *exclusively* to chefs. Lee made the rounds, signing up Trotter, Jean-Louis Palladin, Daniel Boulud, and the Ritz-Carlton hotel chain as customers.

"We had sent Mr. Trotter some samples and things, and he challenged us," Lee Jones says. "He said, 'Here's what you can do for me: I am *over* mesclun. Everybody in the country's doing it. You can even get it in grocery stores and delis now. I want something that is so over the top, so sexy and original, that nobody in the country is going to have seen it before.' Well, three months earlier I'd tried picking some really tiny greens and gotten laughed at by the local chefs, who said, 'Why don't you let it grow up?' But I restarted it, and Mr. Trotter sent some of his team out, and they had some suggestions. Microgreens were basically invented right there. I think it was bull's-blood beet leaves, mizuna, tatsoi, and some tiny spinach and arugula."

AS FOR THOMAS KELLER, the French Laundry was his second attempt at forging his own personal cuisine. Rakel, which opened in 1986, was "kind of that almost grand café type of high-energy meets downtown meets fine-dining" place, he says, the sprawl of his description explaining why the restaurant never quite clicked. Although some of his French Laundry ideas were already in place, such as his technique of butter-poaching lobster out of its shell, resulting in meat with a tender, almost erotically glossy mouth feel, Rakel fell victim to the stock-market crash, poor design, and Keller's own less than even temperament at the time; Colicchio says he was ousted by Keller in a "You can't fire me, I quit!" situation, even though the two were good friends.

Chastened by Rakel's failure and brought back to reality by an unhappy stopgap stint in LA, Keller was alerted by Jonathan Waxman that the French Laundry, already a lovely country restaurant in Napa Valley, run by Don and Sally Schmidtt, was up for sale. Keller moved to get the deal done, and set about making his Fernand Point fantasies come alive. "The vision was simple," he says. "A three-star Michelin French country restaurant."

Except that all of Keller's years of training, and the palpable relief he felt at working in this cheery, vine-smothered, wood-frame house on a quiet street in wine country, allowed him to dream up weirder, kookier ideas than he had before—borderline lysergic food visions that somehow never tipped over into gimmickry. He used pop-culture reference points to inspire him, coming up with a "macaroni and cheese" of butter-poached lobster and mascarpone-enriched orzo, a "bacon and eggs" that was really a soft-poached quail egg served on a spoon with crumbles of bacon on top, a "peas and carrots" of lobster pancakes with a pea-shoot salad and a ginger-carrot emulsion, a "surf and turf" that's a cylinder of monkfish medallion on top of braised oxtail, and a "coffee and doughnuts" dessert that's really a cappuccino semifreddo accompanied by little cinnamon-sugar fry cakes.

"I mean, as children in America, we all grew up with those things," Keller says, alluding to the quotation-marks descriptors. "So, if you create a different reference point for somebody but still accomplish the same flavor profile, what have you done? You've made somebody think differently about it."

The strange thing about all this playfulness and subversive fiddling with perception is that Keller is not a barrel of laughs to be around, not a garru-

lous glad-hander in the manner of many a famous American chef. He's reserved and perpetually furrowed of brow, like he's trying to figure out the
next stage of his perverse experiment on humanity. Famously, he has said that
the tasting menu at the French Laundry is constructed on the basis of "the
law of diminishing returns," the idea being that after one or two bites, the
sensory pleasure of tasting something starts to diminish precipitously. "What
I want is that initial shock, that jolt, that surprise to be the only thing you
experience," he wrote in his *French Laundry Cookbook.* "So I serve five to ten
courses"—often, it's many more than that, even—"each meant to satisfy
your appetite and pique your curiosity. I want you to say, 'God, I wish I had
just one more bite of that.' "

In Keller, the New American concept, brightened by California-fresh
ingredients and executed with the rigor of the old *grande cuisine*, reached
its apotheosis. With the service and the location more than measuring up
to the food, it was, at last, really happening: America's own analogue to
Monsieur Point's La Pyramide. Ruth Reichl, perfectly positioned, as ever, on
the front lines of U.S. gastronomy—she ascended to a national pulpit as *The
New York Times* restaurant critic just a year before the French Laundry
opened—concluded in 1998 that "American restaurants have, finally, come
of age. The cocky young chefs who strutted onto the stage in the 1970s and
eighties have evolved out of the stupid-food stage. No longer fresh out of
school, these American chefs have traveled widely. They have tasted and
learned, and they now have enough experience to produce signature food
without showing off. Heading into middle age, the best of them display both
creativity and restraint." A year earlier, Keller, headed into middle age at
forty-one, had been named the Outstanding Chef in America at the James
Beard Awards.

THE CONFLUENCE OF events in 2004 was too striking and poignant for anyone
in the food world not to notice. Just as Keller was celebrating his return to
New York with his new restaurant, Per Se, the first among equals in a suite

of expensive and expensively constructed ultra-dining restaurants at the Time Warner Center on Columbus Circle, three of the last remaining links to the Henri Soulé era, La Caravelle, Lutèce, and La Côte Basque, served their final meals. (Jean-Jacques Rachou, La Côte Basque's owner, was keeping his space but reconfiguring it as a brasserie.) "The winds that blew La Côte Basque onto the reef are far more volatile than mere actuarial statistics," wrote Bryan Miller in *The New York Observer*. "Some of Mr. Rachou's contemporaries, including several of his protégés, venture that his sclerotic devotion to the verities of Escoffier-style cooking are about as voguish today as a dickey." The current generation of fine-dining enthusiasts, Miller said, "frequent places that serve lighter, cross-cultural cuisine in a casual, often raucous and visually stimulating setting."

The Time Warner restaurants weren't necessarily raucous, but they otherwise fit Miller's description. Keller's Per Se more or less duplicated the French Laundry's culinary adventurism in a modernist, Adam Tihany–designed dining room that looked like the private waiting lounge of the world's most exclusive businessmen's airline, while Café Gray, the return to action of Gray Kunz, the French-Asian fusionist behind Lespinasse, one of the most acclaimed New York restaurants of the nineties, was a chocolate-brown brasserie whose look was conceived by Tihany's chief rival in high-stakes restaurant design, David Rockwell. In addition, there was Masa, the $350-a-head sushi restaurant run by Masa Takayama, who closed his tiny, superexpensive Los Angeles place, Ginza Sushiko, to relocate east, and V Steakhouse by the unstoppable Jean-Georges Vongerichten, with bordello-chic decor by Jacques Garcia, the designer also responsible for the sumptuous, Gustav Klimt–referencing decor of David Bouley's second fine-dining restaurant, the Austrian-themed Danube.*

Another conspicuous feature of the Time Warner restaurants—

---

*Charlie Trotter was supposed to join the constellation of stars in the Time Warner Center, opening a seafood restaurant that was to be less formal than his Chicago flagship, but he bailed out on the project in 2005.

audaciously billed as "The Restaurant Collection" by the center's retail developer, Kenneth A. Himmel, as if they were part of a rewards package formulated especially for holders of the American Express Centurion black card—was that its chefs were all established stars, sought out precisely because of their fame and accomplishment. It was a curious economic model, in which an expensive new shopping center and luxury office-condo complex hoped to attract customers on the basis of chef prestige and restaurant traffic. For Drew Nieporent, who forayed into New York's then dead Tribeca neighborhood in the mid-eighties because the real estate was cheap, the Time Warner Center is a step too far—not the coming-of-age of American restaurants, as Reichl had it a few years ago, or a cluster of American analogues to Europe's Michelin three-star pleasure palaces, as Keller would have it, but "restaurants on steroids." Nieporent has dined at Masa and reveled in the multicourse majesty of Takayama's preparations (which received a four-star rating from *The New York Times*' Frank Bruni), but even though he liked the food, he dismisses the overall concept as "elitist bullshit."

"It's blown up to something that is almost illegal, if you think about it," Nieporent says. "Because what's screwed up this country is all this inflated real estate. It affects everything—food cost, operating cost, the price of your check. Suddenly we all discovered raw fish and rice? I mean, at *$250* it's not right; maybe even at $150 it's not. I mean, Masa, you're in the fuckin' Time Warner building, motherfucker! Before it was in the goddamn strip mall in LA! Which was more fitting?"

These words are especially provocative coming from Nieporent, who, with Robert De Niro, plucked Nobu Matsuhisa from a strip mall in LA (or at least a strip-mall-like stretch of La Cienega Boulevard) and, in 1994, set him up with an elaborate David Rockwell–designed dining room in Tribeca, the site of the first Nobu, home of Manhattan's most desired raw fish and rice. Nobu has since cloned itself ten times over, in locations as far-flung as London, Tokyo, Miami, and Milan, effectively becoming the leading global brand for high-end "New Style Japanese" cuisine, as Matsuhisa himself calls it.

Nieporent admits to being troubled by this willy-nilly expansion. "I'm not about cookie-cutting this stuff," he says. But he argues that, at least, the Nobus rein themselves in with realistic pricing and unpretentious food, unlike the rash of newer, design-aggressive, *Blade Runner* avant-Japanese restaurants that "try to out-Nobu Nobu" and rationalize charging $15 even for edamame—the traditionally cheapo premeal snack of salted fresh green soybeans—by serving the beans still attached to the branch.

ANDRÉ SOLTNER AND Jean-Georges Vongerichten were both born and raised in Alsace, but they're upheld as polar opposites, representations of the old and new paths of the fine-dining chef in America. Soltner was the man of unstinting dedication to his one kitchen, allegedly absent from it only five times in the thirty-four years that he ran Lutèce. (He sold the restaurant in 1994 to the Ark Restaurants group.) He is rumpled and paunchy, as an old French chef should be, and ran Lutèce as a glorified mom-and-pop operation with his wife, Simone, who greeted guests in the front of the house.

Vongerichten is the guy who earned four stars before his thirtieth birthday at the Lafayette; bolted in 1991 to open his own place, Jo Jo, a town-house bistro that served enlivened (and lightened) French food flavored with Asian-style broths and juices; followed up Jo Jo just a year later with another New York restaurant, Vong, in which his Asian influences came to the foreground; scaled the dizzy heights of gastronomy in 1997 with Jean Georges, his ultimate fine-dining restaurant; and then, having achieved all that, went on an entrepreneurial rampage in the late 1990s and early years of the twenty-first century—expanding the Vong brand to other cities across the globe, duplicating Jean Georges in Shanghai, opening a steak house in Vegas, and dabbling in mid-priced restaurants devoted to Puck-style eclecticism (right down to serving tuna-wasabi pizza) and specific Asian idioms (Chinese food, Southeast Asian street food). Streamlined, physically fit, and robotic in appearance—he resembles a member of Kraftwerk, the German synthesizer band—Vongerichten staffs his restaurants with beautiful, icy host-esses, one of whom, an aspiring actress named Marja Allen, became his second wife in 2004.

Alan Richman, GQ's esteemed, long-serving food writer and an early champion of Vongerichten's, contrasted the younger chef unfavorably with Soltner in a scathing broadside published in 2004 entitled "Stick a Fork in Jean-Georges." Throughout the nineties, Richman celebrated the rise of Vongerichten and other entrepreneurial chefs, among them Boulud, Batali, and Lagasse, but he argues now that "the franchising of the fine-dining restaurant is the worst thing that's happened to these guys. I think things peaked in the early nineties, before they all started opening multiple restau-rants"—a sentiment echoed by John Mariani, Richman's longtime counter-part at *Esquire*, who has been even more vituperative on the subject, actively campaigning against the scourge of the absentee celebrity chef.

In the GQ article, Richman noted Vongerichten had become a partner in fifteen restaurants and wrote, "Certainly, such upward mobility is an inspi-ration to cooks who toil in Gulag-type working conditions, stirring stocks long into the night. To those of us who are devoted to dining, it is a disaster. Perhaps I could regard the new entrepreneurial Vongerichten more favorably were he instilling his genius in the chefs who work for him, but this is not tak-ing place." Richman visited several of the restaurants in Vongerichten's port-folio and declared each one to be disappointing, either operating on autopilot or downright shoddy. He portrayed Vongerichten as a fallen hero in the grips of some kind of pathological promiscuity, an unchecked addiction to opening new places: "They say he has little vanity, no ego. They do not know what drives him. They only know he cannot stop."

In Richman's mind, Soltner looms as the guilty conscience of entrepre-neurial chefs like Vongerichten, the man who "haunts every chef living to-day," in the words of Dan Barber, the young chef at New York's Blue Hill restaurant, quoted in Richman's article. "His name is associated with the idea of 'real chef' in every sense of the word," Barber told Richman. "French. Devoted to his craft. A purist . . . Nobody can stand the comparison to a guy whose life was breathing his restaurant, living for his restaurant, engrossing himself in the minutiae of his restaurant. The iconic image of a struggling chef is so glorious."

Vongerichten was gutted by Richman's critique, retiring to his bed for three days after it came out. Today, having regained his color and composure, he says, "I'm not a whore! I'm just a chef who tries to please people, you know? I'm in this business to pamper people. People approach me with things every day, and I want to do things. I have a lot of ideas, so why should I stop? I just wish the foodies like Richman would understand what we do here." He further notes that no one complained when France's first-generation nouvelle cuisine chefs lent their names and reputations to multiple restaurants across the globe in the seventies and eighties—usually in consultancy deals that gave them less control, and required less of their time, than the partnership arrangements to which Vongerichten is committed. Working for Louis Outhier in the late seventies and early eighties, Vongerichten recalls, "I opened ten restaurants for him in, like, six years." David Bouley first caught the attention of Drew Nieporent while serving as the guy who actually did all the day-to-day cooking at Sutter 500 in San Francisco, a restaurant where the nouvelle-cuisine celebrity Roger Vergé's name was played up as the attraction.

What chefs sympathetic to Vongerichten say is that it's disingenuous to compare him with Soltner, since the climate has completely changed since Soltner made his name in the sixties and seventies. Expansionism, says Batali, is as much about "keeping the talented people who work for you from going to work for someone else" as it is about making money. "If you say to your sous-chefs, 'Stick with me and I will get you a slice of the pie,' it empowers them and makes them do better work," he says. And if this system also gives a chef-entrepreneur the manpower to open more restaurants and make tons of money in the process, "Well, that's cool, too," says Batali. "There's nothing in the chef's credo that says 'Thou shalt not make any cash.' "

The chef-entrepreneurs further argue that the talent pool is so much greater today than it was a generation ago that it would be almost churlish not to create opportunities for their staff. "You couldn't find ten cooks who had knife skills and a palate in 1986, but today, the young guys are really seasoned," says Vongerichten, whose stock response to the accusatory question, "Who's cooking at the restaurant when you're not here?" is "The same people cooking when I *am* here."

"The chef world has grown," says Trotter. "People like John Mariani lament that 'This chef's never in his restaurant,' but what difference does it make if the person's in the restaurant or not, unless, of course, you just want to see him? I don't think I've had anything less than a stellar meal at Jean Georges, and I think he's only been there twice out of the eight or nine meals I've had there. And I've been in restaurants where the chef *has* been there— I'm talking about celebrated and noted chefs—and the experience has been abysmal, horrific."

Says Miller, the chef-anthropologist, "The problem with food is that it occupies this existential space that is really personal, yet at the same time, it's also a commercial thing. Food is a very, very personal subject, and it's a very subjective subject. And so it becomes a subject that people have strong opinions about. Somehow, there's this strong idea that these restaurateurs and chefs are polluting the idea of what they do by 'commercializing' themselves. But nobody attacks Armani for having A/X, right? Or Ralph Lauren for licensing his name for fragrance. Or Richard Meier for designing cheap products for Target."

Indeed, there's nothing intrinsically wrong with a chef lending his imprimatur to multiple restaurants as long as his staff's execution is good, the restaurant's conceptualization is sound, and the business plan is solid. As of this writing, Batali, who has seven restaurants in New York with his partner, Joe Bastianich, and two pending in Las Vegas, has not yet had a major slip-up, nor has Colicchio, who, beyond his Gramercy Tavern venture with Meyer, has grown his own brand of restaurants under the Craft name, starting with the Craft fine-dining restaurant in New York, the more casual Craftbar around the corner, and the fast-proliferating Craftsteak and 'wichcraft restaurants—the former devoted to red meat, the latter devoted to high-quality sandwiches.*

But Vongerichten and Puck, the most audacious of the bunch, have had their setbacks. Late in 2005, V Steakhouse became the first of the Time Warner Center restaurants to fail, proving that Vongerichten, if not the damaged sellout that Richman has made him out to be, was perhaps too eager to give life to every half-cocked notion that formed in his head—like his conceptually dodgy "deconstructed" French onion soup, served on a wide plate that held a bowl of onion broth, a separate bowl of bubbling melted Gruyère, and still another bowl containing the croutons; you were supposed to put it all together yourself.

Likewise, in the early nineties, Puck and Barbara Lazaroff lost half a million dollars on a Los Angeles wurstbar and brewery called Eureka, a misbegotten attempt to capitalize on the microbrew craze of the time. And when Puck sold his frozen-food company to the commercial food giant ConAgra in 2001, on the condition that he remain in charge of quality control and that he receive royalties from the sales of the products bearing his name, he was dismayed to discover that the ConAgra versions of his frozen pizzas were not up to the standards he'd set when he owned the company. "They changed everything, because they said they can fabricate it cheaper," Puck says. "I believed them because I thought, 'Well, they have a $25 billion company—they know better than me.' But they fucked it up. So now we just have to restart everything with ConAgra, the way we had it before."

---

*With the Craftsteak brand, Colicchio became the first chef to clone a Las Vegas restaurant in New York rather than vice versa. The original Craftsteak is in the MGM Grand casino hotel in Las Vegas. Gamal Aziz, the president of the MGM, approached Colicchio when the chef was in the process of opening the first Craft in New York. "Gamal said, 'I want a steak house,'" Colicchio recalls. "I said, 'Well, I'm doing Craft.'" He said, 'You can do anything you want as long as there's "meat" or "steak" in the title.' I thought about it and said, 'Well, how about Craftsteak?'" The New York version of Craftsteak sits on a nascent restaurant row on gritty Tenth Avenue, next door to Batali's audacious $10 million attempt at a four-star Italian restaurant, Del Posto, and across the street from Morimoto, the new mega-restaurant from Masaharu Morimoto, an ex–Nobu Matsuhisa protégé who gained fame on the Food Network's *Iron Chef*.

Sometimes, too, Puck's entrepreneurial zeal can get the better of him, leading him to embrace a genuinely stupid idea, such as the prepackaged latte in a self-heating can. In 2005, Puck licensed his name to a beverage company that sold coffee drinks in specially made cans equipped with a button that, when pressed, triggered a chemical reaction that brought the drink's temperature to 145 degrees. Not only was the commercial value of the product dubious—how hard is it to find a hot cup of coffee in the United States?—but Puck grew disenchanted when he heard reports that the cans were exploding, melting, or overheating. (The tech firm that developed the cans questioned the veracity of these reports.)

By dint of having so many irons in the fire, Vongerichten and Puck have been able to overcome their miscues and move on, but other chefs, as they strive to be entrepreneurial like the big boys, may not be so fortunate. Colicchio admits that the possibility of even a single failure "scares the hell out of me. I wake up every morning asking myself, 'What the hell am I doing this for?' " he says. " 'Do I need another restaurant? Do I need a restaurant in Dallas? Christ!' But at a certain point—I don't know if you get addicted to the deal, but you start chasing these deals."

Besides, Colicchio says, he's just rolling with the times and the opportunities they present. "If André Soltner were a thirty-six-year-old chef today," he says, "he would be in Vegas."

"Ehh, maybe not," says Soltner when this idea is put to him. "The Japanese approached me in the eighties and offered me fantastic money to open in Japan. They said, 'We'll use your name, and we'll call it Lutèce.' I said, 'What do you want, exactly, from me?' They said, 'We want you three months a year in Japan.' But then I thought, 'If I go for three months to Japan, I still have the Lutèce in New York, and people will start to say, 'Lutèce is not the same.' When I was working, I went to the theater maybe once every two years or so. I spent the money one time, and the star actor was either sick or tired, I don't know—but he was replaced. I was really disappointed, you know? I never forgot that. Because people came not to Lutèce; they came to André Soltner."

Projecting Soltner into the present day is really a futile exercise, rather like using Elias Sports Bureau statistics to project how Babe Ruth would have hit against Roger Clemens; their eras were so different that it's impossible to draw a valid conclusion. To his credit, Soltner doesn't presume to know how Vongerichten would have functioned in 1963, nor does he knock him for operating the way he does. "You have never heard me criticize Jean-Georges or the others," he says. "Maybe some of them criticize me, but the ones who say I was not ambitious enough—what are they talking about? I left at the top. I had four stars when I retired." Standing in the vegetable garden of his Catskills home, he gestures at the view of Hunter Mountain across the way. "Do you think I did so badly?"

THE EMERGENCE OF Las Vegas as a magnet for celebrity chefs began more or less as a fluke, when Puck was hard up for money. "I used to go to Vegas a lot because I'm a big fight fan," Puck says. "When I went with friends, I'd say, 'Where are we gonna go eat afterward?' and in the hotels, the food was always bad steak or bad continental." So when he was felt out about doing a Vegas restaurant by the real estate developer Sheldon Gordon, he was receptive to the idea.

In the early nineties, Gordon was building the Forum Shops at Caesars Palace, a shopping-mall annex to the casino-hotel complex. The Forum Shops were an exciting, controversial project to be part of, something of a Vegas revolution in that they would offer visitors to the city an attraction that was not gambling-related. Still, after giving the matter some thought, Puck decided he was already overextended, busy as he was at the time with ramping up Granita, his and Barbara Lazaroff's latest restaurant, in Malibu. He called Gordon to say thanks but no thanks.

Then Granita started to experience huge cost overruns. Says Lazaroff, "Wolf always likes to say [*Austrian accent*], 'You know, *Baba-waa* spent too much money building *Gwa-neeta.*' Of course, I wasn't given enough of a budget in the first place." Gordon, who kept a home in Malibu, caught wind of Granita's problems and offered Puck and Lazaroff a $500,000 signing bonus if they agreed to come on board at the Forum Shops. "We used the $500,000 to finish Granita, and then we started to build Spago Las Vegas," Puck says. "We opened there in December 1992."

"It proved very fruitful, and, after that, it made sense to keep going," says Lazaroff. "And, boy, did Las Vegas need some decent food."

When Puck caught wind of the MGM Grand's plan to install a Mexican restaurant on its premises, he thought that the hotel would be better served with "something a little bit more modern, more Southwestern," and recommended Mark Miller to the MGM management. They'd never heard of Miller. "So I called up Mark and said, 'Send them your cookbooks, send them all your press stuff,'" Puck says. "He sent everything, and they built him a Coyote Cafe there. Then they got Emeril to do an Emeril's there, and that pretty much got the ball rolling in Las Vegas."

Within a matter of a few years, chefs were no longer rebuffing the idea of having a Vegas presence, instead viewing it as a mark of their entrepreneurial acumen. Matsuhisa opened a Nobu at the Hard Rock Casino and Resort. Vongerichten opened his Prime steak house in the Bellagio, and was joined there by Todd English, who opened an Olives, and the Maccioni family, which opened a Le Cirque. Mary Sue Milliken and Susan Feniger opened a Border Grill at Mandalay Bay. The Venetian featured not only restaurants by Lagasse (a branch of his New Orleans–based Delmonico Steak House) and Thomas Keller (a second location of Bouchon, the casual bistro he opened down the street from the French Laundry), but a post-Soltner version of Lutèce that survives the original.

The rush of chefs to Las Vegas, which has since grown to include such longtime holdouts as Batali, Boulud, Guy Savoy, and Bocuse, verily infuriated the critic John Mariani, who inveighed against the city's " 'Who-cares-if-the-chef's-never-here?' attitude" in his newsletter, *Virtual Gourmet*. "Does anyone seriously believe these fellows will be spending a major part of their time there?" he wrote in 2004. "Can you see the 78-year-old Bocuse shuttling back and forth between Lyons and Las Vegas every two weeks?"

"John Mariani is living in the seventies," Batali says. "He's still consumed by the fantasy of going to the three-star Michelin restaurant where you're greeted by the mama out front while the papa's in the kitchen, and the little boys are busing the plates. It's a beautiful little world, and there's nothing wrong with it per se, but there's no reason for *me* to live in it."

Batali is realistic enough to understand that his Vegas customers won't be as sophisticated as the ones who come to his New York flagship, Babbo, for fennel-dusted sweetbreads and warm lamb's tongue vinaigrette with chanterelles and a three-minute egg. "I've been to Vegas like everyone else and seen the casino customer with the credit card around her neck on a lanyard, taking puffs of a cigarette through a tracheotomy hole," he says. "But the whole point is, the food that people eat in Vegas now is better than anything that was available to them fifteen years ago. And at the celebrity-chef-owned restaurants, it's all being made by hand. It's not like McDonald's. Our osso buco doesn't come from some central osso buco–expediting place in Kansas."

Clark Wolf, the restaurant consultant, puts it more succinctly. "If this means that people in Vegas are eating at a Spago or a Nobu instead of from a steam-tray buffet," he says, "doesn't that mean that we"—by which he means the children of the food revolution—"have *won*?"

Wolf knows whereof he speaks, because he consulted on perhaps the strangest collision of highfalutin epicureanism and the mammon-sleaze-cheese atmosphere of Las Vegas: the Cypress Street Marketplace. On the surface, there's nothing especially strange about it: it's a dining area adjacent to the Forum Shops at Caesars where tourists are invited to stroll a simulated market street, load up picnic baskets with a variety of fresh foods from various stations—roast turkey from the "Hand Carved" station, bisque from the "Lobster & Chowder Company" station, Carolina slow-roasted pulled pork from "Bar BQ," Chinese pot-sticker dumplings from "Ah So"—and then retreat to picnic-style tables, where attendants help them unload their baskets. Though Wolf frets that the Caesars people didn't execute his vision as well as he'd hoped, he reveals that his model for the venue was none other than . . . Fourth Street in Berkeley. It's a delightful, cosmic food-world joke: the co-opting of the California Birkenstock scene by the Sin City capitalists. The Caesars Palace publicity materials describe how guests enter the marketplace "under a modern interpretation of seven life-size California Cypress Trees," enjoying an "eclectic style [that] marries contemporary elements with Old World Italy and New World Napa Valley."

NO SUBJECT, NOT EVEN Las Vegas or the franchising of fine dining, stirs up more debate between the food world's progressive and purist elements than food television. Right up until the 1990s, TV cooking was predominantly the domain of PBS, its audience a beslippered demographic of "wives and bookish men," in the words of Geof Drummond, who produced Julia Child's 1990s programs.

In the 1980s, Child finally relented to the overtures of the commercial world, appearing regularly on ABC's *Good Morning America* to deliver short reports on American foodways and spar adorably with Charlie Gibson, *GMA*'s co-host. But by that point, no one was going to hold Child's feet to the fire for working with one of the major networks; she hardly made any money off her *GMA* appearances, anyway, and she had become such a sainted figure in the food world, neither a promiscuous endorser like Beard nor a behaviorally erratic misanthrope like Claiborne, that she remained inviolate in the eyes of her fans. Her 2004 death was duly mourned as that of a national treasure.

Besides, Child returned to public television in the twilight of her TV career, collaborating with Drummond on two last-hurrah series in the early 1990s, *Cooking with Master Chefs*, in which Child worked with such professional figures as Alice Waters, Jeremiah Tower, Nancy Silverton, and Michel Richard in their home kitchens (or facsimiles thereof), and *In Julia's Kitchen with Master Chefs*, in which famous chefs pilgrimaged to her Cambridge house, sparing the stooped, eightysomething Child the ordeal of schlepping across the country with a film crew.

PBS remains an important player in food television, and, in Jacques

Pépin and Lidia Bastianich (of the Italian restaurant Felidia in New York), it boasts the two chefs whose programs strike the best balance between authentic instructional value and sheer viewing pleasure. But, as of 1993, PBS had serious competition in the form of the TV Food Network, which was started up by Reese Schonfeld, the founding president of CNN. Because it was an unabashedly commercial, entertainment- and profit-minded enterprise, the Food Network, as it came to be known, became a lightning rod in the food world.

For some old-timers, like Judith Jones, Knopf's grand dame of cookbooks, the notion of watching food television purely for entertainment's sake is unpalatable. Jones says she was appalled to happen upon the Food Network's *Iron Chef America*—an Americanization of a Japanese program in which two famous chefs are pitted against each other and the clock, each chef charged with creating a multicourse meal centered around a "mystery ingredient" whose identity is revealed only once the stopwatch starts ticking. (The play-by-play on *Iron Chef America* is supplied by the amiably dweebish cookbook author and TV personality Alton Brown, who, in a recent episode, breathlessly described a chef racing to make "a last-minute garnish grab.") "I turned it on one night and I couldn't believe it," Jones says. "Bobby Flay running around—run, run, run! You don't cook that way! It's too hysterical."

In its rinky-dink early days, when it wasn't airing black-and-white reruns of old shows by Julia Child and her French-food forebear, Dione Lucas, the Food Network was "throwing everything to the wall to see what would stick," as Schonfeld has recalled. Lagasse actually bombed in his first go-round with the network, shuffling awkwardly through his paces on *Emeril and Friends*, a program in which he was assigned the uncomfortable task (for a chef) of reporting on other restaurants, and appearing on another program, *How to Boil Water*, intended for a demographic of divorced men who wanted to learn how to cook for themselves. "What people don't realize when they criticize me is that I didn't get into television for the money," he says. "Reese Schonfeld approached me himself. I think I was the third employee. They paid me fifty dollars a show."

Batali made his maiden Food Network appearance as a guest on what was then the network's showpiece, a 10 p.m. "after dinner" program hosted by Robin Leach, arguably television's cheesiest personality. Flay says that his initial attractiveness to the network was simply a matter of proximity— "They were looking for local people who cost no more than a taxi ride to get to the studio"—and he made his debut on a program called *Grillin' and Chillin'*, cast as the "city boy" opposite Jack McDavid, a Philadelphia-based, Virginia-bred "country boy" chef who wore bib overalls and a trucker hat. Lagasse, Batali, and Flay all put in their time on a program called *Ready, Set, Cook!*, a sort of ultra-low-budget proto–*Iron Chef America* in which two chefs were given twenty minutes and ten dollars' worth of ingredients to make a meal, with the winner decided by the audience. "There was a very college-radio feel to the whole thing," says Batali.

Lagasse was without a show after *Emeril and Friends* failed, but Schonfeld liked him and thought he still had TV potential. He wasn't the only one to believe this. When he was still little known outside of New Orleans, Lagasse had been one of the younger figures to appear with Child on *Cooking with Master Chefs*. Drummond recalls that "Emeril was just terrific with Julia, and she delighted in him. She loved guys—that was part of it. But he just *had* something—there was a twinkle there, a real graciousness and generosity. The show we did with him, a big crab-and-crawfish boil in the backyard, was so good that even though we had shot episodes with people like Alice Waters, Jeremiah Tower, Jacques Pépin, and André Soltner, Emeril's ended up being the lead show."

In 1996, Lagasse got a second chance on the Food Network with *Essence of Emeril*, in which the New Orleans chef simply prepared Cajun and Creole dishes for the camera, Julia-style. It was on *Essence* that Lagasse happened upon his TV persona—a hammy, exaggerated version of himself that exclaimed "Bam!" or "Let's kick it up a notch!" every time he seasoned something or threw a pork chop in a pan. The public loved it, and Lagasse suddenly found himself getting recognized outside of New Orleans; New York cabbies were rolling down their windows and shouting "Bam!" at him. But the food establishment, whose members had respected Lagasse when he was their little regional secret, the guy whose restaurants you ate in when you were in the Big Easy, was not amused by his catchphrases and new showman shtick. Lagasse became, in essence, the new Graham Kerr, the people's favorite and the intelligentsia's whipping boy.*

"I was humiliated at the Beard Awards," Lagasse says. "This is maybe '96. I was on the ballot for chef of the year, best restaurant, best pastry chef, best wine program for Greg Harrington, who was the youngest guy to pass as a master sommelier since Larry Stone [of Rubicon in San Francisco]. We're all in the ballroom in our tuxedos, and my staff is so proud. Nobu, who's a great friend, is next to us. And Tim Zagat comes up to me, with my colleagues everywhere, press everywhere, and he says, '*You!* You oughta be ashamed of yourself! You're like a used-car salesman on that television program! Why don't you get your culinary dignity back?' And he stomps away. There were only, like, 600 people watching."

As his popularity grew, Lagasse was given a second program on the Food Network, *Emeril Live*, in which he cooked before a studio audience and bantered with his own *Tonight Show*–style band. He became a multimedia juggernaut, putting out cookbooks at a furious pace and launching a series of Essence spice mixes and rubs. But even as he raked in the dough and the Nielsen numbers, his credibility with the intelligentsia eroded further. In 1998, Amanda Hesser portrayed Lagasse in *The New York Times* as a sort of Lawrence Welk of the food world, a schlock merchant whose cornball brand

---

*Between the reigns of Kerr and Lagasse came that of another antichrist of the food elite, Jeff Smith, a cheery Methodist minister from Tacoma, Washington, who hosted a program on PBS called *The Frugal Gourmet*, America's most-watched cooking show in the eighties. "The people who worshipped at Julia's temple did not like Jeff Smith at all. They disliked him intensely," says Drummond, who produced *The Frugal Gourmet* in addition to Child's later programs. "They didn't think he knew enough about food or cooking. They hated his success. It's the same thing that they talk about with Emeril now, except that Emeril at least has the credentials as a chef." And unlike the affable, stand-up Lagasse, Smith was not likable off camera. He was a heavy drinker given to verbally abusing his TV crew, and his career fell apart when, in 1997, seven men filed a lawsuit claiming that, as youths in the seventies, they had been sexually abused by Smith while working in a restaurant he ran called the Chaplain's Pantry.

of entertainment played well with his adoring audience, a mouth-breathing assemblage of heartland rubes too dim to realize how tacky and talent-deficient he was. "Emeril Lagasse, more jester than cook, is catering to legions of gleeful fans," Hesser wrote. "Who can begrudge all the joy he seems to bring?"

Showing no mercy, Hesser begrudged away. Emeril, she reported, spoke like a moron, explaining as he carved a turkey that "You want to slice the breast so that it's, like, edible." The turkey-and-cheese sandwich he proffered to members of his studio audience, which Hesser took a bite of, was "a very bad turkey sandwich. The bread was greasy, the turkey was dry, and the orange mystery cheese wasn't even melted." Michael Batterberry, the editor of *Food Arts* magazine, was tapped for a condemnatory quote, saying that *Emeril Live* "smacks a little bit of the wrestling ring or the roller derby." The food Lagasse made on his show was fattening, gross, and unmethodically prepared, with little step-by-step instruction from the chef, Hesser concluded.

Lagasse was as undone by Hesser's article as Vongerichten would be six years later by Alan Richman's kiss-off. "She came when I was doing a Thanksgiving leftovers show, and because I was using leftovers, she flipped that into 'He can't cook,' " Lagasse says. "I knew that I'd be taking potshots; it comes with the territory. But has she been to one of my restaurants? I mean, I didn't fall out of a plane and someone gave me *Emeril Live*. The bottom line is, go to one of my restaurants."

Lagasse's eyes redden and brim with tears. "*Then* see what a schlocky guy I am! I mean, I'm the only American in the world who has two [*Wine Spectator*] Grand Award wine lists. I mean, tell me I'm not serious?"*

Batali says that it's unfair for any writer or critic to review food that's prepared during a taping, "because it's being made for the cameras, not necessarily as restaurant-quality cuisine. That article made it sound like he was

---

*One person who never wavered in her support of Lagasse, even after he became a multimedia phenomenon, was Child. In her final print interview, given to *CITY* magazine in 2004, she singled him out as someone who "[has] good training, knows what [he is] doing, and [has] fun while in the kitchen."

pulling the wool over people's eyes, when the truth is that he's one of the best chefs in the country"—an endorsement seconded by such chefs as Trotter, Boulud, and Puck. Indeed, Hesser was entitled to her opinions about Lagasse's TV persona and the quality of his cookbook recipes, but, given his track record at Commander's Palace, Emeril's, and NOLA, she was wrong to assert that "Before his meteoric rise on television, Mr. Lagasse had a fairly modest culinary career."

But therein lies the (seven-spice) rub of commercial food television. In its zeal to entertain and find formats that will elicit good ratings, it often obscures the culinary gifts of its stars. Flay, on the basis of *Grillin' and Chillin'*, got pigeonholed as the Food Network's grilling guy, starring in the series *Boy Meets Grill*, *Hot Off the Grill*, and *BBQ with Bobby Flay*, even though he has proven himself capable of three-star cuisine in a variety of idioms in his restaurants Mesa Grill, Bolo, and Bar Americain. "I'm from Manhattan. It's like, how much grilling am I doing in Manhattan?" he says. "It's a funny relationship that I have with the Food Network, because my restaurants are not about that. I want to be thought of as a chef in my restaurants, which are where I am 90 percent of my time. You're not gonna get the food that I cook on TV in my restaurants. Sometimes I have a love-hate relationship with the TV part of my life—but, at the same time, it's also been a great, great thing."

Even cooks who owe their fame entirely to the Food Network, like Giada De Laurentiis, the host of *Everyday Italian*, struggle with their identity. It's easy to see why the Food Network hired De Laurentiis—she came from a famous family (her grandfather is the movie producer Dino De Laurentiis; her grandmother was the Italian film star Silvana Mangano), she ran a successful catering company in Los Angeles, she has an easygoing, camera-friendly manner, and she's a knockout, setting aflutter more hearts even than the voluptuous British TV cook Nigella Lawson. But De Laurentiis is also a classically trained graduate of the Cordon Bleu school in Paris who has long harbored aspirations to open her own restaurant, and who didn't even specialize in Italian cookery at GDL Foods, her catering outfit. "I've struggled with the Food Network thing," De Laurentiis says. "Sometimes I think, 'I didn't go to culinary school to become *this person*.' I have to simplify my technique and language when I'm on TV and not use chef terms. But then I think, do I want to be obscure? Isn't this a good opportunity to get people interested in cooking and better ingredients?"

Says Batali, "Look, it's TV! Everyone has to fall into a niche. I'm the Italian guy; Emeril's the exuberant New Orleans guy with the big eyebrows who yells a lot; Bobby's the grilling guy; Rachael Ray is the cheerleader-type girl who makes things at home the way a regular person would; Giada's the beautiful girl with the nice rack who does simple Italian food. As silly as the whole Food Network is, it gives us all a soapbox to talk about the things we care about."

Batali also notes that the fame and lucre the network generates are often put to nobler purposes than the purchase of beach houses or mint-green Vespa scooters. When his Italian-cooking program, *Molto Mario*, began airing in 1995, Batali had only one modest little Greenwich Village restaurant to his name, Po. It was the sizable advance he got for his first cookbook, *Simple Italian Food*, that enabled him to partner with Joe Bastianich (the son of Lidia) to open Babbo, the Italian restaurant that represents the apotheosis of his gifts as a chef—half rustic-Italian traditionalist, half mad-dog freestyler. "I'd say," he says, "that my book advance was predicated almost entirely on the fact that I was on TV."

CHAPTER TWELVE

TOWARD A
McSUSTAINABLE FUTURE

Our system of public education currently operates in [a] no-context zone of hollow fast-food values. In school cafeterias, students learn how little we care about the way they eat—we've sold them to the lowest bidder. At best we serve them government-subsidized agricultural surplus; at worst we invite fast-food restaurants to open on school grounds.

—Alice Waters, in a speech to the USDA
Nutrition Connections Conference, 2005

Getting your vegetables doesn't have to take a lot of time, especially when you lunch on a tasty McDonald's Premium Salad. Our salads feature up to 16 types of premium greens that may include baby red romaine, baby green leaf, baby spinach, radicchio and arugula.

—excerpt from the McDonald's Web site, 2006

IN THE 1990S AND EARLY YEARS OF THE TWENTY-FIRST CENTURY, THE DEBATE OVER whether Alice Waters had "restaurant chops" and really cooked at Chez Panisse became moot. She shifted into full-time advocate mode, preaching the virtues of sustainable agriculture, farm-to-table connectivity, local foods, and early education about "real" foods vis-à-vis junk foods. The origins of this shift date back to 1983, the year Waters gave birth to her only child, Fanny, the product of a brief marriage to Stephen Singer, a wine and olive oil importer. Jerry Budrick, Chez Panisse's longtime headwaiter, says that Fanny was just one of seven babies born to the Chez Panisse staff that year

PAGE 351: *Whole Foods joins the shopping-mall experience, 2006.*

(including one of his own), and that the restaurant suddenly "became a lot more serious, with less, let's say, recreational intoxication."

As Waters and her colleagues raised their children and experienced firsthand the inbuilt threats of processed, commercial foods and the Mephistophelean seductiveness of Double Meat Whoppers and Cool Ranch Doritos, the great lady of Chez Panisse decided to take action. In 1994, she started the Edible Schoolyard program at the Martin Luther King Junior Middle School in Berkeley, planting a one-acre organic garden in a former parking lot next to the school, so that its students, mostly from lower-income families, could help grow their own food and "transform school lunch into a vibrant expression of education for sustainability," as the program's mission statement puts it.

Some years later, after Fanny Singer had entered Yale, Waters helped instigate the Yale Sustainable Food Project at the university's aptly named Berkeley College, in which students cultivated their own one-acre garden, produce was purchased from local organic farmers, a composting program was established, a chef was brought in to devise seasonal menus, and the first-ever "Sustainable Tailgate" was held at the 2003 Harvard-Yale football game, featuring "Wolfe's Neck Farm grass-fed burgers"—a marked contrast from the collegiate norm of celebrating one's liberation from parental supervision by subsisting entirely on Hostess cakes and Skippy peanut butter eaten straight from an industrial-size tub.

Already a celestial figure in Bay Area and foodie circles, Waters has now been beatified within her own lifetime as Saint Alice, with a court of apostles that includes Marion Cunningham, Ruth Reichl, the *San Francisco Chronicle* restaurant critic Michael Bauer, and *The New York Times* veteran newsman turned gastro-tourist-at-large R. W. "Johnny" Apple. On top of that, her gospel has gained global resonance with the advent of the Slow Food movement, which originated in Italy in 1986 when a man named Carlo Petrini led a protest against the opening of a new McDonald's in Rome. (His followers defiantly held aloft bowls of penne like placards.) Petrini took his movement international in 1989, advocating the preservation of old and endangered foodways, the importance of local and artisanal food products, the sacredness of the family meal as a social rite, and the need for public awareness of the ecological, social, and nutritional evils wrought by industrial, monocultural agriculture. The Slow Food movement's local chapters are known as convivia—because "conviviality is one of the most fundamental aspects of eating together," Petrini explains—and Waters hopped on board early, founding the Berkeley convivium and proclaiming the King School to be a "slow school," a model for her proposed "revolution in public education—a real Delicious Revolution."

No one doubts the worthiness of Waters's goals, especially in a nation where the rates of diabetes and childhood obesity are on the rise, and where municipal governments, desperate for cash, have agreed to such Faustian bargains as Mayor Michael Bloomberg's 2003 deal to make Snapple the exclusive beverage provider of the New York City public school system. And Waters's proposal to let kids "start getting credit for school lunch"—incorporating the daily in-school act of eating lunch into the curriculum, teaching kids about the nutritional value and provenance of the food they're being served—is an inspired idea.

But there are plenty in the food world who admire the message but believe that the messenger lacks the common touch, who feel that Waters is too much of an insulated, ivory-tower dreamer on the one hand and too much of a hardheaded, unyielding dogmatist on the other—"a romantic with a spine of steel," says Betty Fussell, who describes herself as a "Slow Food person with a lot of skepticism. You know, the search for the little tiny Italian fava-bean grower down the road? *Please!* So much of that is really hyped."

The problem is that Waters doesn't realize what more effective celebrity activists, such as Bono, the singer in the band U2, have realized: that politics is about dialogue and compromise, not preaching and obstinacy. Just as the 2004 presidential campaign of the Ohio congressman Dennis Kucinich suffered for its tin-eared cluelessness—his spokespeople said his name "rhymes with spinach, and they're both good for you," effectively extinguishing Kucinich's chances right then and there—so does Waters turn people off with such stock lines as "Give me any kid. In six weeks, they'll be eating chard." That sounds more like a threat than a promise of uplift, and it's characteristic of her sometimes off-key approach, one that takes a fundamentally noble and celebratory premise and turns it into a guilt trip.

"I love Alice, but . . ." is a common refrain among the stars of the food world, who admire her ideals but question her pragmatism. As in "Don't get me wrong, I love Alice, but she's fuckin' out there," the words that come from Emeril Lagasse's lips when it's put to him that she might not approve of his line of California-grown but nationally distributed green-salad blends sold in plastic containers bearing his photo. (There is also a line of Emeril fresh herbs.) A true subscriber to Waters's tenets, Lagasse is told, would recoil from buying non-local produce—with a celebrity chef's mug on it, no less. Waters herself, when asked where an American living in a cold-weather climate is supposed to find salad greens during the winter, says, "I always want to buy from the local small-scale producer who is taking care of the land. During the winter, there are lettuces grown in hoop houses on the East Coast and in the Midwest."

But Lagasse counters, "I got into this because of my children and the crap that's in the supermarket. Look, most people don't live in New York City, where you can just go down the street and get anything you want. Most people have to settle for brown lettuce that's been up there for a couple of weeks, and it's sad."

Working with a commercial grower in northern California called Pride of San Juan, Lagasse claims he's "doing farming two levels above organic. We have this guy that we hired who wrote the laws for the United States government for the FDA on produce, and we hired him to take those standards, and, as I say, kick it up a notch, so that nobody has the standards that we have. We basically have the fields computerized, where we know, based on the weather, the best time that we should pick what lettuce, when we should pick it, what temperature it should be. The lettuces are not gassed. It's totally natural. No chemicals."

Tom Colicchio takes pains to say, "Alice and I have a good relationship," but recalls participating in a panel discussion in which Waters was "going on and on about organic this and local that. I said, 'Alice, I use it whenever I can, but I don't believe that I have to use local ingredients if I can get something flown in from Australia that is great.' And she said, 'Well, if you know how much fuel it takes to fly that in . . .' I said, 'Alice—they're not putting one lobster on a plane just for me!' So then she starts telling us about this wonderful pig that she found up in Oregon. I said, 'Alice, what did you just say? You're in California—how do you consider that local?' She just looked at me and said, 'You're right. I have to stop using that.' I said, 'Why?! *Why?!* You're supporting this farmer who's doing this wonderful thing up in Oregon! Why do you have to not support this person anymore?' It's *insane!*"

Rick Bayless had a much more fraught encounter with Waters after he appeared in a Burger King commercial in 2003, endorsing the fast-food chain's low-calorie Santa Fe Fire-Grilled Chicken Baguette Sandwich, a piece of chicken breast served on a baguette and topped with grilled peppers and onions and a spicy sauce. Bayless says he knew that getting into bed with Burger King was a fraught proposition, but, upon receiving the offer from the company, he thought, "I don't come from the school that says, 'We should just turn our back on the evil giants.' I think we should just get right in the middle of the evil giants' companies and say, 'Hey, you know what? If you take this step, it'll be a good step.' If I can get several hundred thousand people to not eat Whoppers and eat something that's healthier—that's got a brighter, less-processed flavor—then, you know, that's actually a good thing." The money he received for the commercial, Bayless asserts, went straight to his Frontera Farmer Foundation, which distributes money to family farms in the Chicago orbit in the form of capital improvement grants.

Still, for all his forethought, Bayless was unprepared for the kerfuffle his commercial caused. It was a food-world *scandale,* with other chefs wondering if he really pocketed the money for himself, and the chat rooms of eGullet, an online society for hardcore foodies, burbling with indignation. "What is he thinking???" wrote one eGullet member. "What's next, Alice Waters doing a Subway commercial with Jared?"

More seriously, there were reasoned critiques that cast Bayless as either naïve or cynical for promoting a sandwich that was not all-natural, and whose sauce contained high fructose corn syrup, a sneaky ingredient in many processed foods that helps foster obesity. (On this count, Lagasse, who ought to know better, also has a lot to answer for. His Emeril's Original marinades, sauces, and salad dressings, manufactured by the processed-foods giant B&G Foods, are made with high fructose corn syrup.)

BILL NIMAN AND his wife, Nicolette Hahn Niman, who know a thing or two about doing business with fast-food companies, were among those mystified by Bayless's deal with Burger King. Though they sell their pork to the McDonald's-owned Chipotle chain, and though Bill says he would gladly sell his beef to McDonald's itself if the company were interested, what Bayless did was, to them, different.

"It's not that Rick was doing business with the devil—that's not the is-sue," says Nicolette. "It's distinct from, let's say, the concept of Niman Ranch selling something to McDonald's, because Rick was endorsing a product that he was not really involved with. The sauce had corn syrup in it, and that, in itself, is offensive to all the values that he stands for. He was actually going out and—"

"Validating something pretty horrible," Bill says.*

Bayless, taken aback by the reaction, used the Frontera Grill Web site to explain, at length, his actions. "Here is my reasoning in a nutshell," he wrote. "I decided that it's time for those of us in the healthy food/sustainable food movement to applaud any positive steps we see in the behemoth quick-service restaurant chains. Seventy-five percent of our fellow Americans nour-ish themselves in their restaurants at least once a week (an even more serious

---

*All that said, Marian Burros, in a *New York Times* roundup of the fast-food chains' efforts to offer lighter, healthier fare, rated the Santa Fe Fire-Grilled Chicken Baguette Sandwich the best-tasting of the items she sampled.

statistic is that almost 20 percent eat fast food three or more times a week). I can no longer ignore these statistics, and I ask you not to, either."

Bayless believes that, in the end, the controversy was a boon to his food activism, "because it gave me an opportunity to really explain what I was doing, and why I was doing it. People who never listened to me before on the subject of health were suddenly listening to me and going, 'Oh, I guess you've got a point there.' That was great. And now I'm working with the CEO of Burger King about the possibility of the next step, that being an all-natural sandwich, with no preservatives. And he's talking about starting to use organic ingredients in some of the sauces and stuff. How could I have ever gotten that ear if I hadn't gone down that road?"

Whether or not you believe Bayless is sincere—and there have been murmurings that what he's offered is more a rationalization than an explanation—his central point is valid: that the big companies need to be engaged, not excommunicated, if there is to be further progress in America's food revolution. The corporations are not going to fold up and go away. It's Waters's right not to branch out and become a commercial behemoth herself—she has spurned all offers to turn Chez Panisse into a brand, and has opened only one other establishment, a teeny-tiny breakfast spot in a Berkeley strip mall called Café Fanny—but other figures in the food firmament resent how she sits in judgment of their commercial activities.

"Chez Panisse really represents itself as holding value," says Mark Miller. "People even talk about it that way: making a 'pilgrimage' to Chez Panisse. Alice needs to be the goddess figure of the church, in that sense, and hold those values, because they're values that are noncommercial. But she's caught. I think that Berkeley is still sort of stuck in time. Chez Panisse was, at first, a small meeting hall, then it became a sort of church, and now it's this grand cathedral that towers above everything in the Bay Area. At some point, if you don't belong to the sect, or don't want to believe in the beliefs, it's time to move away."

Bayless's heretical actions earned him a rebuke from Waters. "She wrote me this really, really curt, smug e-mail that said, 'There is absolutely no justification for what you've done,' " he says. Actually, the language of her message wasn't that strident. The text of the e-mail that Waters says she sent Bayless reads, "Dear Rick, this is a message from all of us at Chez Panisse. We love you dearly but do not approve of your endorsement of Burger King. No matter how you justify this to yourself and others, it feels like an endorsement of Fast Food Nation, especially coming from one of our champions of sustainability and Slow Food values!"

Couched though it was in smiley language, Waters's critique of Bayless infuriated him. "I've known Alice forever and I really respect what she has done," he says. "But I wrote her back a letter that said, 'I think you're smug, I think you've got your head in the sand, and I think that you can't continue to do this.' When you look at what our restaurant has done through the years, and how we've been exemplary in all things, why couldn't she have just said, 'Well, that seems peculiar, that Rick's doing that. I think I'll ask him why he did it'? Instead of slapping me on the wrist and saying, *'Bad boy!'* "

AT ITS CURRENT JUNCTURE, the story of American food is dominated by two phenomena: the "national eating disorder," to use a phrase coined by the food writer and UC-Berkeley journalism professor Michael Pollan, that finds many Americans obsessing about being thin while getting still fatter, lurching from one faddist diet to the next (such as the Atkins madness that demonized "carbs"), and eating too many processed foods; and the quantum leap forward in ingredient availability and culinary sophistication that is described in this book. The problem is that these two phenomena have been running on parallel tracks, with some segments of the population depending evermore on fast food, and other segments getting deeper and deeper into foodie connoisseurship and/or organic, biodynamic, and "slow" foods.

The trick, the task America faces, is to get these two parallel tracks to converge. For the solution to the national eating disorder lies in the advances and lessons of the American food revolution. The junk-food and diet-food people need to learn that natural and gourmet foods need not be flavorless, expensive, or "elitist"; the foodie sophisticates need to lose their smugness and patronizing tone and embrace capitalist enterprise and engagement with big companies as a good thing, the most effective means of proselytizing on behalf of real, healthful foods.

There are hopeful signs that market forces and moral forces are already effecting precisely these kinds of changes. Slowly but surely, for example, the supermarket is transforming itself from a lowest-common-denominator vendor of pale iceberg lettuce and Spam into a hybrid store that sells both the prepackaged, processed stuff that America will always have an appetite for *and* the fresher, healthier, better-tasting stuff that the premium markets sell.

In the summer of 2004, the venerable A&P company opened its first A&P Fresh Market in New Jersey, an obvious acknowledgment of, and response to, the aggressive expansion of Whole Foods. A&P's promotional materials stated, "The focus is on the fresh department offerings; the wide selection of organic and natural items and the outstanding customer service . . . The signage throughout the store clearly highlights the natural items as those that are minimally processed and contain no artificial ingredients and the organic items, which are produced or grown without the use of harmful pesticides or herbicides, therefore not harming the environment." There was also a prepared-foods department, a cheese department with "over 200 varieties from around the world," a gelato bar that "gives customers a taste of Italy," a bakery that boasts "the scent of freshly baked Artisan breads," and a meat counter offering "store-made sausage and a selection of organic and natural meat products." As this book was being written, A&P was converting several more of its old markets to Fresh Markets. More auspiciously, Wal-Mart, the nation's largest grocery retailer, was embarking on a big push into the organic market, imploring major food companies like Kellogg and General Mills to produce organic versions of their products for the chain's shelves. Wal-Mart's executives made no bones about their motives: to appeal to more affluent customers and upgrade the company's image. Predictably, this unabashedly capitalist stance upset some purists, who fretted that the intrusion of a corporate giant into "OrganicLand" would only loosen standards, dilute the message, and squeeze out small farmers and suppliers. But Michael Pollan, to his credit, resisted the urge to view this new development apocalyptically. Organic, even Corporate Big Organic, is, "for all its limitations, a better agriculture, and, if you care about ingesting neurotoxins and endocrine disruptors and carcinogens, an unambiguously better kind of food to eat," he wrote on *The New York Times*'s Web site. "That more Americans will now be able to make that choice is something to cheer."

Approaching the issue from the corporate side, Ron Burkle, the California supermarket mogul, sensed a paradigm shift afoot in 2005, after his company, Yucaipa, bought shares in both the traditional-supermarket chain Pathmark and the natural-foods chain Wild Oats. "I think traditional supermarkets have to pay attention to the fact that America is more and more conscious of lifestyle," Burkle said, using that old seventies buzz term for upgraded living. "Things have changed, and you have to pay attention to those changes." But not only do the supermarkets need to move in the Whole Foods direction, Burkle argued. "The flip side of the question," he said, "is what do Wild Oats and Whole Foods do to get traditional grocery customers? . . . Whole Foods has to figure out how they can sell Coca-Cola."*

Barry Benepe, the father of the Greenmarket movement in New York, couldn't ignore the fact that Whole Foods opened a superstore on Union Square in 2005, just steps from New York City's most popular farmers' market. "I've always said that if the supermarkets rendered Greenmarket obsolete and put us out of business, that would be a happy day for me," he says. "But I don't see it happening just yet. I went to that Whole Foods, and they still have some ways to go. I don't like their labeling, or lack of labeling. Their produce may be organic, but I didn't know where any of it was from."

Meanwhile, it may be just an incremental step, but McDonald's, spurred to action by public outcry and the good old-fashioned muckraking

---

*You can't get a Coke at Chez Panisse. However, the restaurant does carry lemon and orange Italian sodas.

of Eric Schlosser's book *Fast Food Nation* and Morgan Spurlock's documen-
tary *Super Size Me*, is buying and selling more fruits and vegetables than it
used to. The company now offers apple slices as an alternative to french fries
in its Happy Meals, and its introduction of a line of so-called Premium Salads has suddenly made the Great McSatan of Oak Brook one of the nation's
top five food-service buyers of "spring mix" lettuce, a combo of greens that
includes arugula, radicchio, and frisée; the United States of Arugula, indeed.

The dreamed-of next step—whisper it—would be for McDonald's to
spurn the big commercial farms, and, instead, build up a network of small,
all-natural produce growers, much as Bill Niman has done (albeit on a much
smaller scale) with beef and pork producers. "McDonald's could have a huge
impact," the activist Ronnie Cummins, the director of an advocacy group
called the Organic Consumers Association, told *The New York Times* in
2005. "They could be the company that changes agriculture toward a more
organic and sustainable model." And even if McDonald's did this for less than
pure reasons—like, say, because they discovered that they could make a fortune selling a McNiman Bolinas Burger with organic lettuce and tomatoes
and Marion Cunningham's All-Natural Special Sauce at a three-dollar
markup over a Big Mac—well, what's the harm?

REVIEWING A NEW, painfully correct "local foods" restaurant called Cookshop
in *The New York Times* in 2005, Frank Bruni dryly noted that eating had
"evolved from a matter of survival to a statement of values." The blackboards
in the restaurant listed not the specials of the day, Bruni wrote, but Cookshop's favorite farmers, "an honor roll of principled stewards and good shep-
herds who aren't exhausting their land, immobilizing their livestock,
tweaking genes or toying with hormones."

It does get goofy sometimes, the deployment of the buzz terms du jour
(oh, everything must be "sustainable" nowadays), the self-congratulatory
grandstanding, the trends that bubble up from nowhere, achieve critical
mass, and then get discarded by jaded foodies who've moved on to the next

thing. As this book was being finished, chefs across America were embracing *sous vide*, a French culinary term for Cryovacking, a process in which a foodstuff is vacuum packed in plastic—in some cases, to compact its cells and create an entirely new texture for a familiar food; in other cases, to allow a chef to slow cook the foodstuff to perfection in a water bath, sealing in its flavors rather than letting them leech into the cooking water. Thomas Keller has likened the impact of *sous vide* to that of the Cuisinart. Less rapturously, the food writer Maile Carpenter reported in *San Francisco* magazine that when Keller's waitstaff at Per Se proudly presented her with a whole pink foie gras encased in plastic, the better to impress her with their *sous vide* slow-poaching technology, the experience was akin to having an "organ donor package" shoved in her face.

But for all the unintentional humor the food world gives us, we trivialize this world at our peril. Food is more than just a "lifestyle" choice or fodder for the leisure pages, more than a hobby for *Zagat Survey*–wielding gourmands or a duty for *Ladies' Home Journal* minivan moms. The movements that we've seen embraced headlong and then embarrassedly dismissed as regrettable fads or specious labels—such as nouvelle cuisine, California cuisine, New American cuisine, and fusion cuisine—have actually turned out to have lasting, positive impact. They're nothing to be ashamed of. Our cookery is lighter, our ingredients fresher and better, our tastes more wide-ranging, our palates more adventurous.

James Beard was far ahead of the curve in recognizing that it wasn't silly for us Americans to give serious consideration to what we eat, as the French and Italians do. "While I do not overlook the grotesqueries of American cooking," he wrote in *James Beard's American Cookery*, "I believe we have a rich and fascinating food heritage that occasionally reaches greatness in its own melting pot way . . . We are barely beginning to sift down into a cuisine of our own." Beard was, most probably, off the mark in forecasting the development of a coherent American cuisine, but he was prescient in his optimism and sense of possibility. He knew that we could have it so much better in the United States if we just *cared*. For a long time, though, we resisted caring too much; it was as if there was something wussy, too soft, even un-American about investing one's passion and emotion in what's for dinner. But the tide is turning.

I don't presume, as certain chroniclers of other sectors of American history have, that we've reached some kind of glorious endpoint—that the battle has been won and the Spam banished. We still live in a world where Taco Bell has the audacity to base an advertising campaign on the catchphrase "I'm full!"—the implication being that a) fullness, the turgid state of being stuffed to the gills, is desirable; and b) this state is all the more satisfying when it's been achieved by eating a half-pound, 99-cent beige log of quasi-Mexican food product from the chain's Big Bell Value Menu.

But, like Beard, I'm an optimist where food in America is concerned—buoyed by how far we've come and eager to see where tomorrow will take us. That a healthy debate rages over the merits of a fine-dining chef's alliance with Burger King; that the celebrity chef may soon be joined in the foodie pantheon by the celebrity *farmer*; that even the merciless food-world backbencher Karen Hess cheers the advance of Starbucks as a boon to coffee drinkers; that chefs and parents are finally standing up to the tyranny of the greasy, nasty institutional American school lunch; that the traditional supermarket as we know it is dying and getting reborn as a "fresh market"; that Wolfgang Puck is trying to Puckify airport food with his Wolfgang Puck Express restaurants, positing the Chinois chicken salad as the pleasurable, survivable alternative to the dreaded roller-grill wiener—well, doesn't all this suggest that we're not only getting somewhere but have already gotten somewhere?

ACKNOWLEDGMENTS

HAVING WRITTEN A BOOK ABOUT FOOD, I SUPPOSE I OWE THANKS TO EVERYONE WHO'S
shaped my eating experiences—everyone who's ever fed me, cooked for me,
eaten my cooking, or talked to me about food, right down to the prosper-
ous, terrifying old man I met once in Florida who sat bare-chested in a pa-
tio chair, gnawing on a cold knuckle of meat, and barked at me, "Kid, ham
hocks are the best goddamned meat you can put in your mouth!" (Soon after this encounter, this man's sons opened one of New York's most renowned
restaurants, Gotham Bar and Grill—not that such a fancy place registered in
my suburban, adolescent consciousness.) But I'll stick to thanking those who
have directly influenced the creation of this book.

I owe a debt of gratitude to two great magazine editors, Graydon
Carter of *Vanity Fair* and the late Art Cooper of *GQ*, for their encourage-
ment in this project and their larger roles as mentors and foisters upon me of
grown-up tastes in food and drink. I am grateful to the friends who share my
joy in eating and drinking too much: Marion Rosenfeld and Thomas Jones;
Norman and Lee Rosenfeld; Matt Tyrnauer; Henry Alford (who makes an
excellent case for James Beard as America's foremost unwitting humorist);
Joan Feeney and Bruce Phillips; Peter Richmond and Melissa Davis; Larry
Mufson and Betsy Fillmore; Doug Stumpf; Susan Kittenplan; Adam Platt;
Jim Nelson; Josh Sens; Susi Cahn, the renowned goat-cheese heiress, and her
husband, Mario Batali, the one chef in this narrative whom I consider—
Department of Full Disclosure—a friend (not that this disclosure is painful;
we should all have friends who cure their own meats and pour a generous
glass of Tignanello).

I am grateful to Charlie Conrad, Alison Presley, Bill Thomas, and Steve Rubin of Broadway and Doubleday for patiently and supportively shepherding this "two-year project" through its three-year gestation. I am also grateful to Suzanne Gluck and her deputy at William Morris, Erin Malone, for being my staunchest advocates and doing the dastardly, agenty things that agent people do. I must thank the various people who helped me out with research at different junctures: Cindy Embleton, Claire Smith, Elizabeth Tarpy, Brian Healy, Matt Hermann, and Melissa Goldstein. I am also indebted, research-wise, to Marvin Taylor and his staff at the Fales Library at New York University; and to COPIA, the lovely and hospitable museum and culinary education center in Napa Valley. Eugene Corey deserves special thanks for transcribing hundreds of hours of interviews, many of them with thickly accented Frenchmen. And Jack Mazzola deserves a shout-out for the continuous, shade-grown, stir-brewed, Fair Trade caffeine drip that got me through the writing process. I'm kind to Starbucks in this book because I think it truly elevated the taste experience of coffee drinking in this country, but dedicated local cuppers like Jack go Starbucks one better.

I must acknowledge the direction and insight provided by Nina Planck, Laura Shapiro, Greil Marcus, Bonnie Slotnick, Jonathan Ned Katz, Christopher Hitchens, and Carol Blue. I should add to this list the name of Alan Davidson, the brilliant and endearingly eccentric English food historian behind *The Oxford Companion to Food*, who, shortly before his death in 2003, provided me with some excellent leads, and who tenderly checked in on me after I succumbed, ironically enough, to food poisoning during a visit to London.

There are two longtime food writers and restaurant critics who have been especially helpful in the course of this book's preparation: Alan Richman of *GQ* and James Villas, who was for years *Town & Country*'s knife-and-fork man. Alan and Jim do not share my optimistic outlook about the food world, the former arguing that things peaked in the early nineties, before celebrity chefs started opening multiple restaurants, the latter insisting that it's all been downhill since the sixties, the last period in which elegant service and ardent Francophilia reigned in America's finest restaurants and home kitchens. Despite all this, Alan and Jim were of tremendous help to me as I prepared this (to them) utterly wrongheaded book, offering their thoughts and recollections and invectives free of charge. For their cantankerous good company, for their kindness, for their piquant writing, and for sacrificing their livers and digestive systems over a period of decades so that we could learn from them, I salute these two bibulous cranks.

I must single out Jim and Rosemary Bell for their generosity in letting me pull down volumes from their expansive food and wine library without expecting these books back for months or even years. Rosemary is also the best home cook I've encountered in my life; it's a good thing I married her daughter.

On the subject of family: it wouldn't have even occurred to me to write such a book if my mother and father, along with my sister, Alice, and my brother, Ted, had not been adventurous eaters and home cooks. We had our *Moosewood Cookbook* phase; we had our Julia Child phase; we had our paella phase; we had our "cook every meal in the Crock Pot" phase; and we had our "do everything *The New York Times* Weekend section tells you to do" phase, which always seemed to involve visiting the Lower East Side and eating baked farmer cheese. It was the best preparation a future chronicler of food as popular culture could have wished for.

And finally, I give thanks to the family with whom I spend every day: my children, Lily and Henry, whose concept of kid food—calamari, quesadillas, and avocado rolls—demonstrates how much things have changed since my childhood; and my wife, Aimée Bell, with whom I never go skiing, spearfishing, horseback riding, or windsurfing, because all of those activities pale in comparison with the simple pleasure we derive from sharing a good meal and a bottle of red wine. Looking back on her marriage after her husband had died, Julia Child told her authorized biographer, Noël Riley Fitch, "We did everything together until the end . . . That is why you get married, as far as I am concerned." Julia knew what she was talking about.

D.K.

BIBLIOGRAPHY

IN THE COURSE OF RESEARCHING THIS BOOK, I READ HUNDREDS OF ARTICLES FROM various newspapers and magazines, some still with us, others no longer around. For expediency's sake, I've only included the longer and more heavily leaned-upon articles in this bibliography. However, I'd like to credit the following periodicals for being especially useful to me: *The New York Times*, the *New York Herald Tribune*, *New York* magazine, *The New York Review of Books*, *New West* magazine (and its later incarnation as *California*), *Los Angeles* magazine, the *Los Angeles Times*, the *San Francisco Chronicle*, *Gourmet*, *Food & Wine*, *Saveur*, *Food Arts*, and *Gastronomica: The Journal of Food and Culture*.

Andrews, Colman. "California: Celebrating America's Capital of Food and Wine." *Saveur*, May/June 2001.

Batterberry, Michael, and Ariane Batterberry. *On the Town in New York: The Landmark History of Eating, Drinking, and Entertainments from the American Revolution to the Food Revolution.* New York: Scribner, 1973.

Bayless, Rick, with Deann Groen Bayless. *Authentic Mexican: Regional Cooking from the Heart of Mexico.* New York: William Morrow & Company, 1987.

Bayless, Rick, with JeanMarie Brownson and Deann Groen Bayless. *Mexico: One Plate at a Time.* New York: Scribner, 2000.

Beard, James. *Beard on Bread.* New York: Alfred A. Knopf, 1973.

———. *The Complete Book of Barbecue & Rotisserie Cooking.* New York: The Bobbs-Merrill Company, 1954.

———. *Cook It Outdoors.* New York: M. Barrows & Company, 1941.

———. *Delights and Prejudices: A Memoir with Recipes.* New York: Atheneum, 1964.

———. *The Fireside Cook Book: A Complete Guide to Fine Cooking for Beginner and Expert.* New York: Simon & Schuster, 1949.

———. *Hors d'Oeuvre and Canapés, revised edition*. New York: William Morrow & Company, 1963.

———. *James Beard's American Cookery*. Boston: Little, Brown & Company, 1972.

———. *James Beard's Fish Cookery*. Boston: Little, Brown & Company, 1954.

———. Ferrone, John, ed. *Love and Kisses and a Halo of Truffles: Letters to Helen Evans Brown*. New York: Arcade, 1994.

Becker, Marion Rombauer. *Little Acorn: Joy of Cooking, The First Fifty Years, 1931–1981*. Indianapolis, IN: The Bobbs-Merrill Company, 1981.

Beebe, Lucius. *Snoot If You Must*. New York: D. Appleton-Century Company, 1943.

Belasco, Warren J. *Appetite for Change: How the Counterculture Took on the Food Industry, 1966–1988*. New York: Pantheon Books, 1989.

Brenner, Leslie. *American Appetite: The Coming of Age of a National Cuisine*. New York: HarperCollins, 1999.

Brillat-Savarin, Jean-Anthelme. *The Physiology of Taste*. Translated by Anne Drayton. New York: Penguin, 1994.

Brown, Edward Espe. *The Tassajara Bread Book*, 25th anniversary edition. Boston: Shambhala, 1995.

Brown, Helen Evans. *Helen Brown's West Coast Cook Book*. New York: Bonanza Books, 1952.

Bundy, Beverly. *The Century in Food: America's Fads and Favorites*. Portland, OR: Collectors Press, 2002.

Cahn, Miles. *The Perils and Pleasures of Domesticating Goat Cheese*. New York: Catskill Press, 2003.

Chamberlain, Samuel. *Clementine in the Kitchen* (revised edition). New York: Modern Library, 2001.

Chamberlain, Samuel, and Narcissa G. Chamberlain. *The Chamberlain Sampler of American Cooking*. New York: Hastings House, 1961.

Child, Julia, and Simone Beck. *From Julia Child's Kitchen*. New York: Alfred A. Knopf, 1982.

———. *Mastering the Art of French Cooking, Volume Two*. New York: Alfred A. Knopf, 1970.

Child, Julia, Simone Beck, and Louisette Bertholle. *Mastering the Art of French Cooking*. New York: Alfred A. Knopf, 1961.

Child, Lydia. *The American Frugal Housewife: Dedicated to Those Who Are Not Ashamed of Economy*, 1975 facsimile. Boston: Carter, Hendee, and Co., 1833.

Claiborne, Craig. "Elegance of Cuisine Is on Wane in U.S." *The New York Times*, April 13, 1959.

―――. *A Feast Made for Laughter: A Memoir with Recipes*. New York: Doubleday, 1982.

―――. *The New York Times Cook Book*. New York: Harper & Row, 1961.

Claiborne, Craig, and Pierre Franey. *Cooking with Craig Claiborne and Pierre Franey*. New York: Times Books, 1983.

Claiborne, Craig, Pierre Franey, and the Editors of Time-Life Books. *Foods of the World: Classic French Cooking*. New York: Time-Life Books, 1970.

Clark, Robert. *The Solace of Food: A Life of James Beard*. South Royalton, VT: Steerforth Press, 1993.

Clarke, Paul. *Lessons in Excellence from Charlie Trotter*. Berkeley: Ten Speed Press, 1999.

Colen, Bruce David. "Michael, Throw the Gloat Ashore." *Los Angeles*, July 1979.

―――. "Wolfgang Finds Life After Ma Maison." *Los Angeles*, April 1982.

Cooper, Artemis. *Writing at the Kitchen Table: The Authorized Biography of Elizabeth David*. New York: Ecco/HarperCollins, 1999.

David, Elizabeth. *South Wind Through the Kitchen: The Best of Elizabeth David*. New York: North Point Press, 1998.

Davidson, Alan, ed. *The Oxford Companion to Food*. Oxford: Oxford University Press, 1999.

Davidson, Alan, ed., with Helen Saberi. *The Wilder Shores of Gastronomy: 20 Years of the Best Writing from the Journal "Petits Propos Culinaires."* Berkeley: Ten Speed Press, 2002.

Ephron, Nora. *Wallflower at the Orgy*. New York: Viking, 1970.

Escoffier, Auguste. *Le guide culinaire*. Translated by H. L. Cracknell and R. J. Kaufmann. New York: Wiley, 1983.

"Everyone's in the Kitchen." *Time*, November 25, 1966.

Farmer, Fannie Merritt. *The 1896 Boston Cooking-School Cook Book*, facsimile of 1896 original. New York: Gramercy, 1997.

―――. *The Fannie Farmer Cookbook*, 12th edition. Revised by Marion Cunningham with Jeri Laber. New York: Alfred A. Knopf, 1979.

Ferguson, Priscilla Parkhurst. "Writing Out of the Kitchen: Carême and the Invention of French Cuisine." *Gastronomica: The Journal of Food and Culture*, Summer 2003.

Field, Michael. *Michael Field's Cooking School*. New York: M. Barrows & Company, 1965.

————. *Michael Field's Culinary Classics and Improvisations: Creative Leftovers from Main-Course Masterpieces*. New York: Alfred A. Knopf, 1967.

Fisher, M.F.K. *The Art of Eating*. New York: Collier Books/Macmillan, 1990.

Fisher, M.F.K., and the Editors of Time-Life Books. *Foods of the World: The Cooking of Provincial France*. New York: Time-Life Books, 1968.

Fitch, Noël Riley. *Appetite for Life: The Biography of Julia Child*. New York: Doubleday, 1997.

"Food: The New Wave." *Newsweek*, August 11, 1975.

Franey, Pierre. *60-Minute Gourmet*. New York: Times Books, 1979.

Franey, Pierre, with Richard Flaste and Bryan Miller. *A Chef's Tale: A Memoir of Food, France and America*. New York: Alfred A. Knopf, 1994.

Franey, Pierre, and Bryan Miller. *Cuisine Rapide*. New York: Times Books, 1989.

Fussell, Betty. *I Hear America Cooking*. New York: Viking Penguin, 1997.

————. *Masters of American Cookery: The American Food Revolution & the Chefs Who Shaped It*. New York: Times Books, 1983.

————. *My Kitchen Wars*. New York: North Point Press, 1999.

Gelb, Arthur. *City Room*. New York: Marian Wood/G. P. Putnam, 2003.

Glaser, Milton, and Jerome Snyder. *The Underground Gourmet Cookbook*. New York: Simon & Schuster, 1975.

Goines, David Lance. *The Free Speech Movement: Coming of Age in the 1960s*. Berkeley: Ten Speed Press, 1993.

Goines, David Lance, and Alice Waters. *Thirty Recipes Suitable for Framing*. Berkeley: Saint Hieronymus Press, 1970.

Greene, Gael. *Bite: A New York Restaurant Strategy for Hedonists, Masochists, Selective Penny Pinchers and the Upwardly Mobile*. New York: W. W. Norton & Company, 1971.

Guérard, Michel. *Michel Guérard's Cuisine Minceur*. Translated by Narcisse Chamberlain. New York: William Morrow & Company, 1976.

Halm, Meesha. *The Balsamic Vinegar Cookbook*. San Francisco: Collins, 1996.

Hazan, Marcella. *The Classic Italian Cook Book: The Art of Italian Cooking and the Italian Art of Eating*. New York: Harper's Magazine Press, 1973.

————. *The Essentials of Classic Italian Cooking*. New York: Alfred A. Knopf, 1992.

Hess, John L., and Karen Hess. *The Taste of America*. Champaign, IL: University of Illinois Press, 2000.

Hesser, Amanda. "Under the Toque: 'Here's Emeril!' Where's the Chef?" *The New York Times*, November 4, 1998.

Jacobs, Jay. *A Glutton for Punishment: Confessions of a Mercenary Eater*. New York: Atlantic Monthly Press, 1990.

———. *New York à la Carte: Cooking with the Great Chefs*. New York: McGraw-Hill, 1978.

Jenkins, Steven. *Cheese Primer*. New York: Workman, 1996.

Jones, Evan. *American Food: The Gastronomic Story*. New York: Random House, 1974.

———. *Epicurean Delight: The Life and Times of James Beard*. New York: Alfred A. Knopf, 1990.

Kafka, Barbara. *Food for Friends*. New York: Wings Books, 1984.

———. *The Opinionated Palate: Passions and Peeves on Eating and Food*. New York: William Morrow & Company, 1992.

Kafka, Barbara, ed. *James Beard Celebration Cookbook: Memories & Recipes from His Friends*. New York: William Morrow & Company, 1990.

Katzen, Mollie. *The Enchanted Broccoli Forest*. Berkeley: Ten Speed Press, 1982.

———. *The Moosewood Cookbook: Recipes from Moosewood Restaurant, Ithaca, New York*. Berkeley: Ten Speed Press, 1977.

Keller, Thomas, with Susie Heller and Michael Ruhlman. *The French Laundry Cookbook*. New York: Artisan, 1999.

Kennedy, Diana. *The Cuisines of Mexico*. New York: Harper & Row, 1972.

———. *My Mexico: A Culinary Odyssey with More Than 300 Recipes*. New York: Clarkson Potter, 1998.

Kerr, Graham. *The Graham Kerr Cookbook by the Galloping Gourmet*. New York: Doubleday, 1969.

Kuh, Patric. *The Last Days of Haute Cuisine: America's Culinary Revolution*. New York: Penguin, 2001.

Lang, George. *Nobody Knows the Truffles I've Seen*. New York: Alfred A. Knopf, 1999.

Lappé, Frances Moore. *Diet for a Small Planet*. New York: Ballantine Books, 1971.

Lawler, Edmund. *Charlie Trotter's: An Insider's Look at the Famed Restaurant and Its Cuisine*. New York: Lebhar-Friedman Books, 2000.

————. *Lessons in Service from Charlie Trotter*. Berkeley: Ten Speed Press, 2001.

Levenstein, Harvey A. *Paradox of Plenty: A Social History of Eating in Modern America*. Berkeley: University of California Press, 2003.

————. *Revolution at the Table: The Transformation of the American Diet*. New York: Oxford University Press, 1988.

Liebling, A. J. *Liebling Abroad*. New York: Playboy Press, 1981.

Lucas, Dione. *The Cordon Bleu Cook Book*. Boston: Little, Brown & Company, 1975.

Maccioni, Sirio, and Peter Elliot. *Sirio: The Story of My Life and Le Cirque*. New York: John Wiley & Sons, 2004.

Madison, Deborah. *The Greens Cookbook*. New York: Broadway Books, 2001.

————. *Local Flavors: Cooking and Eating from America's Farmers' Markets*. New York: Broadway Books, 2002.

————. *Vegetarian Cooking for Everyone*. New York: Broadway Books, 1997.

Mariani, John. *America Eats Out*. New York: William Morrow & Company, 1991.

Mariani, John, with Alex Von Bidder. *The Four Seasons: A History of America's Premier Restaurant*. New York: Crown, 1994.

McCully, Helen, ed. *The American Heritage Cookbook and Illustrated History of Eating and Drinking*. New York: Simon & Schuster, 1964.

Mendelson, Anne. *Stand Facing the Stove: The Story of the Women Who Gave America "The Joy of Cooking."* New York: Henry Holt & Company, 1996.

Miller, Mark. *Coyote Cafe*. Berkeley: Ten Speed Press, 1989.

Mondavi, Robert. *Harvests of Joy: How the Good Life Became a Great Business*. San Diego: Harcourt Brace & Company, 1998.

Nelson, Richard. *Richard Nelson's American Cooking*. New York: New American Library, 1983.

Olney, Richard. *The French Menu Cookbook*. New York: Simon & Schuster, 1970.

————. *Simple French Food*. New York: Atheneum, 1974.

Paddleford, Clementine. *How America Eats*. New York: Charles Scribner's Sons, 1960.

Pendergrast, Mark. *Uncommon Grounds: The History of Coffee and How It Transformed Our World*. New York: Basic Books, 1999.

Pépin, Jacques. *The Apprentice: My Life in the Kitchen.* Boston: Houghton Mifflin, 2003.

———. *La Technique: The Fundamental Techniques of Cooking: An Illustrated Guide.* New York: Quadrangle/New York Times Book Co., 1976.

Perry, Charles. *The Haight-Ashbury: A History.* New York: Rolling Stone Press/Random House, 1984.

Point, Fernand. *Ma gastronomie.* Translated by Frank Kulla and Patricia Shannon Kulla. Wilton, CT: Lyceum Books, 1974.

Pollan, Michael. *The Omnivore's Dilemma.* New York: The Penguin Press, 2006.

Puck, Wolfgang. *Adventures in the Kitchen.* New York: Random House, 1991.

———. *The Wolfgang Puck Cookbook.* New York: Random House, 1986.

Randolph, Mary. *The Virginia House-wife.* Columbia, SC: University of South Carolina Press, 1984.

Reichl, Ruth. *Comfort Me with Apples: More Adventures at the Table.* New York: Random House, 2001.

———. *Garlic and Sapphires: The Secret Life of a Critic in Disguise.* New York: Penguin, 2005.

———. "Is This the Best French Restaurant in California?" *New West*, June 18, 1979.

———. "Let 100 Reservations Bloom." *California*, November 1983.

———. *Tender at the Bone: Growing Up at the Table.* New York: Random House, 1998.

Richman, Alan. *Fork It Over: The Intrepid Adventures of a Professional Eater.* New York: HarperCollins, 2004.

———. "Stick a Fork in Jean-Georges." *GQ*, December 2004.

Rodgers, Judy. *The Zuni Café Cookbook: A Compendium of Recipes and Cooking Lessons from San Francisco's Beloved Restaurant.* New York: W. W. Norton & Company, 2002.

Rombauer, Irma. *The Joy of Cooking: A Facsimile of the First Edition.* New York: Scribner's, 1998.

Rosengarten, David, with Joel Dean and Giorgio DeLuca. *The Dean & DeLuca Cookbook.* New York: Random House, 1996.

Rosso, Julee, and Sheila Lukins, with Michael McLaughlin. *The Silver Palate Cookbook.* New York: Workman, 1982.

Ruhlman, Michael. *The Soul of a Chef: The Journey Toward Perfection*. New York: Penguin, 2001.

Schell, Orville. *Modern Meat: Antibiotics, Hormones, and the Pharmaceutical Farm*. New York: Random House, 1984.

Schlosser, Eric. *Fast Food Nation: The Dark Side of the All-American Meal*. New York: Houghton Mifflin, 2001.

Schultz, Howard. *Pour Your Heart into It: How Starbucks Built a Company One Cup at a Time*. New York: Hyperion, 1999.

Shapiro, Laura. *Perfection Salad: Women and Cooking at the Turn of the Century*. New York: Modern Library, 2001.

—. *Something from the Oven: Reinventing Dinner in 1950s America*. New York: Viking, 2004.

Sheraton, Mimi. "Eat American!" *Time*, August 26, 1985.

—. *Eating My Words: An Appetite for Life*. New York: William Morrow & Company, 2004.

Simmons, Amelia. *The First American Cookbook: A Facsimile of "American Cookery," 1796*. With an essay by Mary Tolford Wilson. New York: Dover Publications, 1984.

Sokolov, Raymond. *Why We Eat What We Eat: How the Encounter Between the New World and the Old Changed the Way Everyone on the Planet Eats*. New York: Summit Books, 1991.

Szathmáry, Louis. *American Gastronomy*. Chicago: Henry Regnery Company, 1974.

Terrail, Patrick A. *A Taste of Hollywood: The Story of Ma Maison*. New York: Lebhar-Friedman Books, 1999.

Tomkins, Calvin. "Good Cooking." *The New Yorker*, December 23, 1974.

Tower, Jeremiah. *California Dish: What I Saw (and Cooked) at the American Culinary Revolution*. New York: Free Press, 2003.

Trotter, Charlie. *Charlie Trotter Cooks at Home*. Berkeley: Ten Speed Press, 2000.

Vergnes, Jean. *A Seasoned Chef: Recipes and Remembrances from the Chef and Former Co-owner of New York's Famous Le Cirque Restaurant*. New York: Donald I. Fine, 1987.

Villas, James. *Between Bites: Memoirs of a Hungry Hedonist*. New York: John Wiley & Sons, 2002.

—. "From the Abundant Land: At Last, a Table of Our Own." *Town & Country*, June 1976.

Waters, Alice. *Chez Panisse Café Cookbook*. New York: HarperCollins, 1999.

————. *Chez Panisse Menu Cookbook*. New York: Random House, 1982.

————. *Chez Panisse Vegetables*. New York: HarperCollins, 1996.

Wechsberg, Joseph. *Dining at the Pavillon*. Boston: Little, Brown & Company, 1962.

Weinstein, Jeff. "Puck's Second Coming." *Los Angeles*, April 1997.

Weiss, Mike. "Recipe for Scandal," three-part series. *San Francisco Chronicle*, May 4–6, 2005.

PHOTOGRAPHIC CREDITS

1: © Bettmann/Corbis

2: © Ralph Morse/Time Life Pictures/Getty Images

3: Courtesy of Cecily Brownstone Papers, Fales Library, New York University

4: © Manville-Globe Photos, Inc.

5: © Marc Riboud/Magnum Photos

6: Courtesy of the Bancroft Library, University of California, Berkeley

7: © J. M. Barringer, 1976

8: Courtesy of Celestial Seasonings

9: © Mel Finkelstein/*New York Daily News*

10: © Mario Ruiz/ZUMA Press

11: © Thomas Monaster/*New York Daily News*

14: © NBC/courtesy of the Everett Collection

15: © Marianna Day Massey/ZUMA Press

INDEX

Italicized page numbers refer to photographs.

ABOUT THE AUTHOR

DAVID KAMP has been a writer and editor for *Vanity Fair* and *GQ* for more than a decade. He lives in New York.